DOES YOUR VOTE COUNT?

Studies in the Postmodern Theory of Education

Shirley R. Steinberg

General Editor

Vol. 378

The Counterpoints series is part of the Peter Lang Education list.
Every volume is peer reviewed and meets
the highest quality standards for content and production.

PETER LANG

New York • Washington, D.C./Baltimore • Bern
Frankfurt • Berlin • Brussels • Vienna • Oxford

"For readers familiar with critical pedagogy, Paul R. Carr's book brings together and extends some of [its] core commitments: the eradication of oppression in school and society, making visible and ultimately resisting the effects of militaristic, hegemonic, racist, sexist, colonialist and other oppressive ideologies, and working with students to develop the skills to engage in meaningful and informed examinations about hegemonic practices throughout the world, and participate in robust democratic dialogues about challenging these practices.

For readers who are not familiar with critical pedagogy, …the book contributes a very detailed discussion of democratic (or perhaps democracy) literacy in all aspects of school structures. The book explores a range of examples, questions and case studies that underscore the complexity of democracy discourses as they emerge in a variety of settings.

…Carr's…care and passion for these issues is evident.…Throughout the text, Carr does not lose sight of the blind spots and gray areas that make engagement with democracy a messy art. All of this results in a thoughtfully written book that would make a welcome addition to the critical educator's library."

—*Özlem Sensoy, Simon Fraser University*

"A clear and insightful work that revisits the nature and implications [of] robust democracy in and for education, while offering persuasive justifications for the Freirean tradition of critical education through the use of lived experiences and research. Paul R. Carr provides a refreshing critical discussion of 'econ-ocracy' and the mythology it has created."

—*John Portelli, Ontario Institute for Studies in Education at the University of Toronto*

"In this book, Paul R. Carr does an outstanding job capturing how teachers, researchers, scholars and informed citizens can utilize critical pedagogy to get us beyond the mainstream version of democracy in North America—election politics, polling and parties—that is responsible for perpetuating social inequalities in schools and in the wider society, to engendering a social reality consisting of critically-engaged citizenship, diversity, freedom, hope and justice. Not only does this book highlight the social, economic and political forces behind…entrenched educational and political structures that perpetuate conformity, oppression and intolerance, but it provides readers with pedagogical ideas, original research, and concepts to reflect upon how critical pedagogy can become the cornerstone to creating a reflexive praxis and building an equalitarian society."

—*Brad Porfilio, Lewis University*

"Paul R. Carr's rigorous examination of democracy and critical pedagogy offers timely suggestions for the role education might play in ushering in a less oppressive, less exploitative, less Euro-centric, less barbaric, post-capitalist, post-imperialist world. In a context where one's individual vote arguably has limited political impact on disrupting the basic structures of capitalist power, Carr's emphasis on direct democratic action beyond the voting booth is a necessary reminder of the responsibility of educators to nurture the critical agency and commitment to social justice within their students. *Does Your Vote Count?* should be engaged with by educators and students everywhere."

—*Curry Stephenson Malott, D'Youville College*

Paul R. Carr

DOES YOUR VOTE COUNT?

Critical Pedagogy and Democracy

PETER LANG
New York • Washington, D.C./Baltimore • Bern
Frankfurt • Berlin • Brussels • Vienna • Oxford

Library of Congress Cataloging-in-Publication Data

Carr, Paul R.
Does your vote count?: critical pedagogy and democracy / Paul R. Carr.
p. cm. — (Counterpoints: studies in the postmodern theory of education; 378)
Includes bibliographical references and index.
1. Critical pedagogy. 2. Democracy and education. I. Title.
LC196.C37   370.11'5—dc22   2009044586
ISBN 978-1-4331-0812-9 (hardcover)
ISBN 978-1-4331-0813-6 (paperback)
ISSN 1058-1634

Bibliographic information published by **Die Deutsche Nationalbibliothek.**
Die Deutsche Nationalbibliothek lists this publication in the "Deutsche
Nationalbibliografie"; detailed bibliographic data is available
on the Internet at http://dnb.d-nb.de/.

Cover photo by Wim Van Passel

The paper in this book meets the guidelines for permanence and durability
of the Committee on Production Guidelines for Book Longevity
of the Council of Library Resources.

*Dedicated to the memory of Gunapala Edirisooriya,
scholar, humanitarian, colleague and friend.*

Table of Contents

Figures

Acknowledgements

This book was only made possible through the generous contributions of a number of people who have influenced and supported my thinking over the years. The evolution and growth in my questioning of our society has benefitted from a rich and critical dialog with a number of colleagues and friends, who have challenged me to critique my own critique, and to humbly accept that my own knowledge is extremely limited.

I extend my gratitude to my graduate assistant, Linda Crawford, who has been exceptionally helpful in bringing together the disparate parts of this book. I would also like to acknowledge Mohammed Jadun, Brandi Stillman, Adeel Abass, Donald Masny and Matthew Sprankle of the Instructional Technology Center at Youngstown State University, where I have spent an inordinate amount of time these past few years. Adrian Labra, a student and budding musician, also provided support in the early stages, as did Clarence Howell, who generously culled through a number of details for this project. David Curtis provided some very helpful support at the end of the project to make the manuscript presentable. I have also been supported by my colleagues in the Beeghly College of Education, and am appreciative for the release-time that I have been accorded to work on this book. A friend, Jim Crawford, also provided feedback on an earlier version of the text. I am also indebted to my doctoral students, who, for the past five years, have shared their friendship and critical thoughts through a wonderful and dialectical learning process. The beautiful photos on the front and back covers have been graciously provided by my friend and humanitarian Wim Van Passel (http://www.tijdloze momenten.nl/), who has dedicated his craft to building a more humane and respectful appreciation of the world's ecology.

I would like to thank good friends Darren E. Lund and Brad J. Porfilio for numerous collaborative efforts, Peter McLaren, for his guidance, Shirley Steinberg, for her unwavering support, Richard Townsend, for his longstanding friendship and erudite comments on an earlier draft of the book, David Zyngier, for his partnership in elaborating a global democratic education project, which helped craft some of the thinking contained herein, and many other scholars within the Paulo Freire critical pedagogical orbit, who have offered friendship, support and guidance. Special thanks to Daniel Schugurensky, formerly of the Ontario Institute for Studies in Education at the University of Toronto and now at Arizona State University, and Joel Westheimer, at the University of Ottawa, for the foreword and afterword, respectively, and especially for their support over the years.

I am grateful for the support I have received at my new institution, Lakehead Univesity (Orillia), where Sharon Stone, the Chair in the Department of Sociology, Alice den Otter, Chair of the Department of Interdisciplinary Studies, and Kim Fedderson, Dean of the Orillia campus, as well as many new colleagues, have made my first several months extremely agreeable, which has facilitated the completion of this book.

A couple of friends have been particularly supportive over the past few years, namely Doug Winspear and Hugh Hazelton, who have been amusing (and bemused) lunch partners at the Batory, where we have dissected many geo-political matters beyond our reach, usually ending up at the Social Club for a *bomb* (hybrid between an espresso and *café au lait* in Montréal).

My partner, Gina Thésée, has been the principal recipient of my endless, what I considered to be, epiphanal moments that I have attempted to nuance, always to her epistemologically well-reasoned rebuttal, and I am grateful for the constant dialog that has accompanied the writing of this book. *Merci, mon amour!*

Two people have been paramount in influencing and cajoling my thinking in relation to this book: Joe L. Kincheloe was an intensely gracious, humble, generous and gregarious person, who loved life, and shared it with everyone, and I am extremely grateful to have known him; and Gunapala Edirisooriya, my office-neighbour at Youngstown State University for four years, welcomed and engaged me in morning conversations, shared wisdom, provided friendship, and lived a good life, which will be forever, for me, a memory of the humility and dignity of a great man. To Joe and Guna, I miss you both, and thanks.

To my parents (Chris and Bob), my in-laws (Wes and Cleo), Nat, Tudor and Noah and Luca, and my daughters, Chelsea and Sarah, along with Gina, thanks and *merci* for everything.

The following previously-published articles and book chapters appear in this book in a modified form. The copyright-holders have graciously offered their consent for their usage in this book.

Carr, Paul R. (2007). "Shock and awe and the environment," *Peace Review*, 19(3), 335–343.

Carr, Paul R. (2007). Standards, accountability and democracy: Addressing inequities through a social justice accountability framework, *Democracy and Education*, 17(1), 1–16.

Carr, Paul R. (2007). Experiencing democracy through neo-liberalism: The role of social justice in democratic education, *Journal for Critical Education Policy Studies*, 5 (2). http://www.jceps.com/?pageID=article&articleID=104

Carr, Paul R. (2008). "But what can I do?" Fifteen things education students can do to transform themselves in/through/with education, *International Journal of Critical Pedagogy*, 1(2), 81–97.

Carr, Paul R. (2008). The 'Equity Waltz' in Canada: Whiteness and the informal realities of racism in education, *Journal of Contemporary Issues in Education*, 3(2), 4–23.

Carr, Paul R. (2008). Educators and education for democracy: Moving beyond "thin" democracy, *Inter-American Journal of Education and Democracy*, 1(2), 147–165. http://www.ried-ijed.org/english/articulo.php?idRevista=4&idArticulo=16

Carr, Paul R. & Lund, Darren. (2008). Introduction: Scanning democracy. In Carr, Paul R. & Lund, Darren. (eds.), *Doing democracy: Striving for political literacy and social justice* (pp. 1–29). New York: Peter Lang.

Carr, Paul R. & Thésée, Gina. (2008). The quest for political (il)literacy: Responding to, and attempting to counter, the neo-liberal agenda." In Malott, C. & Porfilio, B. (eds.), *The destructive path of neo-liberalism: An international examination of education* (pp. 173–194). Rotterdam: Sense Publishers.

Porfilio, Brad J. & Paul R. Carr. (2008). Youth culture, the mass media and democratic education, *Academic Exchange Quarterly*, 12(4). http://www.rapidintellect.com/AEQweb/cho4255w9.htm.

Carr, Paul R. (2009). Political conscientization and media (il)literacy: Critiquing the mainstream media as a form of democratic engagement, *Multicultural Education*, 17(1), 2–10.

Carr, Paul R. & Thésée, Gina. (2009). The critical pedagogy of understanding how educators relate to democracy. In Schugerensky, D., Daly, K. and Lopes, K. (eds.), *Learning Democracy by Doing: Alternative Practices in Citizenship Learning and Participatory Democracy* (pp. 274–283). Toronto: University of Toronto, Transformational Learning Center.

Carr, Paul R. & Darren E. Lund. (2009). "The unspoken color of diversity: White privilege and critical engagement in education." In Steinberg, S. (ed.), *Diversity: A Reader* (pp. 45–55). New York: Peter Lang Publishing.

Carr, Paul R. & Porfilio, Brad, J. (2009). The 2008 US presidential campaign, democracy and media literacy, *International Journal of Critical Pedagogy*, 2(1), 119–138.

Foreword

Daniel Schugurensky
Arizona State University

The title of this book (*"Does Your Vote Count?"*), reminded me of Mogens Jallberg's pun: *"In a democracy it's your vote that counts. In feudalism it's your count that votes."* Indeed, in comparison to previous historical periods, it is fair to say that today, at the beginning of the 21st century, people's votes count more than in previous centuries. Furthermore, less than one hundred years ago, in many countries of the world the vote of half of the population not only "did not count," it did not even exist. At that time, which was not so long ago, millions of people were not allowed to vote because they were not considered "full citizens" for reasons that today seem ludicrous. Birth factors such as sex or race were considered legitimate enough by laws of the time to exclude women, people of color and indigenous peoples from the electoral process.

Today, if we look back at that not so distant past, we can say without much hesitation that significant progress has been made in terms of electoral democracy, not only regarding the extension of the franchise to previously excluded groups but also regarding electoral outcomes. In South Africa, for instance, blacks were not allowed to vote until 1994, and since the election of Nelson Mandela that same year all presidents have been black. In Bolivia, indigenous peoples were not allowed to vote until 1952, and the idea of an indigenous president was almost unimaginable. Half a century later, Bolivians elected their first indigenous president, a socialist, environmental and spiritual leader named Evo Morales, who proclaimed a plurinational state that promotes both social and ecological justice. Among other initiatives, Evo Morales called for the first Peoples World Conference on Climate Change and Mother Earth Rights, and appointed a cabinet made up of an equal number of women and men, something very unusual not only in Latin America but across the world. In Brazil, Luiz Ignacio da Silva (Lula), a union activist raised in poverty who began to work at age 12 as a shoeshiner and street vendor, was elected as president of Brazil in 2002, and a few years later was chosen as the Person of the Year by prominent European newspapers. Also in 2002, after centuries of colonalism and decades of brutal occupation, East Timor became a proud, independent nation that soon would be governed by a Nobel Peace Prize recipient, President Jose Ramos-Horta. There are more examples. In 2006, Ellen Johnson Sirleaf became not only Liberia's first female president but also Africa's first elected female head of state. The same year, less than two decades after the long nightmare of Pinochet's dictatorship, and despite the influence of a conservative Catholic Church, Michelle Bachelet, a professed agnostic and single mother of three, was elected the first female president of Chile in 2006. Significantly, Ms. Bachelet completed her mandate with unprecedented levels of popular support and was considered by many as the best Chilean president since the return of democracy. In the United States, universal franchise became effective only in 1965, with the passing of the *Voting Rights Act*, largely as a result of the struggles of the civil rights movement. Despite that achievement, for the remainder of the 20th century probably very few people in that country believed they would witness a black or a female president in Washington during their lifetime. The 2008 elections (discussed in this book), with the energizing primary between Barack Hussein Obama and Hillary Rodham Clinton and the subsequent electoral victory of Obama over John McCain, changed that perception forever. Furthermore, in February 2009, Johanna Sigurdardottir made history when she became not only the first female prime minister of Iceland but also the first openly gay head of state on the planet.

These and many other examples suggest that today popular vote counts more than in previous centuries, that many things that were unthinkable only a few decades ago are now taken for granted as normal part of reality, and that democracy is in better shape than before. At the same time, global civil society is more organized than in the past. The World Social Forum, launched in 2001 in Porto Alegre, Brazil, as an alternative to Davos' World Economic Forum, is just one example of many democratic spaces that bring together social movements from all continents to share experiences and, importantly, to plan collective actions to build a better world.

Other recent developments, like the emerging "new cooperativism"[1] in Latin America, the "people's economy" in Asia, the launch of the Fairtrade Certification Mark, and open source and open access initiatives (Linux, Creative Commons, Wikipedia, YouTube, Twitter, FLISOL[2], etc.) make important contributions to the democratization of economic, political, social and cultural life. Likewise, initiatives like the Earth Charter, the Hague Appeal for Peace, the Transition Towns movement, the World March for Peace, the Millennium Development Goals, and the recent efforts of Bhutan to bring the principles and values of Gross National Happiness into the education system, open new possibilities for an alternative development paradigm that challenges the logic of growth and GNP indicators. In short, if we consider the progress made in the first decade of the 21st century, we can conclude that there are some good reasons to feel optimistic about the health of democracy and the direction of the new trends. At the local level, innovative experiments of participatory democracy are being implemented on all continents. In contexts as different as Venezuela and the UK, for instance, participatory budgeting is now a matter of national policy and is beginning to be put into practice in all municipalities. One might consider that the glass is half-full.

There is, of course, the feeling that the glass is also half-empty. In the domain of representative democracy alone, elections in many countries are characterized by low voter turnouts, which are associated with high levels of distrust of politicians and a notable disengagement with political institutions and political parties. A large survey conducted by BBC-Gallup in 2005 of 50,000 people in 68 countries revealed that two-thirds of people worldwide feel unrepresented by their governments, that less than half feel that elections in their country are free and fair, and that only 13% trust politicians, making them the least trusted group, below military, religious and business leaders. This reminds me of a humorous remark attributed to Charles De Gaulle, himself a very popular politician: "Since a politician never believes what he says, he is surprised when others believe him."[3]

Moreover, despite the encouraging electoral results mentioned in the previous paragraphs, in parliaments all around the world women and ethnic minorities are still largely under-represented. Without entertaining conspiracy theories, it can be argued that in many countries the elected representatives only control the government but the real power is often in the hands of unelected international and domestic elites. This means that, for important decisions, plutocracy, or what Paul R. Carr has labeled *econ-ocracy*, overrules democracy. In many societies, the formal democracy of the law ("all citizens are equal") is contradicted daily by the "real democracy" of the street through labour exploitation, different forms of discrimination (race, sex, caste, age, religion, sexual orientation, national origin, ability, language, etc.) and sizable differences in social, cultural and economic capital that have a clear impact on the structure of opportunities.

Indeed, in terms of economic democracy, during the last few decades income inequality has been rising, and wealth distribution is increasingly polarized. It is estimated that today the richest 10 percent of the world's population owns 85 per cent of global household wealth, while half of the world's population only owns one percent of total wealth, and has limited access to basic goods like water, sanitation, healthcare or education. In this context, it is disturbing (and does not speak highly of us as a mature and caring civilization) that a tiny percentage of global arms spending could provide primary education, water, sanitation and health for all human beings on the planet.[4] Neither does it speak highly of us when we consider how we have treated (and still treat) non-human animals and other living species (ecological democracy), to the point that life itself on the planet is now at risk. I could go on and on with a long list of the contemporary maladies of democracy, but the first section of this book—and particularly the 14 trends observed by Laurence Britt that are presented in Figure 7—does a very good job of summarizing the main problems.

The state of our current democracy, then, underscores that significant progress has been made in the last few centuries but, at the same time, calls our attention to the great challenges that still lie ahead as well as the many obstacles that still need to be overcome. Indeed, the process of societal democratization does not happen by itself: it is the result of long and arduous struggles for freedom and equality carried out daily by a great variety of social movements and community organizations. The process of democratization, in other words, is a permanent interplay of forces of reproduction and forces of transformation, of structure and agency, of oppression and resistance, of exploitation and solidarity, of dogmatic authoritarianism and emancipatory questioning, of banking education and dialogical education.

In this book, which includes chapters in collaboration with Darren Lund, Gina Thésée and Brad Porfilio, Paul R. Carr discusses all of these issues, but pays particular attention to the critical pedagogy of democracy. Central to his argument is the distinction between thick and thin democracy (summarized in Figure 3 of Chapter 1). A related and important distinction proposed by Carr is between a radical, humanistic democracy and what he calls *econ-ocracy*, a term that calls our attention to the influence of neoliberal markets within the psyche and lived experiences of people. Carr argues that there is a clear link between a robust, meaningful democracy and critical pedagogy, and that such a link can be understood through the lens of transformative learning, engagement and action. To build his argument, Carr draws on many sources from the field of critical pedagogy, finding special inspiration in the contributions of Paulo Freire and Joe Kincheloe (who sadly passed away recently while in Jamaica). Following the dialectical tradition of critical pedagogy work, Carr argues that democracy (and education for democracy) must be constantly critiqued and, at the same time, constantly cultivated. He calls for a democratic literacy that brings together political and social literacy, together with traditional forms of knowledge and learning. Democratic literacy can help us to interrogate, as Carr does, the role played by racism, unequal power, war, and blind patriotism in our current democracies.

Raising uncomfortable questions and encouraging reflection and dialog on social issues is certainly an important task of critical pedagogy. In this regard, one of the recurrent reactions to critical pedagogy by university students is that its emphasis on exposing and elucidating structures and dynamics of power as well as oppression is so overwhelming that it often leaves them with a feeling of sadness and impotence. To some extent, every time we see too much structure and too little agency we all experience some version of the "analysis paralysis" syndrome. Students frequently say: "Now I know more than before about all the things that are wrong in the world but what can I do?" In this context, it is very refreshing and useful to see that in a book that is heavy on theory and research, Paul R. Carr includes a chapter entitled precisely "But What Can I Do?" Although in that chapter Carr cautiously warns that lists can oversimplify complex issues (and most of us probably would agree with him), I nonetheless believe that his list of 15 suggestions is very insightful and useful for the everyday practice of critical pedagogy. I hope that these 15 suggestions continue to be refined as others engage with them, and that eventually they become part of our teaching resources for critical pedagogy courses. Not to be accepted as the 15 commandments, of course, but to be carefully examined and discussed one by one, and eventually accepted, rejected or amended. The same can be said about the interesting "100 proposals that could contribute to democracy through education" that are presented in the last chapter of the book. Admittedly, some of these "100 proposals" are not necessarily educational contributions to democracy. They rather belong to the domain of political reform (e.g., #82: social movements should have a place at the decision-making table) or of electoral reform (e.g., #90 politicians and political parties should be prohibited from fundraising; #95: cancel elections with only two political parties).

Some of these 100 proposals make sense and probably would gather strong support, whereas others are more controversial and may generate engaging discussions. Some are more realistic and others are more idealistic but, as a package, all these proposals provide very good input for contemporary debates on policies and initiatives to improve both the health of democracy and the quality of education for democracy. This is an urgent and necessary exercise because, as Carr concludes, paraphrasing the motto of the World Social Forum, *another democracy is possible.* I entirely agree, and would add that *another education for democracy is possible* as well. Moreover, I would argue that both projects are interdependent: more democratic societies and institutions are more likely to improve the quality of education for democracy, and conversely better processes of democratic education are more likely to further democratize institutions and societies.

Epilogue: "Being hopeful in bad times"

While I was writing this foreword, I received the sad news of the passing of Howard Zinn, political scientist, social activist and eminent historian. His book *A People's History of the United States* has been read and discussed in many courses guided by critical pedagogy principles. Although Zinn was acutely aware of contemporary tragedies, he was also convinced of the importance of celebrating people's capacity to make a positive difference, one change at a time, in order to move forward. This text summarizes his optimistic emphasis on hope and agency, which constitutes a great antidote to the feelings of fatalism and cynicism that sometimes arise from certain deterministic analyses that overemphasize structural forces over the capacity of people to act:

> *To be hopeful in bad times is not just foolishly romantic. It is based on the fact that human history is a history not only of cruelty, but also of compassion, sacrifice, courage, and kindness. What we choose to emphasize in this complex history will determine our lives. If we see only the worst, it destroys our capacity to do something. If we remember those times and places and there are so many where people have behaved magnificently, this gives us the energy to act, and at least the possibility of sending this spinning top of a world in a different direction. And if we do act, in however small a way, we don't have to wait for some grand utopian future. The future is an infinite succession of presents, and to live now as we think human beings should live, in defiance of all that is bad around us, is itself a marvelous victory.*

> *Howard Zinn (1922–2000)*

Section 1: Setting the Framework

Chapter 1

Introduction:
Seeking Democracy through Critical Pedagogy

The radical, committed to human liberations, does not become the prisoner of a "circle of certainty" within which reality is also imprisoned. On the country, the more radical the person is, the more fully he or she enters into reality so that, knowing it better, he or she can better transform it. The individual is not afraid to confront, to listen, to see the world unveiled. This person is not afraid to meet the people or to enter into dialog with them. This person does not consider himself or herself the proprietor of history or of all people, or the liberator of the oppressed: but he or she does commit himself or herself, within history, to fight at their side. (Freire, 1973/2005, p. 39)[1]

Is it win-lose, win-win or winner take all?

In a world of supposed infinite hope and possibility, to paraphrase politicians of pretty well every stripe in almost every country at this time (Carr & Porfilio, 2009b), are we still plagued with injustice, discrimination, poverty, famine, war, torment and undeniable sadness at visibly wretched acts of deceit and tyranny? Are we perturbed by the decadence and extravagance of small numbers of people in various lands living out reality-show lifestyles unimaginable to the translucent dreams of the majority, who are obliged to fight their battles, literally and figuratively, all the while supporting the vast inequities that pervade the human condition (Chossudovsky, 2003, 2005)? Can a conscious and enlightened spirit and mind, with or without God and the notion of a superior being, bring to bear a more humane acceptance of the *other*, which could address, as Tinder (2004) puts it, the "perennial questions" plaguing the history of civilization? Are we, individually and collectively, satisfied, ingratiated, comforted and nourished with/by the process of voting for candidates and parties destined to lead us (McLaren & Jaramillo, 2007)? These may seem like discursive and disjointed questions but there is a thread running through them.

Democracy means many things to many people. I start this book contesting the generally accepted wisdom that democracy is unquestionably good, and, conversely, what is not democracy or democratic must, therefore, be unquestionably bad. The *us versus them* paradigm, of democrats and non-democrats, or more crudely put within the American context, Democrats versus Republicans has, I contend, not served us well, has led to extraordinarily unnecessary war and destruction, has effectively produced and (reproduced) structures that have perpetuated oppression and disdain for the human condition, and, lastly, has sought to enshrine what might be thought of as a retrenchment of overzealous and stifling anti-democratic thought, action and outcomes. This sweeping, admittedly provocative, statement does not mean to suggest neither that people are fundamentally evil, nor that there have not been some interesting, important and, even, necessary actions undertaken and achieved through the two-party/winner-take-all/*econ-ocracy* model or system (Chomsky, 2007).

Western society often starts with the notion that we are democratic, and, therefore, it is naturally (more) advanced, developed, superior, preferred, righteous, and justifiable than others, which are considered as the opposite (Gregg, 2000; McLaren, 2005a; Swift, 2002). Our supposed democratic foundation provides a rationale for us to incriminate others for their human rights orientation, all the while covering ourselves with the yolk of a quasi-imperialist glory, which epistemologically decrees that others must conform to our vision of the world or face the wrath of what we can muster, even if that means, unfortunately for the majority of peoples affected, militaristic destruction (Goodall, 2008; Magdoff, 2003; Willinsky, 1998). The goodness of Whiteness (Carr & Lund, 2007) and the (fundamentalist) Christian ethos (Giroux, 2005; Steinberg & Kincheloe, 2009) is normatively inscribed into the hegemonic (supposedly democratic) mindset.

To be clear, I am not against democracy: I am, however, hoping for a more robust, critical, *thicker*[2] interpretation of what democracy is, what it should be, and how it can be beneficial to all peoples (see Barber, 2004, Gandin & Apple, 2002, 2005, and McLaren, 2007, for arguments for a more radical and socially just democracy). I embrace the "critical democratic pedagogy" espoused by Denzin (2009) as well as the visceral hope and passion for a more humane political, cultural and socio-economic space for all (see Darder, 2002, and McLaren, 2007) based on Freire's work).

The problem is not that democracy is not a worthy concept but, rather, that the type of democracy that has received normative, relativistic salience is, in many regards, anti-democratic. Macedo (2009) offers a critical and lucid interpretation of this argument.

> While Western capitalistic hegemonic forces insidiously work to empty out the substantivity of democracy by reducing it to ritualistic voting exercises designed to rectify elite decisions, they expect societies that suffered from centuries of colonialism and

exploitation to implement the Western prepackaged democracy when these societies are forced to spend precious resources in fighting civil wars and political instability fuelled by external powers and market interests that cynically demand democracy. Thus, the term "democracy" is not to be understood within ready-made, Western-developed democracy kit characterized by a blind embrace of asymmetrical market forces, required to be uncritically implemented without analysis or regard to suitability. In this sense, democracy precludes the development of a well-thought-out economic plan designed for the general welfare of all people rather than the interests of the ruling elites, which makes this prepackaged democracy a figment of the Western imagination. (p. 80)

This "figment of the Western imagination" cannot be countered without a vigorous and critically engaged educational experience. Critical pedagogy[3] provides a space to further reflect on the meaning of democracy, and to accept, with humility, that there is not simply one way to conceive of the human condition: the mere act of voting does not make a democracy! Societies are too complex to be reduced to such a caricature: by way of example, India, commonly referred to as the world's largest *democracy*, has massive poverty and impoverishment juxtaposed against Bollywood-style extravagance, military conflicts, a quasi-nuclear arms-race with its neighbour, renowned government corruption, and deleterious social conditions for vast segments of the population not involved in the technological revolution, all of which raises important social and human rights questions. India is but one example, and others will be explored in this book but the point to be underscored is that appreciation of the democratic condition must take into consideration myriad factors and propositions, especially in relation to power and inequitable power relations (see Lund & Carr, 2008; Macrine, 2009).

It would be an affront to all peoples, including indigenous/aboriginal peoples, marginalized groups, and those traditionally kept outside of decision-making circles, if the act of voting could stifle debate about what democracy is simply because elections have provided people with a supposed "free choice." Democracy must be constantly worked and re-worked, with less dependence on the formal process and cycle of elections, and it must reconsider how a more humane, decent, meaningful society can be constructed, outside of the trappings of power elites and constitutional maneuvers that trivialize the legitimate aspirations of all peoples (Chomsky, 1999; Dewey, 1916/1997; Zinn, 2003).

There is ample evidence that democracy needs to be, or must be, linked to social justice (Freire, 1973/2005; Westheimer & Kahne, 2004; Zinn & Macedo, 2005; Macrine, 2009). The book I co edited with Darren Lund in 2008, *Doing Democracy: Striving for Political Literacy and Social Justice* (Lund & Carr, 2008), focuses on this premise, and argues for more creative, diverse, explicit and critical ways of achieving democracy in and through education. The foundation for this type of thinking stretches back in time, where many of the great, and it should be acknowledged from the outset, White, male philosophers raised fundamental questions about right and wrong, how power should be exercised, how we should consider virtues and values, and the meaning of a just and decent society (Tinder, 2004; Kincheloe, 2008b). This book seeks to extend the thinking, analysis and contextualization of democracy in favor of a critical pedagogical vantage point and framework, from which an alternative, yet fundamental, crystallization of democracy can be achieved.

Democracy in Light of, or in Spite of, Education

John Dewey's (1916) contribution to the notion, study and debate related to democracy, buttressed by the salience of the educational project, continues to be an inspirational and insightful commentary on the path toward liberation, or, at least, critical engagement on the part of the masses. Dewey considered the dialectical nature of democracy, which required critical inquiry in and through education, and was critical of the mercantile representation of its role that has vacillated through American society for some time (Simpson & Aycock, 2005). His interest in a humanistic, progressive education, in which authoritarian models of knowledge transmission could be problematized and replaced by experiential efforts, has long been a beacon of light in the dichotomous relationship between reformers and conservatives. Shenton (2009) argues for a return to Deweyian philosophy, maintaining that his fundamental line of inquiry is still the crux of society and democracy: "In 1927, Dewey suggested that a public comes into being when the indirect consequences of transactions between single persons and groups are important, when the effects of these transactions go beyond those immediately engaged and affect others" (p. 436). Thus, the organization of societal encounters, experiences, realities and "transactions" are what constitute, in large part, the fibre of democracy, more so than documents and elections, which might, to varying degrees, seek to underpin a democratic character of a given society.

This juxtapositioning can be exemplified in contemporary times by the (in)famous *No Child Left Behind* (NCLB) legislation, which Gordon, Smyth and Diehl (2008) argue has an ideology linked to war and neo-liberalism, and which Giroux labels as "nothing less than a program of control, both of students and of teachers" (Aronowitz, 2009, p. x). Saltman (2009) links NCLB with "disaster capitalism," which represents an onslaught on public education. Among the critiques of this reform movement tending toward what many consider a vulgar excision of critical engagement, Westheimer (2008) suggests that the more appropriate title for the reform should be *No child left thinking*. Some examples of how NCLB has restricted or prohibited critical engagement, and even critical thinking, given that "In many states, virtually every subject area is under scrutiny for any deviation from one single narrative, based on knowable, testable, and purportedly uncontested facts" (p. 4), include:

In June 2006, the Florida Education Omnibus Bill included language specifying that, "The history of the United States shall be taught as genuine history.... American history shall be viewed as factual, not as constructed, shall be viewed as knowable, teachable, and testable."

Other provisions in the bill mandate "flag education, including proper flag display" and "flag salute" and require educators to stress the importance of free enterprise to the US economy. But what some find most alarming is the stated goal of the bill's designers: "to raise historical literacy" with a particular emphasis on the "teaching of facts." For example, the bill requires that only facts be taught when it comes to discussing the "period of discovery" and the early colonies. Florida is perhaps the first state to ban historical interpretation in public schools, thereby effectively outlawing critical thinking....

More and more, teachers and students are seeing their schools or entire districts and states limiting their ability to explore multiple perspectives to controversial issues. Students and a drama teacher in a Connecticut high school spent months researching, writing, and rehearsing a play they wrote about the Iraq war titled "Voices in Conflict." Before the scheduled performance, the school administration banned the play on the basis that it was "inappropriate." (The students went on to perform the play in the spring of 2007 on an off-Broadway stage in New York to impressive critical review)....

In Colorado, a student was suspended for posting flyers advertising a student protest. In Bay City, Michigan, wearing a T-shirt with an anti-war quotation by Albert Einstein was grounds for suspension....

The federal role in discouraging critical analysis of historical events has been significant as well. In 2002, the US Department of Education announced a new set of history and civic education initiatives that the President said was designed to teach our children that "America is a force for good in the world, bringing hope and freedom to other people." Similarly, in 2004, Tennessee Senator Lamar Alexander (former US secretary of education) warned that students should not be exposed to competing ideologies in historical texts but, rather, be instructed that our nation represents one true ideology. Alexander sponsored his American History and Civics Education Act to put civics back in its "rightful place in our schools, so our children can grow up learning what it means to be an American." Presumably, for Alexander, what it means to be an American is more answer than question. (pp. 4–5)

As Giroux (2009b) argues, despite the trappings of sophistication and techno-logical innovation, we are entering a "new illiteracy in American life."

> The United States is a country that is increasingly defined by a civic deficit, a chronic and deadly form of civic illiteracy that points to the failure of both its educational system and the growing ability of anti-democratic forces to use the educational force of the culture to promote the new illiteracy. As a result of this widespread illiteracy that has come to dominate American culture we have moved from a culture of questioning to a culture of shouting, and in doing so have restaged politics and power in both unproductive and anti-democratic ways.

Thus, the present era could be characterized as one in which *democratic illiteracy* is rapidly usurping the previous capital and democratic fortitude contained within progressive citizenship values and behaviours. Being able to interact with the world—its peoples, cultures, values, differences, decision-making processes, etc.—is no longer a luxury reserved for elites schooled in private vestiges of the colonial past. Literacy must move beyond employment-based technical skills (Giroux, 1988a, 1988b) and seek to problematize the construction of culture by youth (Giroux, 2005a, 2009b), which can tell us a great deal about power and democracy within society. Youth resistance (Giroux, 1997, 2004) must be understood as a reaction to hegemonic forces and not simply the traditional path that needs to be followed (Casella, 2008). How we understand oppositional thinking as well as how we encourage such free thought is critical to the shaping of a democratically literate, engaged and inclusive society (Cook & Westheimer, 2006; Freire, 1998; Portelli & Solomon, 2001).

Being in the moment requires a re-shaping of society that problematizes the prevailing epistemological framework and power structure (Kincheloe, 2008b). Education is something that directly and indirectly affects all citizens (Banks, 2008; Banks et al., 2005). The public good is transparently inter-locked to what transpires in and through schools, and, therefore, Paulo Freire's (1973/2005) notion of *conscientization* needs to be a fundamental pillar to achieving a more humane evolution to what is grounded within the grandiose ambitions of theoretical conceptualizations of democracy. Some of Freire's other, perhaps less well-known, books further explicate *conscientization*, including: *Pedagogy of Indignation* (2004); *Pedagogy of Freedom: Ethics, Democracy, and Civic Courage* (1998); *The Politics of Education* (1985); and *Education for Critical Consciousness* (1973).

Critical Pedagogy as a Way of Interpreting Democracy

While much of the discussion in and around democracy pertains to the political science of political parties, electoral processes, governance structures and the formality of casting a vote, which surely, collectively, play a role in democracy, this book is more concerned with the *critical pedagogy of democracy*. Elections in some form or another are probably with us forever, but the critical pedagogical question of significance is: are these elections and processes relevant in light of oppression, disenfranchisement and a benign neglect of the masses? As per the title, *"Does Your Vote Count?,"* this book will necessarily touch on elections, critiquing them and what they bring to the possibility for uplifting, ingratiating and ameliorating society. Can the two-party system in the US, for example, represent the three hundred million Americans, rich and poor, urban and rural, White and other, powerful and marginalized, warmongers and peaceniks, etc.? Why is the US system considered the model for the world, used as a truncheon to impose, arguably, illegal blockades against Cuba[4], invasions into Iraq, and the tacit omission of Haiti (except in times of catastrophic events such as the January 2010 earthquake that ravaged the country)?

Critical pedagogy offers us a framework to understand political literacy and social transformation, in which static representations of power, identity, and contextual realities are rejected (Darder & Miron, 2006; Denzin, 2009; Giroux, 1997; McLaren 2005b, 2007; McLaren & Kincheloe, 2007). Critical pedagogy is not about providing a checklist against which one can determine the level of social justice within a given society (Carr, 2008a). Rather, it is concerned with oppression and marginalization at all levels, and seeks to interrogate, problematize and critique power and inequitable power relations (Macrine, 2009). Giroux (2007) emphasizes that critical pedagogy "refuses the official lies of power and the utterly reductive notion of being a method.... (It) opens up a space where students should be able to come to terms with their own power as critical agents; it provides a sphere where the unconditional freedom to question and assert is central to the purpose of the university, if not democracy itself" (p. 1).

Critical pedagogy makes a direct, explicit and undeniable linkage between the formalized experience in the classroom and the lived experience outside of the classroom, in which bodies, identities and societal mores influence what takes place in schools (Giroux & Giroux, 2006). Giroux (2007) boldly states that "Democracy cannot work if citizens are not autonomous, self-judging, and independentqualities that are indispensable for students if they are going to make vital judgments and choices about participating in and shaping decisions that affect everyday life, institutional reform, and governmental policy." Significantly, Denzin (2009) provides a number of points that draw together the web of a "critical democratic pedagogy":

> It is not enough to understand any given reality.... (p. 381)

> Pedagogical practices are always moral and practical.... (p. 381)

> ...critical pedagogy disrupts those hegemonic cultural and education practices that reproduce the logics of neoliberal conservatism. (p. 381)

> ...critical pedagogy encourages resistance to the "discourses of privatization, consumerism, the methodologies of standardization and accountability, and the new disciplinary techniques of surveillance" (Giroux & Giroux, 2005, p. 3). Critical pedagogy provides the tools for understanding how cultural and educational practices contribute to the construction of neoliberal conceptions of identity, citizenship, and agency. (p. 381)

> Critical pedagogy offers transformative intellectuals a method, a theory, and a set of practices for putting the critical sociological imagination to work. This project involves constructing and enacting pedagogies of hope and freedom, ways of keeping the idea of a radical democracy alive. (p. 393)

Hence, critical pedagogy can become the cornerstone of democracy in that it provides the "very foundation for students to learn not merely how to be governed, but also how to be capable of governing" (p. 3). Thus, the linkage between a robust, meaningful democracy and critical pedagogy is clearly understood through the lens of transformative learning, engagement and action.

Paulo Freire[5] (1973/2005) is ultimately the leading figure around which a broad range of critical pedagogical scholarship and activism has taken place, theorizing that the conceptualization of education based on traditional modes that enshrine the social order—what he labelled as the "banking model"—can be harmful and destructive for society. Emphasizing the way that power plays out in the "banking model," Freire concludes that "Whereas banking education anesthetizes and inhibits creative power, problem-posing education involves a constant unveiling of reality. The former attempts to maintain the submersion of consciousness; the latter strives for the emergence of consciousness and critical intervention in reality" (p. 81).

Being conscious, able to *read the world*, immersed in humane acts, and engaged in a meaningful interrogation of what the purpose of teaching and learning is should be uppermost in the minds of decision-makers as much as the populace in general (Macrine, 2009). Condemning those who would question hegemonic practices as cynical, negative, uncooperative, unconstructive (even destructive) and corrupted can only further widen the gap between those who enjoy comfort and those seeking a more just conceptualization of society. Education, which, I argue, must underpin democracy for it to be relevant and consequential in favor of the masses, is a political project, one that needs to be understood as such for it to challenge systemically entrenched practices, values, norms and conventions (Freire, 1973/2005; Kincheloe, 2008a, 2008b). Comprehending the dialectical relations between oppressed and oppressor requires a re-thinking of the premise of education, one that properly labels *banking* models of education.

Joe Kincheloe (2008a) puts it quite simply: critical pedagogy is the study of oppression. Some of the components of a critical synthesis of critical pedagogy, according to Kincheloe (2007), are the following:

1. The development of a social individual imagination.
2. The reconstitution of the individual outside the boundaries of abstract individualism.
3. The understanding of power and the ability to interpret its effects on the social and the individual.
4. The provision of alternatives to the alienation of the individual.
5. The cultivation of a critical consciousness that is aware of the social construction of subjectivity.
6. The construction of democratic community-building relationships between individuals.
7. The reconceptualization of reason-understanding that relational existence applies not only to human beings but concepts as well.
8. The production of social skills necessary to activate participation in the transformed, inclusive democratic community.

The inextricable linkage to the establishment of a more decent society is ingrained in the foundation of critical pedagogical work. The desire to enhance human agency, imbued in a process of theory and action, thus underscoring praxis and the libratory potential of critical engagement, is (and should be) a central consideration, not an afterthought. Political literacy and media literacy provide a mandatory platform from which education can be explored, cultivated and transformed (Carr & Lund, 2008; Carr & Porfilio, 2009a; Davies & Hogarth, 2004; Kellner & Share, 2007). Critical pedagogy can assist us in asking questions that are far from the mainstream political process and the corporate media, and, importantly, but which resonate with the lived realities of the majority of people who do not partake fully in the myriad societal, institutional, political, economic and cultural decision-making fora that serve to shape their lives. As a cautionary note, as illustrated by de Lissovoy (2008), critical pedagogy is not disconnected from other critical theoretical frameworks but must be considered from a "compound standpoint," which enhances its relevancy for the multi-disciplinary study of democracy.

This book, building on the seminal work of Paulo Freire and Joe Kincheloe, presents arguments, concepts and propositions that challenge the notion that democracy equates elections, and, moreover, that transformative change cannot and should not take place as a critique of static forms of democracy. Democracy must be cultivated and constantly critiqued, which makes critical pedagogy vulnerable to critiques of its methods, theories, frameworks, and the correctness of its assessment (McLaren & Kincheloe, 2007). Kincheloe (2007) himself, within Freire's spirit and ethos of *radical love*, critiques critical pedagogy as a natural and desirable process of never believing that the final answers have been sought; this dialectical process involves noting, as Kincheloe has done, that critical pedagogy must be open to diverse interpretations and voices from indigenous, minority and marginalized groups, which, ultimately, must be part of the formulation of ideas, truths, realities and experiences. Seeking what Freire calls a *radical democratic humanism* requires a bottom-up movement that is not dependent on the whims of these holding formal positions of power (Aronowitz, 2009). Zinn (2003) reinforces this theme by arguing that change happens when ordinary people organize and create the conditions for change.

While this book is not focused on the debate over Freire's legacy or in refuting attacks on critical pedagogy, it is important to acknowledge that concerns have been raised, and that the advocates for/of critical pedagogy, in many cases, have not been deterred by normative, relativistic interpretations of their work. In some cases, the argument that "people" will never accept critical pedagogy, or that it does not overlap with normative thinking or, equally, that it is too complex should not obfuscate the reason why critical pedagogy developed and has been maintained over the past several decades. Knight and Pearl (2000) unabashedly launch an assault on critical pedagogy in relation to democratic education, arguing that it "wraps itself in the mantle of democracy, but in six generally accepted attributes of democracy (equality, important knowledge, nurture of authority, inclusiveness, participatory decision-making, and rights and a seventh, not normally considered but one that has been the essence of the democratic dreaman optimum environment for everyone), (yet it) offers no direction. In fact, critical pedagogy may be guilty of diversion, division, illusion, and confusion, which are major thrusts of oppression in a 'democratic society'" (p. 197).

Figure 1. Elaboration of Critical Pedagogy by Joe Kincheloe[6]

- Grounded on a social and educational vision of justice and equality
- Constructed on the belief that education is inherently political
- Dedicated to the alleviation of human suffering
- Concerned that schools don't hurt students—good schools don't blame students for their failures or strip students of the knowledges they bring to the classroom
- Enacted through the use of generative themes involve the educational use of issues that are central to students' lives as a grounding for the curriculum
- Centered on the notion that teachers should be researchers—here teachers learn to produce and teach students to produce their own knowledges
- Grounded on the notion that teachers become researchers of their students—as researchers, teachers study their students, their backgrounds, and the forces that shape them
- Interested in maintaining a delicate balance between social change and cultivating the intellect—this requires a rigorous pedagogy that accomplishes both goals
- Concerned with "the margins" of society, the experiences and needs of individuals faced with oppression and subjugation
- Constructed on the awareness that science can be used as a force to regulate and control
- Dedicated to understanding the context in which educational activity takes place
- Committed to resist the harmful effects of dominant power
- Attuned to the importance of complexity—understands complexity theory—in constructing a rigorous and transformative education
- Focused on understanding the profound impact of neo-colonial structures in shaping education and knowledge. (p.10)

It is hoped that the framework presented in this book will soften Knight and Pearl's reticence, and will, moreover, provide some forceful and compelling arguments, examples, conceptualizations and instruments to construct a more meaningful democracy in/through/with critical pedagogy. This is a challenge and a virtue: critical pedagogy does not seek an elevated status on the pantheon of a formalized list of best practices, nor celebratory recognition on the cocktail circuit or at accreditation gala events, which makes it, ironically, a visible and visceral dynamic for internal/external critique, and, ultimately, a desirable, if somewhat uncomfortable, conundrum. However, its outlier status among the accepted and traditional disciplines in the academy make it vulnerable in the sense that its marginalization risks making it a lone voice in the wilderness, delegitimized by an avalanche of neo-liberal policies and wisdom that are infused in the epistemological construction of mass-media thinking. When combined or interwoven with the areas of human rights, antiracism, feminist studies, anti-colonial studies, political sociology, cultural studies, and other interdisciplinary realms, critical pedagogy can represent a powerful antidote to neo-liberal, hegemonic conceptualizations and critiques of *thicker* interpretations of democratic education.

In introductory political science classes, students are told of a simple definition of politics: "the art of the possible." Years later, one understands that neither "art" nor "possible" are easily digestible, nor realizable. Other definitions, which are numerous, include "who gets what, when and how," or how goals are set and influenced, or, even, how values are determined. Seeking to achieve a consensus can be, in many cases, tantamount to aiming for mediocrity, or might underscore oppressive, exclusionary objectives. Can there be a consensus on war, on killing, the death penalty, abortion, gay rights, aboriginal land claims, etc.? Who participates, and to what degree, may determine the parameters of how we frame the salience of consensus government. Critical pedagogy reinforces the reality that politics is messy, and needs to be that way. Moreover, critical pedagogy de-centers the accepted hegemonic wisdom of the ruling classes, and asks questions that encourage introspection, interrogation, empathy, and a critical diagnosis of (all) people as well as their lived experiences, past, present and future.

Epistemology must be reconceptualised, challenging the White, European, male, Christian, heterosexual, middle-class supremacy that has reigned over Western civilization for centuries (Carr & Lund, 2007; Dei & Kempf, 2006). The construction of knowledge must be considered from multiple vantage points, and should avoid the deluge of positivistic measures that have been infused into educational research for decades. Kincheloe (2008b) has developed a critique of this positivist thinking related to knowledge construction and research, which he labels as FIDUROD (see Figure 2).

Figure 2. Kincheloe's Critique of Positivistic Research and Knowledge Construction (FIDUROD)[7]

FIDUROD is an epistemology that stands for knowledge that is
Formal—produced by rigid adherence to a particular research methodology that never changes no matter what new circumstances are encountered, no matter how much these new circumstances might lend themselves to rethinking the mode of inquiry one is using.
Intractable—grounded on the assumption that the world is basically an inert, static entity. What we find today about, say, childhood will be true in all circumstances and will remain true indefinitely. Here childhood (in the same manner as limestone or the chemical composition of salt) is assumed to be a fixed, never changing concept. Of course, such an epistemological stance doesn't account for the ever-changing nature of the world and the observers who study it.

Figure 2 continued. FIDUROD is an epistemology that stands for knowledge that is

---

Decontextualized—constructed by researchers who have removed a phenomenon from the diverse contexts of which it is a part and that grant it meaning. Without these contexts—e.g., the lived world of a student who takes an I.Q. test—the knowledge produced is distorted as it gives a misleading partial picture. The I.Q. tested student may come from a home where her parents were not first English-language speakers and had no formal education, characterized by dire poverty where most energies are directed toward survival not school performance. Might these contextual factors make a difference in the girl's I.Q. test scores? Do they have anything to do with some genetic, inherited notion of intelligence?

Universalistic—what inquirers discover when strictly following the correct epistemology and the research methods it supports applies to all domains of the world and the universe. In pre-Einsteinian physics, for example, gravity was assumed to remain constant in all domains of the cosmos. Einstein's work in the general theory of relativity undermines the universality of gravity as it delineates special circumstances where Sir Isaac Newton's notion of gravity does not work as he postulated—black holes, for example, where nothing can escape the depression in space caused by the concentrated mass of the black hole. There are countless examples one could provide in the social, psychological, and educational sciences to illustrate this same concept. Going back to our I.Q. example, how valid is an I.Q. test in a culture that operates on socio-epistemological assumptions that are profoundly different from Western culture? Another central dimension here is the decontextualization that comes from colonialism-both traditionally and in its new, reconfigured format—that decontextualizes knowledge produced in colonial centers of power by dominant power blocs that dismiss and degrade the knowledges and well-beings of marginalized, colonial groups.

Reductionistic—focusing on those factors that lend themselves most easily to measurement, research/knowledge produced in this context fail to account for the multitude of factors that shape the nature of knowledge produced: the belief and value structure of the researcher, the structural forces that create particular ideological and cultural climates in which the research process operates, the discursive practices of the research community involved in the process, the perspective of numerous individuals from other cultural settings about the phenomenon in question, to name only a few. Such reductionism provides a parochial, limited, and deceptive body of knowledge.

One Dimensional—shaped by the belief that there is one true reality that can be discovered and completely described by following correct research methods. Such an epistemological orientation posits that the walking dimension of human consciousness is the only state worthy of study and use in our daily existence. Thus, the reality that Westerners have depicted via their knowledge production over the last 350 years is a certified reflection of the way the world really is. Anyone who suggests differently has been labeled as crazy, deranged, anti-American, an enemy of Western civilization, or at least a bad scholar. (p.23)

Kincheloe's model of interrogating what has traditionally been considered *truth* and *knowledge* provides a rich tapestry onto which critical thinking can (and should) take place. How are we to understand the vastness, richness and complexity of the human condition without interrogating power? Are manifestations of youth culture through hip-hop, punk and various forms of rock music emblematic of the resistance that is lived but not formally documented within the formal, mainstream democratic structures and strictures (for example, the mass media, government, education)(Kahn & Kellner, 2004; Macedo & Steinberg, 2007; Malott & Miranda-Carol, 2003)? Why is a class-based critique, such as those provided by radical scholars and neo-Marxists (Hill, 2003, 2008; McLaren, 2005a, 2005b, 2007 and 2008) generally rejected, ignored or trivialized in mainstream education circles? Indeed, it would appear that in the US, the words "socialist," "communist," "liberal," "progressive," "radical," "ideological," etc. all seem to carry with them such significant baggage that the mere mention of them is likely to scuttle any discussion related to change (Macedo & Steinberg, 2007; McChesney, 2008). As Kincheloe (2008a, 2008b) has argued throughout a large body of research and practice, epistemology matters: "Thus, Knower and known are inseparable dimensions indelibly connected to anything we call knowledge. With this in mind a critical complex epistemology understands that any rigorous knowledge work involves studying the construction of the selfhood of the knower and the impact it has on what any group of people claim to know." (p.227) Kincheloe (2008b) poses a pivotal question in relation to the essence of knowledge, research, and power: "How, critical researchers ask, can we remain disinterested and anonymous when our concerns, values, experiences, ideology, language, race, class, gender, and sexuality help shape everything we do in a study?" (p. 228) [8]

Freire's (2004) insightful analysis about how *indignation* is not an unnecessary and inappropriate emotion or mode of thinking in relation to oppression further pushes us to re-evaluate our epistemological constitution.

> The dream of a better world is born from the depths of the bowels of its opposite....
>
> The critical position is one where, while epistemologically distancing oneself from the concreteness one is in, so as to know it better, one discovers that the only way out of it lies in the concrete realization of a dream, which thus becomes concreteness anew. Therefore, embracing the dream of a better world and adhering to it imply accepting the process of its creation. It is a process of struggle that must be deeply anchored in ethics. It is the process of struggle against all forms of violence-violence toward the life of trees, of rivers, of fish, of mountains, of cities, against the physical marks of historic and cultural memories. It is also the process of struggle against violence towards the weak, the defenseless, the wounded minorities, violence toward those who are discriminated against for any reason. It is a

process of struggle against impunity, which at the moment encourages crime, abuse, disrespect for the weak, and blatant disrespect for life among us. Otherwise, life itself, in the desperate and tragic form it takes for certain segments of the population, may no longer have any value, or only constitute an unappreciated one. (p. 121)

Ultimately, as will be explored in the subsequent pages, critical pedagogy is not intended to be an idle rant of effusive criticism for the sake of blaming one or another; rather, it seeks to provide, as Freire (2004) argues, *hope* for a more decent life, being and society, to make life meaningful. *Indignation, conscientization, radical love* and enlightenment can lead to the unending dialectical process to achieve various measures of freedom, liberation and humanity. In sum, critical pedagogy is not about acerbic, cryptic, cynical, negative, aimless criticism; it is primarily concerned with the human condition and the critical engagement, analysis, understanding and literacy that is a fundamental part of the process aimed to uplift, not downgrade, the knowledge that we construct.

Formal (Thin) and Lived (Thick) Democracy

What is democracy? How and for whom do we teach about it (Banks et al., 2006; Lund & Carr, 2008a; Parker, 2003, 2006)? How do we reconcile, and teach about, democratic processes in which an unfavorable result conflicts with the mainstream notion of the purity and advantages of democracy over all other systems (Hess, 2004; Parker, 2006)? This raises the question of whose democracy? Should the *democratically* elected Hamas government in Palestine in 2006 be recognized, even though tenets of its platform may seem distasteful to many people? Should US elections be considered democratic when one considers the amount of money required to get elected, not to mention the role of the media, the lack of diversity and representation of the elected officials (especially in terms of race, gender, ethnicity, and socio-economic status), and the restrictive voting processes as well as questionable tabulation practices (the 2000 presidential campaign being an extreme example) (Chomsky, 2008b; McChesney, 2008; Swift, 2002)? How do we consider the cataclysmic economic meltdown on Wall Street with the basic, often unmet, daily needs of the broader populace within a democracy (Prins, 2009)? Can American classrooms debate the US presence in Iraq without being labelled unpatriotic (Kellner, 2007; Westheimer, 2006, 2008)?

Should the intervention in Iraq be characterized as an "invasion," a "military operation," an "occupation" or an "allied rescue mission"? Who are the "freedom-fighters"? The terminology to define the context and conditions of democracy and politics is, to use a military term, a *minefield* of dissent. One example is that FOX News has apparently been reported to have been directed by the owner of the network to refer to "suicide-bombers" as "homicide-bombers."[9] Perspective-taking and a liberal dose of critical reflection on competing visions can enhance democracy, rather than diminish it (Sears & Hughes, 2006). In sum, what are the implications of avoiding "doing" democratic education (Provenzo, 2005; Parker, 2003)? These questions help frame the central role of educators in democratic education process.

With the declining support for elections (this theme is dealt with in some detail later in the book), especially in light of decreasing numbers of young people voting, is there a problem with democracy (Cook, 2004; Cook & Westheimer, 2006; Patterson, 2003)? This is a phenomenon not only in the United States but elsewhere in the Western world as well (Davies & Hogarth, 2004). Swift (2002) has documented how the absence or omission of women from electoral politics is also a concern for representative democracy; somewhat ironically, the US has among the lowest levels of elected women officials in the industrialized world. With the exception of the election of Barack Obama, which is explored later in this book, it is probably more than obvious to emphasize that electoral politics in extremely heterogeneous Western countries remains the almost exclusive purview of Whites (see Carr & Lund, 2007).

The analogy of *thin* versus *thick* democracy, which is a central focus to this book, can be illustrated in diverse ways. Swift (2002) crystallizes the dichotomous relation as follows, using a weak versus strong analysis.

> Two strains can be identified in the history of democratic thought and experience. One is weak democracy where popular sovereignty is hemmed in by the individual right to property that holds sway over the collective rights of the community. This theory is based on a notion of possessive individualism and is a strong market/weak democracy model. The second strain is the notion of strong democracy rooted in the radical republican tradition which emphasizes the self-rule of the political community and the equality of power in democratic decision-making. (p. 35)

The complex debate over economic hegemony, via an unrepentant neo-liberalism in present times, can sway the epistemological, ideological, philosophical and common-sense understanding and appreciation of, and engagement with, democracy (Hursh & Martina, 2003).

As this book argues, voter participation is only loosely connected to the supposed decline in democracy. Many alternative democratic (and social) movements in relation to the environment, rejecting wealth concentration through neo-liberalism, protesting war, denouncing racism, and seeking poverty reduction, among others, have mobilized vast numbers of people internationally, who work outside of the confines of soundbites, interest groups, congressional hearings, and the surreal proliferation of "reality" shows (Gandin & Apple, 2005; Porfilio & Carr, in press; Schugurensky, 2003). The fact that more people voted in/for *American Idol* than did in the 2008 US election is a concern at many levels[10]. Therefore, an important question relates to what knowledge is worth constructing, and whether citizens are as knowledgeable as they should be in relation to democracy.

The epistemological mindset about the "goodness" of the nation, in the US and abroad, often prevents the interrogation of pivotal and necessary questions about the truth concerning the mantra of representing a just cause[11]. Being able to contest a latent or nefarious patriotism manifestly against the best interests of vast swaths of the populace is a fundamental concern within the study of the critical pedagogy of democracy (Giroux, 1997, 2008, 2009b; McLaren, 2007; Westheimer, 2006).

> The history of America is the one story every kid knows. It's a story of fierce individualism and heroic personal sacrifice in the service of a dream. A story of early settlers hungry and cold, carving a home out of the wilderness. Of visionary leaders fighting for democracy and justice, and never wavering. Of a populace prepared to defend those ideals to the death. It's the story of a revolution (an American art form as endemic as baseball or jazz) beating back British Imperialism and launching a new colony into the Industrial age on its own terms. It's a story of America triumphant. A story of its rise after World War II to become the richest and most powerful country in the history of the world, "the land of the free and home of the brave," an inspiring model for the whole world to emulate. That's the official history, the one that is taught in school and the one our media and culture reinforce in myriad ways every day.[12]

Zinn (2003) has elaborated on the importance of re-situating and re-interrogating the *official* version of history, which neglects the diverse racial, class-based, gendered and other representations that have influenced the shaping of society. Further, Westheimer (2006) has cautioned about the potentially oppressive effects of an unchecked patriotism based on limited engagement with the *other*. Education from a critical vantage point is perhaps the most effective way to diffuse the preponderance of fear to question authority, underscoring free speech, which, ironically, is often invoked as the bedrock of American democracy (Carr, 2007b).

Figure 3. Thick-thin Spectrum of Democracy and Democratic Education

THIN	THICK
Voting and elections are the key to democracy	Voting and elections are but one component to democracy, and must be problematized
Studying mainstream political parties, processes and structures forms the core of teaching about democracy	Studying about democracy necessarily involves preparing (and engaging) for democracy, including dialectical critique, and a focus on power
Democratic education is generally concentrated within a single class or subject (i.e., Government, and/or Social Studies)	Democratic education is infused across the curriculum, and involves all aspects of how education is organized (i.e., assemblies, extracurricular, staff meetings, parental involvement, community linkages)

THIN	THICK
Weak connection between democracy and education	Explicit, engaged connection; democracy must involve a politically literate populace
Support for democracy involves an uncritical assessment of foreign policy, militarization, conflicts, neo-liberalism and patriotism	Foreign interventions, war, conflicts, racism, injustice and human rights abuses are critically interrogated, linking local issues/concerns with the international/global context
Politics generally pertains to elections, the predominant political parties, and the agenda set by the mainstream media	Politics pertains to all aspects of education, including decisionmaking, oppression, marginalization and power (what is omitted is as equally important)
Concern that teaching for and about democracy may be contentious, and could even be considered indoctrination	To not teach about and for democracy in a critical fashion is to privilege dominant hegemony; avoiding contentious matter and concepts can lead to great harm (racism, war, injustice, poverty, etc.)
Weak linkage between schools and the broader societal experience	Education is linked to society, and should seek to understand, and, in some cases, transform it
Limited formal curriculum on the vastness, richness, and complexity of democracy, with limited opportunities to experience democracy outside of voting process	Formal and informal opportunities to cultivate, stimulate and inculcate democracy and democratic practices; what is most important here is that knowledge is constructed, not merely conveyed or transmitted (as in the "banking model")
Narrow engagement with alternative visions, movements, concepts and phenomena outside of formal curriculum	Seeking to understand political and social movements not mentioned in mainstream media and the formal curriculum is important; linking what we know with what we do is encouraged
Diversity is generally understood in an essentialized way, with limited linkages to Whiteness, and inequitable power relations	Democracy cannot be understood without a critical linkage to social justice, which problematizes identity, diversity and social change, including intersecting forms of power and privilege
Curriculum is generally prescriptive, with limited emphasis on critical analysis and engagement, and assessment often suffocates dynamic and complex interplay between groups and power-structures; avoids political nature of education	Assessment is not the focus of thick democratic education; seeking critical engagement with authentic encounters, understanding that knowledge is constructed, and accepting that teachers do not have all of the answers are key; Freire's generative themes and Dewey's progressive education underscore the notion that education is a political project
Discussion about and for democracy is limited, contrived and aims for comfort and reassurance rather than questioning complicity, change, and power	Deliberative democracy must be made more authentic with engagement with a broad range of groups/interests/concerns; students should be encouraged to question and challenge problems
Literacy is constructed in limited way, focused on knowledge and skills (→employment is the goal)	Political and media literacy are fundamental pillars, seeking what Giroux calls "emancipatory literacy" and democratic conscientization

Incidences of democratic development historically as well as in the present should be celebrated as much as they should be contextualized (Zinn & Macedo, 2005). Democracy, however it is defined, needs to be re-considered. While strident democratic change was in effect at one level in American society two hundred years ago, the nation also contained within its boundaries slavery, highlighted by many of the Founding Fathers being slave owners. Who writes history, and from what vantage point? Is democracy a litany of battles, dates and victories, or does it also include women, minorities and working-class struggles (Zinn, 2003)?

The history of modern democratic thought, far from the Greek experiences long ago, is generally associated with the United States. Alexis de Tocqueville (2007) wrote of the intricate promise and tensions of early American democracy, almost euphoric about the spirit of a meritocracy as opposed to the traditional heredity-based hegemonic regimes he knew of in Europe. However, he tempered his analysis with concern about meaningful participation, the obvious inequities evident in relation to non-Whites, and "soft despotism" (Gregg, 2000). The infinite quarrel over rights and sovereignty was of concern when de Tocqueville wrote *Democracy in America*, and continues to generate debate. Are rights enunciated on paper *bona fide* rights that enshrine equality? Are the powerful, the wealthy and the elites simply just another voice? How do we know what the truth looks like? Gregg (2000) sums up his analysis of de Tocqueville by suggesting that "we need to convince others that we must love democracy moderately, since it does not deserve our absolute devotion, and that more attention needs to be given to nurturing the type of moral and cultural milieu required by democracy along the lines suggested by Tocqueville over 160 years ago" (p. 43).

In the contemporary time, Robert Dahl (1956, 1972) warned of the excesses of power, providing advice on how to make change within the strictures of a democratic society, critiquing it as a *polyarchy*. Later, I critique some contemporary forms of democracy, including what I call *econ-ocracy*, which is dependent on neo-liberal, hegemonic conceptualizations and influences. The promise of far-reaching equality and equity, opportunities and rights, and security and happiness promised under various iterations of American democracy, witnessed in part by de Tocqueville, has been significantly maligned by the threat of a populace not fully ingratiated within decision-making circles. James Madison, the fourth president of the US, stated that democracy will forever be imperilled and at risk if peace is not foundational to its mission and being: "Of all the enemies to public liberty war is, perhaps, the most to be dreaded because it comprises and develops the germ of every other. War is the parent of armies; from these proceed debts and taxes ...

known instruments for bringing the many under the domination of the few.... No nation could preserve its freedom in the midst of continual warfare."[13]

It should be stressed, at this point, that democracy should not, ideally (or perhaps paradoxically), be an impediment to the human condition. On the contrary, the democratic ideal and project is never completed or achieved. In the course of the past few decades, one can think of incredibly unjust and inhumane policies, practices and experiences that have served to debase societies, cultures and nations: for example, in relation to indigenous peoples, minorities, women, gays and lesbians, and working people. Yet, the prominent narrative of democratic moral superiority has remained intact, beyond reproach, sprinkling an undying allegiance to the flag and political virtue at the national level (Borg & Mayo, 2007; Chomsky, 2008b; Henry & Tator, 2005). Why is there such resistance to critiquing democracy? Why do educators, education systems and governments not favor a more *democratic* approach to education? Why does militaristic hegemony appear to be the ultimate taboo? Why are neo-liberal policies, practices and institutions, which could be considered to be nefarious, disruptive and subversive to the democratic project, not addressed in a critical manner in and through education? Importantly, what are the implications of these questions? This book, using a critical pedagogical vantage-point, approach and framework, seeks to address these questions, hoping to offer alternatives to the traditional, mainstream representation of democracy. The main objective is not to malign the United States nor to diminish and discredit the potential for democracy; on the contrary, a major focus is to facilitate a more meaningful, engaged and critical debate on democracy, allowing for transformative change fulfilling the desires of theoretical democratic.

Re-imagining Democracy

How did democracy end up as being translated into an electoral battle when there is such an unshakable conceptual foundation positioning it to represent the liberation from tyranny? Hartman (2008) details how Dewey's "progressive education movement" has long been a target of Conservative antipathy and the quest for individual rights, which were formulated as being at odds with the broader project of a more democratic and citizenship-based education. The relationship between local/national and international events shaping educational debates has often been underplayed in the minds of Americans, yet the newest incarnation of globalization is but another form of inter-dependency that more explicitly, perhaps through broader technological access, informs the lived realities of Americans and others (Chossudovsky, 2003; Macedo & Gounari, 2006). The conflict with the Soviet Union or communism writ large in the minds of the "West," characterized by the "cold war," is a central point to Hartman's book (2008), and this could lead to some hypothesizing about the use of war and military conflict to pacify local populations. Obliged patriotism, combined with a cultural and political backlash from corporate and government decision-making circles, what Gramsci (Fishman & McLaren, 2005; Grasmci & Forgacs, 2000) has qualified as hegemony, is emblematic through the examples of the 2003 Iraq invasion and the longstanding foray into Southeast Asia through the Vietnam War. The linkage that Gramsci makes to schooling and education is still relevant today, especially in light of the neo-liberalized and long-standing inequitable class structure of education (Bowles & Gintis, 1977, 2001).

Andre Gunder Frank's (1979) dependency theory is also helpful in this discussion to highlight how dependent relations between the periphery and the center, as exemplified through classical colonial relations with the exchange of goods, knowledge and authority being structured in a non-reciprocal fashion to the benefit of the colonizer (for example, Spain with most of Latin America, France with a good part of Africa, England with India), can explain the development of capitalist hegemony in North America and Europe. Other important and fundamental historical events, such as the Berlin Conference (1895), were instrumental in carving up Africa into colonial quadrants that ultimately codified much of the ethnic and cultural conflicts evident today in addition to enshrining corruption, immoral, antithetical values, and a desecration of indigenous cultures (Patterson, 2001). The purpose of education is still being debated, especially in light of the neo-liberal push to swing formal teaching and learning toward a quasi-mercantalist function of supporting the job market, and not contesting hegemonic practices that oppose oppression (see Hill, 2003, Kincheloe, 2008, and McLaren, 2007). Democracy at the most local level, therefore, is viscerally tethered to the broader macro portrait as well as the geo-political, economic, socio-cultural and historic spheres.

The economic meltdown framing the George W. Bush presidency, culminating in the historic election of Barack Obama, focused on bailing out the old capitalist order, has not brought with it a complete re-thinking about how the "free market" has affected the US (Bellamy Foster & Magdoff, 2009; Prins, 2009). With so much energy and resources being ploughed into saving a defunct economic system, with major sums being paid to those who, arguably, assumed only limited risk in the way they handled the savings, the pensions and livelihoods of so many working people, it is intriguing to surmise as to why the (2009) healthcare debate appears to be so much more lively and strident than the proposition that "permanent war" (McLaren, 2007) has caused irreparable damage to the psyche and pocketbook of Americans. The connection between education and democracy is, therefore, unequivocally clear: where is the public, informed and relevant debate on what type of society people actually want? How does education play into hegemonic cooptation of the interests of working people? How does the imbalance in terms of funding, conditions, experiences, outcomes and objectives of schools across the US determine the form and content of debate on all of the major issues of the day?

Dewey's (1916/1997) clarion call for a more critically engaged population, thus, underpins much of the macro-level machinations that continue to serve to re-produce social relations (Bourdieu, 1970; Bourdieu & Passeron, 1990). Asking critical questions, a fundamental component of critical pedagogy, along with an acknowledgment that knowledge is constructed, is as important as the formulation of answers. To understand the state of an education system, it is, therefore, helpful to consider not only what students learn but, importantly, how they learn. Kincheloe (2008a, 2008b) emphasizes the nature of learning and knowledge construction, locating students within their experiential realm, as echoed by Freire's (1973/2005) use of generative themes in learning. The reality that education is a political (and epistemological) project (Freire, 1985) underpins the quest for a more relevant and humane democracy.

Overview of the book

In the subsequent chapters, I seek to present a range of concepts, examples, anecdotes, questions and research in a critical and dialectical manner to underscore the critical pedagogy of democracy. Some of the chapters were previously published as articles or book chapters, and have been re-worked here to more smoothly integrate into this volume. I have been thinking through the linkage between democracy and education over the past several years, trying to better understand how the former can exist without the latter, and, significantly, what the latter actually does to produce a *thicker*, more tangible and meaningful semblance of democracy, one that could assist a society to resolve issues of inequity, power imbalances, oppression, and war. This is not the first book on such a lofty topic. It is hoped that it will, nonetheless, contribute to the critical pedagogical literature on democracy, democratic education and transformational change in education.

There are four sections in this book. The first section aims to set the framework with three chapters that present some basic theoretical, conceptual and methodological concepts on the theme of democracy, democratic education and critical pedagogy. I introduce the concept of *econ-ocracy* to characterize the overwhelming influence of capitalist and neo-liberal markets within the psyche and lived experiences of people, especially those outside of the decision-making circles. These chapters also offer some examples of how democracy is constructed, and how this mainstream perspective can effectively dilute, ironically, meaningful debate on democracy. This section aims to raise questions about the potential for electoral democracy to effectuate substantive change, given the reality of nefarious military and economic machinations that prevail despite the will of major segments of the population.

The second section contains four chapters, which, individually and collectively, strive to enunciate a vision for democracy in and through education. How do we do democracy? What is the role of educators in cultivating democracy? Is it possible to support critical democratic education within the present context, especially in light of neo-liberalism and a globalization that favors the commodification of knowledge? These chapters argue for a more lucid, connected and significant form of *democratic literacy*, one that considers political and social literacy as well as the traditional forms of learning and knowledge. In presenting some original research, I also seek to understand the salience of educators' perspectives, experiences and perceptions in relation to their engagement and conceptualization of democracy within the educational arena. Two of the chapters in this section ask: Should democracy end racism? Can we have a democracy in which racism festers and is unchecked? Does racism undermine the normative and progressive conceptualizations of the democratic project? In focusing on Whiteness, in particular, as a paradoxical concept to interrogate racism (traditionally, race has often been conceptualized as a problem for the people subjugated by it, not those who maintain privilege and power as a result), I raise issues about how democracy and, specifically, democratic education, are interwoven into racialized marginalization. Moreover, it is important to understand how this racialized project has formed a fundamental cornerstone to contemporary visions and versions of democracy. From this research, some interesting findings about social justice boil to the surface. The heading for this section, *Democratic Education: Can It Happen through Osmosis?*, underscores the notion that democracy is a process, and that it must be continually re-thought, cajoled and interrogated.

The third section focuses on democracy and power, still within the context of education. Can we be critical and democratic at the same time? Is there a danger in critiquing patriotism? What are the implications of not understanding how power works? The three chapters in this section address diverse themes: The election of an African-American president: Does this mean democracy is working?; The media, media literacy and the critical pedagogy of democracy; and "Shocked and awed" into and out of democracy: Can there be war and democracy... simultaneously? Together, this section raises concerns about how formal, theoretical and constitutional democracy is not always intertwined with the manifestation of what democracy looks like, for example, within the electoral arena, the media, the military complex, the educational system, and society at-large.

The last section is entitled "The End Is the Beginning," inspired by Joe Kincheloe, whose influence on the thinking in this book has been substantial. Joe ended his last book (Kincheloe, 2008b) with that slogan, and, as is exemplified throughout his vast scholarship, humility is a most remarkable virtue. Rather than (foolishly) claim that this book is the final word on democracy, I seek to underscore that, hopefully, this will be another interpretation, another vehicle from which reflection can be undertaken, and another set of ideas through which educational thinking (and action) might take place. There are three chapters in this section, the first asking "But what can I do?," which offers fifteen suggestions that educators can consider to immerse, or engage, themselves in meaningful action; the second provides some general and specific thoughts on the evolving *critical pedagogical* democratic project, and a final chapter in the form of a postscript that contains a range of quotes about democracy, illustrating that the concept is far-ranging, provocative and problematic. It is easy to despair, to proverbially throw in the towel, to tune out, to reject "politics" in favor of the good times lavishly presented in reality shows and sit-coms aimed at taking away the duress and stress of life, but the challenge of thinking through life's dilemmas can be as invigorating as it is necessary. This book, humbly inspired by Freire, Kincheloe, Macedo, Giroux, Steinberg, McLaren, Dardar, hooks and other critical pedagogues[14], aims to present another version of the truth, another layer of the democratic onion, and another forum in which critical thought, engagement and work can be produced. Critical pedagogy is about liberation, peace, and human decency, themes, I hope, that mesh together throughout the contents of this book in favor of a more democratic society, a more meaningful educational experience, and a more peaceful world.

Chapter 2

Democratic Stripes and Divergent Views of Democracy

The struggle for humanization, for the emancipation of labor, for the overcoming of alienation, for the affirmation of men and women as persons would be meaningless. The struggle is possible only because dehumanization although a concrete historical fact, is not a given destiny but the result of an unjust order that engenders violence in the oppressor, which in turn dehumanizes the oppressed. (Freire, 1973/2005, p. 44)

A Panoply of Democracy

Through a simple Google search, one can find a discombobulating 83,800,000 (in 2010) links for the word *democracy*. There are a plethora of categories, including: direct democracy; Greek democracy; communism; dictatorship; capitalism; monarchy; socialism; and oligarchy. Democracy is linked to numerous concepts, philosophies, systems, governments, movements, operational systems, and as a label for political parties, processes and other remnants within popular culture. With regard to particular forms of government, a broad range of possibilities are enumerated, including: direct; representative; consensus; constitutional; deliberative; liberal; participatory; republican; and social.

Democracy is widely and broadly understood to encompass such things as "majority rule," "government by the people," the "will of the people," and is generally thought to be anchored within a system legitimated by elections. The Merriam-Webster dictionary locates the term within the original Greek *dēmokratia* (*demos* equating people, and *kratos* equating rule or strength), dating back to four or five centuries BC, and defines democracy as follows:

1. a government by the people ; *especially* : rule of the majority b: a government in which the supreme power is vested in the people and exercised by them directly or indirectly through a system of representation usually involving periodically held free elections
2. a political unit that has a **democratic** government
3. *capitalized*: the principles and policies of the Democratic party in the United States ‹from emancipation Republicanism to New Deal *Democracy* C. M. Roberts›
4. the common people especially when constituting the source of political authority
5. the absence of hereditary or arbitrary class distinctions or privilege[1]

The *American-Heritage Dictionary* (2005) echoes these concepts by defining the term as follows:

1. Government by the people, exercised either directly or through elected representatives.
2. A political or social unit that has such a government.
3. The common people, considered as the primary source of political power.
4. Majority rule.
5. The principles of social equality and respect for the individual within a community.[2]

Christiano (2006) outlines the diversity of interpretations for democracy, emphasizing the nuances framing normative approaches.

First, democracy concerns collective decision making, by which I mean decisions that are made for groups and that are binding on all the members of the group. Second, this definition means to cover a lot of different kinds of groups that may be called democratic. So there can be democracy in families, voluntary organizations, economic firms, as well as states and transnational and global organizations. Third, the definition is not intended to carry any normative weight to it. It is quite compatible with this definition of democracy that it is not desirable to have democracy in some particular context. So the definition of democracy does not settle any normative questions. Fourth, the equality required by the definition of democracy may be more or less deep. It may be the mere formal equality of one-person one-vote in an election for representatives to an assembly where there is competition among candidates for the position. Or it may be more robust, including equality in the processes of deliberation and coalition building. "Democracy" may refer to any of these political arrangements. It may involve direct participation of the members of a society in deciding on the laws and policies of the society or it may involve the participation of those members in selecting representatives to make the decisions.[3]

At the philosophical level, historically, there have been vigorous arguments in opposition to, as well as in favor of, democracy. Christiano (2006) outlines how John Stuart Mill (1806–1873) advanced three rationales for which "a democratic method of making legislation is better than non-democratic methods":

Strategically, democracy has an advantage because it forces decision-makers to take into account the interests, rights and opinions of most people in society. Since democracy gives some political power to each, more people are taken into account than under aristocracy or monarchy. ... The basis of this argument is that politicians in a multiparty democracy with free elections and a free press have incentives to respond to the expressions of needs of the poor.

Epistemologically, democracy is thought to be the best decision-making method on the grounds that it is generally more reliable in helping participants discover the right decisions. Since democracy brings a lot of people into the process of decision making, it can take advantage of many sources of information and critical assessment of laws and policies.

Many have endorsed democracy on the basis of the proposition that democracy has beneficial effects on character. Many have noted with Mill and Rousseau that democracy tends to make people stand up for themselves more than other forms of rule do because it makes collective decisions depend on them more than monarchy or aristocracy do. Hence, in democratic societies individuals are encouraged to be more autonomous. In addition, democracy tends to get people to think carefully and rationally more than other forms of rule because it makes a difference whether they do or not. Finally, some have argued that democracy tends to enhance the moral qualities of citizens.[4]

Citing Thomas Hobbes (1588–1679) and public choice theorists, Christiano (2006) also presents a central argument against democracy, emphasizing that the common person is not sufficiently equipped to grapple with all of the intricacies and complexities therein, and also that elites are not simply just another citizen. An analysis of the flaws with democracy emanating from the European context provides the following arguments against the contemporary notion of democracy, suggesting that the perception of democracy does not mesh with the reality of what electoral democracy has produced:

> Democracy does not deserve the semi-sacred status accorded to it. In Europe, democratically elected politicians such as Jörg Haider, Jean-Marie Le Pen, Silvio Berlusconi, Umberto Bossi, Gianfranco Fini and Pim Fortuyn are a reminder of democracy's defects: an anti-racist dictatorship is preferable to a racist democracy. Democracy is expanding globally, but not because of its moral superiority. Military intervention is now the standard origin of democratic political systems. Any universal ideology will tend to crusades and messianic conquest, and democracies feel entitled to 'bring freedom' to other countries.[5]

One can see how these pivotal discussions hundreds of years ago remain germane within the present context, especially given the declining levels of voter participation combined with increasing levels of cynicism related to how elections are conducted (Carr & Porfilio, 2009b; Cook, 2004; Patterson, 2003). Truths that were once presumed apparent must now be questioned, and the power of powerful figures, such as former President George W. Bush, must be re-examined, which can make for a more meaningful democratic experience (Denzin, 2007; Gordon, Smyth, & Diehl, 2008; Kellner, 2002, 2007). Tinder (2004) presents "perennial questions" that have not been resolved over the centuries, highlighting how our thinking about human nature can, and is, linked to our understanding about politics. Political theory, while not readily apparent to many, is grounded in basic beliefs. Tinder (2004, pp. 3–4) points out that most political ideas, perhaps all of them, are based on some particular conception of human nature. The conservative idea that political authority should be strong and highly centralized, for example, is apt to be based on a conception of human beings as selfish and competitive; the liberal notion that extensive social changes can ordinarily be brought peacefully may arise from the premise that human beings are for the most part reasonable."

Tinder (2004) elaborates an intricate model of critical interrogation of our values, beliefs, experiences and epistemology that requires relinquishing commonly held views and perceptions. The critical pedagogy of democracy would, similarly, encourage difficult, problematic, uncomfortable reflection in the hopes of achieving higher levels of understanding and engagement.

In a general sense, the traditional framing of democracy, therefore, focused on rights, freedoms, laws, separation of powers, and systems of government that were intended to be representative (Swift, 2002). Many confounding issues related to minority rights— Who is a minority? How can minority rights mesh with the broader aims and objectives of a just society? What is the balance between majority and minority rights?—still exist in present times. It is clear that there is not simply one way of forming and sustaining a democracy. Historical, traditional, cultural, economic and other factors all shape a society's relationship with democracy. Can a monarchy also be a democracy? Can the Founding Fathers own slaves and prohibit women and minorities from voting and, simultaneously, decree that they are creating a democracy? Was the United States intended to be a democracy in the first place (Chomsky, 2008)? These questions require an interrogation of the values, instruments, practices and outcomes of how a given society grapples with democracy before an assessment can be made before the actual democratic rights and freedoms can be proclaimed (Diamond & Morlino, 2005).

A leading Canadian non-profit, non-partisan group advocating democracy and democratic reform is Democracy Watch[6], founded in 1993, focusing its attention on "government accountability and corporate responsibility": "Its aim is to help reform Canadian government and business institutions to bring them into line with the realities of a modern, working democracy." Democracy Watch's work for democratic reform is based upon the principles of "access to full and timely information about government and business activities," "meaningful rights to participate and be represented in Canada's political system," "easily accessible remedies against government and corporate waste, abuse and misrepresentation," "Accountability measures... (regarding) concentrations of power," and "Measures ...(allowing) Canadians (to) band together as citizens, consumers and taxpayers" Interestingly, while not packaged in the same way, most political parties and leading politicians in Western countries would probably not feel uncomfortable with the guiding principles listed above.

Democracy Watch cautions that even if a range of participation and accountability measures are respected, "It is still essentially impossible to stop three key undemocratic activities, and as a result these three activities even if they only occur at infrequently will always remain a threat to all societies aspiring to be democracies, as follows:"

1. it is essentially impossible to stop secret gifts of money and favor-trading corrupting politicians and government officials;
2. it is essentially impossible to stop secret lobbying of politicians and government officials, and;
3. it is essentially impossible to stop police, security and armed forces from abusing their investigative powers by invading people's privacy and rights.

As is echoed elsewhere in the literature on democracy and democratic reform, the three provisos listed at the end of the Democracy Watch definition highlight some longstanding and important arguments against, or concerns with, the way that democracy is practiced, as opposed to how it is theorized. The notion of accountability must be unpacked related to who determines what, how, by what criteria, and for what ends. Similarly, Dreher, Kotsogiannis and McCorriston (2004) examine corruption internationally using an economic model, deducing that the loss to economic productivity is substantial as a result of corruption. They emphasize the plurality of causes and indicators framing corruption, including political, historical, socio-cultural, and economic factors. Wrage (2007) and Lambsdorff (2007) further flesh out the deleterious nature of corruption in all societies, including those considered the most democratic, which raises important ethical, judicial, political, cultural and philosophic questions about the relationship between elections and democracy.

Figure 4. Democracy Watch's Definition of a Democratic Society[7]

Democracy Watch's mandate, **20 Steps towards a Modern, Working Democracy**, is based upon the following definition of a democratic society:

A DEMOCRACY IS a society in which all adults have easily accessible, meaningful, and effective ways:

1) to participate in the decision-making processes of every organization that makes decisions or takes actions that affect them, and;
2) to hold other individuals, and those in these organizations who are responsible for making decisions and taking actions, fully accountable if their decisions or actions violate fundamental human rights, or are dishonest, unethical, unfair, secretive, inefficient, unrepresentative, unresponsive or irresponsible;
3) so that all organizations in the society are citizen-owned, citizen-controlled, and citizen-driven, and all individuals and organizations are held accountable for wrongdoing.

All children should also have easily accessible, meaningful, and effective ways to hold organizations accountable as set out in #2 above, but it is acceptable in a democracy to limit children's participation rights until they reach adulthood, mainly because psychological research has shown clearly that almost all children below a certain age do not have fully formed brains, and are not capable of reasonable deliberation and discussion.

Some of the types of corruption that are most prevalent include influence peddling, bribery, extortion, graft, nepotism, favoritism, government appointments and nominations, insider-trading through privileged information, and organized activities, such as those related to crime-related gangs and the mafia. The concern over corruption in elections, whether related to the infamous 2000 US presidential election, the recent 2009 Afghani elections, or others in developing countries and elsewhere, renders the actual process of determining issues and leaders to be problematic and even suspicious in some cases. Bradley (2005) provides a critique of the 2004 US presidential election, arguing that voter fraud, combined with the almost non-existent public reaction to it, needs to be critiqued rather than being maligned as some sort of a conspiracy theory. Diminishing corruption, similar to enhancing and strengthening democracy, requires a more critically engaged populace, one that is complicit in determining the shape, scope and direction of the society, and, equally, is not passively standing by waiting to endorse candidates through lengthy and costly electoral campaigns.

Polyarchy as a Challenge to the Affirmation that We Have Democracy

Renowned Yale University political science professor Robert A. Dahl developed the concept of *polyarchy* (in Greek, meaning *many [poly]* and *rule [arkhe]*). The concept describes a form of government in which three or more persons are vested with the power, and, importantly, this "nation-state" must be vigilant in considering the interests of all citizens. While considered desirable for achieving democracy, Dahl has postulated that the major tenets of polyarchy may not be appropriately configured or enforceable to develop in such a way. The reality that small groups of elites may control major "democratic" institutions, combined with the problematic and often discredited nature of the electoral process, should be understood in terms of a broader, systemic analysis of political life, not in a restrained, abstract form that leads to the conclusion that only the powerful, technocrats and the wealthy should determine the direction of a nation.

In outlining the main elements of a polyarchy, Dahl emphasizes commonly held attributes that require further elaboration (what is the extent of free speech, political association and the means to influence the government, especially in the context of a corporate media, stratified class relations, and divergent levels of access to power?)(Figure 5). Dahl provides further clarification of the relevancy of *polyarchy*, outlining the historical, socio-economic and cultural factors that are required to produce it (Figure 6), which, again, suggest that blind allegiance to patriotism (Westheimer, 2006), militarization and hegemonic practices (Chomsky, 2007; Churchill, 1998) can obfuscate the democratic aspirations of all people within a society.

The concept of *polyarchy* has been taken up by Noam Chomsky, who links diminished levels of democratic participation and decision-making to far-reaching catastrophes that can consume a society. Chomsky (2003) warns of the unchecked and blind ambitions of a minority, in this case in relation to the quest for war in Iraq, against the interests of the majority. Building on Dahl's (1972) model, he dissects the intuitive and far-reaching depths of moral thinking juxtaposed against the sophisticated and equally deceptive measures employed to coerce people into a catastrophe they did not want to experience. The manipulation required to cultivate a sentiment of impending danger undermines the prospect of critical, deliberative democratic engagement. First, he lays bare the notion that there was a rationale or justification for invading Iraq, then he presents the case of massive resistance and opposition to any such invasion. Chomsky makes the point that the inference that the US had some sort of democratic right to invade is offensive and dangerous in the light of the foreseeable consequences of such a hegemonic-militaristic foray.

> Controlling the general population has always been a dominant concern of power and privilege, particularly since the first modern democratic revolution in seventeenth-century England. The self-described "men of best quality" were appalled as a "giddy multitude of beasts in men's shapes" rejected the basic framework of the civil conflict raging in England between king and Parliament, and called for government" by countrymen like ourselves, that know our wants," not by "knights and gentlemen that make us laws, that are chosen for fear and do but oppress us, and do not know the people's sores." The men of best quality recognized that if the people are so "depraved and corrupt" as to "confer places of power and trust upon wicked and undeserving men, they forfeit their power in this behalf unto those that are good, though but a few."[8]

Figure 5. Dahl's Characteristics of a Polyarchy[9]

- Control over governmental decisions about policy is constitutionally vested in elected officials.
- Elected officials are chosen and peacefully removed in relatively frequent, fair and free elections in which coercion is quite limited.
- Practically all adults have the right to vote in these elections.
- Most adults also have the right to run for the public offices for which candidates run in these elections.
- Citizens have an effectively enforced right to freedom of expression, particularly political expression, including criticism of the officials, the conduct of the government, the prevailing political, economic, and social system, and the dominant ideology.
- They also have access to alternative sources of information that are not monopolized by the government or any other single group.
- Finally, they have an effectively enforced right to form and join autonomous associations, including political associations, such as political parties and interest groups, that attempt to influence the government by competing in elections and by other peaceful means.

Almost three centuries later, Wilsonian idealism, as it is standardly termed, adopted a rather similar stance. Abroad, it is Washington's responsibility to ensure that government is in the hands of "the good, though but a few." At home, it is necessary to safeguard a system of elite decision-making and public ratification—"polyarchy," in the terminology of political science—not democracy.[10]

Figure 6. Dahl's Conditions for a Polyarchy[11]

1.	Historical Sequence—peaceful evolution within an independent nation-state
2.	Socioeconomic Order-concentration—a competitive regime cannot be maintained in a country where military forces are accustomed to intervening
3.	Socioeconomic Order-level of development
a)	Provide literacy, education, communication
b)	Create a pluralistic social order
c)	Prevent Inequalities
d)	Equalities and Inequalities
4.	Hegemonic regimes reduce public contestation
5.	Inequalities increase the chance comparative politics will displace hegemony
6.	Subcultures, Cleavage Patterns and, Governmental Effectiveness
7.	The Beliefs of Political Activists—treat them as major independent variables
8.	Foreign Control—foreign domination can affect all the conditions and alter available options

The question of political participation raised by Dahl (1972), and further addressed by Chomsky (2008a), is a quintessential piece to the democratic puzzle. How can passive, systemic, nefarious disenfranchisement be tolerated and condoned within a nation proclaiming to be democratic (McLaren, 2005a, 2007)? Clarke et al. (1984) wrote of the *absent mandate* that prevails in the aftermath of elections, postulating that no government ever has a clear mandate due to the confused, dispersed and divergent ways that citizens vote for or against a candidate/party (for example, some may vote based on issues, personal preferences, party affiliation, owing to insufficient knowledge, against someone else or related to other motivations, which may conflict with why other people are voting for the same candidate/party). Gandin and Apple (2005), Schugurensky (2003) and others have questioned whether traditional forms of inclusive participation are sufficient to build truly democratic societies, especially when one considers the agenda-setting potential of the mass media (Bagdikian, 2004; McChesney, 1999). In contemporary times, one might question the predominance of polyarchy within the context of President Obama winning the Nobel Peace Prize, and then presenting a vigorous defense for the intensification of war in Afghanistan at the award ceremony.

Democracy and the Advent of Extremism

Britt (2004) has assembled an arsenal of interconnected criteria underscoring the shift toward more authoritarian, elite-based and politically limiting rule within the US, and has concluded that there are visible signs of a socio-political decline. The word fascism, commonly associated with the horrors of World War II, is based on some specific ideological girders buttressing a governmental and political framework (Figure 7). Each point in this framework taken individually would be highly debatable. As an ensemble of arguments, Britt's analysis raises questions about the salience of the Republican-Democrat polyarchy as well as concerns about the impact of citizen voice, resistance and engagement. Goodhall and Wiener (2008) argue that some of the communications strategies, "such as the suspension of reality, propaganda techniques, and the use of movement opinion to subvert, transform, and replace fact" (p.135), that have been promoted by the Republican party and the conservative movement exhibit some of the characteristics of totalitarianism (Goodall & Weiner, 2008; Steinberg & Kincheloe, 2009).

The blurring of the democratic lines camouflaged by well-organized and publicized elections that produce, in many cases, less than hospitable regimes has commonly been overlooked in mainstream politics as well as, importantly, the formal school curriculum. Is the United States sliding into a quasi-fascistic state? The question itself would be swatted like a fly by the governing elites but needs to be considered, should such a diagnosis be undertaken based on lived realities? Related to Britt's formulation of democratic extremism, Kaplan (1997) argued some fifteen years ago that "democracies are not value-neutral," and, moreover, that they may not be good for everyone all of the time: "Hitler and Mussolini each came to power through democracy. Democracies do not always make societies more civil, but they do always mercilessly expose the health of the societies in which they operate." Kaplan (1997) further submits that, in many cases, serious harm, conflict and even genocide occur as a result of what the West has perceived as democratization, often crudely translated into multi-party elections (Schmitz, 2006).

> The very fact that we retreat to moral argumentsand often moral arguments onlyto justify democracy indicates that for many parts of the world the historical and social arguments supporting democracy are just not there. Realism has come not from us but from, for example, Uganda's President Yoweri Museveni, an enlightened Hobbesian despot whose country has posted impressive annual economic growth rates—10 percent recently despite tribal struggles in the country's north. In 1986 Museveni's army captured the Ugandan capital of Kampala without looting a single shop; Museveni postponed elections and saw that they took place in a manner that ensured his victory. "I happen to be one of those

people who do not believe in multi-party democracy," Museveni has written. "In fact, I am totally opposed to it as far as Africa today is concerned.... If one forms a multi-party system in Uganda, a party cannot win elections unless it finds a way of dividing the ninety-four percent of the electorate [that consists of peasants], and this is where the main problem comes up: tribalism, religion, or regionalism becomes the basis for intense partisanship." In other words, in a society that has not reached the level of development Tocqueville described, a multi-party system merely hardens and institutionalizes established ethnic and regional divisions. Look at Armenia and Azerbaijan, where democratic processes brought nationalists to power upon the demise of the Soviet Union: each leader furthered his country's slide into war. A coup in Azerbaijan was necessary to restore peace and, by developing Azerbaijan's enormous oil resources, foster economic growth. Without the coup Western oil companies would not have gained their current foothold, which has allowed the United States to increase pressure on neighboring Iran at the same time that we attempt to normalize relations with Iran "on our terms." (Kaplan, 1997)

The pivotal underpinning of democracy, at least as argued in this volume, concerning a meaningful, critically engaged, vibrant and socially just education, thus the critical pedagogy of democracy, often appears to be missing from the equation of how societies (can) become democratic. As Martin (2005) puts it, "you can't be neutral on a moving bus."

Thus, the potential drifting of a non-participatory, thin, polyarchish form of democracy, infused with the neo-liberal components earlier defined that are associated with *econ-ocracy*, could blend into passive or more aggressive forms of fascism if political and democratic literacy and participation levels are considered negligible. If voters participate reluctantly, do not fully believe in the electoral process, are ill informed and disengaged, and are troubled by the integrity of the process, then it may be doubtful how their best interests are actually served. Similarly, if conflicts of interest are not easily identifiable, and there is an air of corporate malfeasance, then the actual system in place to ensure democracy may become a barrier to achieving emancipation, liberty and transformation. Therefore, as will be elaborated throughout this book, Freire's (1973) concept of *conscientization* is a fundamental component to facilitating *bona fide* democratic participation.

War and Democracy

A pivotal concern in relation to democracy is whether or not it can exist, flourish and function effectively within a mindset of militarization, framed as the *military-industrial complex* by senior business, government and military officials (Chomsky, 2008a, 2008b). Figure 8 outlines the massive funding and support provided by taxpayers/citizens to the US military as well as militaristic objectives (the US spends more on military purposes than the next fifteen countries combined, including China, Russia, Britain, France, Japan and Germany). With such substantial concern around the cost of healthcare, it is nothing short of bewildering that massive funding can be allocated to militaristic ventures without there being a vigorous, even rancorous, debate over the moral, ethical, economic, political and humanistic objectives of such decisions/priorities that ultimately involve all American citizens, both directly and indirectly. With approximately half of the US budget being directed to militaristic purposes, can there be room for meaningful debate on patriotism, the distribution of wealth, the focus of education, etc., when this would conflict with the present power configuration? Bellamy Foster, Holleman and McChesney (2008) peg the annual US military expenditure at $1 trillion, and contextualize the pervasive hegemonic effect of what they characterize as the "military/industrial/media triangle," which serves to further entrench inequities and, ultimately, the antithesis of democracy. The gravity and salience of having an economy, a political structure and a societal framework buttressing the "goodness" and necessity of such an expansive and powerful (military) presence throughout society is explored, and questioned, in this book.

Figure 7. Britt's Fourteen Points of Fascism[12]

<table>
<tr><td>

1) Powerful and continuing nationalism
Fascist regimes tend to make use of patriotic mottos, slogans, symbols, songs, and other paraphernalia. Flags are seen everywhere as are patriotic symbols on clothing, public displays....

</td></tr>
<tr><td>

2) Disdain for the recognition of human rights
Because of the fear of enemies and the need for security, the people in fascist regimes are persuaded that human rights and civil liberties can be ignored in certain cases because of "need." The people tend to look the other way or even approve of torture, summary executions, long incarcerations of prisoners without trial, etc.

</td></tr>
<tr><td>

3) Identification of enemies/scapegoats as a unifying cause
The people are rallied into a unifying patriotic frenzy over the need to eliminate a perceived a common threat or foe: ethnic or religious minorities, liberals, communists, terrorists, etc.

</td></tr>
<tr><td>

4) Supremacy of the military
Even when there are widespread domestic problems, the military is given a disproportionate amount of government funding, and the domestic agenda is neglected.

</td></tr>
<tr><td>

5) Rampant sexism
The governments of fascist nations tend to be almost exclusively male dominated. Under fascist regimes, traditional gender roles are made more rigid. Opposition to abortion is high as is homophobia, and anti-gay legislation as national policy.

</td></tr>
</table>

Figure 7. continued

6) Controlled mass media
Sometimes the media is directly controlled by the government, but in other cases, the media is indirectly controlled by government regulation, or sympathetic media spokespeople and executives. Censorship, especially in war time, is common.

7) Obsession with national security
Fear is used as a motivational tool over the masses.

8) Religion and government are intertwined
Governments in fascist regimes tend to use the most common religion in the nation as a tool to manipulate public opinion. Religious rhetoric and terminology is common from government leaders, even when ... religion is diametrically opposed to the government's policies and actions.

9) Corporate power is protected
The industrial and business aristocracy of a fascist nation often are the ones who put the government leaders into power, creating a mutually beneficial business/government relationship for the power elite.

10) Labor power is suppressed
Because the organizing power of labor is the only real threat to a fascist government. Labor unions are either eliminated entirely or are severely suppressed.

11) Disdain for intellectuals and the arts
Fascist regimes tend to promote and tolerate hostility to higher education and academia. It is not uncommon for professors and other academics to be censored or even arrested. Free expression in the arts is openly attacked, and governments often refuse to fund the arts.

12) Obsession with crime and punishment
Under fascist regimes, the police are given almost limitless power to enforce laws. The people are often willing to overlook police abuses and even forego civil liberties in the name of patriotism. There is often a national police force with virtually unlimited power in fascist nations.

13) Rampant cronyism and corruption
Fascist regimes almost always are governed by groups of friends and associates who appoint each other to government positions and use governmental power and authority to protect their friends from accountability....

14) Fraudulent elections
Sometimes elections in fascist regimes are a complete sham. Other times elections are manipulated by smear campaigns or even assassination of opposition candidates, use of legislation to control voting numbers or political district boundaries, and the manipulation of the media. Fascist nations also tend to use their judiciaries to manipulate or control elections.

Conclusion

Democracy takes many shapes and forms, and must be continually debated (Held, 2006). The Western world, in large part based on neo-liberal conceptions of progress and development, would probably concur with Fukuyama's (1992) conceptualization of his widely cited work *The End of History and the Last Man*. His central hypothesis contends that liberal democracy is the most suitable model to advance social and political development.

> The triumph of liberal democracies over rival political forms would seem to stand as confirmation that liberal democracy is the form of government which most closely reflects certain timeless and universal human aspirations. Liberal democracy would also seem to be the political form which most closely coincides with certain aspects of human nature, and certain ideals which have been recurring themes throughout Western political thought. In particular, the origins of the twin ideals of liberty and equality, can be traced along a path of intellectual development which extends from ancient Greece through the American Revolution. As the form of government in which these ideals achieve their fullest expression, liberal democracy stands as a monument to Western political thought, and to the humanist intellectual tradition more generally.[13]

In postmodern and critical theory, one might ask for whom is liberal democracy most suitable, who benefits, who determines its meaning, and how do we understand the experiences of those in the opposition or who are marginalized by the application of such theoretical models? To this end, Khan (2003) argues that the notion of liberal democracy is Western-based, and that what is required is the development of universal democracy and values, which can allow for different conceptualizations and an acceptance of non-Western traditions.

> Universal values are not abstract philosophical notions without any practical utility. They are indeed the tools and necessities of ordinary life that the state must protect. For example, the right to life, liberty and security of person is a universal value that no state should arbitrarily revoke or suspend. Likewise, prohibitions against slavery, torture, arbitrary arrest, and exile are universal values that no state can regard with impunity. In more recent years, electoral democracy has emerged as a universal value as the peoples of the world aspire (for) their governments to be accountable and removable.... Recognizing these and other universal values, Universal Democracy offers a theory of government rooted in the reality of human condition as well as human aspirations. (p.2)

Figure 8. US Military Spending[14]

<table>
<tr><td>

US Federal budget 2009 (fiscal year) (billions of dollars)
Total Outlays (Federal Funds)—$2,659B
MILITARY: 51% (details below)—Non-MILITARY: 49%

</td></tr>
<tr><td>

Human Resources—$789B (30%)
• Health/Human Services • Soc. Sec. Administration • Education Dept.
• Food/Nutrition programs • Housing & Urban Dev. • Labor Dept. • other H.R.

</td></tr>
<tr><td>

Past Military—$484B (23%)
• Veterans' Benefits—$94B • Interest on national-debt (80%) due to military spending, $390B

</td></tr>
<tr><td>

General Government—$304B (13%)
• Treasury, including 20% interest on debt ($97B) • Government personnel • Justice Dept. •
State Dept. (partial) • Homeland Security (15%) • International Affairs • NASA (50%) •
Judicial • Legislative • other general government.

</td></tr>
<tr><td>

Physical Resources—$117B (6%)
• Agriculture • Interior • Transportation • Homeland Security (15%) • HUD
• Commerce • Energy (non-military) • Environmental Protection • Nat. Science Found. • Army
Corps Engineers • Fed. Commerce Com. • other physical resources

</td></tr>
<tr><td>

Current Military—$965B (28%)
• Military Personnel $129B • Operation & Maintenance $241B
• Procurement $143B • Research & Development $79B • Construction $15B
• Family Housing $3B • DoD miscellaneous $4B • Retiree Pay/Healthcare $70B
• DoE nuclear weapons $17B • NASA (50%) $9B • International Security $9B
• Homeland Security (70% military) $35B • State Dept. (partial) $6B
• other military (non-DoD) $5B
• *"Global War on Terror" $200 billion*

</td></tr>
</table>

Barber (2004) speaks of strong (and *thick*) democracy, emphasizing participation at all levels. Participatory democracy eclipses representative democracy in many ways, but the quality, as opposed to the quantity, of participation is, ultimately, the key consideration. In this regard, political literacy and *conscientization* should be *de facto* requirements to be engaged in a functioning democracy. Putnam (2001) articulates the issue of perceived and real declines in political participation as being connected to social capital, arguing that, to use his metaphor, although more people are bowling today, they are doing it alone and not in organized leagues, which poses a problem for cohesive social movements. The individualism and materialism ingrained in *econ-ocracy* and tacitly endorsed through polyarchy can have the effect of diminishing meaningful (democratic) engagement. Putnam's research[15] is important because it raises issues about social group identity, salience and integration, which has consequences for ethno-cultural, racial and immigrant groups that largely characterize the contemporary heterogeneous nature of Western societies. Understanding how social capital contributes to political and democratic meaning is fundamental to the debate around democratic education (Schugurensky, 2003). Ultimately, education bleeds into an analysis related to universal values, participation, social capital and the quest for a more democratic ideal and engagement for all citizens (Agostinone-Wilson, 2005; Dewey, 1917/1997; Macrine, 2009; Parker, 2003). Problematizing war and peace, justice and injustice, the theoretical as opposed to the lived experience, and the potential for meaningful change are, therefore, all relevant aspects of a critical pedagogy of democracy.

Chapter 3

Discursive Thoughts on the Irreproachability of Democracy

Who are better prepared than the oppressed to understand the terrible significance of an oppressive society? Who suffer the effects of oppression more than the oppressed? Who can better understand the necessity of liberation? They will not gain the liberation by chance but through the praxis of their quest for it, through their recognition of the necessity to fight for it. And this fight, because of the purpose giving it by the oppressed, will actually constitute an act of love opposing the lovelessness which lies at the heart of the oppressors' violence, lovelessness even when clothed in false generosity. (Freire, 1973/2005, p. 45)

Why Democracy, and Can We Be Critical of It?

Some propositions, which synthesize some of the arguments presented in the first two chapters, are helpful here to discuss a re-defining of democracy:

- Democracy is important, it should be studied, and, for it to be meaningful and tangible, it must be fully cultivated throughout the educational experience (Kurth-Schai & Green, 2006; Westheimer & Kahne, 2002, 2003, 2004);
- Elections are but a very small part of democracy, they are highly exaggerated, can lead to disenfranchisement, and can smother the universal quest for a more humane and decent existence (Lund & Carr, 2008a; Palast, 2004; Putnam, 2001);
- Democracy is not, nor should it be, dissociable from social justice, and if the two are not connected the relevance of democracy should be questioned and re-evaluated (Nieto, 1999; Portelli & Solomon, 2001; Sleeter, 2007; Spring, 2004);
- The media does not play a passive, objective, neutral role in sustaining democracy, and the impact of misrepresentation, omission and corporate control of information can have a deleterious effect on public debate (Bagdikian, 2004; Chomsky, 2008b; Herman & Chomsky, 2002; McChesney, 1998a, 1999b, 2008);
- When formal democracy blends into the neutralization of marginalized groups from power and decision-making processes and centers, this can enshrine a stealth-like contamination and disenfranchisement of the masses (Kincheloe, 2008ab; Lintner, 2007; Macrine, 2009; McLaren, 2007);
- Doing democracy requires embarking on a process of critical interrogation, engagement and action, cognizant of our limitations in terms of knowledge, experience and philosophy, and open to constructive new and alternative paths to hegemonic interpretations of power (Kincheloe, 2008b; McLaren & Kincheloe, 2008; Parker, 2002, 2003, 2006).

I am intrigued as to how educators perceive, understand and experience democracy because, I believe, there is a (direct/explicit and indirect/implicit) connection between our own relationship to, and understanding of, democracy, at the individual and collective levels, and how we will, ultimately, engage in/with democracy in and through education. My concern, as inspired by Paulo Freire (1973/2005, 1973, 1985, 1998, 2004), is whether this engagement is critical, substantive, and meaningful. Do we seek transformation or merely to reproduce social relations (Bourdieu, 1970; Bourdieu & Passaron, 1990; Kincheloe, 2008b)? Or is our involvement with power mitigated by the mainstream notion that individuals, supposedly, cannot change anything (Carr 2008a)? Can we change democracy if we are only weakly aware of what it is all about?

Can we have democracy if we have poverty? Racism? Sexism? Illogical, counter-productive and debilitating war? Systemic, entrenched impoverishment in a time of unprecedented wealth accumulation by the thin wedge represented by the postmodern, mercantilized-induced jet-set (Prins, 2009)? A number of critical pedagogues have written widely on the hollow shell of American hegemony, unearthing the deleterious effects of the neo-liberal confederacy (see McLaren & Kincheloe, 2007). Maintaining the boundaries of the US empire requires a constant stream of misinformation, propaganda and militaristic manipulation, all of which serves to disenfranchise democratic tendencies in society (Kincheloe & Steinberg, 2006). Yet, their work, unfortunately, is not generally well known in departments/ministries of education, nor through formal venues of educational decision-making, which is not to say that their ideas have not, or will not ultimately, be germinated within the broader societal Petri dish.[1] Although, for example, enslavement and colonization may not have been readily questioned at the height of their time, significant change has occurred, often with substantive struggle, always accompanied by visionary thinkers expounding on a different version of the truth (Zinn, 2003; Zinn & Macedo, 2005).

Figure 9 situates some of the characteristics, variables and concerns related to how we might achieve a more robust, *thicker* democracy—what I refer to below as *democratic conscientization*. This model attempts to illustrate some of the stages, or phases, that people may enter and pass through as they seek higher levels of *democratic conscientization*, building on Freire's (1973/2005) work.

This model seeks to underscore the complex, problematic and nuanced challenges, obstacles and experiences that one faces when critically assessing democracy, which is a much more encompassing, power-laden enterprise and political project than the limited, and thin, existence of elections. More importantly, this model underscores the fundamental role played by education—formal, informal, experiential—in cultivating a thicker interpretation and more critically engaged relationship to democracy, with the active and dialectical interplay between epistemological inquiry and critical action, ensconced in a vibrant democratic praxis. *Democratic conscientization* is a never-ending process, one that acknowledges differences, power imbalances, hegemonic forces and the non-neutrality of formal political and educational structures. Moving through the stages, one can also relate to some of the seminal research undertaken by Westheimer and Kahne (2004), which seeks to have students understand their political agency as well as reasons for inequity.

Figure 9. Democratic Education Change Model

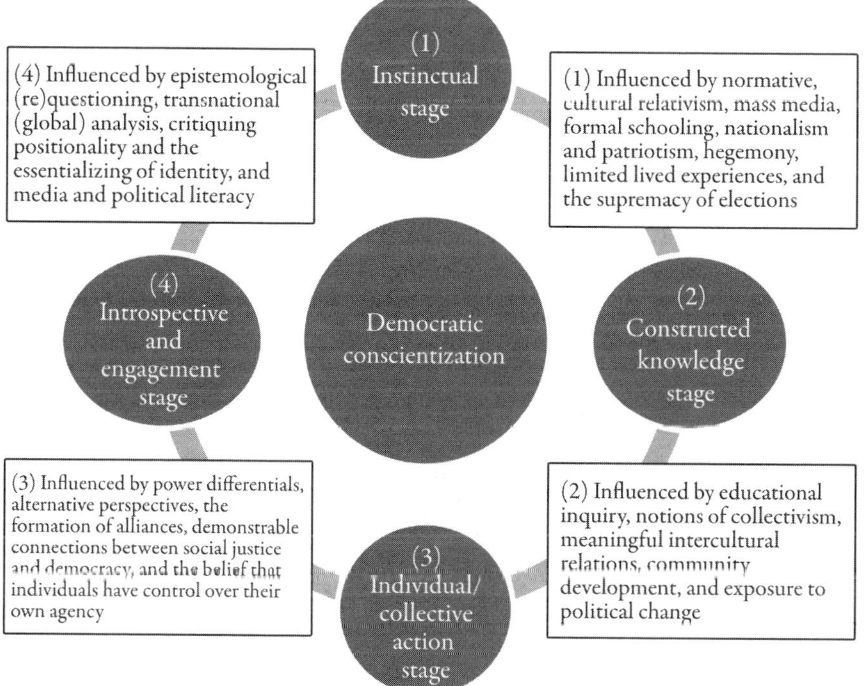

Can we have democracy when only approximately half of eligible voters vote, not to mention the less than *bona fide* participation that the majority actually experiences (Cook, 2004; Patterson, 2003)? Can we have democracy with limited public debate (Parker, 2006)? Can we have democracy when the supposed cornerstone (elections) is fraught with serious systemic problems, such as the necessity to raise funds, the limited choice (two parties), the limited breadth of debate (a corporate media generally focused on the same issues from the same vantage points), the lack of opportunity for engagement, the quasi-consensus that there are no alternatives, etc. (Carr & Porfilio, 2009b; Macedo & Steinberg, 2007)? Is there now a "pulpless generation," as Agger (2009) suggests, whose politics are decidedly different than one or two generations ago, including a detachment from books in favor of *cyber-democracy*? In outlining *econ-ocracy* and various conditions, issues and determinants related to democracy, this chapter provides some examples (*American Idol*, Haiti, the Olympics, and development assistance to the South) of how facile interpretations of democracy have had nefarious effects on more structurally relevant concerns related to power.

Econ-ocracy as the New Neo-liberal Democracy

Econ-ocracy focuses on limited, often trivial, interests that divert attention from broader forms of democracy aimed at inclusive, transformative, participatory movements, and are inclined to address systemic inequities and marginalization. It refers to how theoretical conceptualizations of democracy rooted in epistemological interrogation and dialectical debate have been supplanted by *common sense, us versus them*, arrogance over humility, a bottom-line approach, and a disdain for critical anything, including critical thinking. *Econ-ocracy* relies on the marketplace to sort out the whims of culture and the human condition. However, *econ-ocracy* is also dependent on exploiting inequitable power relations and advancing the hyperbole of neo-liberal thinking that competition is the only way of achieving collective gains, and, moreover, that we can and should quantify everything, including the education of children. Ultimately, *econ-ocracy* is dependent on the full weight of hegemony being pressed onto the backs of the working class, the marginalized, indigenous peoples and other outliers from the center of power.

The issue of meaningful participation and engagement in the electoral process, combined with the role of the media, political (il)literacy, and the distribution of public and private funds, together, raise the question of what kind of democracy, or *econ-ocracy*, we are creating. Ironically, although the Iraq war/invasion was a pivotal issue in the 2008 presidential campaign, there was relatively scant attention actually paid to life in Iraq, let alone the rationale and objectives, of the military infiltration. Hartnett (2008) decries the manipulation and audacity of militaristic patriotism within a perceived awning of democracy, highlighting that "the president (Bush) won reelection in November 2004 by running a campaign emphasizing military strength, hunting terrorists, homophobic attacks on gay marriage, and tax cuts for the rich. It was a campaign of chest-pumping imperial bravado spiced by remarkable amounts of deception and much talk of God" (p. 187). "Lying in politics" is often acceptable because of the fear of being labeled a dissenter, perilously contesting hegemonic power, as was the case throughout the rationalization phase for the Iraq War/conflict/invasion (Kellner, 2005, 2007; King, 2009). However, the alternative media profiled an almost endless amount of evidence, insight and critique, which was broadly ignored by official channels as well as the mainstream candidates.[2]

As Chomsky (2003, 2007, 2008b; Herman & Chomsky, 2002) has effectively argued, the media play an effective role in "manufacturing consent." Corporate control (Bagdikian, 2004) and a nebulous editorial direction (McChesney, 1999, 2008) should create compelling arguments for schools to develop robust media literacy programs. A politically literate populace would, and should, be able to decipher the freshly wrapped veneer of the pervasive mainstream media message, which envelopes patriotic fervor in order to make democracy something more than a epiphany of expensive hair-cuts (the furor over the $400 spent by candidate John Edwards during the 2008 election[3]), celebrity vignettes (the insatiable appetite for reports on the pastor at Obama's church during the same campaign[4]), and beer summits (the several-week drama over comments made by President Obama in 2009, which eventually culminated in a very photo-opportunistic scene of four men and a couple of beers[5]). Endless energy and resources consecrated to banalities and insignificant trivia is the hallmark of a media-manipulated society, in which propaganda is something associated with the most barbarous regimes and not, supposedly, our own governments and marketeers in the business world.

Writing a blog throughout the two-year electoral campaign culminating in November 2008, I can see how the daily meanderings I was writing about can be quickly usurped and swept away in a trivial manner. Yet, over time, the constant flow of meaningless banter seems to characterize the mainstream political discourse/analysis. One of my first thoughts, which was not questioned throughout the campaign, concerned who could actually compete to be president. How is it possible for those running for office to maintain their full salaries and benefits of their elected offices, as was the case for almost all of the candidates in the 2008 and other elections, and, simultaneously, raise funds and generally be unavailable to do the former in a quest to seek other elected positions? The mere notion that a teacher, a social worker, a public servant, or virtually anyone would maintain the benefits and integrity of their employment, not to mention the full remuneration, while campaigning for elected office is so obviously objectionable that it is almost surreal that the mass media did not raise this as a concern, let alone a point of contention. Everyone competing for the office of president was more than double-dipping; they were actually using the employment of one publicly funded position (most predominantly as a senator) to seek another, without ever declaring a conflict of interest.

Sex also seems to titillate, obscure and play heavily in political coverage. During the campaign period, the mainstream media maintained a central focus on the private meanderings of the freshly deposed governor of New York,[6] then launched into a sensational foray about the extracurricular activities of his replacement,[7] who acknowledged that he had already had extramarital affairs during his inaugural press conference, a pseudo preemptive strike against the presumed anti-investigative journalism of the new era. The most infamous case of sex dominating the political agenda, with impeachment being a direct consequence, relates to the tenure of President Bill Clinton, whose mandate was significantly derailed as a result (Mbakpuo, 2005).[8] Perhaps somewhat surprisingly, there is a long history of sex scandals among elected officials, including presidents, although there has traditionally been a code of silence among journalists (Boertlein, 2010).

One often hears that democracy is the best of the lot, the system that works to achieve the most for the most people. Former British Prime Minister Winston Churchill is well known for having stated that "Democracy is the worst form of government except for all those others that have been tried".[9] Is it majority rule, and, if so, what do we do about minority rights (i.e., for women, racial minorities, the disabled, etc.)? If we are free to say what we like, who will listen? How do we know what to say? Why are so many voices muted? So, what is the point of democracy? Are elections, ultimately, the best way of securing democracy?

Democracy can be exemplified at one level by the reverse pyramid, effectively illustrated by economic theorists. For example, there are studies in Canada dating back to the 1960s (Porter, 1965) in relation to social class, discrimination, and the *vertical mosaic*. In the US, Bowles and Gintis (1977, 2001) have produced seminal work on capitalist schooling and how disadvantage is ingrained within society, and Jonathan Kozol (1992, 2005) of the US has tirelessly documented systemic inequities in his work on *Savage Inequalities*. These inequities place marginalized groups (those of color, lower socio-economic status (SES), African-Americans, Puerto Ricans, aboriginal peoples, and diverse configurations and intersections of gender, class, race and other variables)—the majority—on the bottom of the societal rung. This Marxist critique of power postulates that the 1–2 percent at the top are generally inter-meshed in private schools, private clubs, elitist institutions, economic centers of power, etc., and network throughout business/government/media/cultural sectors in order to sustain inequitable power relations despite the notion of democracy. Henry and Tator (2005) develop the theme of democratic racism, in which societal norms, values and institutions color-blindly accept racism as part of its ethos, laws, culture and power structure.

If we took money out of the American political system, would it matter? Would elected officials then not be relieved of the unbearable pressure of constantly seeking funds, which, ultimately, culminates in offering unparalleled access to their time and services to those who have provided for their campaign war-chests? The media covers the politicians endlessly, regardless, so would there be a loss of coverage if politicians were not able to pay for political advertisements? Would the removal of money from the formal political system open the way for more diverse representation outside of those willing and able to raise large sums? The economics of democracy is important, but it is not the only consideration for opening up the system to more meaningful, legitimate, transformative and *democratic* potential. A challenge to *econ-ocracy* must, therefore, include a vigorous and critically engaged educational process.

American Idol *and Democracy*

While I have never seen the television show *American Idol* (at least that's what I say publicly), I know a fair amount about it. Students talk about it, the media is obsessed with it, it has become part of the political vernacular, and, of course, it is considered to be nothing but good news. A quick public narrative could be that it is simply people coming together to sing and enjoy the *American dream*. It seems that if you do not know about *American Idol*, you have somehow missed a significant part of (pop/popular) culture. It would be easy to surmise that *American Idol* is what brings out the best in society: it is promoted as being nothing less (or more) than a little friendly competition, some passion, and lots of emotion. We can actually see people of different races cajoling and mixing. This reflection of American society makes us feel connected to the youth, who work with diverse folks in trying to realize their dreams. The personalities are larger than life. Should it be surprising, as noted earlier, that more people vote for their Idols than for candidates in US elections?[10] The level of analysis that is funneled into how the Idols dress, walk, dance, sing, enjoy life, etc. is extensive, and many people seem to be (critically) engaged as to who these people are. This raises questions about why so many people willingly say that they are "not political," or are "not interested in politics" (see Carr, 2008a). The judges certainly add to the spectacle, and, no one, the argument goes, is coerced into watching or being a part of it. Is it worth considering how *American Idol* is not just a subtle, feel-good representation of the American ideal?

Hidden away from the glitter and lights of the show, referenced only sparingly but in a glamorous way, the *American Idol* website[11] branches out into good deeds. A video in 2009 on *American Idol*, in attempting to highlight the charitable works that emanate from the show, portrayed a very poor girl in Somalia, who was separated from her brother, another street child. The narrative and filming expose an easily understood saga: the children live in poverty, they really do not have much to look forward to, Somalia is not a friendly place to look at (not, at least, through this video), and, thanks to *American Idol*, a very luxurious SUV was able to drive the young girl around town to try and find her brother. Some food and clothing are also provided. In brief, the message is clear: *American Idol* is making a difference.

Where does one start with all of this? That *American Idol* is backed by official sponsors not necessarily well known for poverty reduction (Ford, AT&T, Exxon Mobil, Coca-Cola), that the FOX network—the centerpiece for *Idol* dissemination—has not been normally associated with the elimination of inequities, and that the fact that the program is premised on "average" folks providing the funds, rather than profits from the conglomerates making money for the show, may seem a little shallow.

Is it good to give? Yes. Is it good to give without getting an intellectual and political handle on the systemic problems underpinning poverty? This is more contentious. Charity is nice, and it is important to help out. This is, or should be, a basic and fundamental part of humanity, but there is a difference between taking a can of beans to a food-bank, and working on changing the root causes of poverty (Westheimer and Kahne, 2004).

Apart from the good times, *American Idol* is about making money, about supporting patriotism, and about not questioning social problems, especially decisions related to military conflict. Some might argue that there is no requirement for people to be engaged and to help others, or that entertainment need not have a direct political message. How much of the millions that the hosts earn are being dedicated to this (welfare) program, and how much of the billions that the sponsors earn will be earmarked for poverty reduction? Should there be full disclosure, and if not, why not?

Figure 10. The *American Idol* Foundation

Idol Gives Back Foundation is a new not-for-profit organization established by the producers of *American Idol* and FOX to raise money and awareness for children and families living in poverty and at risk in the US and abroad. Idol Gives Back Foundation is harnessing *American Idol*'s ability to capture America's hearts and the power of entertainment to benefit some of the poorest and most vulnerable people in the world.

Foundation Functions

• To make grants for charitable endeavors that touch and change the lives of children and their families in the US and abroad

• Focusing on the provision of health, education and services for those in poverty and at risk

Guiding Principles

Idol Gives Back Foundation's grant selection is guided by the following criteria:

• Young people living in poverty and at risk • Basic needs • National Awareness • Broad appeal • Clear, measurable results

How We Do It

Idol Gives Back Foundation harnesses *American Idol*'s ability to capture America's hearts and the power of entertainment to benefit some of the poorest and most vulnerable people in the world.

Who We Are

Idol Gives Back began as a meaningful way for those behind *American Idol* and FOX to give back in a significant way to children's causes worldwide. Idol Gives Back was successfully launched as a charity event in 2007 and has grown into a foundation comprised of Fox Broadcasting Company, FremantleMedia North America and 19 Entertainment.

Perhaps it is not polite to say that poverty is a political problem but, ultimately and arguably, it is. Social inequities are not choices that people wish to make, although many choices are factored into the equation. A baby does not choose poverty, for example. Poverty reduction is about politics. The trillion or more dollars being spent in Iraq[12] has had implications for those affected by the sub-prime crisis stateside, with thousands of people losing their homes (Prins, 2009). In other words, politics is about establishing priorities and making decisions. *Econ-ocracy* characterizes the pivotal linkage between political and economic power.

Despite the widely-held myth that people on welfare and people in developing countries receive endless bounty for no good reason except that "we like to help others," the actual amounts spent on poverty-reduction, as exemplified later in this chapter, are comparatively small. For instance, Africa pays more in debt-servicing than it receives in developmental assistance. It would not be surprising to discover that, after months of *American Idol* throwing its weight behind its good works program, an amount equivalent or less to one day's worth of militarization in Iraq had been expended. Democracy morphs into *econ-ocracy* when sophisticated campaigns to mask inequity and suffering are paraded about to convince the masses that we are all working together to achieve positive change when, importantly, the recipients of this change may quite compellingly argue the contrary. Gordon, Smyth and Diehl (2008) argue that the "many of the same techniques used by the Bush Administration in the build up to the Iraq War and in science have been adapted to control education in the US under the guise of 'evidence-based educational reform'" (p. 173).

At a personal level, I could not help but feel for the little girl being driven around in the air-conditioned SUV, being used for a very slick and heart-wrenching photo-op. Rather than interrogate how Somalia, or any other country, has been mired in poverty, and our own implication in ensuring that the poverty is almost irreversible, the favored option is to point to how much the good folks are helping out. How did Somalia become a country replete with social, economic and political problems? Are we implicated in any misery that they might experience? Is it relevant to know that there have been accusations of Western countries dumping toxic waste in the waters bordering Somalia, that incursions from Ethiopia have been endorsed and promoted by the US, and that international efforts at supporting peaceful transitions in that country have not been cultivated with the same vigor and seriousness as in many other regions of the world[13]?

Should we stop making and selling military weapons and bombs as a protest for the poverty that we see here and abroad, or are we obliged to continue on this path because of the economic benefits? Peter McLaren's (2007) summation that we are in a "permanent war on terror" represents a clarion call for a more concerted and comprehensive educational strategy aimed at political literacy. As alluded to earlier, Westheimer and Kahne (2004) argue that to do charity work without some critical political contextualization can lead to contrary effects, culminating in the donor having a limited emotional reaction without understanding that change can be made to stop the very reason for the identified charity in the first place. In the *American Idol* scenario, an important question that is overlooked by the emphasis on the *goodness* of the donor is: How are Americans and the US government complicit in the poverty evident in Somalia?

Haiti and Democracy

In late April, 2008, there were a series of sporadic reports on the famine taking place in Haiti. Granted, these reports have ranged from short clips showing how "out of control" Haitians were to more elaborate pieces that discussed how we are now experiencing a world-wide food shortage.[14] There has been no sustained reporting and, more importantly, no significant analysis of the "story." The reports almost always left the impression that it is "their" fault, and not "ours."

Haiti is problematic for a host of reasons. The classic book *The Black Jacobins: Toussaint L'Ouverture and the San Domingo Revolution* by C. L. R. James (1989) documents the almost unbelievable story of slaves taking back their freedom, culminating in the world's first Black republic. Figure 11 contains my 60-second history of Haiti, which is not intended to capture all of the nuances, actors, events and full dynamism of the society but does attempt to highlight how other nations and peoples are vested in the Haitian reality (from slavery to revolution to independence to dictatorship to dependence, through various phases of underdevelopment). What is most disturbing about Haiti now is that the world doesn't seem to care. More is spent in a few days of militarization in Iraq than is donated in development assistance to Haiti in one year (see Taft-Morales & Drummer, 2007).

Haiti was, arguably, not permitted to develop, to shed itself of dictators, or to opt for more reasonable and socially just policies. Why? Because it posed a threat? Because it is a country of Black people? Because it has no oil? Because it is easier to simply let it slip away into decay? Farmer (2005) documents the insidiousness of neglecting the cries and pleas for humanity in relation to Haiti and, significantly, the role played by the US in codifying incessant degradation in the lives of Haitians. Is there a democratic responsibility to know, understand and engage with Haitians, many of whom are held hostage to intolerable levels of poverty (Taft-Morales & Drummer, 2007) resulting from political regimes that have been beholden to foreign interests (Farmer, 2005)?

Haiti has, despite everything that has gone wrong, a rich, dynamic and joyous culture: art, music, literature, language, customs and cultural conventions that uplift the soul.[15] Why do so few people know of this, and, yet, other countries—Cuba comes to mind—are known around the world for their contribution to the world's cultural heritage? Tourism to Haiti was once a vibrant and promising enterprise, but it is not even a trickle today. Once considered the "Pearl of the West Indies" with tourist numbers outpacing its neighbors, today fears of being kidnapped, violence, criminal activity and corruption have virtually dried up all tourism from non-Haitians.[16] Adding to the degradation, Haiti has practically no trees left (see Thésée & Carr, 2008), which effectively translates into erosion of the earth, less agriculture, more health problems, inadequate housing (in a mountainous country), and an extremely problematic social dynamic for those crowded into relatively small living spaces.

Figure 11. Quick History of Haiti

After a bloody and sustained revolt, slaves overthrew the White elites that ruled Haiti in 1804 (James, 1989). The French left their mark through colonial domination, exemplified in modern times with the French-Creole linguistic struggle, and the massive reparations that Haiti was obliged to pay to France. With the Whites vanquished, Mulattos filled the void, and racialization become the order of the day (at the time of the Revolution, there were some 144 racial classifications used to categorize people) (James, 1989). All kinds of turbulence characterized the decades leading up to the 1950s, culminating in the enhanced dictatorship of "Papa Doc" Duvalier, a ruthless tyrant supported by the US (Farmer, 2005). Slowly but surely hundreds of thousands of educated and professional Haitians left the country, further entrenching social class differences, and eliminating potential resistance. "Baby Doc," the off-spring successor, carried the torch into more devastation (Schmitz, 2006). "Baby Doc's" wife is said to have had a specially-designed, air-conditioned room in the presidential palace to care for her fur coats, an intriguing necessity in a tropical climate. "Baby Doc" was finally chased from power, pillaging a few billion dollars along the way (the Haitian dictatorial team rivals the Marcos in the Philippines, Mobuto in Zaire, and Pinochet in Chile, all, coincidentally, vigorously supported by the US) (Stockton, undated). Jean-Bertrand Aristide was welcomed home from Canada, became president in 1991, was chased out, came back to power, and then was removed by force through a convoluted US military intervention. He was sent into exile in Africa, and chaos and instability have reigned ever since. Haiti has no military, with the United Nations being charged with keeping public order. Aristide is accused of drug trafficking, although it is not clear why the democratically elected president could be forcefully removed from office. Aristide was not pro-American, which may explain part of his predicament. Over time, Haiti has faced economic pillage and catastrophe. Economic, social and political exploitation have been a common theme since the founding of the world's first Black republic. Images of contemporary Haiti include unsightly portraits: locked into slave-like conditions in Dominican sugar plantations; young girls indentured as "reste-avec"; the infamous boat people who throw themselves into rubber tubes in the hopes of making it anywhere; the poor masses fighting for a meal (Taft-Morales & Drummer, 2007); and the drum-beat of silence from developed countries (Canada is not a neutral player in this game) all mesh to make the west side of the island of Hispaniola an explosive cocktail. There are a few people (some say 11–12 families who essentially dominate the Haitian economy) who live extremely comfortably in Haiti, and are disaffected by the throngs clamoring for more. Haiti is tantamount to a state without a state, the absence of a functioning government being a palpable reality. The horror of the January 2009 earthquake that caused massive damage and loss of life in the capital raised concerns about Haiti, and also the world: how did Haiti become what it is?

So, why Haiti? Why is it so easy to forget Haiti? Is the Haitian diaspora, especially in Montreal, New York and Miami, a beacon of hope? Why should people fighting for rice in Haiti be our concern? How did we contribute to the present situation? Elsewhere, I (see Thésée & Carr, 2008) have elaborated a framework to examine the vulnerability of racialized/marginalized populations in relation to natural, militaristic and economic disasters. The connection to democracy here is clear as Haiti has been used and abused by other countries (in particular, the US, France and Canada), these very countries that tacitly supported years of an unstable, chaotic political climate, tacitly maintaining an unsightly dictatorship.

Generations of ex-pat Haitians are living with the reality that they may never be able to see their country, and this is a tragic phenomenon for many people who seek to understand and validate their identities, not to mention others, who may not have a multi-dimensional understanding of Haiti. If globalization means letting some countries, cultures and peoples be swept away as a casualty of the proverbial "marketplace," then it may be time to question the collective sense of living/being (see Chossudovsky, 2003; Macedo & Gounari, 2006). The place of all peoples is fundamentally important if democracy is to have a significant resonance in a practical, tangible way, beyond the theoretical constructs and commitment to "one man, one vote." Haiti deserves better.

The Olympics and Democracy

Much can be said about the Olympics. Nations competing with one another to advance cultural connections, striving to be the strongest, the fastest and the best, and putting aside all that ails us in order to immerse the human condition in challenges as well as the undeniable quest for peace, are noble and decent goals. One way of surmising a global event such as the Olympics is that if we are all in the same proverbial sandbox together, playing, then we cannot be out in the street, fighting. One year before the stunning ($100M) official opening of the Olympic Games in Beijing in 2008, President Bush declared that he would attend, as a "sports fan"[17]: for him, apparently, this is not about politics (although the infamous boycotting of the Moscow Olympic Games in 1984 was tinged with other considerations than simply sports).

What is not political about the Olympic Games? How the host city is selected (and how potential host cities lavish International Olympic Committee members with a bevy of treasures) cannot be considered outside of the realm of the Olympic spirit. How athletes are funded, supported, promoted and portrayed (some athletes live on the poverty line while others earn $20M salaries playing professional basketball)? How the Games seem to be an endless buffet of mind-numbing advertisements from "official" sponsors (is it possible to conceive of VISA, Coca-Cola, McDonald's, etc., being genuinely concerned with the welfare of the masses?)? How some issues are front and center as if they are the only political concerns on the planet (the smog in China was constantly referenced, but significantly underplayed were human rights, the distribution of wealth, perverse visions of globalization, and militarization, etc.)?

It is interesting how the focus can be, in a marginalized way only, on Tibet, without any substantive interrogation on a host of US allies, which have well-documented and dubious human rights records. If Darfur, for example, is a problem, and China is supporting Darfur, then why do the US and others not raise the issue in an explicit way? If Myanmar (Burma) is a problem, and China is supporting Myanmar (Burma), then why do the US and others not raise the issue in an explicit way? If poverty and impoverishment are a problem in Africa, and Western countries pay only scant attention to the issue, then why does the world's only "superpower," the head of the G-8, the country that wields supposed infinite moral authority, the US, not vigorously attack those who would not advocate a full-throttle assault in favor of those living without? Why should there be privileged, high-level, favored-nation trading status for China because, according to official dogma, this is what will make them "democratic" (the infamous "constructive engagement" philosophy), and the exact opposite is the fifty-year-old recipe for Cuba, which is unproblematically ignored?

The International Center for Media and the Public Agenda (ICMPA) at the University of Maryland undertook a comprehensive study of the media coverage ("68 newspapers, in 10 languages, in 29 countries, across six continents") of human rights at the 2008 Olympic Games in Beijing, and concluded that human rights issues/abuses were significantly downplayed, despite pre-Games concerns enunciated by pro-Tibet and other groups.[18]

I am not suggesting that there should not be any Olympics, only that there should be a more frank discussion on what the Olympics represents. Every country has human rights issues, not just those believed to be less democratic by the *developed* countries. What would Canadian Prime Minister Stephen Harper, who boycotted the opening ceremony but sent his minister of external affairs and a host of other underlings, say if the international community boycotted the 2010 Vancouver Olympic Games as a protest for the treatment of Aboriginal peoples by the Canadian government? Ultimately, the normative, epistemological, ideological and political values linked to human rights and vested interests, over-riding the saliency of democracy, can be determining factors concerning which regimes are to be scrutinized for human rights violations.[19] This tendency to obfuscate and rationalize such inequities and inconsistent assessments could be characterized as *democratic marketizaton*, in which supposedly neo-liberal free market principles dictate which issues, realities and events will be addressed.

The political economy of the Olympics is effectively examined by Toohey and Veal (2007), who underscore the widespread financial negotiations required to win the right to hold the Games. They argue that political considerations underpin the decision-making required to convince local and national populations to build stadiums, infrastructure, transportation and other necessities to comfortably welcome the world to the host city. As for the economics, the costs almost systematically balloon past bid estimates, and revenues, which are substantial, often have trouble covering the investments made. The Olympics relates to *econ-ocracy* in the following way: the more money involved, the further it strays from the true, fundamental underpinning of the philosophical raison d'être of the Games themselves.

So, can the Olympics lead to peace? Does the cost of holding the Games (Athens has a substantial debt from its 2004 Games, it took Montreal some thirty years to pay off its stadium from the 1976 Games, and almost all developing countries are prohibited from making a bid to hold the Games because of the financial spreadsheet) make it worth it (Toohey & Veal, 2007)? Similarly, McHugh (2006) presents a cost-benefit analysis that questions the economic advantages of holding the Olympic Games.

Which country has earned the most Olympic medals per capita? Would it be surprising to know that, using this indicator, the US ranks 28th overall, well back of many smaller countries, including Cuba, Jamaica and all of the Scandinavian countries?[20] What are the short- and long-term costs of engaging in the Olympic Games? This speaks to what we know to believe to be the truth, and how our knowledge construction (epistemology) is always limited by our experiences, education and critical interrogation of our beliefs, perceptions and realities. Critical pedagogy prompts us to further examine the glossy exterior of phenomena, such as the Olympics, *American Idol* or impoverishment in Haiti.

The North, the South and Democracy?

Some fifty years ago, the nations of the world agreed that by the mid-1970s *developed* countries would allocate to *developing* countries, at that time considered as the *Third World*, a modest 0.7% of their GNPs.[21] Some four decades on, only a few countries have achieved this objective (mainly the Scandinavian ones), which raises serious concerns about the perceptions people in the Western world have about the developing world as well as the aid that is provided. As Figure 12 illustrates, developed countries, in general, do not provide infinite amounts to the developing world. The funds provided by the US, despite commonly held views that "charity begins (or should begin) at home" and an unflattering portrayal related to how American *largesse* is liberally sprinkled throughout the world while there are unmet needs at home, represent a rather small percentage of its GNP (Gross National Product) and GNI (Gross National Income); in fact, it is the smallest per capita donation of all of the world's most developed nations. What is more significant, however, is that much of the aid that is sent to developing countries comes with strings attached.[22] Funding projects that are often more beneficial to donor-countries does not necessarily support development, can underpin the hegemony of dictatorial regimes, spurring on corruption, and can also be premised on geo-politics and military maneuvers more so than considering humanitarian, socio-cultural, economic and development considerations (Figure 12).

Figure 12. Official Development Assistance (ODA) (in $M)(GNI = Gross National Income)

		ODA in US $ millions				ODA as % of GNI			
	Country	2005	2006	2007	2008	2005	2006	2007	2008
1	Australia	2,005	2,443	2,669	3,038	0.25	0.3	0.32	0.34
2	Austria	1,805	1,679	1,808	1,555	0.52	0.47	0.5	0.42
3	Belgium	2.264	2,209	1,953	2,214	0.53	0.5	0.43	0.47
4	Canada	4,476	4,008	4,080	4,577	0.34	0.29	0.29	0.32
5	Denmark	2,410	2,482	2,562	2,570	0.81	0.8	0.81	.082
6	Finland	1,037	935	981	1,047	0.46	0.4	0.39	0.43
7	France	11,599	11,846	9,884	10,168	0.47	0.47	0.38	0,39
8	Germany	11,369	11,592	12,291	12,994	0.36	0.36	0.37	0.38
9	Greece	450	476	501	636	0.17	0.17	0.16	0.2
10	Ireland	830	1,129	1,192	1,269	0.42	0.54	0.55	0.58
11	Italy	5,834	4,061	3,971	4,059	0.29	0.2	0.19	0.2
12	Japan	12.055	10,918	7,679	8,310	0.28	0.25	0.17	0.18
13	Luxembourg	302	323	376	382	0.79	0.9	0.91	0.92
14	Netherlands	5,818	6,036	6,224	6,522	0.82	0.81	0.81	0.8
15	New Zealand	305	305	320	355	0.27	0.27	0.27	0.3
16	Norway	3,373	3,287	3,728	3,638	0.94	0.89	0.95	0.88
17	Portugal	440	445	471	570	0.21	0.21	0.22	0.27
18	Spain	3,569	4,291	5,140	6,138	0.27	0.32	0.37	0.43
19	Sweden	3,884	4,441	4,339	4,508	0.94	1.02	0.93	0.98
20	Switzerland	1,904	1,750	1,685	1,794	0.44	0.39	0.37	0.42
21	UK	12,519	13,938	9,849	12.217	0.47	0.51	0.35	0.43
22	USA	29.611	24,166	21,787	25,439	0.23	0.18	0.16	0.18

From a critical pedagogical perspective, how do we even frame the problem of development assistance? Are we concerned with the effect on the recipients (see Moyo, 2009, for a critique of the deleterious impact of development assistance on Africa, arguing that it has not been effective in spurring on development)? Do we care if our governments are involved in providing vast sums of *development assistance* in the form of military aid (see Figure 13)? How do we choose who should receive the aid, in what format, and how should the success of aid projects be measured? What is the connection between aid and development, and, within a Western context, between the critical interrogation of aid and education? It is interesting that it would appear that the average citizen is ill informed about how his/her government is involved in providing development assistance, especially in relation to the military component (see Figure 14 for the primarily military aid that the US has provided to Israel since 1949). These important matters are largely overlooked during election campaigns, smothered by the personalities and media-driven issues that are presented as being the most salient.

Figure 13. US (Military) Foreign Aid[23] (the top six countries)

Country	Aid	Purpose
1. Israel	$2.4 B	Virtually all funds are used to buy weapons (up to 75% made in the US). Beginning in 2009, the US plans to give $30 billion over 10 years.
2. Egypt	$1.7 B	$1.3 billion to buy weapons; $103 million for education; $74 million for health care; $45 million to promote civic participation and human rights.
3. Pakistan	$798 M	$330 million for security efforts, including military-equipment upgrades and border security; $20 million for infrastructure.
4. Jordan	$688 M	$326 million to fight terrorism and promote regional stability through equipment upgrades and training; $163 million cash payment to the Jordanian government.
5. Kenya	$586 M	$501 million to fight HIV/AIDS through drug treatment and abstinence education, and to combat malaria; $15 million for agriculture; $5.4 million to promote government accountability.
6. South Africa	$574 M	$557 million to fight TB and HIV/AIDS; $3 million for education.

Another fundamental feature to this discussion is the reality that the *developed* world is not simply, benevolently, assisting the *developing* world. According to the UK-based non-governmental organization Share the World's Resources, the South has paid to the North almost $8 US trillion in debt repayment since 1979, an amount that far outweighs the development assistance it has received.[24] The amount that developing countries pay and repay to developed countries, private donors and banks has the general effect of suffocating development efforts, leaving little, if any, resources to cultivate basic services, such as universal health care and education, food production, and a stable economic base. There have been, within a neo-liberal lens, positive economic developments, such as in China and India, but in both cases rampant poverty, poor wealth distribution, inadequate health care, education, housing and other services, and a weak democratic impulse to resist militarization have been notable factors. This condition of perceiving the *goodness* of the North as juxtaposed against the insufferable incompetence of the South, channelled through popular culture and education, is an outcome of *econ-ocratic* democracy (Moyo, 2009). The vast militarization of the South, with limitless arms sales from the North, further frames the development quagmire, one which ultimately leads to mass migration, civil unrest, conflict, deleterious human rights and problematic electoral regimes that are incessantly propelled to imitate the two-party American model or risk isolation, sanctions or worse.

Figure 14. US Aid (Grants) to Israel Since 1949 (billions of dollars)[25]

Year	Total	Military Grant	Economic Grant	Immigration Grant
1949–1996	68	29	23.1	.87
1997	3.1	1.8	1.2	.08
1998	3	1.8	1.2	.08
1999	3	1.9	1.1	.07
2000	4.1	3.1	.95	.06
2001	2.9	2	.84	.06
2002	2.9	2	.72	.06
2003	3.8	3.1	.6	.06
2004	2.7	2.2	.48	.05
2005	2.7	2.2	.36	.05
2006	2.5	2.3	.24	.04
2007	2.5	2.3	.12	.04
TOTAL	102.2	53.6	30.9	1.5

NOTE: The $600 million in housing loan guarantees, $5.5 billion in military debt reduction loan guarantees, $9.2 billion in Soviet Jew resettlement loan guarantees, and $9 billion in economic recovery loan guarantees are not included in the tables because the United States government did not transfer funds to Israel. The United States underwrote loans to Israel from commercial institutions.

Patriotic Democracy and Unsavory Regimes

At the macro political level, there have been many attempts to label a nation/regime democratic or something incongruent with democracy.[26] Some of the countries deemed to be *undemocratic* can be destined to be marginalized (i.e., a 50-year US blockade against Cuba), face sanctions (i.e., Iran) or even be subjected to invasion (i.e., Iraq in 1991 and in 2003). The operative word above *can* qualifies the inconsistent and nefarious actions of some countries, which choose to support "dictatorial" or presumed "undemocratic" counties. The US, for example, considered Saddam Hussein to be a staunch ally during Iraq's war against Iran in the 1980s, supplying him with arms and figuratively "turning the other cheek" when it was made aware of human rights abuses, and used "deceptive tactics" and "subterfuge" to coerce and manipulate the American public into accepting a nefarious militaristic ideology (Gordon, Smyth & Diehl, 2008). Moreover, the US has supported a range of brutal regimes[27] in Latin America, Africa and Asia (see, for example, Chomsky, 2007; Galeano, 1973; Magdoff, 2003; Perkins, 2007; Schmitz, 2006, Zunes, 2007). Democracy, ironically, was not always invoked as a rationale to condemn unsavory regimes, nor was it an instrument used to support and mobilize change in governing structures that were known to have tortured, killed and oppressed local populations. The throngs of refugees fleeing these regimes is well known, and one can debate the direct causal linkage to the foreign policy of countries in the North. Figure 15 provides a portrait of some of the dictatorial regimes supported by the US as well as some of the diverse military actions undertaken under the guise of supporting the national interest. Interrogating the direct and indirect linkage to democracy would seem to be a necessary component to education, which will be explored in subsequent chapters.

There are many similarities in the dictatorial regimes selected in this figure, including: the dictators are almost always men; the US support has often come in the form of tacitly or actively orchestrating the overthrow of democratically elected regimes (the Allende government in Chile being one of the most salient examples); the media coverage, general knowledge and educational approach in exposing such linkages to dictatorial regimes has been, arguably, very thin; there is always an exodus of refugees from dictatorial countries; the cost for such support in terms of dollars, human rights, morality, legality and local economic development has been high, conflicting with the normative conception of US democratic ideals.

Figure 15. US Foreign Policy, Democracy and Un-democratic Activity[28]

Date	Country	Regime	Outcome
1931–1944	El Salvador	Maximiliano Hernandez	Assassination of political officials/civilians; repression
1936–1980	Nicaragua	Anastasio Somoza & sons	Political repression; civilians attacked
1941–1979	Iran	Shah of Iran	Repression, corruption and instability
1954–1959	Cuba	Fulgencio Batista	Torture, women raped, repression, and killings
1954–1982	Guatemala	Armas, Fuentes, Montt	400 Mayan villages razed; rape and torture
1954–1989	Paraguay	Stroessner	Widespread torture; political repression
1957–1986	Haiti	Papa Doc Duvalier & son	20,000–60,000 murdered; political repression
1965–1967	Brazil	Banco	Rebels executed; students tortured
1967–1998	Indonesia	Suharto	100,000–500,000 dead; violent repression
1969–1988	Zaire	Mobutu	Stole $3–5B; repression leading to bloodshed
1970–1978	Bolivia	Hugo Banzer	Drug production and trafficking; repression
1973–1990	Chile	Augusto Pinochet	3,000 murdered; 400,000 tortured
1975–1989	Angola	Jonas Savimbi/ UNITA	Killed/displaced millions
1976–1981	Argentina	Jorge Rafael Videla	30,000 murdered;repression
1978– present	Egypt	Sadat, Mubarak	Civilians killed in rebellion; corruption; repression
1979–1988	Iraq	Saddam Hussein	Repression; 1 million killed in war with Iran
1983–1989	Panama	Noriega	Support to contras; repression
1990– present	Uzbekistan	Kamirov	Rebels executed; conspirators tortured
1999–2007	Pakistan	Musharaff	Repression; political censorship; torture

As will be discussed later, a passive, neutral, non-critical appreciation of patriotism generally serves the hegemonic interests that dominate working people.
Donaldo Macedo (see Zinn & Macedo, 2005) underscores the danger of a passive
acceptance of indoctrination:

> If one were to argue that patriotism involves a lot more than a jingoistic display of waving the flag—that it is more patriotic to work to make the country more democratic, more just, less racist, and more humane—one would probably be accused of a lack of patriotism or even of being anti-American. If one would point to the vulgar commercialism of the flag after September 11, ranging from American flag thong underwear to condoms designed in red, white, and blue, one would also be charged with a lack of patriotism. If one pushed the envelope further and pointed out that the leaders of our country were hiding behind the flag to promote one of the largest shifts of wealth from the poor to the rich via tax cuts and corporate subsidies ($15 billion to the airline industry alone) while cutting services to the poor and elderly and slashing funds for education and social services, including benefits for the very troops that the administration is asking us to support, the reaction would again be more finger-pointing about one's lack of patriotism. And if one went so far as to link the undemocratic nature of US foreign policy with the present worldwide hatred of the United States, the possibility for further dialog just might collapse. (p. 8)

Zinn (Zinn & Macedo, 2005), one of the US' most recognized progressive historians, who has advocated for a more genuine and inclusive account of history, argues that classism is a fundamental girder underpinning American patriotism.

> If you look at the laws passed in the United States from the very beginning of the American republic down to the present day, you'll find that most of the legislation passed is class legislation that favors the elite, that favors the rich. You'll find huge subsidies to corporations all through American history. You'll find legislation passed to benefit the railroads, the oil companies, and the merchant marine and very little legislation passed to benefit the poor and the people who desperately need help. So the Law should not be given the holy deference that we are all taught to give it when we grow up and go to school, and it's a profoundly undemocratic idea to say that you should judge what you do according to what the Law says—undemocratic because it divests you as an individual of the right to make a decision yourself about what is right or wrong and it gives all of that power to that small band of legislators who have decided for themselves what is right and what is wrong. (p. 130)

Thus, how we look at the complexity of society, all of its contours, struggles, differences, inequities, achievements and relations with others in addition to power, can translate into the depth and scope of democracy in a given state. Clearly, this involves a much more rigorous analysis than the standard Gross National Product (GNP) of a country, which does not take into account socio-economic and political inequities.

Cookie-cutting Democracy and the Quest to Categorize

One of the best-known, and most effectively argued, rankings in relation to democracy is produced by *The Economist*. In 2008, it published its second *The Economist*

Intelligence Unit's Index of Democracy, providing a methodology and analysis underpinning the listing of countries that it evaluated. Specifically, it examined five categories: "electoral process and pluralism; civil liberties; the functioning of government; political participation; and political culture. Countries are placed within one of four types of regimes: full democracies; flawed democracies; hybrid regimes; and authoritarian regimes" (p. 1). *The Economist* qualifies the criteria by emphasizing that "Our Index embodies a wider concept than is the case with some other measures of democracy. Free and fair elections and civil liberties are necessary conditions for democracy, but they are unlikely to be sufficient for a full and consolidated democracy if unaccompanied by transparent and at least minimally efficient government, sufficient political participation and a supportive democratic political culture" (p. 1). The review echoes the sentiments above that "A combination of double standards in foreign policy (autocrats can be good friends as well as foes) and growing infringements of civil liberties has reduced the effectiveness of Western governments' calls for democratization" (p. 2).

The Economist is thorough in substantiating how it assembled its analysis, and constructive debate could be entertained to critique the underlying assumptions. The focus of this book, being on the critical pedagogy of democracy, leads one to question the preponderance and credence that *The Economist* has placed in the free-market and neo-liberal economic policies. It does acknowledge that "The standard modernisation hypothesis that economic development leads to, and/or is a necessary precondition for democracy, is no longer universally accepted. Instead it has been argued that the primary direction of causation runs from democracy to income" (p.3). Acknowledging that civil rights during a time of enhanced preparedness against terrorism have been problematic in the US and Great Britain, not to mention low levels of "voting turnout, membership of political parties, willingness to engage in and attitudes to political activity," and the increased visibility of extreme right-wing movements and parties in many European countries, *The Economist* keeps its focus primarily on the economic ball, so to speak. Revealingly, despite the astonishing detail consecrated on this study, *The Economist* confirms that:

> There is no consensus on how to measure democracydefinitions of democracy are contested and there is an ongoing lively debate on the subject. The issue is not only of academic interest. For example, although democracy-promotion is high on the list of US foreign policy priorities, there is no consensus within the US government on what constitutes a democracy.
>
> Although the terms freedom and democracy are often used interchangeably, the two are not synonymous. Democracy can be seen as a set of practices and principles that institutionalise and thus ultimately protect freedom. Even if a consensus on precise

definitions has proved elusive, most observers today would agree that, at a minimum, the fundamental features of a democracy include government based on majority rule and the consent of the governed, the existence of free and fair elections, the protection of minority rights and respect for basic human rights. Democracy presupposes equality before the law, due process and political pluralism. A question arises whether reference to these basic features is sufficient for a satisfactory concept of democracy.

Thus, while there is debate around thin and thick interpretations of democracy, the instrument provided by *The Economist* privileges elections to the behest of social and economic well-being. The distinctions between and within countries are not effectively made, nor is there (much) room to incisively critique how poverty, racism, sexism, homophobia, classism, etc. serve to undermine the interests of those citizens located in *democracies*.

The introspective discussion that *The Economist* initiates characterizes the complexity and problematic nature of democracy. How are we to understand it, engage in it, critique it, and, significantly, thread the education needle through it? According to *The Economist* (2008, p. 17), "Democracy is more than the sum of its institutions. A democratic political culture is also crucial for the legitimacy, smooth functioning and ultimately the sustainability of democracy. A culture of passivity and apathy, an obedient and docile citizenry, are not consistent with democracy. The electoral process periodically divides the population into winners and losers. A successful democratic political culture implies that the losing parties and their supporters accept the judgment of the voters, and allow for the peaceful transfer of power." It also emphasizes the importance of citizenship participation as well as inclusionary measures.

The model derived by *The Economist*, which rates North America and Western European countries as being the most democratic, raises many questions (if considered legitimate, why are so many regimes labeled as authoritarian such staunch allies of the West, and why are some other regimes hived out for special (negative) attention? What is the role of education in cultivating democracy, something that appears to be largely absent from this economic-centered model?). Yet, this attempt at unearthing the foundation of formal democracy seems more advanced than some of the other, more election- and economics-based approaches.

A radically alternative version of the traditional model expounded by *The Economist* is that used by Bhutan, which favors happiness as it organizing principle. Developed in the 1970s, the Royal Kingdom of Bhutan has sought to counter the widely accepted neo-liberal Gross National Product (GNP) measure for development (Center for Bhutan Studies, 2009b).

...a GNH society means the creation of an enlightened society in which happiness and well-being of all people and sentient beings is the ultimate purpose of governance....

...happiness is an indicator of good development and good society. He (the King) also believed in the legitimacy of public deliberation, public discussion, and public opinion in defining any goal, including GNH, through democracy and nlightened citizenship.

...Across the world, indicators focus largely on market transactions, covering trade, monetary exchange rates, stock market, growth, etc. These dominant, conventional indicators, generally related to Gross Domestic Product (GDP) reflect quantity of physical output of a society.

...The almost universal use of GDP-based indicators to measure progress has helped justify policies around the world that are based on rapid material progress at the expense of environmental preservation, cultures, and community cohesion.

...Once people are familiar with GNH indicators, they can have a practical effect on consumer and citizens behaviour. The behaviour changing function can emerge in significant ways when there are appropriate indicators that direct attention towards both the causes of problems and the manner in which behaviour and decisions can prevent and solve those problems.

... Our understanding of how the mind achieves happiness affects our experience of happiness by influencing the means we choose in striving towards it. In some branches of the behavioural sciences, the mind is conceived of as an input-output device responding to external stimuli. One consequence of this model is that happy and pleasurable feelings are seen as dependent solely upon external stimuli. Happiness is perceived as a direct consequence of sensory pleasures. ...With such an overemphasis on external stimuli as the source for happiness, it isn't surprising that individuals are led to believe that being materialistic will increase their happiness.[29]

Within each of the nine dimensions in Bhutan's GNH index, there are a number of indicators, which contain various measures. Conceptually, the GNH is easily understood based on a more holistic, humanistic and counter-hegemonic notion of development, yet the actual formulation, conceptualization and measurement formula is intricately complex. Respecting the environment and non-materialist factors underpins the engagement required by the populace to produce the data that feed into the overall analysis. There are nine dimensions to Bhutan's GNH index: psychological well-being; time use; community vitality; culture; health; education; environmental diversity; living standard; and governance.

From a critical pedagogical vantage point, it is relevant and, I would argue, necessary to explore diverse conceptualizations of development, and to problematize the political, economic and social factors and considerations that frame our thinking on what constitutes democracy. The United Nations Development Program's Human Development Index Reports[30] provide a vast range of measures that contextualize the differentiated development of countries that surpasses the neo-liberal economic indicators. Normative values related to what democracy should resemble must be interrogated in order to allow for a broader analysis and understanding of the plurality of democratic models. Focusing on the needs, rights and conditions of working people, minority and marginalized groups and majority populations necessitates different paradigms that place less of an emphasis on the disjointed nature of economic growth (Hill, 2003). Regardless of the model, in order to determine the democratic experience it is important to determine how wealth accumulation and distribution can help all people within a given society.

Concluding Thoughts

The epistemology of democracy is laden with normative values about the meaning of freedom, justice, liberty, fairness, and empowerment. Our knowledge about the lived experiences of others plays a fundamental role in pivotal decisions that are made about our relationships at the micro and macro levels (Freire, 1973/2005; Kincheloe, 2008b). This can flow into major decisions that deal with war and peace, migration, economic issues, health matters and environmental concerns that know no boundaries (Klein, 2008). It can also have a direct and tangible effect on what we learn in schools, how we develop intercultural relations and how we strive to build communities as well as the prospect to openly engage with the world (Kurth-Schai & Green, 2006). The examples, or vignettes, illustrated in this chapter—*American Idol*, the Olympics, Haiti, the North-South divide, and the categorization of democracies—seek to provide some analysis in support of the critical pedagogy framework, which forms the cornerstone of this book.

Critical pedagogy offers a lens, perspective and approach to reconcile some of what our epistemological foundation is unable to diagnose. Accepting that our understanding of the world, or as Freire (2005) puts it, "our ability to read the world," is limited, an open, dialectical, critical process of reflection, interrogation and engagement (*conscientization*) would be beneficial to achieving a more substantive and meaningful form of democracy. In sum, a more holistic and dynamic approach—pedagogical, experiential, political, social, economic and cultural—is a necessary step to attaining a more "decent society," as Tinder (2004) has set out through his dialectical interrogation of *perennial questions*. It is inconceivable that we will never have peace (and justice) without a more human, dignified and humble engagement with diverse historical and contemporary forces and realities.

Chapter 4

Framing Democracy in Education[1]

Paul R. Carr in collaboration with Darren E. Lund

The oppressed suffer from the duality which was established itself in their innermost being. They discover that without freedom they cannot exist authentically. Yet, although they desire authentic existence, they fear it. They are at one and the same time themselves and the oppressor whose consciousness they have internalized. The conflict lies in the choice between being wholly themselves or being divided; between ejecting the oppressor within or not ejecting them; between human solidarity or alienation; between following prescriptions or having choices; between being spectators or actors; between acting or having the illusion of acting through the action of the oppressors; between speaking out or being silent, castrated in their power to create and re create, in their power to transform the world. This is the tragic dilemma of the oppressed which their education must take into account. (Freire, 1973/2005, p. 48)

Can There Be Democracy Outside of Elections?

As argued in the first section, the notion that democracy equates elections is highly problematic. Despite the mainstream media obsession with the electoral politics that pervades the public psyche, another perspective, which was advanced in the first few chapters, one that should not appear to be overly radical or unusual, notwithstanding the commonly accepted formulation of the concept, is that, for democracy to be meaningful and tangible, it must be connected to education as well as social justice (Chomsky, 2003; Dewey, 1916/1997; Portelli & Solomon, 2001). A democracy that does not discourage (or is ambivalent about) racism, sexism, homophobia, homelessness, poverty, religious/linguistic/ethnic discrimination, and the torment of macro- and micro-level legislation or government policies that further marginalize individuals and groups must be taken to task (Banks et al., 2005). In other words, apart from the all-consuming electoral periods which seem to stretch virtually from one election to the next and which, inevitably, consume precious resources while diverting attention from serious problems, there need to be broad, and meaningful, entry points in which average citizens can, and should necessarily, partake in the democratic experience (Demaine, 2004).

Although it may not be promoted on the nightly news or in mainstream media sources, students, workers, citizens, groups, associations, and myriad other collectives in society can, and must, engage themselves, to varying degrees, in politics, attempting to have their voices heard, to change society, and to present alternatives that may not be readily recognized as standard, "textbook" democracy. Through their collective efforts, which may not be synchronized with the formal, elite-centered democratic notion of freedom and equality, people can effectuate some measure of change in their lives (Carr, 2008a). The passive acceptance of majority rule from above can also have the effect of constraining and pacifying the public (Chomsky, 2003; Gramsci, & Forgacs, 2000). Since the lens of formal democracy is often focused on formal structures and events, it is questionable how education is, and should be, immersed in shaping the political, economic, and cultural life of society, especially in relation to democratic participation and engagement (Lund & Carr, 2008; Gandin & Apple, 2005; Portelli & Solomon, 2001).

Democracy in Education

I approach this project with the firm belief that democracy needs to be cultivated, critiqued, demonstrated, and manifested throughout the educational experience (Carr, 2007a, 2008b; Dewey, 1916/1997; Lund & Carr, 2008a; Westheimer & Kahne, 2004). As elaborated in a previous work (see Lund & Carr, 2008a), there is still much to be learned about we actually *do*, or *should do*, democracy in education. Do we know how to *do* democracy, how to talk about it, how to engage with it, and how to accept, as Schugurensky (2000) has argued, that it is more of a work in progress than a fixed object that we have achieved? Is democracy merely something that is isolated to a singular course or discipline, often bottled up within social studies or civics? Parker (2003) argues that democracy needs to be infused in everything that happens at school, from the curriculum to the extracurricular activities, through the formal organization and structures, including interaction with parents and communities, and also comprising the infinite number of issues that blend into the realms of decision-making, participation, and shaping the identity, culture, and outcomes of the educational experience. At the theoretical level, to recapitulate a concept presented in the first section of this book, Gandin and Apple (2005) have hypothesized that, building on the work of Barber (1984), there are *thick* and *thin* notions of democracy, and teaching about and for the latter generally avoids doing critical work and engagement destined to reinforce democracy. My understanding of, and support for, a *thicker* interpretation of democracy involves a more authentic, encompassing and critical democratic engagement, participation, and educational experience. This analysis is respectful of the work of Daniel Schugurensky (2008), who seeks a broadening and deeping of our engagement with democracy, incorporating peace education, environmental education and participatory democracy.

Kurth-Schai and Green (2006) offer some fundamental questions in relation to how democracy and education should be considered, and these queries further assist us in building a critical framework to examine the educational project within a *bona fide* or perceived democracy.

- Given the importance afforded throughout our history to foundational concepts of "education" and "democracy," why does the gap between our aspirations and our achievement persist?
- Given the dimensions and dynamics of contemporary social and educational concerns, what, beyond rational problem solving, is necessary?
- Given the prevailing philosophic and pragmatic commitments to individualism, what is the meaning and purpose of social learning?
- Given the costs and consequences of failure, how can we responsibly risk innovation in an increasingly dangerous world?

Kurth-Schai and Green (2006) suggest that re-envisioning democracy involves a multitude of forces, considerations, creative forays, and ethical and aesthetic processes, which, together—given the argument that I am advancing that democracy is an amalgam of factors, processes, structures, and phenomena, rendering it a philosophy, a culture, a way of thinking and living, and a political system that is flexible and responsive to the needs of a diverse society—point to a more complex, nuanced version of how students need to relate to their own implication, participation, and engagement with the society that they form (Darling-Hammond, French, & Garcia-Lopez, 2002).

The context for interrogating democracy in education is, as Shapiro (2005) effectively points out, the crisis-like situation characterizing schools in the United States and elsewhere:

> Issues such as the growing administrative control over teachers' lives, allegations about mediocrity of American schools, the crisis of funding, concern about what is called educational *excellence*, the impoverishment of increasing numbers of children and adolescents, the influence of the media on young lives, fears about moral degeneration, school violence, bitter contention over the nature of the curriculum and of school knowledge, and widening disparities in educational achievement among ethnic and racial groups must all be seen, at the same time, as both critical issues in American education and as metaphors for the larger human and societal situation. (p. ix)

When universal concerns, including the environment, racism, AIDS, war and military conflict, migration, and inequitable power relations in general, are added to the dynamic context characterizing pluralistic societies, it is easy to see how democracy, democratic values, and the democratic experience are as vulnerable as they are contested (Paehlke, 2003). It is necessary to *do* democracy in education because to do otherwise will, ultimately, lead to apolitical, hyper-patriotic societies with only a limited understanding of what is becoming increasingly a multicultural citizenry (Kymlicka, 1995).

Democratic habits and values must be taught and communicated through the dynamic intercultural, interracial interclass and other relations of our society, our legal institutions, our press, our religious life, our private associations, and the many other agencies that allow citizens to interact with each other and to have a sense of efficiency. The best protection for a democratic society is well-educated citizens (Ravitch & Viteritti, 2001, p. 28). Patrick (2003) argues that successful democratic education must include several interconnected components:

> Effective education for citizenship in a democracy dynamically connects the four components of civic knowledge, cognitive civic skills, participatory civic skills, and civic dispositions. Effective teaching and learning of civic knowledge, for example, require that it be connected to civic skills and dispositions of various kinds of activities. Elevation of one component over the otherfor example, civic knowledge over skills or vice-versais a pedagogical flaw that impedes civic learning. Thus, teachers should combine core content and the processes by which students develop skills and dispositions. (p. 3)

Similarly, Laguardia and Pearl (2005) identify seven themes or attributes of a democratic classroom: "(1) persuasive and negotiable leadership; (2) inclusiveness; (3) knowledge made universally available and organized for important problem solving; (4) inalienable student and teacher rights; (5) universal participation in decisions that affect one's life; (6) the development of optimum learning conditions; and (7) equal encouragement" (p. 9).

Parker (2003) further fleshes out the conceptualization of democratic education:

> First, democratic education is not a neutral project, but one that tries to predispose citizens to principled reasoning and just ways of being with one another. Second, educators need simultaneously to engage in multicultural education and citizenship education.... Third, the diversity that schools contain makes extraordinarily fertile soil for democratic education.... Fourth, this dialog plays an essential and vital role in democratic education, moral development, and public policy.... Fifth, the access/inclusion problem that we (still) face today is one of extending democratic education to students who are not typically afforded it. (pp. xvi–xvii)

Parker (2003) elaborates on the seamless nature of citizenship, democracy, and diversity, and how teaching democracy must be synchronized with many of the same issues that are enmeshed in multicultural education. This interpretation of democracy is strongly aligned with the work of (Dewey, 1916/1973), who believed in the notion of democratic education as enabling people to live productively together, and also as a vehicle to resolve social problems (Simpson, Jackson, & Aycock, 2005).

Teaching, Learning, and Democracy

The fundamental core of democratic education at the classroom level is the teacher, which invariably places certain responsibilities on teacher education programs (Solomon, Portelli, Daniel, & Campbell, 2005). Teacher educators have encountered numerous challenges in inculcating democratic values in the curriculum as well as through practical experiences. Simpson et al. (2005) illustrate how the teacher can play multiple roles in cultivating, nurturing, and engaging in what they call the "art of teaching," which can reinforce the democratic experience for students.

Elsewhere, I (Carr 2006a, 2007b, 2008c) have found that many teacher-education students and teachers focus the majority of their attention on the electoral process in relation to their notion of teaching about democracy and, moreover, that most of the teacher education students and teachers in my study had only a limited democratic education experience while they were in elementary and secondary school. In particular, I have developed a number of themes from the research project on democracy and education in which I have been involved since 2005 (Figure 16).

Therefore, preparing those who will be teaching diverse students one day is a fundamental part of ensuring that democracy is cultivated in education (Simpson et al., 2005). Solomon, Portelli, Daniel, and Campbell (2005) have documented the limited understanding and engagement of White preservice teachers in relation to social justice, which underpins the need for a greater focus on White power and privilege in education at the policy, institutional, curriculum, and training levels (Carr & Lund, 2007a; James, 2003). Further, as Lund (1998) has argued, creative ways must be found to engage all students in the struggle for social justice in schools as a way of nurturing the kind of engaged and critical forms of democracy that can attend to equity concerns. Preparing the future teachers of these students to be open to engaging the next generation in new forms of activism has proven to be rewarding work, with tremendous potential for progressive social change (Lund, 2005). Understanding the reticence of some educators to teach for social justice and (*thicker*) democracy is a challenge that is not always addressed in contemporary educational reforms.

Figure 16. Carr's Research and Overview of Literature in Democratic Education

A critical appreciation and analysis of democracy as a philosophy, ethos, political system, and cultural phenomenon is only thinly articulated by participants. There is little commentary on critical thinking, politics as a way of life, power sharing, decision-making processes, the role of the media, alternative systems, and social responsibility (Gandin & Apple, 2005).
Almost all of the participants focus on elections as the pivotal underpinning to democracy. Almost all participants, although extremely supportive of democracy in the US, are dissatisfied with a number of aspects associated with democracy (i.e., elections, issues raised, elected officials) (Patterson, 2003).
US democracy is often considered to be a model, far preferable to what exists in other systems/countries. However, there does not appear to be a strong understanding of what democracy looks like elsewhere (Holm & Farber, 2002).
An excessive emphasis is placed on presidential politics when talking about democracy, eclipsing local, regional and international issues.
There is extreme reticence about "politics" being part of education, with many participants mentioning a concern about "indoctrination" (Sears & Hughes, 2006).
Civic engagement is understood in very narrow terms, concentrated within a specific class/course or associated with elections (Galston, 2003).
The connection between education and democracy is a nebulous one, with many participants questioning the foundation of such a linkage (McLaren, 2007).
The critical area of social justice, especially in relation to race and poverty, is not fully supported as an integral part of the teaching about/for democracy (Portelli & Solomon, 2001).
The study underscored significant differences between White and non-White participants in relation to the place and significance of social justice in education (Carr & Lund, 2007b).

Democratic Education within the Context of Neo-Liberalism

As Osborne (2001), Karumanchery and Portelli (2005), and McLaren (2007) have argued, the notion of democracy cannot be disconnected from capitalism and neo-liberalism. Hill (2003) has warned of the pervasive nature of neo-liberalism in forcing a corporate, business agenda into the curriculum, the educational policy development and decision-making processes, and the myriad areas that shape the educational experience. The result is a mild, somewhat superficial, and *thin* exposure to critical democracy and engagement, especially in relation to social justice. Sleeter (2007) complements this analysis by arguing that the present corporatacracy, imbued within the neo-liberal yolk, is further distancing education from democracy under the guise of greater *accountability*. Lipman (2004) maintains that:

> School accountability policies undermine critical thought and dialog and human agency.
> They discipline students and teachers alike to the power of central school authorities and

create a coercive climate in which teachers and school adminitsrators are afraid to speak up against educational practices they privately abhor. They sort students and schools based on the superficial images constructed out of test scores and promote simplistic binary thinking. They create a culture of fear and individual blame and erode social solidarities. The authoritarianism of these policies is particularly meted out in public to students of color and their schools and communtiies, definign them as deficient and in need of regulation.

The neo-liberal model of education involves a range of free-market principles—rationalization and cost cutting, declining investments, a limited selection of curricular options, privatization, the specter of school choice—the No Child Left Behind (NCLB) legislation in the United States is the best example, and a general assault on teachers in relation to effectiveness and efficiency levels (Carr, 2007b; Gordon, Smyth & Diehl, 2008; Hill, 2003; Torres, 2005). Saltzman (2009) sums up the problematic nature of NCLB as "set(ting) schools up for failure by making impossible demands for continual improvement. When schools have not met Adequate Yearly Progress (AYP), they are subject to punitive action by the federal government, including the potential loss of formerly guaranteed federal fudning and requirements for tutoring form a vast array of for-profit Special educatioanl Service provider" (p. 30). Similarly, a major focus of neo-liberal education is the unwavering devotion to standardized testing, standards, and (supposed) accountability, all of which isolate and diminish the place of democracy and social justice in education (Sleeter, 2007).

The multiple tentacles masked in a foray of supposed prosperity, economic growth, freedom, and independence that are so skillfully articulated within the neo-liberal discourse serve to undermine meaningful debate and engagement on democracy (Walsh, 2009). The premise for a more critical (and critical pedagogical) approach is, therefore, biased toward a more active and activist role for educators and others involved in education in order to fully embrace critical engagement and political literacy. As Freire (2005) has suggested, education is a political enterprise, so it would, therefore, be necessary to understand, interrogate, and act upon political matters (Bourdieu & Passeron, 1990). Students are much more than the "empty vessels" of Freire's banking education critique, needing to be filled with knowledge; they need to be engaged with how power works (Delpit, 1996) as well as being positioned to challenge, reshape, and transform society (Ayers, Hunt & Quinn, 1998; McLaren, 2007). As Westheimer (2006a, 2006b) has pointed out, this academic vacuum in which democracy and social justice can be quickly replaced with the suffocating scent of patriotism serves to homogenize thinking and dampen the plurality of opinion and experience that is required for a highly heterogeneous society, such as those that exist in North America and Europe.

Sleeter (2007) summarizes some of the confusion around how democracy is considered within the educational context, emphasizing that "where one stands on the relationship among individual rights, group claims and cultural identities, and shared common interest has implications for the extent to which one will view standardization of schooling and school curricula as a just and democratic means of promoting excellence for everyone" (p. 5). Sleeter (2007) also raises the significant concern of the "relationship between democracy as a governance structure and capitalism as an economic structure" (p. 5). Linking these issues has implications for educators and decision makers who can shape the texture and shape of democracy in education through their own understanding and experience with democracy. Here, the question of whether educators can *do* democracy if they do not have a belief in the importance of formalizing democratic education and experiences through critical engagement and the interrogation of controversial issues is pivotal (Carr, 2006a, 2007b, 2008c).

Measuring Democracy in Education

Diamond and Morlino (2005) illustrate how difficult and problematic it is to assess the quality of democracy, introducing a range of concepts as measures and indicators, including the usual components related to voting, political parties, and alternative sources of media as well as an emphasis on procedure, content, and results. They continue to identify eight "dimensions on which democracies vary in quality": five procedural dimensions, including "the rule of law, participation, competition, and accountability, both vertical and horizontal"; two dimensions that are substantive in nature: respect for civil and political freedoms and the progressive implementation of greater political (and underlying it, social and economic) equality"; and the "last dimension, responsiveness, links the procedural dimensions to the substantive ones by measuring the extent to which public policies (including laws, institutions, and expenditures) correspond to citizen demands and preferences, as aggregated through the political process" (p. xii).

Arguably, education must be a factor in assessing democracy, in how it is constructed, shaped, and lived, and, importantly, how it facilitates or restricts participation in the evolving processes that Diamond and Morlino (2005) present above. Deconstructing the meaning of elections as equating democracy in a "globalized," neo-liberal society requires a nuanced, critical understanding of, and engagement with, democracy through education.

Banks et al. (2005), in their analysis of *Democracy and Diversity: Principles and Concepts for Educating Citizens*, have compiled a checklist to frame effectively the discussion around teaching for and about democracy (Figure 17). It is clear that, based on the comprehensive synthesis provided by Banks et al. (2005), democracy in education reposes on a strong theoretical, conceptual, and applied engagement with diversity, which is supported by the seminal anti-racism work of George Dei (1996), James Banks (2008), Christine Sleeter (2007), Sonia Nieto (1999), and others. Their checklist (Figure 17) also responds effectively to many of the findings in Torney-Purta's (Torney-Purta, Schwille, & Amadeo, 1999; Torney-Purta & Richardson, 2002) groundbreaking studies related to measuring civic attitudes internationally. This comparative work has demonstrated not only the need for greater political literacy and engagement in, and through, education but also, at the methodological level, the need for more research and the establishment of measures to determine and assess how and what students are learning about civic and citizenship education. One obvious shortcoming in the flood of neo-liberal education reforms is the absence of a clear, critical focus on democratic education that includes attention to social justice, with the requisite resources being made available.

Democratic Education and Political Literacy

Do schools aim for political literacy (Davies & Hogarth, 2004)? Do they formally and informally cultivate political literacy? Is there a place for political literacy within an educational milieu that has been submerged in the hazy clouds of neo-liberalism (Hill & Boxley. 2007; Schugurensky, 2000)? If we are not teaching about and for political literacy, what then is the mission of the school (Parker, 2003)? Is it to foster the skills and knowledge to prepare students for the world of work? Does it flow over to attitudes and behaviors so that students can live in harmony within a pluralistic society (Provenzo, 2005)? Are teachers trained, prepared, and able to be engaged in such a process (Fenimore-Smith, 2004)? Do curriculum policy documents nurture this order of thinking? What is inherently critical about the educational experience? Is the mantra of critical thinking embedded in the notion of schools being potential sites of transformational change, or is it simply loaded jargon to appease those who clamor for a more holistic educational experience?

As noted by Freire (2004), who crystallizes the notion of a socially just, politically literate society, in elaborating the conditions for a more decent society, democracy involves negotiating the limits of authority and freedom:

> I am convinced that no education intending to be at the service of the beauty of the human presence in the world, at the service of seriousness and ethical rigor, of justice, of firmness of character, of respect for differencesno education intending to be engaged in the struggle for realizing the dream of solidaritycan fulfill itself in the absence of the dramatic relationship

> between authority and freedom. It is a tense and dramatic relationship in which both authority
> and freedom, while fully living out their limits and possibilities, learn, almost without respite, to
> take responsibility for themselves as authority and freedom. It is by living lucidly the tense
> relationship between authority and freedom that one discovers the two need not necessarily be in
> mutual antagonism. It is from the starting point of this learning that both authority and freedom
> become committed, within educational practice, to the democratic dream of an authority zealous
> in its limits interacting with a freedom equally diligent of its limits and possibilities. (p. 9)

Likewise, Giroux (1988) argues for "critical literacy as a precondition for self- and social-empowerment" and dissects the way that traditional forms of literacy, especially when imbued within the web of neo-liberalism, serve to further marginalize the marginalized. He maintains that "the language of literacy is almost exclusively linked to popular forms of liberal and right-wing discourse that reduce it to either a functional perspective tied to narrowly coerced economic interests or to a logic designed to initiate the poor, the underprivileged, and minorities into the ideology of a unitary, dominant cultural tradition" (p. 61). Ultimately, in order to become engaged in democracy, there must be political literacy, the absence of which would make the prospect of meaningful social justice in society less likely.

Other authors have also emphasized the strong need for political literacy to enhance social justice. Tarcov (1996), for example, situates democratic education within the framework of popular political participation:

> To think clearly about democratic education, we must reconsider the meaning and the
> goodness of democracy. It is sometimes said, and even believed, that democracy is the
> ultimate political criterion, good, or aspiration, and that all political evils should be
> attributed to the absence of full democracy and their cure sought in more democracy.
> That view is usually accompanied by an understanding of democracy that insists on the
> maximum of immediate and unlimited popular rule and the exclusion of any elements of
> other forms of government. Such a view sees democratic education as directed toward the
> propagation and actualization of such an understanding of democracy. (p. 1)

Davies and Hogarth (2004) argue that political literacy must be resituated as the focal point of citizenship education. Their vision of political literacy surpasses the "compound of knowledge, skills and procedural values" to also include "such areas as respect for truth and reasoning and toleration as opposed to substantive values which could mean that pupils would be told what to think about particular issues" (p. 182). They reject previous political literacy models, such as the "civics" model centered on "factual knowledge and a didactic teaching methodology" as the modus operandi (p. 182), and the "big issues" model in which adversarial political debates take place in class. For this latter approach, there is concern that issues will only be examined at a superficial level without serious follow up. Rather, they favor the "public discourse model," which "seeks to induct pupils into the language, concepts, forms of arguments and skills required to think and talk about life from a political point of view, emphasizing both process and product. Factual knowledge is important but is made subservient to other aspects that are centrally important to political literacy" (p. 183).

Figure 17. Banks et al.'s (2005) Checklist for Teaching for and about Democracy

Principles

1. Are students taught about the complex relationships between unity and diversity in their local communities, the nation, and the world?
2. Do students learn about the ways in which people in their community, nation, and region are increasingly interdependent with other people around the world and are connected to the economic, political, cultural, environmental, and technological changes taking place across the planet?
3. Does the teaching of human rights underpin citizenship education courses and programs?
4. Are students taught knowledge about democracy and democratic institutions and provided opportunities to practice democracy?

Concepts

1. Democracy: Do students develop a deep understanding of the meaning of democracy and what it means to be a citizen in a democratic society?
2. Diversity: Is the diversity of cultures and groups within all multicultural societies explicitly recognized in the formal and informal curriculum?
3. Globalization: Do students develop an understanding of globalization that encompasses its history, the multiple dimensions and sites of globalization, as well as the complex outcomes of globalization?
4. Sustainable Development: Is the need for sustainable development an explicit part of the curriculum?
5. Empire, Imperialism, and Power: Are students grappling with how relationships among nations can be more democratic and equitable by discussing the concepts of imperialism and power?
6. Prejudice, Discrimination, and Racism: Does the curriculum help students to understand the nature of prejudice, discrimination, and racism, and how they operate at interpersonal, intergroup, and institutional levels?
7. Migration: Do students understand the history and the forces that cause the movement of people?
8. Identity/Diversity: Does the curriculum nurture an understanding of the multiplicity, fluidity, and contextuality of identity?
9. Multiple Perspectives: Are students exposed to a range of perspectives on varying issues?
10. Patriotism and Cosmopolitanism: Do students develop a rich and complex understanding of patriotism and cosmopolitanism?

The Juncture between Democracy, Education and Citizenship

There has long been a robust debate, in both the public and academic domains, on the role that citizenship education can or should play in the fostering of democratic ideals. For example, according to the Corporation for National and Community Service (2005), effective citizenship education should prepare young people in three areas:

- Civic literacy: Fundamental knowledge of history and government, political and community organizations, and public affairs; skills for making informed judgments, engaging in democratic deliberation and decision making, influencing the political process, and organizing within a community.
- Civic virtues: Values, beliefs, and attitudes needed for constructive engagement in the political system and community affairs, such as tolerance, social trust, and a sense of responsibility for others.
- Civically engaged behaviors: Habits of participating and contributing to civic and public life through voting, staying politically informed, and engaging in community service.

In a related vein, Santora (2006) examined why cooperative learning often failed to promote democratic behavior among culturally diverse students and found that students reacted to knowledge provided by the teacher in multiple ways, including finding avenues to dispute or complement such knowledge with that acquired in/from their families, the environment, and the media. Her study demonstrates how power, as it affects knowledge construction, is locally reproduced or reconstituted through classroom interaction.

The analysis above reflects Delpit's (1996) work on how minorities are systemically excluded from the decision-making process in the classroom, as well as in the broader society, through myriad processes that codify the implicit and explicit ways that power works. Within this context, we might ask the following questions: Why is there exclusion, who defines it, how do we measure it, and what can be done to remedy it? What are the implications of sustained marginalization? What formal and informal processes are in place to effectively bring together and to ensure constructive engagement between peoples from different races, social classes, ethnicities, religions, etc.? What is the responsibility of those who have access to power and decision making?

Gilmour (2006) raises a fundamental issue when considering the salience of citizenship education: "(It) has the potential to open up new and controversial areas of debate and, within the critical whole-school approach, can advance anti-racist developments. In Britain, however, the dominant tradition has been for citizenship education that reinforces the status quo by binding students to a superficial and sanitized version of pluralism that is long on duties and responsibilities, but short on popular struggles against race inequality" (p. 99).

In her work on citizenship and service learning, Waggener (2006) elaborates on this dichotomy between the political and social components of citizenship, and concludes that "more attention must be given to service learning projects that teach about the structure of governments and encourage students to engage in political action" (p. 4). Simon (2001) complements this research by effectively elucidating the dilemma of constructing meaningful democracy and citizenship:

> To be a citizen is not just to hold a legal status in relation to a particular nation state; rather it is to possess the capacities, and have access to the opportunities, to participate with others in the determination of one's society. This means being able to take into account the inter-related character of culture, politics, and economics. If we want people to be citizens, not subjects (i.e., those to whom economics, politics, and schooling simply happen), we will need to have young people think critically and be able to participate in society so as to transform inequities that impede full participation in democratic life. (p. 12)

Portelli and Solomon (2001) further tease out the distinction between *thin* and *thick* democracy. They emphasize "common elements such as critical thinking, dialog and discussion, tolerance, free and reasoned choices, and public participation ... which are associated with equity, community, creativity, and taking difference seriously ... [a] conception [that] is contrasted with the notion of democracy that is minimalist, protectionist, and marginalist and hence promotes a narrow notion of individualism and spectacular citizenship" (p. 17).

Westheimer and Kahne (2003) have cogently argued that the emphasis on patriotism and community service in the post–September 11 era may effectively diminish the level and intensity of democracy in society, and may even be anti-democratic. They point to the formal, governmental push for volunteerism and charity as a potential lever that, despite creating the impression that society is becoming more democratic, does not achieve *bona fide* critical civic engagement. Friedland and Morimoto (2005), in their study of volunteerism, found that for "middle- and upper-middle-class high school students 'resume-padding' is one of the motivating factors driving the increase in volunteering," and it is "shaped by the perception that voluntary and civic activity is necessary to get into college; and the better the college (or, more precisely, the higher the perception of the college in the status system) the more volunteerism students believed was necessary" (p. 1). Therefore, as illustrated by Westheimer and Kahne (2004), there must be an authentic (and political) ring to the conceptualization and implementation of service learning for it to have any value for the students. Kahne and Westheimer (2003) have formulated a typology to interrogate some of the fundamental questions that should be asked when engaging democratic education (Figure 18).

The absence of democratic citizenship (or rather the presence of an extremely nuanced approach to it) is evident when considering that only three US states have specific standards for civic education, although almost half of them have addressed at least some components of civic education in their social studies curricula and standards (RMC Research Corporation, 2005, p. 7).

Figure 18. Broad Priorities of Successful Democratic Educational Programs (Kahne & Westheimer, 2003)

	Commitment	*Capacity*	*Connection*
W	*Why* should I be committed to actively engaging issues in my community and beyond?	*How* can I engage issues?	*Who* is going to engage issues with me?
T	For example: show students that society needs improving and provide positive experiences seeking solutions.	For example: engage students in real-world projects; teach civic skills and provide knowledge through workshops and simulations so students can be effective civic actors.	For example: provide a supportive community of peers and connections to role models.
R	I am committed to civic engagement.	I have the skills, knowledge, and networks I need to act effectively for change in my community and beyond.	I know and admire people who have made a difference in the past and feel connected to those who want to make a difference now, and I want to work with them.

Legend: W=what students ask?; T=teaching democracy; R=results

Similarly, Galston (2003) has found that there is only limited civic knowledge among American students:

> The National Assessment of Educational Progress Civics Assessment has revealed major deficiencies in the overall results: For fourth-, eighth-, and (most relevant for our purposes) 12th-graders, about three-fourths were below the level of proficiency. Thirty-five percent of high school seniors tested below basic, indicating near-total civic ignorance. Another 39% were at the basic level, demonstrating less than the working knowledge that citizens need. (pp. 31–32)

O'Toole, Marsh, and Jones (2003) have found, despite the contention to the contrary, that young people are not apathetic, nor are they disinterested in politics, but they are discouraged from participating because of the way the current system seems to present issues; interestingly, they note that "politics is something that is done to them, not something they can influence," and "inequalities based on class, gender, ethnicity and age are crucial features of the lives of our respondents: they are not variables, they are lived experiences" (p. 359). In sum, the present neo-liberal configuration of educational curricula, standards, expectations, and testing concurrently has a tendency to isolate political literacy and places a premium on a type of learning that can disenfranchise many students.

For a Critical Democratic Education

Understanding and being able to participate in society in a critically engaged manner should not be a sidebar item on the educational agenda. Without question, students need to master certain skills and knowledge, they need to become literate in certain areas, and they also need to learn certain basic notions about society. However, as cultural capital (Delpit, 1996) plays a significant role in shaping the education experience of students, there is also the concern as to how educators understand difference and identity in doing democracy in education (McLaren, 2007). Missing out on focusing on validating and transcending boundaries, barriers and (lived) experiences can serve to further entrench injustice, inequity and antidemocratic thinking, values, and manifestations (Banks et al., 2005; Dei, Karumanchery, & Karumanchery-Luik, 2004; Parker, 2003). Westheimer and Kahne (2004) have argued for a more engaged, relevant and critical involvement during their educational experience, based on some extensive research with schools in the US (see Figure 19).

Contrary to commonly held views of democracy being based around elections, freedoms and rights, the focus of the critical pedagogy of democracy is that it is an ethos, an ideology, a set of values, a philosophy, a contested terrain of action and debate, and a complex, problematic, dynamic framework and terrain in which diverse forces, interests, and experiences intersect to develop relations and relationships that continue to evolve over time, space and epistemological transgression. No singular or simplistic definitions characterize the breadth of democracy, the consequent-laden valley of human decisions and predispositions that coalesce to underpin how we have resolved to live, either in struggle or solidarity, resisting or embracing change, oppression and human-made conditions (Freire, 1973/2005; Shapiro & Purpel, 2005). An unequivocal focus on social justice needs to be incorporated within the broad and uneven strokes that paint the democracy tableau. Although securing a place within the socio-polotical debate on and around democracy, elections need to be problematized, lest the general populace may be lulled into believing that their best interests are always at hand simply because they have voted.

There is a concern that if we do not *do* democracy in education there will be clear and obvious consequences for society as a result. Is there a connection between a high degree of political literacy and a lower level of patriotism, for example, or at least a more critical vantage point concerning monumental decisions that lock societies into generations of ill will and decline because of weak engagement and understanding of politics? Are people less likely to be manipulated if they have higher levels of political literacy? Would people likely be more critical of the media, and of democracy for that matter, if they were more fully engaged in the critiquing, experiencing, and fostering of democracy in schools? The contributors to this book collectively seek to answer affirmatively that education can and must be a vehicle for advancing a more critical engagement in democracy, one that effectively advances social justice and political literacy for the good of all citizens.

Looking Forward from the Doing Democracy Project

In a previous work (Lund & Carr, 2008a), and based, in part, on original research (Carr, 2007a, 2008b), a book entitled *Doing Democracy: Striving for Political Literacy and Social Justice* was published in 2008. Given the critical, international and directly related content, it may be useful to highlight some of the salient points in order to exemplify the broad range of thinking on the topic of how we do democracy, especially as it relates to a thicker version that far outpaces the obsessive focus on elections (see Figure 20). Although there is a range of theoretical, conceptual, and methodological approaches adopted and advocated by the contributors to this book, they all follow the same thread of articulating a version and vision of democracy in education. An explicit attempt to offer such a critical assessment of democracy forms the cornerstone of this volume. Similarly, all of the contributors to the *Doing Democracy* book sought to underscore the importance of social justice in their analysis of democracy in education.

Figure 19. Kinds of Citizens (Westheimer & Kahne, 2004)

	Personally responsible	*Participatory*	*Social-justice oriented*
D	Acts responsibly in their community Works and pays taxes Picks up litter, recycles, and gives blood Helps those in need, lends a hand during times of crisis Obeys laws	Active member of community organizations and/or improvement efforts Organizes community efforts to care for those in need, promote economic development, or clean up environment Knows how government agencies work Know strategies for accomplishing collective tasks	Critically assesses social, political, and economic structures Explores strategies for change that address root causes of problem Know about social movements and how to effect systemic change Seeks out and addresses areas of injustice
S	Contributes food to a food drive	Helps to organize a food drive	Explores why people are hungry and acts to solve root causes
C	To solve social problems and improve society, citizens must have good character; they must be honest, responsible, and law-abiding members of the community	To solve social problems and improve society, citizens must actively participate and take leadership positions within established systems and community structures	To solve social problems and improve society, citizens must question and change established systems and structures when they reproduce patterns of injustice over time.

Legend: D=description; S=sample action; C=core assumptions

Figure 20. Themes from Doing Democracy: Striving for Political Literacy and Social Justice (Lund & Carr, 2008a)

<table>
<tr><td>

Dave Hill, from Great Britain, argues for a new type of education in/on democracy, one that resists neo-liberal global capitalism. In elaborating a framework that critically analyzes the political and ideological orientation of neo-liberalism, Hill points out how it has become increasingly difficult and problematic to integrate social justice into the formal curriculum and educational experience. He also provides evidence of the "growth of undemocratic (un)accountability," which has served to further drive a wedge between the social classes while reinforcing racism and marginalization. Hill concludes with three potential arenas of resistance: within the education and media apparatuses; working outside of the classroom; and mass action as part of a broader movement for economic and social justice.

</td></tr>
<tr><td>

Michael O'Sullivan, from Canada, offers a critique of critical pedagogies and global citizenship education in the era of globalization, interrogating the meaning of democracy in education as well as its positioning within the school experience. Underpinning his analysis with Dewey's (at the time) revolutionary notion of education being the lever for collective, participatory, and emancipatory action, O'Sullivan stresses how much neo-liberalism is a "dominant anti-democratic ideology" and proposes a framework for introducing ideas, concepts, and experiences aimed at critical democratic work through, and under the auspices of, global citizenship education, which can be found in the formal curriculum.

</td></tr>
<tr><td>

Jennifer Tupper, from Canada, interrogates citizenship and democracy in education, seeking to examine the implications for disrupting universal values. She questions the essentialist notions of universal citizenship that are infused into what students learn in, and through, formal education. In elaborating on the concept of "commonsense," Tupper challenges the beliefs/stories of those in power or who have privilege in society, which are considered "cultural truths" and are simply seen to "just make sense"; she writes, "the uncritical acceptance of commonsense (embodied in curriculum) shifts down possible alternative visions for what society might look like by consistently reifying a dominant vision."

</td></tr>
<tr><td>

Ali Sammel and *Gregory Martin*, from Australia, in their chapter entitled "'Other-ed' pedagogy: The praxis of critical democratic education," build on some of the themes identified by Hill, namely the application of neo-liberal reforms in education, especially the impact at the classroom level. Sammel and Martin focus on notions of White privilege among teachers, and draw conclusions, based on their study in Australia, that have implications for teaching and learning in relation to democracy.

</td></tr>
<tr><td>

Reinaldo Matias Fleuri, from Brazil, discusses the notion of rebelliousness in relation to democracy, and raises important concerns about the role of power within the educational context. Using a conceptual framework based on the work of Michel Foucault to understand discipline and transgressive behaviors, Fleuri also builds on the work of Paul Freire and Céléstin Freinet to help explain the pedagogical context and experience as well as the potential for democratic experience.. Fleuri presents the notion of resistance and rebelliousness to discipline in an attempt to analyze the impact and relationships that are created, and which ultimately affect the texture of, and potential for, democracy in education.

</td></tr>
<tr><td>

From an aboriginal point of view, *Jason M. C. Price*, from Canada, writes about "Educators' conceptions of democracy," identifing four interconnected and interdependent core qualities of democracy in education (voice; critical thinking, reflection, and action; community, cooperation, and consensus; and nondiscrimination and nonoppression), explored in conjunction with the backdrop of Red Democracy. Price concludes by stating that "rather than equating democracy with process-related practices (votes, political parties and elite representation), the educators [in his study] emphasized the core qualities of democracy as being related to values, attitudes, approaches to decision making and the importance of generalized, empowered and active discursive participation by all community members."

</td></tr>
</table>

<table>
<tr><td>

Figure 20 continued

Alexandra Fidyk, a Canadian teaching at an American university, elaborates on "Democracy and difference in education: Interconnectedness, identity, and social justice pedagogy." Fidyk emphasizes that "attending responsibly to democracy and difference in education requires a shift (ontologically) in the way we perceive, interpret, and respond to events." She explores how heightened consciousness and love can be translated into meaningful action in the classroom. Fidyk's approach to democratic education calls for an intensive process of conscientization, one that may lead to the peaceful resolution of numerous conflicts that occur in pluralistic societies.

Lisa Karen Taylor, from Canada, discusses "Beyond 'open-mindedness': Cultivating critical, reflexive approaches to democratic dialog" and illustrates how students can become engaged through critical pedagogy. Her starting point is illuminating: "Within Liberal and neo-liberal conceptions of democratic societies, therefore, citizens are imagined as either unfettered by difference (being of dominant, unmarked gender, class, ethnoracial affiliation, ability, etc.) or as needing to overcome and set aside their difference from normative dominant identities through presumed neutral, universal forms of reasoning."

Alireza Asgharzadeh, a Canadian of Iranian origin, discusses "Secular humanism and education: Re-imagining democratic possibilities in a Middle Eastern context." He raises a number of pivotal questions about how problematic it is to achieve democratic education in contexts that reject secular humanism. Asgharzadeh emphasizes that "schools can play a major role to this end by educating young people to be open-minded, to think critically, and to respect universal values, such as human rights, peace, difference and diversity." Tackling the issue of fundamentalist thinking raises a number of related questions about normative values and power relations, thus extending the study and existence of democracy.

Glenda Tibe Bonifacio, a Canadian of Filipino origin, discusses "Doing democracy and feminism in the classroom: Challenging hegemonic practices." This chapter shines a light on how gender is an integral part of how we understand democracy and social justice. Arguing that "teaching feminism in the classroom is inherently doing democracy" and, moreover, that it "constructively builds on citizenship practice, and grounds democratic values and processes in education," Bonifacio argues that identity is an indispensable component to any interrogation of the value of democracy.

Njoke Nathani Wane, a Canadian of Ghanian origin, writes about primary education for girls in Kenya, and stresses the impact of colonialism in shaping the present context, something that is a significant factor in influencing the education of hundreds of millions of students in developing countries. In elaborating on the notion of democracy, Wane explores the salience of indigenous African education, highlighting the barriers for the education of girls. In repositioning democracy from the typical North American vantage point, Wane concludes by arguing that "there is a powerful correlation between low enrolment, poor retention and unsatisfactory learning outcomes, and this requires nothing less than the integration of gender, class, regional and outcomes into the design and implementation of relevant inter-sector policies and strategies."

Sarah E. Barrett and *Martina Nieswandt*, of Canadian and German origin, respectively, and who both teach in Canada, explore the role of science education in fostering democracy. They critically assess the potential for science educators to be engaged in teaching and learning, emphasizing social justice, ethical responsibility, the implications for scientific research, and the possibility of empowering students. They raise pivotal questions about how teachers should approach controversial issues, such as global warming, nuclear weapons, nuclear power, and the exploitation of nonreusable resources including oil. Barrett and Nieswandt conclude by suggesting that teachers need to explore cognitive, activist, and critical approaches to teaching science education in their teacher education programs.

</td></tr>
</table>

Figure 20 continued

Mary Frances Agnello and *Thomas A. Lucey*, from the United States, explore the notion of critical economic literacy, which is compatible with political literacy. Agnello and Lucey emphasize how the propensity for testing has limited the scope and critical nature of economics in schools. They also point out that the array of standards blanketing education in the United States does not adequately address the study of economics, which further diminishes the possibility for meaningful and contextualized learning in the field. Last, they provide evidence of only an extremely limited reference to social class issues in history, geography, and economics textbooks used in US schools.

Karim A. Remtulla, from Canada, discusses the pedagogical paradoxes of online activism, highlighting the potential for social justice through electronic networks and technology. Underscoring how the integration of electronic media has created a "digital divide," and is far from being neutral, Remtulla elucidates some of the issues for democracy in the classroom related to critical pedagogy and civic engagement. He introduces various angles of the problematic, including the implications for race, gender, and subjectivity, as well as for citizenship, community development, and participation.

Suzanne Vincent and *Jacques Désautels*, from Quebec, Canada, discuss "Teaching and learning democracy in education: Articulating democratic citizenship in/through the curriculum." They clearly situate the role of the school within contemporary education: "the School's work of 'providing an education' can be considered to be a sociopolitical project or agenda in that it evinces the intentions underlying not only a given society's preferred model of development but also the type of citizen that this same society aspires to produce." They conclude with an analysis on the importance of addressing the hierarchy of the subject-disciplines in education, intertwined with the role of power in diminishing the impact of education on diverse groups in society, particularly if the school is not attuned to the need to achieve greater student conscientization.

Patrick Solomon and *Beverly-Jean Daniel*, from Canada, focus on the challenges of democratic engagement while reporting on a study of preservice teachers during their field-based experiences. Distinguishing between theorized and actualized democracy they find that the former affects the latter; teacher "candidates' theoretical notions of democratic education provide them with an effective lens for critiquing educational practices within varied contexts, including their teacher education program, their practicum school, and community placements." Solomon and Daniel make a strong case for a more explicit pedagogy and experience in the preservice teaching program in relation to democracy, including taking advantage of antidemocratic predispositions and actions in students' field based sites.

Georg Lind, from Germany, writes about "Teaching students to speak up and to listen to others: Fostering moral-democratic competencies," emphasizing the importance of cultivating skills, comportments, and experiences to be able to discuss issues with a view to resolving conflicts peacefully. Lind stresses that "to be effective, democratic competencies must be rooted in an unconscious cognitive structure." He further elaborates on three strategies or principles for ensuring that effective discussion takes place in school—the constructivist principle of learning, the principle of maintaining an optimal level of arousal through alternating phases of support and challenge, and the principle of mutual respect and free moral discourse in the classroom—which makes the task of engaging students in democracy attainable as well as meaningful.

Figure 20 continued

Heidi Huse, from the United States, tackles the issue of fostering democratic literacy, arguing that apathy, combined with a reluctance to *do* democracy in education, has imperiled the political debate and prospects for critical engagement at several levels. Huse starts with an overview of how little university students, in general, know about democracy and social justice, all the while stressing that they seem to be intonating, according to the title of her text, "Don't teach me what I don't want to know." She emphasizes how student resistance to democratic literacy is twofold, encompassing simple disinterest and outright hostility, and she presents strategies to engage students in writing and thinking about democracy.

Shazia Shujah, from Canada, elaborates on "A pedagogy for social justice: Critical teaching that goes against the grain." Situating the analysis on the curriculum in Ontario, Shujah advocates for a more thorough examination of lived identities in order to develop critical democratic literacy, especially since the formal requirements laid out by the government are largely silent on the issue of engaged citizenship. While highlighting the role of educators in the process of democratizing education, she states that democratic education "must commence with the premise that race, class, gender, sexuality, ablism, among other social markers, are all factors that continue to influence education."

Section 2:
Democratic Education:
Can It Happen through Osmosis?

Chapter 5

Standards, Accountability and Democracy in Education[1]

> The solution cannot be achieved in idealistic terms. In order for the oppressed to be able to wage the struggle for their liberation, they must perceive the reality of oppression not as a closed world from which there is no exit, but as a limiting situation which they can transform. (Freire, 1973/2005, p. 49)

Introduction

For a number of years, and especially since the introduction of the *No Child Left Behind (NCLB)* legislation in 2001, many educators have been guided toward being centrally focused on achieving "high academic standards" (Bales, 2006). Giroux (2009a) questions the relevancy of neo-liberal education reforms, arguing that the pervasive context for them is leading to a muzzled and anti-democratic postsecondary education sector. The frenzy around the need to improve educational achievement has arguably forced educators to concentrate almost exclusively on raising grades (Kincheloe & Steinberg, 2006). Increasingly, education in the United States is being re-shaped to remunerate high-achieving schools while punishing those that do not meet the proverbial grade[2]. This chapter discusses the other side of the standards debate, and proposes a framework to develop and implement social justice in education[3].

With the heightened emphasis on academic outcomes, it is unclear how education systems consider and deal with social justice in its broadest sense (Baltodano, 2006). Should public education not address both explicitly and implicitly, in a holistic manner, the notion of democratic education, which is broadly focused on reinforcing and building a citizenry immersed in strengthening social cohesion, equity, anti-discrimination, and, ultimately, a critical reflection on the human condition (Guttman, 1999; Portelli, 2001)? A key question, therefore, is: what is the function of education in contemporary society? Some have offered the critique that it is intended to re-produce, or results in the re-production of, the social order (Bourdieu & Passeron, 1990), creating an able workforce to support capitalist exploitation (Bowles and Gingis, 2001).

Advancing such a position that education needs to be centered as much on social justice as it does on academic achievement would likely face little resistance from marginalized and progressive sectors (Ayers, Hunt & Quinn, 1998; Howard, 1999; Sleeter, 2007). One review of a range of studies found that an emphasis on social justice supported and helped increase academic grades (Collaborative for Academic, Social and Emotional Learning, 2003). However, the neo-liberal educational reform movement has been highly influential in its attempt to force educational decision-makers to quantify and measure education (Hill, 2003). Standardized testing is the order of the day, and the ideology of accountability has been infused into what many decision-makers consider to be a prerequisite to achieving excellence in education (Brosio, 2004; Kim and Sunderman, 2005). These are realities that influence the public mind-set, and, significantly, promote and craft legislation, policies and trends in education. Therefore, in constructing a *Social justice in education accountability framework*, this chapter argues in favor of a critical democratic citizenship (Gilborn, 2006; Hyslop-Margison & Thayer, 2009), one that explicitly addresses the multitude of issues that characterize long-standing social concerns and problems within a multicultural society (Banks, 2008; Banks et al., 2005; Guttman, 1999; Osborn, 2001).

Key Considerations for Social Justice Education

How should social justice be conceptualized in contemporary times? Social justice considers the human condition, discrimination, equity, racism, and other forms of oppression and difference and, within the educational policy context, is concerned with inclusion, representation, processes, content and outcomes from a critical perspective. The term "equity," although there are some nuanced interpretations, is used as a complement to social justice herein. Vincent (2003) focuses on identity in her definition of social justice, and this is also to be considered pivotal to under-standing how social justice takes shape. While the social construction of race, with a key focus on Whiteness (Carr & Lund, 2007), is a critical aspect to social justice, equally important is the notion of the intersectionality of identity, including gender, class, sexual orientation and other markers of identity (Kincheloe, 2008a).

For this chapter, I wish to extend and amplify the meaning of social justice in education, bringing into the fold the dynamic nature of institutional culture, including decision-making processes and inequitable power relations. This conceptualization of social justice in education includes four pillars, all of which center around, and feed into, the notion of democratic citizenship. Figure 21 provides a visual representation of the key considerations for understanding social justice education and social justice *in* education, which underpin the *Social justice in education accountability framework* to be presented later.

The first pillar concerns the need to establish, and highlight, linkages with the broader socio-economic and political context, given the myriad, intricate relations and inter-dependencies that inform, cultivate and are infused into the local experience. The values, philosophy, relations, and workings, as well as the commitment of societies, institutions and individuals to work toward social justice, must be factored into the equation. For instance, Klein (2005) has critiqued the organization of, and impact on, labor and the circulation of capital in the globalized world, stressing the inequities, impoverishment and corruption that characterize the international drive for profits. Similarly, Giroux (2005a) provides an analysis of the corporatization of public schooling, arguing that "Schools are an important indicator of the well-being of a democratic society" (p. 143). How we understand social justice locally must, therefore, be considered within the confines of international events and movements, including wars, famine, conflicts and the migration of peoples. An example of this might be the need to contextualize such events as 9/11; September 11, 1973, is commemorated in Chile as the day when a democratically-elected government was overthrown by a right-wing military dictatorship, with backing from the US.

Figure 21. Broad Conceptualization of Social Justice Education

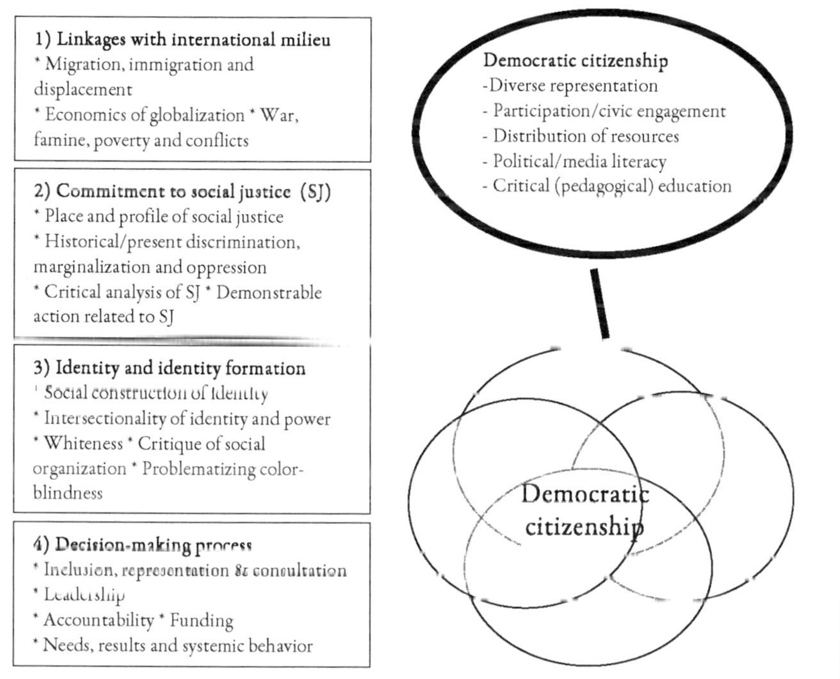

A second pillar relates to societal understanding and commitment to social justice. What are the culminating, cumulative, features that define a society? How do minority rights figure into the constitution, laws, conventions and history of a given society? What events shape the destiny of the inhabitants of a geographic space? For instance, what is the sort of Aboriginal people in the US (or in Canada, Australia, New Zealand or throughout Latin America)? Is it just and reasonable to consider English to be the one and only national language of the US if Aboriginal peoples spoke their languages there for over ten thousand years before the arrival of Europeans? Henry and Tator (2005) have developed a theory of "democratic racism," which serves as an important critique of how society accepts, enshrines, and cultivates racism in democracy, building on populist-based epistemological and experiential foundations. Sleeter (2000) complements this concept with her analysis of how White teachers are disconnected from their largely diverse classrooms. In sum, it is necessary to determine how the formal society—its institutions, the media, and the elites who have disproportionate access to power—as well as the disparate forces representing diverse communities and interests, understand, and are engaged in, social justice.

A third pillar relates to identity and identity formation as well as an appreciation of how identity is socially constructed. One might question for whom is social justice intended? If there are discrimination, marginalization, oppression and different experiences in society, what are these experiences based on? How does (socially constructed) identity shape one's location, voice, salience, opportunities, impact and meaning in society? Whiteness is, ultimately, an important consideration in understanding privilege and power in society (Carr & Lund, 2007; Feagin & O'Brien, 2003; McIntosh, 1988). Tatum (1992) writes about the complexity of racial identity formation and how it is difficult to transcend levels of sensitization. Similarly, Applebaum (2005) has demystified the traditional myths used to propagate White privilege, including the merit principle and the strongly held belief that individualism always trumps collective identity. For there to be social justice, citizens, educators, students and decision-makers must be able to understand identity and difference, common and differing values, the problematic nature of finding a terminology to discuss issues, and also, significantly, the context to deal with issues of identity in a meaningful and critical way.

The fourth pillar of this conceptualization of social justice concerns the decision-making process. Who is involved in decision-making, how, when and where? Is the process inclusive, representative, and responsive to the needs of marginalized groups? Is accountability taken as seriously for social justice as it is for academic achievement? Are systemic issues identified in addition to individual situations and phenomena? How is funding amassed and distributed? Schugaransky (2003) highlights broad community involvement, and participatory democracy, in education as a way of reducing individualism, which could have the effect of diminishing conflicts. Lipman (2004) critiques the notion of accountability in education, arguing that the mainstream conceptualization of the concept does not serve to cater to the interests of marginalized groups (Hoover & Shook, 2003; Sleeter, 2007). In effect, social justice is not only about outcomes but, significantly, also must reconcile the processes that strive to inculcate values of equity, human dignity and fairness. Moreover, it is critical to diagnose and monitor both the formal and informal realities framing institutional and societal behavior (Carr, 1996a, 2007b, 2008c; Lund & Carr, 2008a).

These four pillars function in a dynamic and critically inter-dependent way. Each pillar has an intimate relationship with the other, with a central focus on the notion of democratic citizenship, which is the manifestation and application of the values, theories, philosophies, laws, policies, and commitment to a society not only supportive of but also engaged in democracy. Are citizens engaged during and, more importantly, before and after elections? Are diversity, equity and human rights enshrined, codified and implemented as guiding principles in society? Is patriotism countered by a critical reflection of problems and issues? Westheimer and Kahne (2002, 2003, 2004) question the linkage between citizenship and educating for democracy, emphasizing the unique role that schools can play in supporting and promoting social justice. The democratic citizenship identified here related to the *democratic conscientizaton* elaborated earlier, building on Freire's work (1973/2005).

To have democratic citizenship, the appropriate conditions must be established so that teaching and learning can be a liberating process, not a re-productive one (Bourdieu & Passeron, 1970; Freire, 1973/2005; Kincheloe, 2008b). Gutman (1999) views democratic education as being "political education," which can de-center traditional approaches to learning. Rury (2005) further expands on Gutman's (1999) analysis by arguing:

> Within schools, democracy cannot be reduced to a topic in the academic curriculum or an object of extracurricular activities. Gutmann suggests that it must permeate the institution, infusing relations between teachers and students, affecting the students themselves, and extending outward to the larger community. Democracy demands diversity and requires deliberation and discussion to flourish. It also enjoins authority, particularly in schools. Democracy is not license, and it entails a responsibility to community and humanity, (p.47)

Therefore, the broad conceptualization of social justice in education presented herein largely surpasses the notion of elections supporting democracy, freedom of the press, laws that are codified but may not be enforced, and, in general, the tradition of maintaining that politics has no place in education. Portelli (2001) makes a useful distinction between "participatory, public, and critical democracy, on one hand, and representative, privatized and managed/market democracy, on the other hand" (p. 280). He further elaborates that the former is "associated with equity, community, creativity, and taking difference seriously" and "the latter is protectionist and marginalist, and leads to an extreme form of individualism and spectator citizenship" (p. 280). In sum, this vision of social justice within democratic citizenship is intended to be broad and inclusive, supported by critical engagement and education, and responsive to diversity and the dynamic and intricate inequitable power relations in society.

Constructing a Social Justice Accountability Framework

It is questionable how the central focus on accountability through NCLB and in contemporary education, in general, has captured the essence of social justice in education (Baltodano, 2006; Saltzman, 2009). In tandem with, and as a counterweight to, mainstream accountability policies and measures, I propose a comprehensive framework for education systems, which aims to reinforce democracy, address concerns raised by marginalized groups, improve social cohesion, ameliorate and render more responsive decision-making processes and the allocation of resources, and also lay the foundation for a more critical, inclusive, and relevant democratic educational experience for all students. Globally, it is necessary to simultaneously consider the educational experience as well as the processes framing the classroom, pedagogical and institutional experiences, all of which serve to provide a more accurate portrayal of school success than standardized tests.

Despite various, disparate efforts, it is apparent that formal, institutional social justice accountability frameworks, where they exist, face significant challenges. Where some semblance of a strategy might exist, it is often undermined, underplayed and under-emphasized. It would seem that there is always another priority, another set of circumstances, another funding imperative or another election that will change and peel back the momentum and resources gained to promote a strong, comprehensive, supported social justice framework (Carr, 2006b).

Figure 22: Social Justice Accountability Framework

	1. Inclusion	2. Representation	3. Decision-Making Process	4. Communication	5. Funding	6. Data-Collection Processes	7. Accountability	8. Monitoring/Review
1-Strategic Policy								
2-Leadership								
3-Curriculum								
4-Extracurricular								
5-Service Learning								
6-Community Involvement								
7-Training								
8-Evaluation								

This proposed *Social justice accountability framework* can be visualized and operationalized in the form of a matrix (Figure 22). On one side, there are eight substantive content components (strategic policy; leadership; curriculum; extra-curricular; service learning; community involvement; training; and evaluation), complemented by eight functional criteria along the top of the matrix (inclusion; representation; decision-making process; communications; funding; data-collection and analysis; accountability mechanism; and monitoring and review).

It is important to acknowledge, from the outset, that any given accountability framework requires careful, strategic planning, resources and (political) commitment. Therefore, if this proposed *Social justice accountability framework* seems complex and burdensome, we must also consider the costs, not only in relation to finances but, more importantly, in human terms, of not moving forward, past the rhetorical commitment, to achieving equity and social justice. One could also argue that it would be as equally complex and problematic to avoid establishing a comprehensive social justice framework in education.

How is the framework operationalized? The evaluation of each of the components, along with standards and targets established for each, provide a roadmap for further reflection, analysis and restructuring in order to foster a more equitable and democratic educational system. If we are able to set targets for graduation rates, literacy levels, academic achievement, class size and spending, why should we not be more dedicated to establishing formal measures and procedures to guide us in achieving social justice in education? The question (or objective) of establishing a *thicker*, rather than a *thinner*, democratic educational experience is key in this analysis. It is worth reiterating that this framework is for the entire education-system of a given jurisdiction, as there are innumerable connections and linkages between the highest and lowest levels representing a state department of education, school boards and the schools. Figures 23 and 24 provide some of the questions that each of the *content* and *functional* areas address.

Phases in the Accountability Review Process

This accountability framework will function best when there are intersecting reviews as well as input taking place in a cyclical manner. In rotating Review Teams, involving diverse and inclusive representation of key stakeholders (students, teachers, administrators, parents, marginalized groups) from the entire education system of a jurisdiction (schools, school boards, and state department of education), a detailed analysis and rating for each of the content areas, juxtaposed against each of the functional criteria, contained in the framework matrix, would be undertaken. The Review Teams would draft reports containing qualitative and quantitative information, as well as recommendations, on all of the variables and configurations having a connection to the *Social justice accountability framework*. The chief objective during this Phase is to engage the sector through outreach, dissemination of information, public fora, and action research. The Review Teams would attempt to establish a benchmark from which targets and goals could be measured. The state level might be more preoccupied with policy development, resource allocation, and leadership while the school board level would focus more specifically on program delivery, processes, and educational outcomes. At the school level, local issues of concern as well as teacher and parent perspectives could come to the fore. All of the school reports for a district would subsequently be rolled up to enhance the school board wide review. If there are no objectives, targets, standards and measures for social justice, are education-systems likely to achieve a high level of social justice?

To illustrate the type of work required using the *Social justice accountability framework* presented here, committees would critically and comprehensively assess each of the component-areas in the social justice matrix. For instance, for the

Content component related to Curriculum, a systematic review would be undertaken using each of the functional criteria in the matrix (Inclusion, Representation, Decision-making Process, Communications, Funding, Data collection and Analysis, Accountability Mechanism, and Monitoring and Review). In practical terms, this would mean determining how inclusive the curriculum is, how representative it is, whether or not the decision-making process employed to formulate and develop the content of the curriculum is mindful of social justice considerations, if the communications around the development and implementation are appropriate, whether the funding required is allocated to ensure that there would be an engaging social justice core to the content, how data are collected, managed and analyzed in support of social justice, what accountability mechanisms permeate the entire curriculum process to enable high-quality as well as critical teaching and learning, and, finally, what monitoring and review mechanisms are in place, and are used. The review process would focus on quantitatively and qualitatively addressing all of these items, establishing targets, measures, objectives and standards, and then working through the process of striving for, and, ultimately, achieving social justice.

Both the decision-making process and the institutional culture are, therefore, considered as indispensable as the program content and academic outcomes. In this framework, accountability is, thus, dismantled from the Total Quality Management (TQM) lock on profit margins to become a tool of empowerment for marginalized groups as well as for systemic change in relation to social justice. One of the chief barriers to achieving accountability is the plethora of exposing problems (for example racism and/or academic underachievement for minority groups, for fear of being blamed, labeled or saddled with the problem). By extension, are school administrators normally rewarded for indicating that their schools did not meet the "standards"? What are the implications for school enrollment, teacher retention, funding, etc., if such problems and issues are exposed?

The overall expectation is not to magically eliminate racism, discrimination, inequity, marginalization, inappropriate and ineffective learning programs, and systemic barriers of all sorts. As McGinn (1994) has argued, in relation to the pitfalls of educational policy development, there are at least three reasons for which plans for progressive change encounter significant challenges: the process used for implementation; the failure to mobilize a focused and sustained political commitment; and the weak content of the initiative. This is the social justice goal, however, toward which great energy would be consecrated, based on the presented framework. With the mobilization of collective action and resources, such goals would become more attainable than the present splintering of efforts have been, however well-intentioned they may be. To have *bona fide* democracy, in which meaningful, participatory citizenship is a functioning reality, a multiplicity of diverse, inclusive, critical approaches, initiatives and individuals is required.

Discussion

This chapter has argued for a broader understanding of the purpose of education within the standards debate (Gilborn, 2006; Hill, 2003; Hursh & Martina, 2003). Strong academic achievement is important, but it should not preclude the need to have a healthy and invigorating effect on the human condition, on the salience of social justice in society, and how citizenship is cultivated in a democracy (Westheimer and Kahne, 2004). Compatible with the *social justice accountability framework* presented herein, Alexander (1999, p. 191) suggests that "The key to peaceful and successful growth and transformation in the emerging global and transnational society is to embrace the strengths of the growing diversity and to anchor change in our oneness, realizing that, as individuals and as a global society, we are in a constant state of becoming." In sum, understanding how citizenship is becoming a multicultural concept (Kymlicka, 1995) as well as the role of diversity in transforming our reality is pivotal to appreciating the place of standards and accountability in education. Meaningful participation and political enlightenment, as outlined by Guttman (1999) and Schugaransky (2003), is required for education to achieve a sense of democracy.

The present neo-liberal reform agenda has not appropriately or effectively considered accountability for social justice. Hoover and Shook (2003) make a distinction between the types of standards that are driving educational policymaking:

> Current reform-based accountability policies ignore the diversity of communities and deny the wisdom of allowing a multi-factored approach of assessment to accommodate and pay respect to the differing needs both within school districts and across school districts.... Authentic accountability, properly framed and requiring multiple indicators, serves the democratic ideals of public schools that embrace inclusion as a key focus of their vision, unlike government schools that have exclusion as their primary purpose and effect. ... Today, with the re-forming of public schools into government schools through the powerful hegemony of the accountability movement, the threat to teaching, experiencing, and realizing democratic ideals has never been more real, especially as teaching convention is driven almost entirely by invalid proficiency tests and pseudo-accountability mechanisms. (p.8)

Kim and Sunderman (2005) argue that the "accountability requirements of the *No Child Left Behind Act* of 2001 place high-poverty schools and racially diverse schools at a disadvantage because they rely on mean proficiency scores and require all subgroups to meet the same goals for accountability." (p.3)

Accountability hinges, in large part, on leadership (Levin, 2005). As Fullan (2005) has suggested, it is critical to develop targets and measures in order to strategically position an educational system. Bjork and Alsbury (2005) have focused on normative expectations for democratic leadership in the superintendency, and have found that educational leaders face a number of challenges and conundrums within a political environment. What is pivotal, however, is that leaders understand, and are capable of, connecting and working with social justice (Leithwood and Riehl, 2003). Accountability will not be achieved if education leaders are not able to immerse themselves into the institutional culture of their school-systems in such a way as to reverse passive resistance and intransigent behaviors that will not allow for democratic transformation (Carr, 1999, 2006b). Significantly, Baltodano (2006) found that NCATE, while encouraging more hiring of non-White faculty, did not strive for, nor did it achieve, a thicker sense of social justice, generally over-looking the critical questions related to power.

Decisions on resources, process, program content, evaluation, staffing, and school climate all involve politics. For the proposed *Social justice accountability framework* to be meaningful, decision-makers would have to acknowledge this fact, and also be prepared to become genuinely engaged in democracy. It would be counter-intuitive to introduce this framework into a jurisdiction, and then not provide the direction, support, authority and resources to solidify the required systemic change. This process would be most effective when the schools, school boards and the state department of education are all partners in diagnosing issues of concern, setting targets, establishing standards, and reviewing progress on education from the classroom level on through the decision-making processes, which design and prescribe the quality, content and substance of education. The cost of implementing this framework, it could be argued, would be minimal compared to the cost of not having accountability for social justice. Social justice is not a cancer bringing down high academic achievement; it is the medicine needed to push all of our children toward the notion that learning can be a liberating, not alienating, process. To the very pertinent critique that this type of engagement might only further entrench the neo-liberal grasp on education (McLaren, 2005a, 2007, 2008; McLaren & Jaramillo,

2007), it is important to acknowledge that something can, and should, be done within the contemporary education system that may serve to ameliorate conditions and possibilities for a range of people, while simultaneously positioning the debate toward a more conducive arena in which more radical change can take place (Macrine, 2009).

Figure 23. Content Components for a Social Justice Education Framework

1. **Strategic Policy** (What are the explicit policies, directives, and pronouncements directly and indirectly articulating a vision, direction, and administrative and legislative framework regarding social justice? How does the institutional culture influence the shaping of strategic policy?)

2. **Leadership** (How are senior levels perceived throughout the system, and what do leaders do to inculcate and support behaviors, attitudes and actions bolstering social justice education? What are the requirements—moral, legislative, administrative and institutionally—for leaders to provide ethical, effective and accountable leadership concerning social justice?)

3. **Curriculum** (How does the curriculum (Social Studies and all other courses) effectively address social justice? How is Civics dealt with? What quality assurance mechanisms are in place to ensure the most effective teaching and learning of the curriculum?)

4. **Extracurricular** (What extracurricular activities exist and why? Are there clubs, associations, student governments, sports, etc., and how are they managed and connected to the curriculum and service-learning? Are there student exchanges, school-twinning arrangements, and activities of a broader national and international flavor?)

5. **Service learning** (What programs, policies, and activities are in place to promote, support, and ensure effective service learning? Is there an explicit linkage between service learning and the curriculum and extracurricular activities? Who is involved, and what is done to prepare them to understand and support social justice and democracy?)

6. **Community Involvement** (How is the community involved in shaping and supporting social justice? How is this involvement evaluated? How does the system ensure that the appropriate segments of the community have been involved, and how does it rectify the lack of participation in some quarters, including among parents?)

7. **Training** (What type of training is provided, how is it determined, and how is it evaluated? How is the connection to leadership, policy, curriculum, community involvement, and other areas ensured through training? Is there a self-reflective critical social justice component attached to training?)

8. **Evaluation** (In light of the social justice framework, how are students, teachers, administrators and department of education staff evaluated? What processes are in place to ensure that this evaluation is effective, and supports social justice in education?)

Figure 24. Functional Criteria for a Social Justice Education Framework

1. **Inclusion** (What processes, guidelines and strategies are employed to ensure that there are no barriers, systemic or otherwise, excluding groups and/or individuals, and what is the result? How is inclusion defined and understood by diverse stakeholders, and how do educational institutions continually strive to align their interests with the broader community?)

2. **Representation** (Who is represented in various spheres of leadership, policy development, program delivery, teaching, training, consultation, etc. in relation to gender, ethno-cultural origin, race, social class, and other identifiers, and what is the result?)

3. **Decision-making Process** (How are decision-making processes structured and implemented, and what is the result? What rights to appeal and review exist for decisions, and are there legal/budgetary/policy limits placed on decision-making processes?)

4. **Communications** (How are communications planned and delivered, and what is the result? How does the system ensure the effectiveness of communications? Is there a *bona fide* link between what is publicly said, and what actually takes place?)

5. **Funding** (What, and how, is funding provided? Are "value for money" and "cost-benefit" analyses undertaken to ensure the effective use of funding? Is funding provided directly and indirectly for social justice activities?)

6. **Data collection and Analysis** (What, and how, are data collected? How are the data analyzed, and what is the utility of this analysis? How are social justice implications considered regarding the collection of data?)

7. **Accountability Mechanism** (What mechanisms are explicitly in place to ensure fairness, effectiveness, and accountability? Are students, teachers, administrators, state department of education and others permitted and encouraged to question accountability processes and results?)

8. **Monitoring and Review** (What are the policies and processes in place to ensure over-sight and follow-up? How are diverse constituencies involved in monitoring and reviewing of social justice?)

Chapter 6
Neo-liberalism, Political (Il)literacy
and the Quest for Democracy[1]

Paul R. Carr in collaboration with Gina Thésée

Consciously or unconsciously, the act of rebellion by the oppressed (an act which is always, or nearly always, as violent as the initial violence of the oppressors) can initiate love. Whereas the violence of the oppressors prevents the oppressed from being fully human, the response of the latter to this violence is grounded in the desire to pursue the right to be human. As the oppressors dehumanize others and violate their rights, they themselves also become dehumanized. As the oppressed, fighting to be human, take away the oppressors' power to dominate and suppress, they restore to the oppressors the humanity they had lost in the exercise of oppression. (Freire, 1973/2005, p. 56)

Making a Market out of Our Place: Neo-liberalism

As outlined earlier, neo-liberalism is a concept, philosophy, and operating system that, together, serve as a template for the world's political economy (Tabb, 2001; Treanor, 2005). In some quarters, globalization has been reduced to a series of inexpensive "midnight-madness" sales at Walmart without any meaningful socio-cultural interchange. Economics, within the energized neo-liberal era that makes little attempt to mask the rawness of its capitalist underbelly, rules the day, at least that is the way politics is presented in the current quest for democracy (and to lay the template to democratize) in the West and around the world (Hoffman, 2006). McLaren (2007) defines this neo-liberal economic quagmire as

A corporate domination of society that supports state enforcement of the unregulated market, (which) engages in the oppression of nonmarket forces and anti-market policies, guts free public services, eliminates social subsidies, offers limitless concessions to transnational corporations, enthrones a neo-mercantilist public policy agenda, establishes the market as the patron of educational reform, and permits private interests to control most of social life in the pursuit of profits for the few (i.e., through lowering taxes on the wealthy, scrapping environmental regulations, and dismantling public education and social welfare programs). (p. 27)

There is an implicit, underlying residue to the neo-liberal agenda stressing that the collective is much less important than the individual, which poses an obvious and not so delicate problem of how we are to consider social justice and democracy, especially within the educational context (Hill, 2003; Hursh & Martina, 2003). If we are all individuals, as noted previously, can we then bear collective responsibility for such pervasive realities as racism, sexism, classism, homophobia, xenophobia, etc. (Dei, Karumanchery, & Karumanchery-Luik, 2004; Kincheloe, 2008a, 2008b)? An important backdrop to this chapter is an obvious and viscerally entrenched socio-economic system that blends inequities, marginalization and vastly differentiated experiences (i.e., employment, housing, education, wealth accumulation, crime rates, travel, etc.) alongside a hegemonically induced belief that there is hope, freedom and fairness in our society (see Smiley, 2006, and McLaren, 2007, for summaries of the numerous ways that race and class, in particular, are important predictors of marginalization). Critical, political literacy can become an indispensable tool for citizens outside of elite circles to counter hegemonic oppression (Freire, 1973/2005; Kincheloe, 2008a; Giroux, 1988).

Public education (K-12) is pivotal in this discussion because this fundamental period of formal learning in young peoples' lives can help them critique, deconstruct and become engaged in society, or, conversely, it can make them passive consumers, patriotic supporters of war, and enthusiastic adherents of the "marketplace" (Westheimer & Kahne, 2004; Westheimer, 2006). The process of teaching and learning is critical to supporting or diminishing the drive toward the complete marketization of society (Dermaine, 2004; Hill, 2003; McLaren & Kincheloe, 2007). The disenfranchisement of large portions of society in and through the educational process beckons the call for greater political literacy as a counter-measure to pre-packaged curricula and evaluation reforms that emphasize conformity as well as underplaying the importance of social justice (Holm & Farber, 2002; Hursh & Martina, 2003). Understanding identity, marginalization and social justice (Vincent, 2003), therefore, becomes a critical feature to the leveling of the proverbial playing field for students and others, who are not privy to the decision-making processes that shape and control public education. Similarly, it is imperative that the prevailing notion of color-blindness be challenged (Carr & Lund, 2007), especially since "racism and racial inequality undermine democracy in any form, especially in its radical and inclusive versions," and, further, "neither racism nor racial inequality can be systemically contested or transformed unless the power of neo-liberalism is simultaneously contested" (Robbins, 2004, p. 1).

This chapter attempts to make the connection between neo-liberalism and political literacy in education (Rossatto, 2005), focusing, in particular, on social justice in education (Darling-Hammond, French & Garcia-Lopez, 2002; Hyslop-Margison & Thayer, 2009). Some of the questions that will be addressed include:

Do we teach for political literacy (Schugurensky, 2000)? What are the considerations for teaching, or not, political literacy (Giroux, 1988; Provenzo, 2005)? How does political literacy relate to neo-liberalism (Hursh & Martina, 2003; McLaren, 2007)? How are educators and students engaged in political literacy to construct their roles in shaping democracy, and how does this democracy relate to social justice (Carr, 2007b, 2008c)? Must political literacy be taught in an explicit way, or can it be learned through osmosis (Davies & Hogarth, 2004)? What are the implications for society of neglecting political literacy in education (Parker, 2003)? Political literacy is a critical component to this discussion because of the lurking danger of neo-liberal education to further destabilize marginalized groups and re-entrench vastly inequitable power relations, which would have obvious consequences for a democratic society (Westheimer and Kahne, 2004; Parker, 2002, 2003).

Building on Freire's work (1973/2005), Giroux (1988) has been one of the most prolific writers arguing for "critical literacy as a precondition for self and social-empowerment," as well as "literacy as a form of cultural politics." Some two decades ago, Giroux (1988) framed the context for how literacy has been reformulated in a narrow, functionalist way, compatible with what we now know as neo-liberalism:

> The language of literacy is almost exclusively linked to popular forms of liberal and right-wing discourse that reduce it to either a functional perspective tied to narrowly coerced economic interests or to a logic designed to initiate the poor, the underprivileged, and minorities into the ideology of a unitary, dominant cultural tradition. In the first instance, the crisis in literacy is predicated on the need to train more workers for occupational jobs that demand "functional" reading and writing skills.... In the second instance, literacy becomes the ideological vehicle through which to legitimate schooling as a site for character development; in this case, literacy is associated with the transmission and mastery of a unitary Western tradition based on the virtues of hard work, industry, respect for family, institutional authority, and an unquestioning respect for the nation. (p. 61)

The incessant and all-encompassing ideology pushing the working classes to believe that K-12 public education is a meritocratic, transformative enterprise is evident in schools at several levels. Kozol (2005) has long advocated for a more critical approach to understanding the organization and structure of schools, how resources are allocated, the relevancy (and control) of the curriculum, and the redundancy of accountability measures that effectively constrain teachers from teaching and students from learning. Kozol has been particularly effective in underscoring the marginalization of minority groups within the broader society, questioning the perceived *sagesse* of avoiding tackling basic issues, such as the availability and quality of the environmental and physical infrastructure housing students, including the technological, library, physical education, cafeteria, and other fundamental services. Kozol compellingly argues that minority and socio-economically marginalized groups have long lost out in receiving a just and equitable share of the required and available resources. Accordingly, the public mantra of equal opportunity within a neo-liberal context serves to dissuade many young people from achieving the very standards decision makers proclaim are the goal for all students. Therefore, the need for critical and emancipatory engagement (Freire, 1973/2005; Giroux, 1988; McLaren, 2007; Rossatto, 2004), surpassing the basic reading, writing and numeracy skills so often trumpeted in contemporary curriculum standards is inextricably connected to democracy and social justice in the broadest terms (Vincent, 2003; Gross & Shapiro, 2005).

There are three sections to this chapter: first, some of the primary tenets of neo-liberalism, as they relate, primarily, to the US context, are presented so as to frame the following sections as well elucidating why political literacy in education is imperative; second, the question of political literacy in education, especially in relation to social justice and accountability, is contextualized, making linkages with democracy and citizenship; and the concluding section offers an analysis of some of the vantage points that could constructively shape the discussion.

Neo-liberalism and the Human Condition

Decrying the role of US hegemony and quest for empire in the new mania for globalization (McLaren, 2005a; McLaren & Jaramillo, 2007), Hoffman (2006) defines the neo-liberal agenda as broad, encompassing and extremely divisive in terms of the center and the periphery. Part of this re-restructuring involves relinquishing unprecedented leverage and rights to transnational corporations, eliminating large swaths of the economy in developing countries, reducing other sectors to intolerable conditions and highly uncompetitive wages, and becoming submissive economically to international bodies, such as the International Monetary Fund, the World Bank, and the World Trade Organization, which do not prioritize socio-cultural development or a genuine respect for the world's environment (Hill & Boxley, 2007; Martinez and Garcia, 1996).

Hoffman (2006) effectively summarizes the world's reaction to this new US hegemony after 2001 as follows:

The US and much of the rest of the world fell out over America's new unilateralism and its refusal to accept the International Criminal Court, the Kyoto Protocol, and arms control generally. Most nations were appalled by America's flaunting of its dominance; its use of preventive war, particularly the invasion of Iraq, was wisely seen as proof of a will to reshape and dominate the Arab world. America's new mixture of patriotism and religiosity annoyed many secularists at home and abroad, and the American way of fighting terrorism by bombing and torturing Iraqis and mistreating Afghans shocked many previously well-disposed allies. (p. 60)

Hoffman (2006) goes on to critique the rather flimsy notion of the "free market" economy that will bring peace and prosperity to all corners of the globe, as proposed by the US, which subsidizes some sectors while concurrently abolishing the social safety net. The surprisingly high number of US citizens who have no or limited healthcare coverage, while a small minority of individuals reaps untold profits, often in an illegal manner (i.e., Enron, World.com, the savings and loans banking crisis), is a case in point.

The contradiction inherent in US foreign policy, as well as domestic policy, belies the polished veneer proudly presented as American meritocracy. Hoffman (2006, p. 60) decries the disjointed hegemonic forces that marginalize debate, freedom and solidarity with the impoverished: "Abroad the US support of dictators and its failure to protect victims of genocide in Rwanda and Darfur have contributed greatly to anti-Americanism. Foreigners can observe for themselves, on the one hand, the weakness of public services throughout the US, the cult of low taxes, and the distrust of any redistributive role of government and, on the other hand, the formidable apparatus of American military and intelligence services throughout the world and in the US itself."

There are visible signs of anti-Americanism cresting throughout the four corners of the globe, epitomized by the rejection of the US dollar in favor of the Euro, vacillating numbers of foreign students to the US, a wave of countries opting for a less than friendly approach to the US in Latin America (in the last few years, Venezuela, Argentina, Brazil, Chile, Bolivia, Nicaragua and others have elected left-wing governments critical of the US), and a general decline in American prestige in cultural terms, in large part owing to the American intervention in Iraq, Afghanistan, and elsewhere.

Ultimately, neo-liberalism is an all-encompassing mind-set that is predicated on having no permanent physical infrastructure, since capital and free-market capitalism are encouraged to shift into and out of local, regional, national and international economies, seeking endless profit while downplaying the relevance of the environment, social justice and the basic needs of the masses (Hill, 2003; McLaren, 2005a, 2008). It is, therefore, not surprising to witness social policy predicated on the basis of maximizing economic gain, as is the case in such policies as workfare for welfare recipients, and the over-arching emphasis on business and "employability" in education (Porfilio & Malott, 2008). This can be juxtaposed with the limited emphasis placed on the social aspect of the human condition in education, including the capacity to participate in and influence society, to appropriate mechanisms in place to ensure that discrimination, poverty and civil strife are addressed at all levels, and, significantly, to ensure that democracy, social justice and equity resonate with all sectors in society, not just those able to financially find a place at the decision-making table (Lund & Carr, 2008; Westheimer & Kahne, 2004).

While Hill & Boxley, (2003) seem to be focused on the macro-level political and economic issues, it is, importantly, appreciably intertwined with the culture and daily living conditions of people in their respective societies. How could neo-liberalism be sustained if people did not support it? Are people led to the proverbial well, as Herman and Chomsky (2002) suggest, to sing and dance, but not to think and act owing to sophisticated and systemic media that they characterize as "manufacturing consent" (Engles, 2007; Goodall, 2008; Ivie, 2005; Kellner, 2002)? In other words, would people not naturally resist something that they consider to not be in their best interests, as some of the more visible parts of neo-liberalism have clearly demonstrated (see Gramsci's work on hegemony (Burke, 2005), and Kincheloe's work on epistemology (2008b))? Or, rather, are people even aware of their rights and interests in a society that discourages them to organize to fight for social justice? Are teachers able to engage themselves and their students in the struggle for an education that will be liberating and decisive for society, as articulated by Freire (1973/2005)? Why are the numerous groups and movements at the local and international levels (for example, those focused on human rights, development, peace, fighting the spread of AIDS, and racism) not more broadly incorporated into the formal learning process in schools? Thus, the potential of a politically literate population, supported and nourished through public education, is a key consideration in the discussion on neo-liberalism (Davies & Hogarth, 2004; Provenzo, 2005).

Perspectives for a More Politically Literate Education

Tabb (2001) identifies the key threads of neo-liberalism as being a driving force behind the disintegration of education as a public good in the turbulent waters of the marketplace, emphasizing three key factors:

making the provision of education more cost-efficient by commodifying the product; testing performance by standardizing the experience in a way that allows for multiple-choice testing of results; and focusing on marketable skills. The three elements are combined in different policies—cutbacks in the public sector, closing "inefficient" programs that don't directly meet business needs for a trained workforce, and the use of computers and distance learning, in which courses and degrees are packaged for delivery over the Internet by for-profit corporations.

Lopez (2000) highlights that neo-liberalism aims specifically to promote the privatization of education services. This tendency to make education a commodity involves increasing "user fees and private contributions to educational costs," creating "more flexible hiring methods and teachers salaries, and at the same time developing) centralised state evaluation systems," and striving to enhance "the productivity of teachers by augmenting the number of students per class" (Lopez. 2000).

The ideological tendency of neo-liberal supporters is to over-emphasize that the education system is broken and "bankrupt," and also to argue that only radical profit-oriented, business practices can restore integrity and support for public education. It is telling that with the election of a decidedly pro-market, conservative government in Ontario, Canada, in 1995, after five years of a moderately left-wing social-democratic government, the new minister of education immediately pronounced that he intended to "create a crisis in education," and, consequently, the educational climate for the next several years was known for an abrupt and radical elimination of any commitment to equity and social justice (McCaskell, 2005; Carr, 2006b).

The neo-liberal model of education is, therefore, characterized by severe rationalization and cost-cutting, reduced investments, more students in fewer programs (for example, it is not uncommon to witness the elimination of music, physical education and arts programs), privatization, expanded school choice (the *No Child Left Behind* legislation in the US is a classic example), which diminishes the strength and integrity of the public education system, and an attack on teachers, both at the effectiveness (quality of teaching) and efficiency (costs) levels (Hill, 2003; Torres, 2005). Hursh and Martina (2003) stress how "this testing and accountability system (NCLB) has resulted in increased inequality," buttressed by an untenable situation in which the federal government is responsible for funding only a small portion of education but "has determined what subject areas take precedence, limits the ways in which they may be taught, and designates what reform options are available to schools and districts that fail to improve sufficiently their test scores" (pp. 1–2), all of which diminishes the role and capacity of local jurisdictions to manage education. Clearly, social justice and political literacy are not central components to these broad and far-reaching reforms (McLaren, 2007).

Referring to the infiltration of neo-liberalism in education in the US (Hursh & Martina, 2003), Torres (2005) points out that the two principal political parties, the Republicans and Democrats, essentially share the same values and orientation, and, in relation to NCLB, are not at odds (Macedo, 2009). To this end, it is worth questioning how schools present and inculcate political literacy so that students are able to effectively dissect what bipartisanship actually means, and whether two political parties functioning in the same socio-economic landscape and mindset can actually relate and respond to the needs of the entire population, including those traditionally not involved in power-sharing. Further, Torres (2005) documents other significant shortcomings and contradictions in NCLB, including the inadequate funding levels, the sanctions on schools in poorer communities that do not meet standards, the lack of prescribed scientifically based instructional practices, the support of vouchers and charter schools, and "provisions that try to push prayer, military recruiters, and homohobia into schools while pushing multiculturalism, teacher innovation, and creative curriculum reform out."

Morse (2006) unearths several social justice problems with NCLB, which relate specifically to the marginalization of disadvantaged children and minorities. A case in point is how many children are not counted in Annual Yearly Progress (AYP) reports simply because they were asked to stay home on the day of testing, a measure that is surprisingly common in those schools striving to reflect high performance standards without having to contend with potentially low scores from disadvantaged or minority children. Further, she notes that "the tests which are designed to measure AYP are based on a naïve realist assumption that the 'knowledge worth having' is easily identifiable and can be validly and reliably tested in a multiple choice format" (Morse, 2006).

NCLB has effectively reduced the ability of teachers to provide students with intrinsically motivated curricula, replacing it with formalized programs from commercial developers (Hoover & Shook, 2003). As teachers and administrators prepare for the standardized testing required for compliance with NCLB, the need for scripted materials appears to be increasing (Saltzman, 2009). However, most teachers decry the use of such materials as not representing the true needs of their students, especially in the urban areas, claiming that there is too much attention on obedience to authority as well as on rote memorization. In advancing a neo-liberal agenda antithetical to the needs and concerns of teachers, NCLB "assumes that the capitalistic model of businesses competing for market share is appropriate for public education, although there are many ways in which public education is unlike the capitalist model of business" (Morse, 2006).

In sum, there are many deficiencies in the new and enhanced interpretation of the role of education in the twenty-first century, and it is increasingly questionable how neo-liberal hegemony will provide for social justice and democracy during and after the formal education experience. As Hill (2003, p. 2) notes, the capitalist class in Britain and the USA have a:

a. Business Plan *for* Education: this centers on socially producing labour-power (people's capacity to labour) for capitalist enterprises,
b. Business Plan *in* Education: this centers on setting business 'free' in education for profit-making,
c. Business Plan for Educational Businesses: this is a plan for British- and US-based Edubusinesses to profit from international privatizing activities (p. 2).

The issue of formal accountability, therefore, seems to focus on spread-sheets and budget-items more than the actual educational experience of the students, while students' understanding and engagement with the structures, processes and manifestation of power is increasingly an isolated but critical feature to educational attainment for all students (Sleeter, 2007).

What Do We Learn, and What Should We Learn?

Rather than simply considering education as a means of euphemistically achieving "higher standards" and developing a "qualified workforce," it is imperative to interrogate the foundation of education. How do we teach and train teachers for education (Davies & Hogarth, 2004)? What are the specific aims or purposes of education in society (McLaren, 2007)? What are the implications of emphasizing employment skills over citizenship (Schugurensky, 2000)? Can we have education without focusing on society's problems and the lived experiences of the students (Lund & Carr, 2008)? How do we measure what we are learning, especially in relation to political literacy (Parker, 2002)?

The US National Institute for Literacy (2006), for example, produces reams of data and research on literacy but does not delve into the area of political literacy. There is a purposeful de-emphasis on political literacy, the explicit and implicit processes of engaging in critical thinking and action to shape and influence one's environment. For some decision-makers, curriculum developers and educators, there should be no place for, what some perceive to be, "indoctrination" in education (Carr and Lund, 2008a). For others, the main feature of education should be helping students to become workers or employees in a market-based economy. For this group, the key is learning the skills and knowledge required for the workplace through a re-jigged curriculum emphasizing business skills, comfortably woven into a framework referred to as employability. However, there is evidence that greater political literacy can improve academic outcomes, improve the educational culture and experience, and reduce unacceptably high drop-out rates, especially for marginalized groups, that have plagued the education system for generations (Dei, Karumanchery, Karumanchery-Luik, 2004; Ryan, 2006).

In examining the issue of indoctrination in relation to citizenship education, Sears and Hughes (2006) are critical of the present trend in Western countries to superficially respond to concerns about citizenship development, denouncing the "promotion of single, assailable views, and the shunning of evidence" (p. 4). This closed discourse buttressing indoctrination is characterized by: creating false crises, sloganeering, setting up false dichotomies, grossly over simplifying both problems and solutions, and the demonizing of opponents and alternatives. The cult-like mantras that sometimes dominate our discourses are consistent with a doctrinaire approach to citizenship education in that they are much more focused on creating true believers than on listening to alternatives or making substantive arguments (Sears and Hughes, 2006, p. 5). Sears and Hughes (2006) conclude their analysis by exposing how measures, when they are evident, taken by governments to develop citizenship education curriculum and programs are lacking at several levels, and there is virtually no empirical evidence to demonstrate success. Demaine (2004) further echoes the problematic nature of developing meaningful citizenship education programs that seek political understanding and engagement.

Westheimer (2006a) meshes the potential for indoctrination with the advent for nefarious types of patriotism, as illustrated by the authoritarian perspective in Figure 25, which can lead to anti-democratic values, behaviours and experiences.

To "do" democracy in education, as Westheimer and Kahne (2004) have articulated in their research, it is necessary to formally connect tangible learning experiences in a political way to the educational experience. They provide evidence that not making explicit linkages with the political side of civic engagement can serve to reinforce and undermine democracy. The example of Ontario's 40-hour mandatory voluntary experience component (Ontario, 2002) required to meet graduation requirements is pertinent in this regard because it is not explicitly linked to the learning experience, is not funded nor supervised by educators, and leaves the impression that doing anything is sufficient to meet the rigors of developing a well-rounded student (Westheimer and Kahne, 2003). This raises the important question of the place of citizenship and civic engagement in the formative years of students (Osborne, 2001; Sears & Hughes, 2006). An important part of this learning necessarily involves engaging students in discussions about politics in a process that entices, encourages and challenges youth to listen, argue and become effectively part of the process of understanding and taking action on controversial issues (Hess, 2004; Parker, 2003). Therefore, it is incumbent to have some formalization to the process of fostering and legitimating political literacy within a formal context, notwithstanding the concerns of trivialization and cooptation that arise when some educational and political leaders may wish to simply fabricate a policy response in order to placate enunciated concerns for change (Gilborne, 2006).

Figure 25. Westheimer's Politics of Patriotism (Westheimer, 2006a)

	Authoritarian Patriotism	*Democratic Patriotism*
I	• Belief that one's country is inherently superior to others. • Primary allegiance to land, birthright, legal citizenship, and government's cause. • Nonquestioning loyalty. • Follow leaders reflexively, support them unconditionally. • Blind to shortcomings and social discord within nation. • Conformist; dissent seen as dangerous and destabilizing.	• Belief that a nation's ideals are worthy of admiration and respect. • Primary allegiance to set of principles that underlie democracy. • Questioning, critical, deliberative. • Care for the people of society based on particular principle (e.g., liberty, justice). • Outspoken in condemnation of shortcomings, especially within nation. • Respectful, even encouraging, of dissent.
S	• My country, right or wrong. • America: love it or leave it.	• Dissent is patriotic. • You have the right to NOT remain silent.
H	• McCarthy Era House Un-American Activities Committee (HUAC) proceedings, which reinforced the idea that dissenting views are anti-American and unpatriotic.	• The fiercely patriotic testimony of Paul Robeson, Pete Seeger, and other before HUAC, admonishing the committee for straying from American principles of democracy and justice.
C	• Equating opposition to the way in Iraq with "hatred" of America or support for terrorism.	• Reinforcing American principles of equality, justice, tolerance, and civil liberties, especially during national times of crisis.

Legend: I=ideology; S=slogans; H=historical example; C=contemporary example

Anti-racism and Leadership

Elsewhere, I (Carr, 1999) have examined the state of anti-racism education in the Toronto Board of Education in the 1970–1995 period, focusing on the institutional culture and the representation of race as well as the formulation of educational policy in the Ontario government during the 1990s when there was a widely publicized anti-racism education policy in effect (Carr, 2006b; Carr & Lund, 2007). I found an intricate and sophisticated labyrinth of systems, processes and mechanisms that reinforced the systemic discrimination and marginalization of non-White individuals and groups (Carr, 1999, 2006b, 2008c; Carr & Klassen, 1997; Carr & Lund, 2007a). This is not to say that all Whites accrue the same advantages, nor that all racial minorities suffer from the same disadvantages. However, over time, there is an inherent, although manifestly subtle at certain levels, power imbalance (Carr, 1999). How decisions are made, how resources are distributed, how teachers are trained, how students learn, who is able to access the system, how accountability is determined, and other similarly important questions all constitute a framework for diagnosing the issue of anti-racism and social justice in education (Carr, 2007a).

Focusing more on the pedagogical implications, Thésée (2003) has found that Black students in Montreal encountered a range of individual and systemic barriers in relation to their relationship to, and success in, science education, a key gateway subject to advanced university studies, which paralleled findings from Carr's (1999) research. Her study (Thésée, 2003) underscored the lack of role models and teachers in education as well as a general incompatibility with guidance counseling and leadership, in particular, which served to further marginalize some students "of color."

The education system could be considered to be *democratically* racist (Henry and Tator, 2005), in that there is a consensus on the worldview, which is overwhelmingly White as well as male, European, Christian and heterosexual. Thésée (2006) questions identity and power from an epistemological vantage point, surmising that our notion of knowledge needs to be problematized in order for there to be the appropriate conditions to resist neo-liberalism. Similarly, Carr and Klassen (1997) found that White and racial minority teachers in the Toronto Board viewed and experienced race quite differently, with the former devaluating its salience and the latter maintaining that (socially constructed) race was an extremely important factor in defining one's lived experiences. Elsewhere, Carr and Thésée (2006) have also illustrated how even the usage of the terminology related to race can be highly contentious. The importance of racial minority teachers in diverse, as well as non-diverse, contexts is immeasurable, yet there are a number of obstacles to recruiting, integrating, retaining and promoting racial minority teachers (Carr & Klassen, 1996). The issue of Whiteness (Carr, 2006b; Carr & Lund, 2007; Sleeter, 200, 2005), therefore, requires understanding how education systems have favored a Eurocentric vision, how meritocracy is not necessarily firmly anchored into our conception of democracy, and significantly, how Whites may have the power and privilege to avoid considering the lived experiences of non-Whites.

Ultimately, leadership becomes a pivotal issue in ensuring any meaningful change or reform in relation to anti-racism and social justice (Carr, 1997, 1999, 2007a, 2008a). The willingness of educational leaders, who are largely White, to embrace diversity, including the plurality of issues, concerns and identities intersecting with race (gender, class, sexual orientation, religion, language, etc.), is limited, yet the risk of not doing so is substantial (Ryan, 2006). If educational leaders do not experience nor understand the issues related to social justice, and they are reluctant to be out of step with the over-arching discourse which profoundly de-emphasizes the social conditions from which students originate, how can progressive change be made (Fullan, 2005; McLaren, 2007)? In sum, political literacy can become an indispensable lever for ensuring that public education is not simply reduced to the reproduction of social relations (Freire, 1973/2005; Provenzo, 2005).

Democracy, Citizenship and Educational Experience

The issue of democracy and citizenship in education is pivotal in that how students are engaged in these areas during their formative education years will impact on their commitment to, and engagement in, society afterwards (Sears & Hughs, 2006). Diamond (1997) discusses educating for democracy, emphasizing that "To improve democracy and make it work, citizens must have not only democratic knowledge and values but also skills and propensities to organize with one another for common ends, to stir one another to action, and to voice their concerns in speech and writing." Understanding and working against intolerance, marginalization, injustice, and prejudice are key to preventing people from feeling unworthy and less deserving of a place in society, and, therefore, a more explicitly political approach to learning is considered beneficial for all students (Giroux, 1988).

Strama (1998), in analyzing youth participation and electoral politics, states that low voter turnout among youth is countered by more youth engaging in community service: "The wiring of American democracy is disconnected. Americans no longer believe that ours is a government of, by, and for the people." Strama (1998) points to the influence of money in the formal political process as being one of the key alienating factors in diminishing youth involvement in elections. Therefore, it is critical to dissect the formal propensity to reduce political education to the knowledge of elections and political parties in favor of a broader and more developed understanding of how everything has a political dimension, and that, moreover, students and citizens can "do" something to shape their environment (Stevick & Levinson, 2008).

Schugurensky (2000) has studied adult citizenship education, particularly regarding the connections between citizenship learning and the redistribution of political power, focusing particularly on knowledge, skills, attitudes, closeness to power, and resources. He claims that these areas are inter-related but that average citizens may not have a high-level capacity in more than one of them (Schugurensky, 2000). This analysis speaks to the cultural capital that students bring to their educational experience, and the concomitant need to equip all students with insight into the intricate workings of power so as to de-mystify the notion of a color-blind, meritocratic society (Delpit, 1988; Kincheloe, 2008a).

Dudley and Gitelson (2002) present a number of salient as well as cautionary points concerning political literacy in education, stressing, in particular, the merits of service learning (Westheimer & Kahne, 2003, 2004) being connected to the curriculum, acknowledging the hidden curriculum (Apple, 1996). They illustrate the need for research about how political knowledge underpins civic engagement. Building on this research, O'Toole, Marsh and Jones (2003) highlight the concern that decision-makers and researchers often have a narrow view of youth (non-)participation, which does not adequately consider how young people define politics and political engagement. Their research found that young people feel marginalized and disconnected from mainstream politics, especially decision-making processes, and, similarly, that they did not sense that they are encouraged to participate in political life, nor are they appropriately represented. However, O'Toole, Marsh and Jones (2003) conclude that young people are not apathetic, nor are they disinterested in politics, but they are discouraged by the way the present system seems to present issues: interestingly, they note that "politics is something that is done to them, not something they can influence," and "inequalities based on class, gender, ethnicity and age are crucial features of the lives of our respondents: they are not variables, they are lived experiences" (p. 359). In sum, the present neo-liberal configuration of educational curricula, standards, expectations and testing concurrently isolates political literacy, and places a premium on learning that disenfranchises many students, often discounting *bona fide* youth resistance and activism (Porfilio & Carr, in press).

Davies and Hogarth (2004) argue that political literacy must be re-situated as the focal-point of citizenship education. Their vision of political literacy surpasses the "compound of knowledge, skills and procedural values" to also include "such areas as respect for truth and reasoning and toleration as opposed to substantive values, which could mean that pupils would be told what to think about particular issues" (p. 182). They reject previous political literacy models such as the "civics" model centered on "factual knowledge and a didactic teaching methodology" as the modus operandi (p. 182), and the "big issues" model in which adversarial political debates take place in class. For this latter approach, there is concern that issues will only be examined at a superficial level without serious follow-up. Rather, they favor the "public discourse model," which "seeks to induct pupils into the language, concepts, forms of arguments and skills required to think and talk about life from a political point of view, emphasizing both process and product. Factual knowledge is important but is made subservient to other aspects that are centrally important to political literacy" (p. 183).

Demaine (2004) examines the subject of citizenship education and globalization, highlighting that, *de facto,* the world is confronted with interdependent economic (and, therefore, political) relations, which have been an area of inquiry and concern since the writing of the *Manifesto of the Communist Party* by Karl Marx and Frederick Engels in 1848 (p. 202). While both concepts—citizenship education and globalization—are problematic and need to be problematized, there is significant concern about how to teach about and for the international changes and machinations that are shaping local realities. Teachers, therefore, have a substantial role in preparing and engaging students for a world that is increasingly less focused on uniquely local and/or national concerns (Portelli & Solomon, 2001).

Santora (2006) examines why cooperative learning often fails to promote democratic behavior among culturally diverse students, and has found that students reacted to knowledge provided by the teacher in multiple ways, including finding avenues to dispute or complement such knowledge with the knowledge acquired in/from their families, the environment, and the media. Her study demonstrates how power, as it affects knowledge construction, is locally reproduced or reconstituted through classroom interaction: "Controversial issues relevant to students' lives considered within the groupwork structure can, depending on the type of dialog and student engagement within its 'disturbing spaces,' silence some students while empowering others." This analysis reflects Delpit's (1998) work on how minorities are systemically excluded from the decision-making process in the classroom as well as in the broader society through myriad processes, which codify the implicit and explicit ways that power works (Bourdien & Passeron, 1990).

Ogbu's (1991) research also questions the interpretation of Black student underachievement, challenging the notion that the education system is neutral and, further, asserting that individuals may encounter difficulty to succeed in spite of their effort and abilities if power-imbalance issues are not factored into the equation. The case of a portion of the young Black male population arguing that it is not "cool" to succeed at school speaks to the institutional culture in education vis-a-vis those who contest inequitable power relations, thus highlighting the need for a re-invigorated approach to critical engagement and political literacy. Some questions that might be raised include: Why is there exclusion, who defines it, how do we measure it, and what can be done to remedy it? What are the implications of sustained marginalization? What formal and informal processes are in place to effectively bring together and ensure constructive engagement between peoples from different races, social classes, ethnicities, religions, etc.? What is the responsibility of those who have access to power and decision-making?

Discussion

This chapter has sought to situate the problematic nature of neo-liberalism within the context of an increasing need for political literacy in education. Greater political literacy can be the starting point for more dialog, partnerships, solidarity, and, ultimately, action to re-define the supposed meritocracy, color-blindness and democracy under-pinning society. Critical thinking and engagement require thoughtful, well-resourced and inclusive decision-making (Lund & Carr, 2008a; Provenzo, 2005). There are many ways of understanding political literacy— epistemology, institutional culture, curriculum, and student engagement, all of which were alluded to in the preceding analysis. Is there a place for political literacy in the neo-liberal education agenda? How will this be developed and effectuated?

Writing about confronting and undoing neo-liberalism is a daunting, cathartic, destabilizing proposition. We live in a society shaped by myriad contradictions and ethical quagmires: how do you talk to people about peace when you are simultaneously accused of "not supporting the troops" and being "non-patriotic"? Can we seek the truth in our teaching, if the truth lies in endless interrogation, reflection and dialectical, critical thought, and not in standardized testing and supposed accountability? Yet, there is a cultural ethos supporting simplistic reasoning and sloganeering. Popular culture is full of get-rich-quick schemes, with a plethora of mind-numbing so-called reality shows preoccupying the minds of large portions of society. People, and students, are focused on their economic livelihood, and questioning is sometimes misconstrued as being hostile to the social environment (being critical is often labelled as being "cynical"). This is not to say that we need to dismiss the cultural manifestations of the various groups constituting society, only that we should be critical. For instance, we are concerned about a woman who steals food for her children and learn about her shortcomings through soundbites and trivial comments in the media, but we often do not learn of or question the poverty in which she lives, nor the broader, more significant issues around how infinite resources can be found for a war in a country that most Americans cannot identify on a map; similarly, we do not question why schools are underfunded, or how it is that there are intolerable levels of violence in schools and neighbourhoods, especially in racialized, poorer areas, which does not excuse individual acts but does provide relevant context and background to how power is formulated. Thus, there is concern that political literacy should involve many intricate components. Would poverty, racism, war, disproportionate wealth accumulation and other manifestations incompatible with a democratic society be effectively remedied with more political literacy in schools? An important conclusion from this work is that the process of and support for becoming engaged would undoubtedly work toward more dynamic and meaningful participation in the identification and resolution of problems. Politics must be considered more than an economic equation, and the multiple interconnections between peoples and nations require more extensive, lucid and critical examination in schools.

We are challenged by students who reject the notion that society may not be as fair and balanced as they were led to believe. One student told me at the end of an undergraduate course in the bachelor of education program, "Why did no one tell us about this (racism, and how our education system can reproduce inequities) before?" Other students proclaimed that they were unaware that the social construction of identity had such a huge influence on how we are educated. Surprisingly, as a Canadian teaching at a mid-sized US city in Ohio, I have found that many students have not overly considered their own implication in racism, nor do they (the majority of whom is White) consider it a priority to become engaged in improving the situation. Many are of good faith and believe in the sanctity of fairness as the basis of US values, which complicates their "shock and awe," to embolden the terminology used by the US government to describe its military assault on Baghdad, of how the myriad stories of those who have not benefited from integration into American society have been systemically down-played throughout their lives (Spring, 2004). Some students are openly hostile to the point of claiming that one might be disrespectful to even talk about the war in Iraq. The epistemological starting point for many is not considered: the important questions about who is an immigrant, how the working class has been treated, the complicity in suffering abroad, and the not-so-cushy inner-lining of the esteemed 'marketplace' are rarely subjected to critical discussion (Kincheloe, 1997, 2003).

Gross and Shapiro (2005), in their analysis of Democratic Ethical Educational Leadership (DEEL), aim to create an action-oriented partnership, privileging open dialog, free speech, community involvement, and participation toward the common good, and call for a more direct approach to political literacy in education: "upon reflection colleagues around the nation and around the world are coming to a different conclusion: there is no democracy without social justice, no social justice without democracy and that these mutually inclusive concepts are indispensable ingredients to school improvement worthy of the name."

Ultimately, for there to be meaningful change in education at the social justice and political literacy levels, several inter-twined actions and processes are required. In the neo-liberal context, it is questionable whether there is room for educational policymaking that is original, progressive and in touch with a holistic, humanistic approach to education, which is open to constructively including a range of interests, groups and research that would effectively advance an agenda more aligned with the needs of society as opposed to the market. Thus, in conclusion, there is a pressing and indispensable need for a re-configured vision and framework for accountability for political literacy, and this process must consider how and why we teach and learn what we do in schools (Carlson, Gause, Steinberg & Kincheloe, 2007).

Chapter 7

Democracy, Critical Pedagogy and the Education of Educators[1]

Banking education (for obvious reasons) attempts, by mythicizing reality, to conceal certain facts which explain the way human beings exist in the world; problem-posing education sets itself the task of demythologizing. Banking education resists dialog; problem-posing education regards dialog as indispensable to the act of cognition which unveils reality. Banking education treats students as objects of assistance; problem-posing education makes them critical thinkers. Banking education inhibits creativity and domesticates (although it cannot completely destroy) the intentionality of consciousness by isolating consciousness from the world, thereby denying people their ontological and historical vocation of becoming more fully human. Problem-posing education bases itself on creativity and stimulates true reflection and action upon reality, thereby responding to the vocation of persons as beings who are authentic only when engaged in inquiry and creative transformation. In sum: banking theory and practice, as immobilizing and fixating forces, fail to acknowledge men and women as historical beings; problem-posing theory and practice take the people's historicity as their starting point. (Freire, 1973/2005: p. 84)

Introduction

The debate over democracy in education could be characterized in terms of *representative* versus *participatory* democracy, with the former highlighting electoral processes (*thin*), and the latter focusing on critical engagement and social justice (*thick*). This chapter reports on research I have undertaken (Carr, 2007a, 2008b; Carr & Thésée, 2009) involving college of education students at a university in the midwestern US and faculty of education students at a university in Quebec, Canada, in relation to their perceptions, experiences and perspectives of democracy[2]. Four broad themes are highlighted: 1) how education students understand democracy and politics; 2) the potential for, and limitations to, *doing* democracy in education; 3) the importance of understanding power and difference in relation to democracy; and 4) the nebulous linkage between democracy and social justice[3], with the overriding fear of bias, values-dissemination and indoctrination. Using a critical pedagogical framework, concerns are raised as to how education systems and teachers conceptualize the citizenship-based, lived experience of democratic education[4], as opposed to standardized testing and the never-ending quest for high academic achievement that has become the hallmark of neo-liberalism (Hill, 2003; Kincheloe, 2008a). The meaning of political literacy within the context of democracy in education is, therefore, a primary concern (Carr & Thésée, 2008b). The chapter culminates with a proposal for conceptualizing democracy in education, highlighting, in particular, what educators can do to become more critically aware and engaged.

Education in, for and about Democracy

Discussions on democracy often result in platitudinous affirmations that it is naturally desirable, and, as a corollary, anything that is not democratic is considered virtually irrelevant. Yet, it is apparent that there is no one universal definition of democracy (Karumanchery and Portelli, 2005), and, further, that many people have only a superficial conceptualization of what democracy is or should be (Gandin & Apple, 2005). Thus, the notion of *thin* as opposed to *thick* democracy, in addition to the epistemological and analytical tenets of critical pedagogy, as exposed in this book, allow us to conceptualize the visible tension between the superficial features often associated with democracy and the fundamental scaffolding, which, on the other hand, permits people to appropriate the deeper meaning of the term (Gandin & Apple, 2005). An examination of democracy in education, therefore, should incorporate the educational context, especially given the neo-liberal architecture framing most contemporary education reforms (Torres, 2005). As Karumanchery and Portelli (2005) point out, globalization, despite the typical "meta-narrative," is neither apolitical (neutral) nor equitable, and it is highly questionable as to how the human dimension is appropriately reflected in the marketization of education.

It is important to highlight the distinction between what democracy looks like, in the minds of research participants, and what it could look like in a more political and critical pedagogical framework. As Stevick and Levinson (2007, p. 6) argue, "A focus on culture also allows a shift from such norm-laden questions as 'Is this teaching practice effective?' to the more interpretive question 'What does this practice mean to the people engaged in it.'" In sum, while critically assessing the views and experiences of participants in this study, a critical pedagogical approach, moving beyond a norm-laden analysis of how they might be or are not supportive of democracy, will be used to suggest strategies, concepts, and issues that could inform a framework aimed at cultivating *thick* democracy.

Stevick and Levinson (2007) summarize the cultural dimension of the quest for democracy in education as follows:

> Democracy is not an abstract system that can be dropped into any new context and be expected to function, nor is it a set of institutional arrangements that can be evaluated satisfactorily simply by examining a flowchart in a document. Democracy is rather the product of interaction, the interaction of a system and its institutions with the cultural context and the people who make them real. Institutions and practices are infused with culture. And so are schools, educational practices, and the debates that surround them (p. 2).

A general hypothesis for this chapter, therefore, is that progressive, critical, democratic education work in classrooms and schools, along with the resultant experience for the students, will be greatly diminished if teachers have a weak or disaffected attachment to democracy themselves. While there are numerous factors involved in the formulation and framing of democracy in schools, it is argued herein that educators have an important role to play in cultivating and shaping the educational experience for students in relation to their present and future attitudes, behaviours, ideologies and engagement regarding democracy.

Rationale for the Study

As Kahne and Westheimer (2003) ask, "Is it important to learn math, history, English, and science? Yes. Is this focus enough to sustain a democratic society? No" (p. 63). Connected to this point, and central to this chapter, is the question of whether we can have democracy without social justice. While a range of definitions and interpretations exist for both democracy (Levin, 2005) and social justice (Vincent, 2003), there does not appear to be a consensus on how the two are intertwined in education (Portelli & Solomon, 2001; Soder, 1996). This is troubling because what takes place in schools will have a significant effect on how adults understand and are engaged in democracy. The role of the educator in preparing students is paramount, but few studies have been undertaken on the perspectives, experiences and perceptions of educators in relation to democracy (Apple, 1996; Sears & Hughes, 2006).

To understand how current and future teachers might teach about democracy, it is important to first grasp how they conceptualize democracy. Democracy, like education, is political, laden with values, biases, judgments, predispositions, and ideological tendencies, and is based, to a varying degree, on lived experience (Westheimer & Kahne, 2004). What people experience may often shape, confirm or disprove, augment, and, generally, inform their belief in something (Dei, Karumanchery, & Karumanchery-Luik, 2004). Repeated experiences of a similar phenomenon may lead to the construction of theory. The meshing of theory and practice—praxis—can be a powerful formula in promoting social change (Freire,

1973/2005; McLaren, 2007). Having meaningful, critical dialog and undertaking cogent analysis, on a particular matter, sometimes referred to as *deliberative democracy*, can lead to transformative learning (Hess, 2004; Parker, 2006). Walsh (2009), using a framework building on Freire and Dewey's work, emphasizes the usages of language and discourse in mediated education for democracy, making a clear distinction between training and education, which relates to the thicker, deliberative democracy that is possible to construct. Therefore, understanding how current and future teachers perceive and experience democracy is relevant to the multi-layered student democratic experience in education.

Holm and Farber (2002) question the linkage between democracy and education in the US, especially following September 11, and examine the geo-political knowledge and global awareness of education students. Their study found that US student-teachers have a limited understanding of the global relationships, actions and realities that have a direct impact on Americans. While emphasizing that a "democratic public space for deliberations about the directions and impact of globalization" (p.141) requires having teachers who are both engaged and knowledgeable, their study raises concerns about the Eurocentric curriculum and conceptions of democracy. This tension, which is highlighted throughout the literature (Dei, Karumanchery, & Karumanchery-Luik, 2004), can be delineated as competing visions of *thin* as opposed to *thick* democracy, with the latter being characterized by more of an inclusive, holistic, critical engagement than the former (Gandin & Apple, 2002).

One area that has been under-emphasized in the literature on civic and democratic engagement in education relates to social justice. How do different racial, ethno-cultural, religious and other minority groups relate to education initiatives to address as well as inculcate a sense of democracy? Does the identity of the teacher play a role in how they understand, experience and deal with democratic education? How is Whiteness theorized and applied so as to frame democracy in education (Carr, 2006b; Carr & Lund, 2007a)? How does identity shape the democratic educational experience? In general, is there a correlation between the understanding of, involvement in, and beliefs about democracy among teachers, on the one hand, and the quality of the educational experience for students in relation to democracy, on the other (Maitles & Gilchrist, 2005)? These questions help lay the foundation for the research presented in this chapter.

Research Methodology

This section is divided into two areas, representing the methodology for the two samples: a) college of education students in the US; and b) college of education students in Canada. The Canadian sample commences the process of comparative analysis.

a)   US College of Education students

This research sample includes 129 students at a college of education in a university in Ohio[5]. Education students were the target group for this research because of their obvious role and impact in educating young people; although other disciplines, such as law, medicine, social work, engineering, etc., would also be interesting and important to study, the focus on education students was felt to provide a more distinct linkage into how democracy is constructed within schools and the broader education field. The vast majority of participants, who self-identified, are undergraduates, under the age of 21, and White, with about ten percent of the sample being racial minorities (see Carr 2007a for details on the methodology).

Working with colleagues in the college of education, a detailed survey questionnaire containing approximately thirty open- and closed-ended questions was distributed to roughly 400 students in October 2005, with completed surveys being returned at the end of the same year. Therefore, the return rate of roughly 30 percent is considered significant, given the voluntary nature of their participation, in order to acquire an environmental scan and some representation for the sample population.[6]

In addition to providing a quantitative score based on a Likert scale[7], the survey instrument invited respondents to expand on their answers. Several participants noted that the survey made them reflect on issues that they were not always confronted with in relation to democracy and education. This chapter focuses primarily on the narrative comments, alluding occasionally to the quantitative scores as a means of simply providing an overview of sample.

The university in question serves primarily a regional constituency, with over three-quarters of the roughly 14,000 students coming from the surrounding area. Many of the students are the first in their families to attend university. It is relevant to underscore that this is a predominantly working-class university, and that the data reflect and are shaped by the lived experiences of the research participants. Approximately fifteen percent of the students at the university, and ten percent in the college of education, are non-white. Approximately 90% of the students are enrolled in undergraduate programs.

The survey instrument, for both samples, contains four sections: 1) an introductory section requesting demographic information; 2) questions on democracy and education; 3) questions on citizenship and education; and 4) a final section allowing respondents to add any additional comments on democracy and citizenship, or on the questionnaire. Specific questions on the area of social justice and racism are presented in sections 2) and 3). The questionnaire did not define such terms as democracy, citizenship, and social justice to participants but, rather, asked them to do so. The aim was to ascertain the perceptions, experiences, and perspectives of participants in relation to democracy without judging the level of sophistication they demonstrate through their responses. In order to succinctly describe and accurately associate narrative comments to participants, the following system is employed: a number for each participant (up to 129), followed by the gender ([M] and [F]), followed by a racial origin identifier (White [W], African-A [A], and other [O]), followed by the age (under 22 [1], 22–25 [2], 26–30 [3], 31–40 [4], 41–50 [5], and 51+ [6]). For instance, (81/F/W/1) would represent participant 81, who is an undergraduate, White female, under 22 years of age. All students in this sample are at the undergraduate level.

In cases where participants seemed unsure or less equivocal in their answers, I note the potential ambivalence and seek to test the strength of these assertions through the responses provided by others. The data-analysis phase included reviewing the quantitative scores for each question, then breaking down the scores based on gender, age, race and status. From this point, all of the narrative answers for the open-ended survey questions were read with a view to coding and triangulating some of the more salient themes that developed. In complementing Berg's (2007) approach to triangulation, I reviewed narrative answers, seeking to make linkages to certain themes. A theme gained salience based on the number and intensity of how respondents elucidated points that could be subsumed in a particular category. Throughout the content analysis, I tested responses to determine how they fit in relation to my research questions and the theoretical framework presented in the first section of the paper.

b)   *Methodology for Canadian College of Education Students*

It is important to underscore the different linguistic, cultural, political and geographic location of the Canadian sample, which facilitates the beginning of a comparative analysis with the US sample. The Université du Québec à Montréal (UQAM), a major French-language university in Quebec, where the Canadian sample took place, has a unique mission connected to the social, economic and cultural development of the Quebecois society. UQAM's Faculty of Education is the largest in Quebec, enrolling 30% of the province's education students, and some 70% for the city of Montreal, the largest city in the province. With over 110 tenure-track professors and roughly 5,000 full- and part-time students, the faculty of education is engaged in a number of projects, programs and initiatives. Almost 80% of the faculty of education students are female.[8]

Concerning the profile of the students, the University gathers data based on gender, status and area of study. It is, therefore, difficult to ascertain the exact proportion of immigrant, foreign, racial minority and other types of students[9], which is important to consider when examining democratic education. As per the model used in the US sample, participants were asked to self-identity. However, ethno-cultural diversity has started to become a more visible and pressing concern in Québec, as evidenced by the recent Bouchard-Taylor Commission on Reasonable Accommodation[10]. The debate over the place of immigrants has spurred on a number of programs, often under the rubric of interculturalism, and has proven to be a point of concern in education circles. Increasingly, the issue of race and racialization, in addition to the ethnocultural and linguistic realm, is situated within the context of French-English relations (Carr and Thésée, 2006), but such a debate has been problematic at several levels, given the real and perceived minority status of French-speaking Québécois within Canada and North America.

The participants in this study—undergraduate education students at UQAM—are largely under 23 years of age and are White Francophones born in Quebec (12% of the respondents are visible minorities). Some 261 students participated, on an anonymous basis, by completing hard-copy (n=50) or electronic format (n=211) questionnaires in late 2007. It is important to note that students overwhelmingly agreed that the detailed questionnaire was "thought-provoking" and "interesting," and also emphasized that, for many, they had not reflected on the connection between democracy and education in a critical way before. It is significant to point out that the detailed questionnaires provided almost 7,000 textual entries into a database (Sémato) that offers the possibility to undertake extensive discourse analysis.

In order to differentiate the various participants, as per the system used for the US college of education student sample, the following identity markers have been formulated: a number (1–252) indicating the participant, the gender (male [M] or female [F]), the age range (1=<22, 2=22–30, 3=31–40, 4=41–50, and 5–51+), place of birth (simplified here as C=Canada or O=other), racial origin (W for White or non-visible minority, and VM for visible minority or non-White), and ethnic origin. For example, (51-F-2-Q-W-C) would translate to Participant 51, who is female, in the 22–30 age range, born in Quebec, White, and of Canadian ethnic origin. Although these indicators are more complex than a simple pseudonym, it is felt that the additional information helps further characterize and nuance the narrative comments provided by participants.

One study of note on democracy and education in Quebec, building on the citizenship education research indicating that youth are increasingly becoming disengaged in formal democracy, was conducted by Lebrun (2006), who surveyed 110 teacher-education students at UQAM in relation to their representation of the notion of democracy. Employing a multi-layered approach to engage participants in discussion and reflection, Lebrun (2006) distinguishes between "formal democracy," "fundamental democracy" and "substantial democracy," which demonstrate how youth are becoming less committed to state-driven interventions as the primary mobilizing force for democratic engagement (p. 645). In general, as eluded to throughout this book, the subject of how teacher-educators conceptualize, experience and perceive democracy in education has not received a great deal of attention, either in Quebec or elsewhere in North America (Lund and Carr, 2008).

While both teacher-education samples (US and Canada) are formed of largely White individuals, there are also some obvious differences: the national cultures and education-systems differ; the Canadian sample is made up of French-speaking participants who form a linguistic minority in North America; there are more immigrants in the Canadian sample; and the US sample has unique features, such as the number of African-American participants as well as the socio-economic class of the majority of the students whereas the Montreal sample is more reflective of a large, cosmopolitan society.

Figure 26. Main Themes Arising from the US College of Education Sample

<table>
<tr><td>a)</td><td>the particular conceptualization of democracy, with an overriding focus on elections;</td></tr>
<tr><td>b)</td><td>the democratic educational experience of teachers in relation to their appreciation of democracy in education;</td></tr>
<tr><td>c)</td><td>the concern about teaching controversial issues, combined with the fear of being labelled doctrinaire, is a serious concern for the majority of participants; and</td></tr>
<tr><td>d)</td><td>the understanding of democracy, and linkage to, social justice is considered nebulous and problematic.</td></tr>
</table>

Findings

a)   *US College of Education Sample*

A fuller analysis is provided herein for the US sample, more so than the Canadian one, which is still ongoing. In general, this research raises a number of concerns about, and opportunities for, democratic education and, importantly, education for democracy. It is noteworthy that other studies (CIRCLE, 2003) have high-lighted national problems with the teaching of and about democracy that are not incompatible with the problems identified here. Each of the main research themes below, within the *thin* versus *thick* spectrum, is illustrated by narrative comments from research participants along with an interpretive analysis.

a.   *Conceptualizing Democracy*

An initial area of inquiry in the survey was to gage how respondents defined democracy. While most respondents conceptualized democracy as "freedom" and the "right to choose," a primary focus for the majority of respondents was on elections, and many maintained that this correlated with a high level of democracy. Participants high-lighted that "We live in a democratic society! We elect the officials we want and have a chance to make our opinions known" (22/M/O/1), and "for the most part we are able to vote on all issues that affect our lives and others. We vote people into office that share our concerns and beliefs" (38/F/W/1).

Anger and apathy in relation to the electoral system seems to be overridden by the sentiment that elections in and of themselves connote a semblance of a progressive, advanced, democratic society. There was little analysis of the limited choices available to citizens in relation to the two predominant political parties, which seem to resemble one another in a multitude of ways. The national election in 2004, in which Ohio played a significant role in determining the outcome, may have made research participants more cynical or jaded. The almost unreserved reference to the Democrats and Republicans without any commentary to other political parties and movements leads one to surmise that the formal political system has, to a certain degree, dissuaded many working-class educators from being engaged at that level. Hill's (2003) analysis of neo-liberalism meshes well here in highlighting the prevailing view that citizens are discouraged from political engagement as a result of the predominance of the market-place in determining priorities in the classroom.

In some cases, reference was made to the notion that "It's (Democracy) what the US was founded on, and is still active this way today" (64/F/W/1), "Democracy is the basis from which our country runs. It is the structure that allows and guarantees freedom" (31/F/W/1), and "We hold elections and trials in this country which remain for the most part un-biased and geared towards upholding our nation's specific beliefs" (35/M/W/1). The predominant reference to the deep roots established during the founding of the US conflicts greatly with the true history involving the removal and quasi-genocide of Aboriginal peoples, the enslavement of African-Americans, the assimilation and marginalization of Mexicans and Puerto Ricans, and a slew of other undesirable actions related to a number of minority groups (Spring, 2004; Zinn, 2003). Therefore, an uncritical examination of US history can lead to a sensationalistic appreciation of contemporary democracy. Lintner (2007) suggests using critical race theory to de-mask the normative understanding of history classrooms as being neutral: "The representation of marginalized groups within history classrooms is dependent upon the willingness of individual teachers to present material that accentuates contributions, challenges historical givens, empowers the marginalized, and, above all, raises awareness of and reflection upon race and racial images and the impact they have on the historical interpretation of American history" (p.103).

From the quantitative responses, interestingly, the two racial identity categories representing African-Americans and other non-Whites provided scores significantly lower than all other groups in relation to how democratic participants felt the US actually is. This reflects the notion that peoples' lived experiences, complementing the social construction of identity, will determine how democratic their experience within society may be. "People of color" may, generally speaking, experience American society in ways that Whites do not understand (Carr & Lund, 2007; Gilborn, 2005; McIntosh, 1988). Overall, participants demonstrated a fuzzy notion of democracy, often expressing commonly held mainstream virtues, and rarely critiquing the extremely nuanced nature of democracy.

When considering engagement with democracy, again the African-American and other non-White categories provided lower scores than the entire group, which was already at a very modest level of appreciation. At one level, this would appear to be an extremely low level of engagement in or with democracy, which returns us to how participants define democracy and why they consider their involvement in it to not be substantive. Does the response from "people of color" suggest that "formal" democracy is perceived to be primarily for White people? The visible symbols and nomenclature of formal democracy seem to appear to be overtly White (and male), judging by the national heroes, presidents, military history and so on that are emphasized in the curriculum, and this somewhat superficial veneer of democracy prevents many citizens from seeing themselves reflected in the national identity (Carr & Lund, 2007). Of course, the historic election of Barack Obama, which is addressed in a subsequent chapter, raises questions about racial identity and the possibility for transformation in and through democracy. It should be noted that the US and Canadian studies were undertaken before Obama's election.

A primary consideration for participants in relation to their engagement in democracy is the centrality of voting. Some participants simply noted that this act was the extent of their participation in democracy, offering that "I vote but do not actively participate" (11/F/W/1), "I vote and do some stuff like that but I'm not very engaged" (31/F/W/1), "Sometimes I vote, but I pay very little attention to politics" (86/M/W/3), and "The only time I am engaged in democracy is when I vote on Election Day. Other than that day, I don't pay much attention to politics" (74/M/W/1). As future teachers, one has to wonder how these individuals might understand intricate international issues and how they might take on the task of engaging students to talk about, for example, the military interventions in Iraq and Afghanistan or the impact of global warming on all societies (Holm & Farber, 2002). Can teachers move beyond the temptation to teach compliant patriotism (Westheimer, 2006)?

While respondents were often critical of the level and texture of American democracy, a small number pointed to the perceived lack of democracy elsewhere as proof that the US is decidedly more democratic and even superior than other nation-states. Although no examples were given of the shortcomings of other systems, one insight might be that respondents are not as well informed or educated about democracy within the international context (Holm & Farber, 2002). Is democracy understood to be a one-size-fits-all type of proposition for the average educator? Participants noted that "There are many opportunities provided to people (in the US) because of our rights and freedoms, whereas other countries do not have such opportunities" (33/F/W/1), "We vote, not a dictatorship" (102/F/W/1), "Democracy is what made this country so great and outlast our former fellow super power the USSR. Let's keep promoting it" (18/M/W/1), and "Most democratic and free country in the world. If you don't break the law then you are free to do just about anything you wanted" (70/M/W/1). The connection to the international environment is often considered secondary to domestic issues, and the inner workings of the narrowly defined curriculum serve to accentuate the possibility of teachers finding innovative and critical ways of engaging students in macro- as well as micro-level problems (Gandin & Apple, 2005).

b.   Democratic Experience in Education

Responding to the question of the level of democracy in education, using the Likert scale, respondents generally felt that their democratic experience in education was moderate, with the African-American and non-White categories, again, providing a rating lower than the entire group. The overall scores in relation to the high school experience having an impact on participants' thinking about democracy were slightly lower than those pertaining to the level of democracy in the education system. Narrative comments fleshed out these scores, illustrating that participants have a range of concerns about how democracy is actually shaped and delivered in education.

Some participants admitted to not seeing a link between education and democracy, often referring to their discipline as being disconnected from teaching democracy. For example, participants highlighted that "I am a math (science) major" (46/F/W/1), "I'm going into gym" (51/M/W/1), and "As a music education major, citizenship is not a subject in my curriculum" (42/F/W/1). It is troubling that future teachers would discount the pivotal role of democracy, however that may be defined by them, in the lives of their students. The implications are numerous in light of the already significant social problems (racism, poverty, violence, under-achievement, disenfranchisement, hyper-development combined with underdevelopment, political illiteracy) that are evident in schools across the nation (McLaren & Kincheloe, 2007).

A predominant thread to the answers provided by participants pointed to a decidedly negative experience in school, some ridiculing the notion that democracy was part of the mandate of the institutions in which they were educated. For instance, some participants stated that "I remember high school 'government' and history classes as being somewhat of a joke. the teachers 'taught,' the students 'learned' and dialog was pretty much non-existent" (124/F/W/5), "I went to 2 high schools that never talked about the government and even in my social studies classes" (114/F/W/1), "Hell no, went to a city school; football there had an impact on democracy for me" (68/M/A/2), and, in a somewhat detached way, "I didn't fall into the crowd" (16/M/W/1). The connection between the negative democratic experiences in schools to the prevailing view that democracy should not be openly addressed in teaching is clear, although there is undoubtedly a patriotic flavor that further reinforces the schism (Westheimer, 2006).

Another prevalent comment about democracy in education was that the teacher is not necessarily democratic. Pointing to the perceived autocratic style of teachers, participants underscored that "The students do not govern the classroom; the teacher is the dictator. The students do not vote for the teacher; the teacher is appointed"

(18/M/W/1), and "In fact, it was an essentialist environment where teachers and administrators were more like dictators than those of today. Students had no input into education; it was a set curriculum determined entirely by the school bureaucracy" (124/F/W/1). The notion of a teacher working with and providing authentic leadership seems to be conflated to that of a political dictator. The comments, however, are a testament to the prevailing view that most of the participants did not perceive their teachers to be practicing, in an explicit way, democratic education, something that requires effort, practice and planning (Hess, 2004).

Fewer respondents had an unequivocally positive democratic experience in education, but some did mention that "My school was full of supportive and outspoken people that helped to acquaint me with politics" (1/F/W/1), "I began thinking for myself in high school and realized for the first time that the things I agreed with were really my thoughts, not my parents" (19/F/W/1), and "My teachers taught me to be open minded and ask questions, especially when it comes to government" (22/M/O/1).

A large part of this positive experience can be attributed to a single "government" class in which students were exposed to some of the formal workings of democracy. The comments stressed that "My last class in high school was government and I think this was the most effective" (43/F/W/1), "my government class opened my eyes to it" (15/F/W/1), "My senior year government class really had an impact on my thinking of democracy because it made me more knowledgeable" (89/F/W/1), and "The mandatory gov't class for seniors teaches a great deal about citizenship and almost everyone knows a lot more when they leave than when they entered" (18/M/W/1). Channelling all of the democratic work into a single class is a sure-fire way of undermining and misrepresenting democracy to students (Parker, 2003; Banks et al., 2005). With the neo-liberal pressures to "teach to the test" and "achieve the standard," teachers are under increasing pressure to limit constructivist, situational and context-based learning (Kincheloe, 2008a, 2008b).

c.   *Teaching about and for Democracy*

Concerning the area related to inculcating a sense of democracy in students, participants generally felt strongly about this, providing a relatively high quantitative score. Interestingly, the survey found that the notion of teachers playing a role in transmitting values becomes more relevant with age. There are, however, a number of nuances and subtleties to the interpretation of what participants mean by inculcating "a sense of democracy in students."

Participants in favor of teaching democracy pointed out that they are, and should be, positive role models. Some participants assumed that this would be a natural extension to their mandate of communicating the formal curriculum, noting that "I want the kids I teach to be instilled with the morals and beliefs that keep our great nation sustained" (35/M/W/1), "We as teachers must show that it is through dialog that we reach agreement and air our opinions. Everyone's opinion is important—the teachers' as well as the students'" (124/F/W/5), and "They should because it is important and yes, teachers are capable of establishing democratic values in students" (90/F/W/2). The implications for citizens after they matriculate are duly noted, which renders not teaching for and about democracy extremely problematic. This concern can have the effect of, as Gilmour (2006) coins it, using citizenship education as a placebo to actually doing social justice work.

When talking about democracy, some participants, again, emphasized that schools and teachers should be focused universally on the electoral process and voting. Participants emphasized that "Getting kids to vote is a big thing" (68/M/A/2), "Voting is the key" (66/M/W/1), "my senior class was encouraged to vote as well as (be) informed on current issues allowing interest to be taken. We were also provided with voting registration forms by our teacher" (67/F/W/1), and "Yes, (teaching democracy is important) by presenting information about all election issues and showing examples of how federal issues affect us on a personal level" (42/F/W/1). What is most disconcerting is that this perspective does not appear to be centered on a critical understanding of elections and democracy but, rather, on promoting participation in the electoral process and a neo-liberal view of politics (Lund & Carr, 2008).

An important *proviso* to any attempt to broach the notion of teaching democracy, according to a large number of participants, is the concern about imparting values and indoctrination. Participants cautioned that "They should teach students their rights, but not instill this 'sense of democracy' to the point where the students are indoctrinated" (11/F/W/1), "No, because when they try to do so their political views come out" (25/F/W/1), "I think teachers should inform their students but need to be careful not to pursue any answers" (84/F/W/1), and "Teachers should never be allowed to (present) information to their students about choosing democracy over anything else. A student should have their own right as to which party they would be a part of" (74/M/W/1). As Sears and Hughes (2006) point out, this exaggerated and misunderstood formulation of indoctrination is, in effect, preventing the teaching and learning of critical aspects related to democracy and citizenship, while undermining political literacy (Banks et al., 2005). The concern about being misrepresented and, subsequently, being considered as doctrinaire is clouded with the contemporary socio-political context, which encourages a compliant patriotism and discourages critical, class-based analysis that would unfavorably position neo-liberal education reforms (Westheimer, 2006).

For many of the participants, their formal school experience had only a limited, if any, influence on the democratic character of their attitudes. With reflection and critical analysis, it is possible that participants might re-evaluate their educational experience in a more positive light over time, but it would appear that this process has not yet been undertaken (Parker, 2003). Meanwhile, the university experience, it is hoped, will help participants raise important issues related to social justice and democracy so that their future teaching will more fully and effectively accommodate the myriad issues and concerns therein (Torney-Purta, Kland Richardson, & Henry Barber, 2005). The educational experience of future teachers is extremely important, owing to the numerous trickle-down ripples that will occur with their students in the classroom.

In this regard, as reinforced by critical pedagogy, the *context* for teaching and learning is as important as the content (Carr, 2008a). With the intense focus on standards and accountability in the neo-liberal era (Hill, 2008; Hursh & Martina, 2003), do participants in this study perceive themselves to be caught up in a windmill of prescriptive outcomes? In other words, will they determine that their own experiences, which often spurred them on to become teachers, despite the negative undertones, serve to motivate them to be more attentive to the needs of their own students in terms of critical engagement? Extrapolating from that point, will these future educators in the study have a stronger commitment to social justice and democracy because of the lack of such a focus in their own educational experience? This presupposes a knowledge base and capacity as well as an interest to do so but that central motivation could come to light if it is cultivated throughout the teacher-education program (Nieto & Bode, 2008; Torney-Purta, Kland Richardson, & Henry Barber, 2005).

A common theme to the favorable democratic educational experience that some of the participants revealed relates to a singular class in secondary school that focused on government, with a significant emphasis on elections. A minority of participants highlighted how this class facilitated advanced thinking on subjects that they had not previously been exposed to. It would appear that the school culture, in general, did not reinforce the learning taking place in the more focused Government classes. The CIRCLE (2003) report, *The Civic Mission of Schools*, one of the pre-eminent portraits of the state of civic education, emphasizes the following:

> We do not recommend renewing stereotypical civics classes. For some people, "civics class"
> conjures up an image of a teacher instructing students on the minutiae of federal legislative

procedure or election law, without encouraging them to wrestle with larger public issues,
underlying principles, and ways for them to participate in local government and civil society.
While there is no evidence that this is the standard approach in today's schools, it is important
to underscore that teaching only rote facts about dry procedures is unlikely to benefit students
and may actually alienate them from political participation, including voting. (p 20)

Therefore, while some participants in this study did benefit from their "Government" or "Civics" class, it is conceivable that many others viewed that singular experience as the totality of their democratic experience at school. The concern here is that teachers and students alike may be led to the false assumption that democracy can and should be taught in only one class and that it is not a dynamic, critical, cross-disciplinary phenomenon and subject.

How participants view teaching for, and about, democracy elicited a common concern that discussing democracy, in and of itself, could be perceived as indoctrination (Sears & Hughes, 2006). This was not a concern qualified according to varying levels of approach, context, and content; rather, it seemed to reflect the notion that addressing democracy in the classroom could lead to problems, and potentially be perceived as anti-patriotic (Westheimer, 2006). Such an attitude could reflect the current public chill against critical interrogation of the actions of the US government and its hegemonic role in the world (Hoffman, 2006). This misconception, that it is better to say nothing than to engage in debate, is troubling. There is ample evidence that preparing and facilitating dialog, especially on controversial subjects, can be of great benefit in the educational environment, especially for the students (CIRCLE, 2003; Hess 2004; Nieto & Bode, 2008; Parker, 2003). Educators need to develop the requisite skills and competencies to feel comfortable in addressing controversial issues as well as allowing students to become engaged in deliberative debate. Yet as Agostinone-Wilson (2005) emphasizes, the propensity to seek "balance" on all issues has left a gaping hole in the critical learning process of students. For instance, what would be the balance in discussing the pros and cons of rape, genocide, or incest? Although there are many perspectives, this does not mean that debate should be cloistered into the rigid and alienating Republican-Democrat stricture, in which a variety of intelligent and diverse perspectives are neglected in the name of "balance."

It is unclear whether these future teachers are prepared to confront a conservative institutional culture in schools, where they will be positioned to educate and engage students. After all, most of the participants in the study confirmed that schools were inhospitable to them as students in relation to democratic education. Compatible with the notion that democracy equates elections, many participants favorable to teaching about democracy felt that the primary, if not exclusive, focus should be on teaching about elections. This limited, *thin* interpretation of democracy could lead students to the false belief that there are few actions to be taken to mold and shape democracy outside of voting (Gandin & Apple, 2005).

Deliberative democracy is an important skill, concept, and disposition that needs to be cultivated. Another key thread that emerges in defining the comportment and experience of participants in the study is that there is, for a significant number, a reluctance to be engaged with democracy and politics, on the one hand, and an even more central feeling of disenfranchisement and apathy, on the other (Gandin & Apple, 2005): "I watch news but never really pay attention," (37/F/W/1); "I'm not too involved. I'm not a huge fan of politics," (41/F/W/1); and "I could be more active by voicing my concerns, but I don't have time for that" (17/F/W/1).

This sentiment would clearly make it difficult to develop critical democratic engagement lessons, activities, and programs in and for the classroom (Banks et al., 2005). But what is behind these sentiments? Is there an expression of social class alienation from the broader, macro-level decisions that seem to be made in spite of visible public alienation? The disinterest among future teachers is disconcerting because this only serves to reinforce the perception that education is, or rather should be, apolitical. Agostinone-Wilson (2005) discusses the "threat of neutrality" in education, emphasizing that teacher-education programs need to address directly and indirectly, in an infused manner, a range of concepts, approaches, and perspectives that collectively serve to reinforce critical dialog. This disinterest in politics can ultimately reveal a reluctance and resistance to dealing with pivotal democratic issues of power, identity, and social justice; such disinterest, ultimately, can orient itself haphazardly toward the drum-beat of a nefarious patriotism.

d.   *Democracy and Social Justice*

A primary concern of this research has been the place of social justice in democracy, especially within the context of education. Participants were asked directly for their views concerning social justice and racism in relation to democracy. Interestingly, for the former, in relation to its importance, the overall response is relatively significant, and is higher than the score provided for the latter. However, the African-American and non-White categories provided a lower score for the social justice question but a much higher one for the question related to racism. For both questions, it would appear that age was an important indicator of agreement that social justice and racism are integral components in/to democracy.

For some participants, understanding racism is critical to democracy. It is obvious that the two components are inextricably linked, evidenced by comments that "I feel we will have a female president before a Black one" (47/M/W/1), and "It's sad to me that people still judge each other on appearance, but I cannot deny it still goes on. If racism didn't impact democracy then why have we not had an ethnic president?" (71/F/W/2). The predominance of Whiteness in shaping the debate around race, racism and racialization was not specifically alluded to, which raises questions about the university education respondents are exposed to (Carr & Lund, 2007).

An interesting connection to systemic inequities, especially in relation to social class, was made by a number of participants. The understanding of privilege based on class, as opposed to race, is evidenced through comments such as "Rich people seem to always have more than poor people when it comes to politics and rights" (17/F/W/1), "The more important or even 'rich' a person is, they can get away with more things than an average person would" (35/M/W/1), "Those who have power and influence—and 'know people'—can usually achieve things others cannot. Getting out of trouble, favors, etc." (43/F/W/1), and "I still believe that in our society it does make a difference where you come from and who your parents are, it's hard to be a minority with the same right as a respectful figure" (44/F/W/2).

A point that seemed to resonate with a number of participants is that there is significant injustice within the American political system based on social class. Many participants did not make the natural linkage between disenfranchisement based both on social class and race, which, in effect, downplays the intersectionality of identity (Dei, Karumanchery & Karumanchery-Luik, 2004). In other words, marginalization can take place at a number of levels, within a range of contexts, and the reluctance to focus on race is supported by the ideology of merit, individualism, and color-blindness exemplified by Whiteness (Carr & Lund, 2007): "Rich people seem to always have more than poor people when it comes to politics and rights" (17/ F/W/1); "The more important or even 'rich' a person is, they can get away with more things than an average person would" (35/M/W/1); and "Some laws are skewed to favor people. The people in power make the laws so they are the ones who get the most out of them" (71/F/W/2).

Working-class White students have direct experience with social and class disadvantage, but the common linkage to other types of marginalization—in other words, the intersectionality of identity—is not readily perceived or understood. The internalization of Whiteness, again, can play a nefarious role in perpetuating the re-production of unequal social relations through education, without addressing critical issues required to engage and transform society (Carr & Lund, 2007).

These statements reflect, in part, the lived experiences of Whites, who generally have meaningful knowledge and experience of social class inequities more so than the racial discrimination (Fine, Weis, Powell Pruitt, & Burns, 2004). Similarly, they demonstrate the contradictory notion of their commitment to democracy, that the US is democratic but that there are numerous manifestations of systemic anti-democratic behaviour and action. Importantly, they also speak to the obvious and extremely nuanced nature of social class in contemporary American society. While it is clear that society is stratified, it is more difficult to problematize social class, and how it is intertwined with other forms of marginalization. Many people feel that there are serious problems with democracy in the US, and yet there has been a relatively uncritical endorsement, and even support, for, as McLaren (2007) characterizes it, the "permanent war on terror," which effectively disadvantages the working class more than other sectors of society. Similarly, Goodall (2008) analyzes the "global war on terror" (GWOT), linking contemporary hegemony with that of the Cold War period, threading together a deceitful narrative that has served to reinforce the notion of empire and superiority.

Another layer of responses questioned the reality of racism in the US, arguing that equal rights were the foundation of the nation. White participants noted that "I don't see how it (racism) affects democracy" (20/F/W/1), "Why would racism be an issue in democracy nowadays?" (26/M/W/1), "Race doesn't matter, everyone is equal" (102/F/W/1), "Racism is only an important issue if someone makes it one. In the end, votes have no color" (126/F/W/1), and "It shouldn't be an issue. An American citizen is an American citizen. Americans of all races should take advantage of our democracy" (19/F/W/1).

Although the sample size for African-American respondents was small (n=11), it is revealing that on certain questions, using exclusively the racial variable, the variation between African-Americans and the other respondents is significant. This is particularly the case when discussing whether the US is democratic, if the educational system in which respondents were educated was democratic, the importance of elections in democracy, and, particularly, the question of racism and social justice in relation to democracy. Lindner (2007) argues that an uncritical examination of race in history paves the way for political illiteracy when examining contemporary issues, including the place of race in current events.

b) Findings from the Canadian College of Education Sample

The Quebec sample[11] identified many of the same themes as in the US study, although an exhaustive analysis of the French-language participants has not yet been undertaken. However, the French-language participants differed in the detail they provided, owing to, one might speculate, their particular context, including the notions of solidarity and sovereignty, which were not mentioned by American participants. The unique linguistic minority experience clearly plays a role here. Interestingly, few participants in either study focused on education as a key determinant in democracy. The most predominant themes in defining democracy, including some illustrative narrative comments, are as follows:

i.   *Power of the People, with an Emphasis on Government*

Many participants formulated their understanding of democracy in relation to a political system that exercises decision-making power and, interestingly, "sovereignty." For example, (216-F-1-Q-W-C) offers that "For me, democracy involves an organization where decision-making power (sovereignty) belongs to each person or the collective (of citizens, of a people, of a class…)"; similarly, (130-F-1-Q-W-C) maintains that "For me, democracy is a political regime in which the people exercise their sovereignty themselves, where they hold a certain power to make decisions." This interpretation differs somewhat from the US sample in that symbols such as the Constitution were barely referenced by the Canadian group, and, moreover, the reference to sovereignty, which was not made in the American study, holds a special significance for the French-language participants. At this early stage, it could indicate some reference to the sovereignist movement in Quebec, where there have been two referenda in the last thirty years in an attempt to separate from Canada, or to a more collectivist notion of governance whereas the US sample was more replete with affirmations of individualism as a presumably logical counter-balance to government.

ii.   *Participation of People, Especially through Voting*

Participants reiterated the mainstream belief that "Democracy is one person=one vote. Each citizen has the right and the responsibility to vote" (24-F-1-Q-W-C), and that "Power is in the hands of the citizen who exercises his/her right to vote on the services, organizations, rules concerning the direction of his/her country." (2-F-1-Q-W-C) Although voting was certainly a strong and relevant factor in defining democracy for the Canadian sample, it was not mentioned as frequently or with as much force as it was in the American study, where voting was often construed to equate, as in the comment above by participant 24, the totality of democracy. Whereas voting is a part of democracy, Lund and Carr (2008) argue, as illustrated earlier in this book, that it is over-emphasized as a contributing force to democracy and is also conflated to diminish the importance of critical engagement in relation to social justice. However, Cook and Westheimer (2006), in the Canadian context, and Patterson (2003), in the US context, have underscored the reality that youth involvement in elections is on the decline, and that their future participation is key to legitimating societal support for democracy.

iii.   Voting for Representatives Represents Democracy

The Canadian sample, like the American one, emphasized that voting for representatives, who would then carry out the primary tasks of a democracy, was a key feature to democracy. (53-M-1-Q-W-C) believes that "Democracy is a political system in which all individuals of age in a society, through voting, relegate freely the political power to a person or a group a specific mandate," and another participant echoed that "Democracy is the possibility to vote for candidates. These candidates should be able to speak on our behalf in the legislative assembly" (64-F-2-Q-W-C). What is interesting in both samples is how many participants also hold negative views of these representatives (the term/word "politician" is used in a pejorative sense in some circles). The reference to voting here is perhaps emblematic of the normative ways that democracy is portrayed in the mainstream media but it also raises questions about how education-students learn about, and are engaged in, democracy throughout the educational experience. In the American sample, Carr (2007a; 2008) found that participants, generally, did not have a robust democratic educational experience: most of the participants noted that learning about voting was the main component of their engagement with democracy, and, moreover, any substantive discussions about democracy were principally constrained to a single class on Government. It goes without saying that what participants do outside of their formal educational experience also contributes greatly to their understanding and involvement in democracy (McLaren, 2007).

A common refrain expressed in this study is the general notion that "democracy is about freedom of expression" (211-M-1-Q-W-C) and that "democracy is freedom of expression. It allows everyone to have an opinion on what is best for themselves and others" (171-F-1-Q-W-C). This theme was equally highlighted by the US sample and echoes a common sentiment enunciated by political elites. While noting that the principle of freedom of expression or other types of freedoms was integral, a critical assessment of how these freedoms are constituted or manifested themselves was not as evident. As Carr (2008) found in his research on the American sample, it is important to problematize such statements to determine their non-neutral and highly political connotations. For example, do all people have the same freedoms, the same access to power, the same ability to influence public debate, and the same interest in achieving social justice? Furthermore, it is critical to have present and future educators become engaged in the culture, ethos, philosophy and process of cultivating democracy, far surpassing the naming of rights. This is not to say that the participants in this study will not become effective teachers but, rather, that it is important to underscore that naming commonly held beliefs about democracy must be accompanied by critical engagement, such as being able to resist patriotism and war as the only option to resolve problems (Westheimer, 2006).

iv.   *Majority Rule is the Key Principle in Democracy*

The contention that majority rule constitutes democracy was also prevalent in both the Canadian and US surveys. As noted by the Francophone participants, "(Democracy) is a political system that is based on majority rule" (56-M-4-Q CA-VM-O), and "Democracy can be translated into the will of the majority population in relation to laws and political decisions" (102-M-1-Q-W-C). Although more prevalent in the US sample, it is interesting to note that majority rule is highlighted within the Canadian sample, especially given the obvious reality and sanctity of minority rights. This raises the question of who is the minority: is it the French-speaking Quebecois within the Canadian context, or ethnocultural and racial minorities within the Quebecois context? More importantly, how are minorities protected if it is only up to the majority to decide what laws will be passed (for example, in relation to protection for gays and lesbians, against racism, for equal rights for persons with disabilities, etc.)? As Lund and Carr (2008) have noted, it is problematic to discuss democracy without connecting it to social justice and political literacy (Banks et al., 2005).

v.   *Democracy Is a Better System than What Exists Elsewhere*

In a limited number of cases in the Canadian sample participants noted that Canada was democratic because other countries were not, thus illustrating the comparative and normative value of democracy. For instance, (181-F-2-Q-W-C) commented that "We are lucky to be in a democratic country because some countries in the world are not," and (36-F-1-Q-W-C) added that "Despite the shortcomings in our system, we are quite developed compared to totalitarian systems that some countries unfortunately have." In the American study, it was found that participants had not, generally speaking, studied or experienced other systems, and, apart from enunciating that one system was preferable over another, little evidence could be provided to justify this statement. This raises the question of what students learn and should learn about diverse contexts, and also how some values have been relativized and rendered normative without critical assessment (Holm and Farber, 2002). For example, one might argue that Canada and the United States are more democratic than some other countries but how do we substantiate this for those who have been marginalized in North America, including Aboriginal peoples?

vi.   Critical Perspectives on Democracy

A small number of participants underscored their critique and criticism of the way that democracy is portrayed, and these comments generate themes of particular interest that require further exploration. A few participants spoke of the "lack of participation" (48-F-2-Q-W-C), and the need for citizens to have access to "pertinent information in order to be able to take an enlightened position" (13-F-2-Q-W-C). Another area of concern is that the "democratic principle has disappeared for some time because of manipulation by elites" (35-F-1-Q-W-C), and, quite simply, "it's anarchy... The present democracy is far from being the power of the people, by and for the people" (138-F-1-Q-W-C). Still, others questioned the existence of democracy because of economic inequities: "democracy reposes on human rights—an oppressed people, constrained, cannot have access to democracy" (187-F-1-Q-W-C); and "with the propulsion of globalization, (democracy) has disappeared. I imagine that the fundamental principles are 'by and for the interest of the people' and that (democracy) could be defined as a political entity favoring equity, sharing, justice but, like all good things, aberrations end up infiltrating the system" (23-F-2-Q-W-C). Lastly, a few participants argued that democracy is a utopian and abstract concept, characterised by: "democracy is a policy that seeks equality for all citizens but, in reality, it is a representative of an ideal model because the true democracy does not exist" (31-F-1-Q-VM-LA); and "the vision of democracy is abstract.... Our vision of democracy is that which one wishes to see, that of the West: a North-American democracy" (61-M-1-Q-W-C). What is striking about these notes of dissent or, rather, the critical assessment of democracy by participants, is how few there are. These critical comments were even sparser in the American sample. Why are participants reluctant to critically deconstruct and assess the merits of democracy, or why do they more freely and seemingly instinctively conceptualize democracy in a more formal sense of electoral processes and formal representation?

Discussion

The research presented in this chapter encourages us to reflect on how democracy should be cultivated and undertaken in schools. A case can be made that democracy should be supported by education, yet in the current neo-liberal bias toward testing, standards, and accountability, which largely excludes concerns about democracy and social justice, no such agreement exists around the philosophical and practical applications of education for democracy. There are, therefore, obvious concerns related to how teachers understand democracy, how they teach for democracy, and how school systems support such democratic engagement. Stevick and Levinson (2007) connect the debate on democracy with a *thick* notion of democratic citizenship: The question of "what kinds of knowledge are needed," however, is not just a question for researchers but is also a question for the education of citizens anywhere. Just as the free, fair, open, regular, and contested elections constitute a minimal conception of democracy, a minimal conception of responsible citizenship requires "the capacity for informed, reasonable, deliberative and freely made choices in response to competitive public elections and contested public policy issues" (Patrick, 2002, p. 17). Thus, the overriding theme and framework of (inequitable) power relations must be understood in order to do democracy.

Elsewhere, Kincheloe and Weil (2004) argue that "previously neglected perspectives, sociocognition, issues of political economy, complexity theory, and critical theoretical notions of epistemology and power theory" need to be brought to light in order for critical thinking to be more fully integrated and valued in education. Perhaps going against the grain of their own educational experiences, in which cultural influences promote patriotism (Westheimer, 2006) and an avoidance of critical debate (Agostinone-Wilson, 2005), teacher educators should work diligently to disrupt the myth that democracy and social justice are side-bar issues reserved for social studies teachers. A more global approach to understanding these broad concepts will lead to better as well as more engaged teaching and learning (Parker, 2003). Ryan (2006), in writing about inclusive education and inclusionary practices in urban school settings, cautions that inauthentic attempts to simply demonstrate change by inserting actors of various origins into the mix will ultimately fail.

One of the answers is that the game itself—the system—has to change. It has to acknowledge the contributions of not just the regular or traditional contributors, but also what others have to offer. Meaningful inclusion involves more than engineering minor problems; it can only be achieved when the structural and inherent features of an already unequal system are changed. Doing this means not only permitting access for all, but also allowing the accessed to shape the game so that they will be able to contribute and benefit from the game just like everyone else. New players need to be empowered so that they will gain confidence and develop skills to control their participation and contributions and their own lives (p.24). Thus, the issue of power is decisive in determining who will succeed, how decisions will be made, and what the educational experience will resemble. Dei, Karumanchery & Karumanchery-Luik (2004) write on the inequitable power relations that frame the macro- as well as the micro-educational context for students, parents, educators and other interlocutors, and caution educators to concern themselves with how and why marginalized groups do not succeed in public education. One message from the research in this paper is that White students need to be exposed to diverse and authentic experiences that will help them comprehend better and to work more effectively with heterogeneous student bodies. Campbell (2000, p. 205) has pointed out that there are several ways of teaching for democracy:

1) teaching "about civic responsibility, the electoral process, and the US Constitution";
2) "using social participation strategies...";
3) "promote democracy in the classroom (is) by developing in students a preference for fairness, justice, and mutual respect...";
4) "teach students to work together to resolve problems and to achieve goals."

The range of democratic practices, therefore, involves a process as well as a systematic and explicit effort to inculcate democratic values. Stopping this process at the formalized and limited first step of conveying information resembles Freire's "banking" concept, which institutionalizes a passive and neutralized approach to democracy, apt to counter any progressive engagement. The results from the study presented in this chapter conclude that more focus and energy is required throughout the teacher-education program to prepare current and future teachers to be comfortable with developing democratic values and in assisting students to become critically engaged in democracy (CIRCLE, 2003). Galston (2003) makes the connection between civic education and political participation, arguing that schools must focus more on basic democratic and citizenship skills in order to endear youth to the formal democratic apparatus in society. Similarly, Westheimer and Kahne (2004) have documented how schools do democracy, concluding that there are various approaches (like service learning, for example) that may not have a meaningful impact if a more explicit political interpretation is not introduced.

The findings from this research speak to the need to further flesh out the salience of democracy in education at several levels: in schools, in general, in teacher education, in educational policymaking, and in the vigorous debates that take place in society in relation to the sense and orientation of contemporary public education. Cook and Westheimer (2006) provide a broad scan of the state of democracy in Canada and argue that "If people are not born democrats, then education surely has a significant role to play in ensuring that democrats are made" (p. 348). The findings in this paper also reinforce the notion that democracy is not, nor should it be, a static, fixed objective. Rather, for democracy to exist, it must be continually messaged, questioned and, especially, experienced (Westheimer and Kahne, 2004). The emphasis that participants in this study, similar to the themes elucidated in the American study preceding it, placed on the commonly held signposts of formal democracy, such as elections, freedoms and majority rule, may not be surprising but the lack of depth and critical assessment of the shortcomings in Canadian, and American, society is relevant to note. Moreover, the relatively weak appreciation for education as a key aspect to bringing about critical engagement and experience in democracy, combined with the pivotal feature of social justice, underscores the general sentiment that future educators may not be experiencing a strong, or "thick," democratic educational experience throughout their formative schooling (Gandin and Apple, 2005).

There are many factors to explore to further substantiate the foundation of democratic education, but this study complements the findings from the American study, even though there are some nuances to each samples' responses. The themes that flow from the research are similar in both contexts, yet the depth and resonance of the findings reflect certain values, histories and experiences of each locale. Several of the themes highlighted in this research were also brought to light in Lebrun's (2006) study, which involved in-depth discussions among teacher-education students, including: the choice of government through free elections; guaranteed fundamental rights; the obligation of the majority to respect the opposition; and the principle of majority rule (p. 644). This indicates that these common themes are understood broadly in diverse contexts, yet it is unclear the degree to which the enunciated statements and values are translated into critical engagement, especially in relation to political literacy and social justice.

In sum, the commonality of the North American experience can be explained, in part, by the prevalence of neo-liberal policies and realities that have affected youth, students and educators on both sides of the border (Gandin and Apple, 2005; McLaren, 2007; Kincheloe, 2008). Similarly, these findings support the introduction of a critical pedagogical approach in education that could not only better prepare future educators for the challenge of engaging students in the classroom but also, importantly, framing their experiences so as to be able to confront diverse political realities themselves (Kincheloe, 2008a). In line with Freire's work, education is a political project, and avoiding embracing such a notion can only diminish the educational and democratic experience for all students. In an increasingly multicultural society, as exists throughout North America, it is important to problematize the meaning of ethnocultural and racial pluralism within a context of democratic education. What are the implications for society, as argued throughout the paper, if critical, democratic engagement (a *thicker* interpretation of democracy) is not the focus, or one of the pillars, of public education?

Proposal for Framework to Elaborate a Thicker Democracy

Based on the findings from this study on democracy in education, there are a number of areas that could benefit from further examination. Below are some of the questions that could form the basis of a framework focused on political literacy, critical engagement, and a *thick* democracy that takes social justice matters fully into consideration.

In order to critically engage students in, and about, democracy in schools, educators need to feel supported to do so during their university training, as well as within the institutional settings where they find themselves as teachers. What seems to be fundamental here, as exemplified in the research presented in this chapter, is the need to articulate engagement and a critical conceptualization of democracy. A typically *thin* view of democracy seems rather ingrained, in large part through experience in schools and also through formative life experiences. An important consideration, therefore, for developing critical democratic values in schools is how educators conceive, construct, and experience democracy, since this will influence what they do in the classroom and within the school culture.

The study presented in this chapter raises concerns about the degree to which educators can and do explore democracy, particularly in relation to engaging students in meaningful and critical democratic activities. The implications for achieving and promoting political literacy in schools are multifold. Through the practice of critical pedagogy, a critical assessment of the ideology and cultural acceptance of neo-liberalism in education should be undertaken in order to avoid the deleterious effects of less democracy in schools. Adopting a critical approach to understanding and constructing democracy in education, as suggested by the above framework of inquiry, would assist educators to grapple with contentious issues and, possibly, to transform education.

Figure 27. Framework to Elaborate a Thicker Democracy

a. Educational curricula

i. What is explicitly asked of teachers and students through curriculum and other policy documents with regard to democracy, citizenship, and social justice?

ii. Who is involved in developing the formal and informal curricula of schools?

iii. How can the myth of social studies as the only area to explore politics best be rectified?

b. Teacher preparation

i. How are educators prepared to understand and interact with democracy?

ii. What types of ongoing support are provided to teachers to undertake critical work?

iii. How are educators evaluated to ensure that they are able to effectively engage in democracy?

c. Institutional culture

i. How do educational systems support, cultivate, and demonstrate leadership for democracy?

ii. What is, and should be, done to encourage a culture of democracy in schools?

iii. How are macro issues defined, articulated, and funded and what is the linkage to social justice within the institutional culture of educational systems?

d. Accountability

i. What leadership measures are in place to ensure that democratic policies, practices, and outcomes are obtained?

ii. How are academic standards connected to democracy, citizenship, and social justice? iii. How are decision-making processes evaluated to ensure that social justice will be an authentic concern in schools rather than a mere written policy directive?

e. Civic engagement

i. How should students become engaged with democracy at school?

ii. What should be done to forge a stronger linkage between US citizens and communities and international matters?

iii. How should the formal curriculum recognize the importance of civic engagement?

f. Political education

i. How can controversial issues be addressed without the fear of being labelled antipatriotic?

ii. What can be done to introduce students to the complexity of politics, including problematizing the electoral process?

iii. What strategies, measures, activities, and experiences should be infused into the formal and informal educational experience in order to support and integrate political education and political literacy into schools?

Conclusion

To teach about politics, democracy and civic engagement in schools, do educators need to be more politically aware and involved? Giroux (1997, 2007) argues affirmatively that teachers need to be more activist and politicized in order to counter the plethora of inequities perpetrated in society. Similarly, McLaren (2007) maintains that teachers must refuse to take a neutral posture that is antithetical to the needs of the working class. The challenge of providing a space for such engagement is enveloped in the moral imperative of providing ethical and, as defined by Ryan (2006), inclusive leadership, which conceptualizes the curriculum, standards and accountability in a more socially just way (Fullan, 2005). Teacher education programs need to be cognizant of the dangers in being too focused on standards and not enough on the teaching and learning processes leading to social justice and critical engagement (Wilson Cooper 2006). Part of the equation of pushing mainstream education into a more critical, radical, transformative sphere requires accepting that traditional conceptions of democracy are limited, constraining and deleterious for the development of a vibrant civil society. To this end, Brosio (2003) argues for a more meaningful engagement with radical democratic perspectives, including those of the Marxist and Freirian traditions.

Chapter 8

Can There Be Racism (and Democracy) in a "Color-blind" Society?[1]

Only by abolishing the situation of oppression is it possible to restore the love which that situation made impossible. If I do not love the world-if I do not love life-if I do not love people-I cannot enter into dialog. (Freire, 1973/2005: p. 90)

Introduction

Canada has long perceived itself to be a country in which multiculturalism, and a concomitant respect for diversity, is a unique and defining feature of its identity (Reitz & Banerjee, 2006). Moreover, Canada has often been regarded as a country that has more openly and effectively embraced pluralism than other societies[2]. Although Canada is a *de facto* multicultural country, owing to its rapidly evolving demography and the explicit notion of multiculturalism enshrined in its Constitution, there remains a plethora of problems and issues related to equity, diversity and human rights (Carr & Lund, 2007). A major focus to any discussion of diversity necessarily concerns social justice, and acknowledging its existence has been a contentious and arduous process (Fleras, 2002; Dei, Karumanchery, & Karumanchery-Luik, 2004). As governments become more intertwined and submerged in neo-liberal policies, there is an obvious shifting from somewhat explicit social justice approaches toward less direct concepts (citizenship, character and civic education), or some other standards-based program, as a response to widespread, systemic social concerns, such as racism (Hill, 2003; McLaren, 2007). Lauder, Brown, Dillabough and Halsey (2006) further frame the arguments around the potential for development and social change through education within a globalized economic context. As Banks et al. (2005) have outlined, being critically aware of, and engaged with, diversity needs to become a fundamental disposition and competency for students in addition to the other commonly designated priorities in education. Thus, addressing the core concern of neo-liberalism and globalization is considered an integral feature to countering the apolitical nature of education, and, moreover, to enhancing a critical approach to social justice (Kincheloe, 2008a). The direct linkage to democracy and democratic education is a fundamental concern for the debate around the existence of racism and what we should do about it (Carr & Lund, 2007; Lund & Carr, 2008).

The naming of, and focus on, marginalization in, what is commonly thought to be, a democratic society may be extremely nuanced and underplayed, which can lead to conflict, given the lack of validation of diverse identities (Banks, 2008; Nieto & Bode, 2008). Governments have become increasingly skilled at coding language so as to present an inclusive and progressive face while perpetuating the *status quo* (Lund, 2006). The metaphor of the "equity waltz," which symbolizes the complexity of race relations, symbolizes the back-and-forth, almost hypnotic, seemingly effortless motion, floating on the dance floor, which could also be applied to the way racism is approached within the Canadian context: dynamic, considered fluid, and constantly being addressed, but easily swept aside in order to focus on the meshing of bodies, and generally understood to be light-hearted rather than systemically debilitating. The relationship to the American and European contexts is direct, despite national boundaries. The premise of White power and privilege, which is explored herein, is that racial discrimination, within education as well as within the societal context, is not merely the work of a "few bad apples" but has a broader, more far-reaching underpinning that, ultimately, relates to inequitable power relations (Carr & Lund, 2007; Feagin, Vera & Batur, 2001; Sleeter, 2000, 2005).

This chapter explores the relevance of race, racialization and racism in education, especially in relation to the prospect for democracy. White power and privilege, and the lived experiences, perceptions and identities of marginalized groups, provide a backdrop to the analysis. One important consideration is that the intent, or articulation of the problem, must be considered within the context of the actual outcome in terms of equity in education; in other words, the cleavage between the rhetoric and reality of racism must be critically interrogated. The chapter contains five sections: 1) framing the context for discussing race and identity; 2) Whiteness as a conceptual model for understanding the racial problematic in education; 3) defining anti-racism; 4) analyzing anti-racism programs in education, with a focus on Ontario; and 5) considerations and perspectives for policy development and research with a linkage to democracy.

Framing the Context for Discussing Race and Identity in Canada

As the world becomes more globalized, more people, representing a multitude of ethno-cultural, racial, linguistic, religious and other minority groups, are migrating, seeking exile, emigrating and leading lives that were previously unheard of in terms of studying, living and working in diverse locations (Fleras, 2002; Vincent, 2003). Canada is a dynamic reflection of this trend (Reitz & Banerjee, 2006).

Canada is a country of immigrants, despite the historical foundation known as the "two founding nations" (Great Britain and France), which has been increasingly contested over the years. Significantly, the Aboriginal peoples claimed Canada, and North America, as their ancestral homeland for 10,000–20,000 years before the arrival of the Europeans some five hundred years ago (Royal Commission on Aboriginal Peoples, 1996). The following sections contextualize the diversity inherent in and permeating the Canadian state and identity, which serve as a fundamental precursor to discussing educational policy development. It should be noted that this chapter elucidates only some of the groups forming the diverse demography of Canada; at the same time, it is openly acknowledged that identity is extremely complex, dynamic and problematic (Vincent, 2003).

Not all people of one origin or another experience a phenomenon the same way, which frames the notion of identity as being socially constructed (James, 2003). Similarly, the intersectionality of identity infers that there are several components—including race, ethnicity, gender, class, sexual orientation, physical ability, religion, language, family, etc.—that work concurrently to shape one's reality. Therefore, in discussing identity, it is important to provide the cautionary note that the objective here is not to stigmatize or essentialize groups but, rather, to elucidate the problematic of racism in society. It is equally pertinent to highlight that this chapter deals with the social manifestation of identity (and race), and does not advocate for a scientific or biological interpretation of race (Dei, 1996, 2007, 2008). Since racism exists in society, I argue that it is critical to understand how and why it manifests itself, and, moreover, what can be done to diminish and, ultimately, eliminate it. Given the visible and invisible inequities in society, an examination of the role of identity seems to be fundamental to the cause of achieving a more meaningful and fruitful educational experience. Thus, the discussion in this chapter on White power and privilege is a key piece of the equation to grappling with educational policy development and the oversight of our schools and also to achieving some semblance of *thick* and critical democracy.

Aboriginal Peoples

Aboriginal peoples, often referred to as First Nations, are not a homogeneous group, and include a range of nomenclature: on-reserve, off-reserve, Métis, Inuit, dozens of bands and tribes, and various territorial and treaty-rights groups, which are spread throughout the country and represent a number of linguistic and cultural perspectives. The relationship with Aboriginal peoples since the beginning of European contact is a history shrouded in exploitation and disregard for the indigenous population. In the early years of Confederation, the Indian Act ensured control over Aboriginals by prohibiting the *potlatch* ceremony (1884) and the *sun dance* (1885), and, in 1885, introduced a "pass system" prohibiting outsiders from entering reserves without permission from an Indian Affairs agent and also restricting movement of Aboriginals off-reserve (Royal Commission on Aboriginal Peoples 1996). Despite the diverse regional conditions, there have been disputes, principally concerning treaty rights, characterized by roadblocks, protests, occupation of land, and even killings, across the country. The Royal Commission on Aboriginal Peoples (1996) concluded that: "Aboriginal people's living standards have improved in the past 50 years—but they do not come close to those of non-Aboriginal people," emphasizing the gap in life expectancy, education, housing, health care, access to water and sanitation, employment, and incarceration rates. More than a decade later, Mendleson (2006) confirms that Aboriginal peoples face a number of entrenched systemic barriers to accessing and achieving high educational outcomes as well in other areas of socio-economic concern (Canadian Council on Social Development, 2003). The disconnection between high academic standards and achievement for Canadians as a group, on the one hand, and the lived experience and formal and informal realities of First Nations, on the other, speaks directly to the need for a critical examination of the place of identity in education policymaking. The effect of Whiteness on the educational, cultural, political and economic development of Aboriginal peoples is indisputable (Carr & Lund, 2007).

African-Canadians

Little known for many Canadians is the fact that Blacks have formed an important part of the Canadian identity from the outset of the European arrival to Canada[3]. With the arrival of Samuel de Champlain in 1604 came Mathieu de Costa, a Black man from the Caribbean, who served as an interpreter with the Micmac peoples. Numerous Black communities arose in places like Chatham, Ontario, and Buxton, Halifax, and, perhaps somewhat surprisingly, in the mid-1800s Toronto had a significant Black population[4]. The existence of slavery in the Canadian ethos is often downplayed or ignored despite it being a significant part of the nation-building process. Therefore, the history of African-Canadians is rich and deep, although underdocumented and not celebrated, and speaks to a reality that is not fully understood or accepted by mainstream Canada nor the decision-making elites (James, 2003). Longstanding issues of racial discrimination in education (Dei, Mazzuca, McIsaac & Zine, 1997) and employment, segregation, overrepresentation in prison, marginalization from decision-making, and racial profiling (Smith, 2004) are a testament to the legacy of uncomfortable race relations in Canada (Fleras, 2002). The recognition of the Ontario Royal Commission on Learning (1995) that Black-focused schools should be considered, further, reveals the need to understand the racial variable within the educational context, and, importantly, also underscores the prevalence of Whiteness.

Racial and Ethnic Diversity in Canada

The formal Canadian identity includes a multitude of symbols, milestones, laws and cultural phenomena underscoring that, in terms of power, it is principally structured as a White country (Carr & Lund, 2007). A number of important events and practices illustrate how, despite the pivotal role that they have played in constructing Canadian society, immigrants to Canada have faced a plethora of formal and informal obstacles (Fleras, 2002). For instance, Canada has discriminated against the Chinese (1903—Head tax), East Indians (1914—refused admittance), socialists (1918— declared illegal), the Doukhobors, Mennonites and Hutterites (1919—prohibited entry), Jews (1939—ship denied entry), Japanese-Canadians (1942—internment), and other groups. Canada has a multicultural population, but the most diverse sectors are centralized in its three largest cities, Toronto, Vancouver and Montreal, which distinguish themselves from the rest of the country, owing to their extremely heterogeneous populace (Ornstein, 2000; Reitz & Bannerji, 2006). Ornstein (2000) has provided ample evidence of higher rates of unemployment and poverty for certain racial minority groups compared to White, European-origin Torontonians, and the situation is most likely more pronounced outside the most diverse city in the country.

Sentiments Related to Racism

To conclude this section on Canadian demography, it may be helpful to briefly underscore the national sentiment concerning racism. Canadians are, generally speaking, fond of deflecting complaints of racism by pointing to the less than enviable history and present-day reality in the United States (Carr & Lund, 2007). In their study of racial inequality and social cohesion in Canada, Reitz and Banerjee (2006) found that visible minorities, especially Blacks, reported experiencing discrimination at 3–4 times the rate of White Canadians. Ironically, their study also revealed that "greater experience in Canada seems to lead to a larger racial gap in the perception of discrimination" (p. 11), which would appear to contradict the prevailing view that second- and third-generation visible minority immigrants integrate more seamlessly. With the ample evidence of racial discrimination (prejudiced attitudes; human rights cases; field tests of discrimination; statistical analysis of earnings gaps), Reitz and Banerjee (2006) highlight studies illustrating how White Canadians, to a lesser degree than visible minorities, acknowledge that racism does, indeed, exist in Canada. Therefore, the different manifestations of anti-racism in Canada and the US are not necessarily cause for celebration as every context contains its own unique particularities, and underscore, rather, how racism is situational, shaped by historical forces, and subsumed in the torment of neo-liberalism.

Whiteness in a Color-blind Society

Is it possible to speak of anti-racism, or social justice, without contextualizing Whiteness? Whiteness has to do with power and privilege, and is a fundamental construct to understanding how inequities are formed and perpetuated (Dei, Karumanchery & Karumanchery-Luik, 2004). While emphasizing the social construction of identity, the lived experience of being White is considered pivotal to unblocking injustice (McIntosh, 1988). Women have long argued that men have been out of touch with their realities, and, therefore, a broad range of measures have been introduced attempting to rectify systemic, institutional and individual discrimination. However, at the programmatic and institutional levels, it has been mainly White, middle-class women who have benefited from these gains, not women of color. The Toronto Board of Education vigorously pursued a policy of affirmative action for women in the 1980s, with the result being that today a large percentage of the principals in elementary and secondary schools are women, predominantly of the White race (Carr, 1996b; Carr & Lund, 2007). Solomon, Portelli, Daniel and Campbell (2005) document how White teacher education candidates in Canada resist and downplay their own racial identities. Using an American lens, Marx and Pennington (2003) highlight the confounding relationship between being "good" and being "racist":

> Thus, naming racism within themselves (White pre-service teachers) was at first cause for great concern. This is the point where guilt, fear, and even trauma came into the picture. Because they viewed goodness and racism as a dichotomy, their first glimpse of their racism led them to the conclusion that they must be horrible people. It seemed that, in coming to terms with their own racism, our students/participants necessarily had to make the connection that they could still be good be people and still be racist.... Moreover, despite their altruistic hearts and their efforts to "hide" their racism, it is still possible for their racism to hurt the children they teach. (p.105)

Elsewhere, in a study of the perceptions of race in education in the Toronto Board of Education, I (Carr and Klassen, 1997) found that White and racial minority teachers had significant differences in how they viewed anti-racist education and discrimination in education. The major finding of that study highlights the importance of lived experience and *bona fide* access to power as being key determinants in framing the educational institutional culture as it pertains to social justice.

Thompson, (2003) argues, as do Dei, Karumanchery, and Karumanchery-Luik (2004) within the Canadian context, that Whiteness must be challenged for there to be meaningful change in education:

This (decentering Whiteness) means relinquishing our cherished notions of morality: how we understand fairness, how we understand what it means to be a good person, how we understand what it means to be generous or sympathetic or tolerant or a good listener. When we are challenged for our whiteness, our tendency is to fall back on our goodness, fairness, intelligence, rationality, sensitivity, and democratic inclusiveness, all of which are caught up with our whiteness .(pp. 16–17).

As co-editors of *The Great White North? Exploring Whiteness, Privilege and Identity in Education* (2007a), Darren E. Lund and I pose several questions "that seem self-evident and yet confound our work":

Do most White people even know that they are White? Do they use their own privilege to deny or ignore their racial identity and, simultaneously, infer inherent racial attributes to the "Other? If White people do not know they are White, how can those in positions of power, many of whom are White, effectively understand and challenge racism and unearned privilege? (p. 2)

I frame the notion of Whiteness, as illustrated by Reitz and Banerjee (2006), around the particular Canadian context in which the general sentiment is that the United States is more of a historically racist society than is Canada. Yet, Canada has been home to a litany of racist events, actions, policies and legislation. Solomon and Daniel (2007) further flesh out the problematic of White privilege in documenting how little Canadians generally know about racism in Canada, and also emphasize the importance of meaningful, critical and engaged education as a means to bringing about social justice in the classroom. Therefore, to develop educational policy that is responsive to the construction of *thicker* democracy, it is imperative to acknowledge, understand, critically diagnose and realign structures and processes to take into account crucial variables, such as lived experience, the social construction of identity, the distribution and exercise of power, the political nature of society, and, importantly, the conceptualization and manifestation of social justice.

Defining Anti-racism in Canada

Anti-racist, or anti-racism, education, as a philosophy, a concept, and an approach, started to take shape in Canada, borrowing from the British example, in the early 1980s (Dei, 1996; Carr & Klassen, 1997). As it evolved, anti-racism was deemed a more critical and political response to diversity and equity in Canada than the well-entrenched multiculturalism that had permeated the mainstream of society (Dei, 1996). One of the first practical guides in Canada to espouse an anti-racism pedagogical approach is Enid Lee's *Letters to Marcia* (1985), which echoed the prevailing sentiment of the day that "Raising the topic (of racism) might be compared to breaching a code of conduct. Some of us believe that the more we talk about racism the worse it becomes" (p. 6).

Whereas multiculturalism was traditionally perceived to support the "social contact" theory (getting diverse people to interact with one another), tolerance, openness, and exposure to different cultures, traditions and origins, anti-racism was conceptualized to address systemic, structural inequities, and, importantly, to focus on power relations, with a particular interest in racism. To this end, issues of differential outcomes for various groups (for example, African-Canadians and First Nations), the underrepresentation of some groups in the teaching and administrative fields, and a Eurocentric curriculum, all become pivotal concerns. However, it is important to point out that critical approaches to multicultural education have overlapped with the primary tenets of anti-racism in many regards, and the strict definitions once used are no longer applicable (see, for example, Joshee & Johnson, 2007, and Banks, 2008). Ghosh (2001) and Fleras (2002) have provided comprehensive texts on multiculturalism that summarize the range of issues that have often been packaged under the rubric of diversity, and which also mesh with anti-racism, although the tone may be less sharp than those advocating a more obvious critical pedagogical approach (Kincheloe, 2008a; McLaren, 2007).

One of the most prominent anti-racism theorists in Canada over the past fifteen years has been George Dei, who teaches at the Ontario Institute for Studies in Education at the University of Toronto. The fundamental premises of Dei's conceptualism of antiracism education (see Carr & Klassen, 1997, p. 49) concern the social effect of "race," the intersectionality of various forms of social oppression, the salience of White (male) power and privilege, recognizing that students are not "disembodied" individuals but that their background and identities are implicated in the schooling and learning processes, acknowledging the pedagogic need to confront diversity and difference, and questioning explanations of pathological family and home environments as a source of school problems.

The construction of anti-racism is not devoid of criticism, as Pon (2000) highlights the need to "(Conceive of) power... to (understand) present-day race and racism in Canada and the United States and (get) beyond the paradigms of Black/White race relations and majority/minority cultures" (p. 149). Similarly, in advocating a broader and more fluid conceptualization of identity, he argues for a more nuanced interpretation of the manifestation and exercise of power, something at the core of the conceptualization of anti-racism education. Similarly, Yon (1999) is concerned about the tendency to privilege notions of difference between groups as a means of structuring debate and reality, which can serve to undermine action related to inequitable power relations. As a response to concerns about the weakness of anti-racism to address social justice, Dei (2007) has promoted a vision of integrative anti-racism, which incorporates the intersectionality of identity, and also emphasizes the salience of White power and privilege.

In sum, the multiculturalism/anti-racism debate thus provides a context for understanding racism in society, and also serves as a useful starting point for diagnosing, critiquing and taking action to improve the education system, especially with a view to addressing the key concern of social justice. One of the main tenets of anti-racism is to allow individuals and groups the space and voice to articulate who they are as well as being cognizant of the power and privilege to name the "other" (Dei, 1996). Being involved in the decision-making process to determine racial, linguistic, ethnic and cultural categories is, therefore, integral to public policy development (Carr, 1999). Avoiding recognizing difference can only compound pervasive systemic barriers (James, 2003). It should be noted that Kincheloe (2008a) Banks (2008), Nieto (1999) and McLaren (2007), from an American vantage point, have advocated for a *critical multiculturalism* that meshes with many of the concepts enunciated by Dei in the Canadian anti-racism debate.

Analyzing Anti-racism Programs in Education

When looking for tangible, comprehensive policies dealing with anti-racist education in Canada, one is struck at how sparse the terrain actually is. There are usually preambles in policy documents inferring a commitment to equity, but the actual funding, processes, staffing, content and, significantly, accountability, are not predominantly featured, nor are they transparently visible (Carr, 1999; James, 2003). To underscore this point, the whole area of social justice is not generally placed on a similar plane as the multitude of areas that are formally tested and for which generous resources are provided to develop, implement and assess curriculum, achievement and institutional standards (Carr, 2007b; McLaren, 2007). Are educational systems in Canada preoccupied with ensuring that students receive a holistic, inclusive, anti-discriminatory education immersed in social justice, as exemplified by how and what they learn as well as the activities that characterize their educational experience inside and outside of the classroom (Westheimer & Kahne, 2004)? How does the neo-liberal policy agenda account for social justice? Can the Canadian education system strive for high academic achievement and also aim for broad accessibility and critical learning (equity) concurrently (Leithwood & Riechl, 2003)? Ultimately, anti-racism involves a political engagement that surpasses symbolic measures.

The Ontario Case in the 1990s

An example of the *equity waltz,* to extend the analogy employed in the title, is the rather rapid, tumultuous shifting of climate and context in Ontario in the mid-1990s. Progressively, for a number of years, the Toronto Board of Education (TBE) developed a staff complement, research base, policy framework and institutional culture favorable to the equity agenda (Carr, 1999; Carr & Klassen, 1997). The TBE had a multitude of mandated committees, initiatives, research projects and public displays of formal and informal support. While the TBE was open to criticism, other jurisdictions often were reluctant to consider discussion of the matter. McCaskell (2005), a student program worker in the Board's Equal Opportunity Office, has reported on the inner turmoil and struggles related to advancing social justice in the Board, and concludes that the challenges were monumental but that some important, far-reaching equity work was being accomplished. Some of this innovative work by the TBE included multicultural/multiracial residential camps for secondary school students (McCaskell, 2005), and the collection, analysis and dissemination of data on achievement and educational experience of students based on identity (for example, Brown, 1999), which was virtually unheard of in Canada throughout the 1980s and 1990s.

As the Toronto Board distinguished itself as a leader, both nationally and internationally, with its vigorous equity programs, which included race relations, gender equity, working-class issues, curriculum development, community outreach, research and other institutional measures, the Ontario government, for the 1990–1995 period, for the first time in history, was led by a left-leaning, more openly social justice-based New Democratic Party (Carr, 1999, 2006b). One of the pillars of the government's policy agenda was anti-racism, and a plethora of policies, programs and structures were put in place, all with the requisite funding. This translated into assistant deputy minister and director positions for anti-racism and ethno-cultural equity in the ministry of education, both filled by former TBE employees, and a government-wide Ontario Antiracism Secretariat, which was placed under the leadership of another former employer of the TBE (Carr, 2006b).

Along with the training, communications, and overall shift in institutional culture, however contested, the Ontario Ministry of Education produced an anti-racism and ethno-cultural equity policy for school boards, which mandated boards to plan for and implement strategies to address important social justice concerns, including the curriculum, training, leadership, staff development, evaluation, harassment, and school-community partnerships (Ontario Ministry of Education, 1993). This policy went farther than previous articulations of the problem within the Canadian context in relation to the existence of racism, stating boldly that it is "based on the recognition that some existing policies, procedures, and practices in the school system are racist in their impact, if not their intent, and that they limit the opportunity of students and staff belonging to" (Ontario Ministry of Education, 1993, p. 5). The policy can be considered *avant-gardiste* in a number of ways: 1) it presented a plan of action; 2) it emphasized social justice, which some considered to conflict with high academic standards; 3) it contained provisions for accountability; 4) it aimed to address systemic barriers in addition to individual attitudes; and 5) it sought to bring into the decision-making fold marginalized groups, which was rejected by those claiming that "merit" should be the only criterion for participation in educational policymaking (Carr, 2006b).

The government produced an impressive range of committees, reports and initiatives, particularly the discussion document *Changing Perspectives* (Ontario Ministry of Education, 1992), which invited an open dialog on the issue of race and ethnicity in education. Subtitled *A Resource Guide for Antiracist and Ethnocultural-Equity Education*, it laid the groundwork for discussing a more activist, inclusive role for education and also articulated a clear vision of antiracism, which "will enable all students to" "feel that their culture and identity are affirmed by the educational system" and also "accept and appreciate diversity and reject prejudiced and discriminatory attitudes and behaviour" (Ontario Ministry of Education, 1992, p. 3). The document also clarified that "Antiracist education calls for educators to recognize how discrimination, distortions, and omissions occur; to correct distortions and remedy omission and discriminatory conditions; and to establish practices and procedures consistent with the goals of equity education" (Ontario Ministry of Education, 1992, p. 2). Therefore, with the formal recognition of a Eurocentric, White bias in education, educators were encouraged and, in a policy sense, required, to adhere to ministry of education guidelines aimed at inculcating equity in education.

The trickle-down effect throughout the educational system in Ontario, to school boards, schools, and educational associations, including administrators, teachers and other stakeholders, stemming from the formal articulation of a social justice focus, was as impressive as it was expeditious (Fielding, 2002). Not all those involved were as equally engaged, nor did they seek the same level of change but the focus was considered to be favorable to the equity-seeking public (Corson, 2001). The education system was required to follow suit in order to continue receiving funding and, at a strategic level, to have access to decision makers. One example of this was the resource guide produced by the Ontario Secondary School Teachers Federation (Coelho, Costiniuk and Newton, 1995), entitled *Antiracism Education: Getting Started, A Practical Guide for Educators*. This is a visible testament to the power of government to control the language of public discourse, acknowledging anti-racism instead of multiculturalism or some other nomenclature, and also to push stakeholders into a more equity-positive mind-set. On June 8, 1995, the Progressive Conservatives, under the leadership of Mike Harris, won the provincial election, and, within days, formally dismantled years of equity work. The employment equity legislation, which was labelled incompatible with the "merit principle" (Klassen & Cosgrove, 2002), was immediately abolished, the Ontario Anti-racism Secretariat soon followed, the ministry of education's Anti-racism and Ethno-cultural Equity Branch was phased out, and funding for all of the previous activities was cut off (see Corson, 2002).

The anti-racism policy in education (Ontario Ministry of Education, 1993), while not formally revoked, was never implemented or monitored, despite there being a requirement for boards to submit annual progress reports, with which none instinctively complied. The Conservative government also put an end to several well-developed curriculum initiatives, including an Aboriginal antiracism education document, an anti-racism teacher's resource-document, and a guideline for principals to detect and deal with hate crimes in schools (see Carr, 2006). The new business plans under the Conservatives did not contain any equity provisions, and this meant that work from the inside would become exceedingly difficult. A direct consequence is that boards and stakeholders that did fashion a progressive take on equity, such as the TBE, slowly downsized operations, unable to counter the will and direction of the chief funder and decision-maker at the provincial level (McCaskell, 2005). At the curricular level, the Harris government re-wrote the entire curriculum, emphasizing high standards and a decidedly business flavor, effectively removing any significant reference to equity and anti-racism (Fielding, 2002). Black (2003), in his review of anti-racism in education in Ontario, found that "The word "racism" cannot be found within the curriculum for any compulsory course," "'Racism' appears in only two of 22 ministry-approved Canadian history textbooks published prior to 2000," and "Courses and workshops in anti-racist teaching methods are elective, so only those teachers already interested receive advanced instruction on the topic" (p.1).

The Conservative government's framework policy document overseeing the reform at the secondary level, *Ontario Secondary Schools, Grades 9 to 12, Program and Diploma Requirements* (Ontario Ministry of Education, 1999), offered a detailed and prescriptive overview of all of the major aspects for the teaching and learning of students. Significantly, all of the principle touchstones of neo-liberalism are highlighted (i.e., "high standards," "accountability," "expectations," "education and work," "independent, productive, and responsible members of society," "measurable results" and "parental responsibility"), framing the importance of creating a competitive workforce ("employability") for the "twenty-first century." The 82-page policy document consecrates only one page for "antidiscrimination education," which is sufficiently vague and non-prescriptive, avoiding accountability, in that it does not carry any proportionate weight in comparison to other tangible requirements such as the Individual Education Plan (IEO), the Teacher-Advisor program, and the Annual Education Plan. It highlights, for example, "equal opportunity," and "asks," not "requires," that "Students entering the system should be given the support they need to adjust to the new environment," and "Teachers, including guidance counselors and teacher-advisors, should give support to students that is appropriate to their strengths, needs, and backgrounds so that all students have a chance to succeed" (p. 59).

What is most striking here is that the previous anti-racism educational policy is not mentioned, nor is there any *bona fide* accountability mechanism identified to ensure that students will receive an education appropriate for their needs (Carr, 2006a). Additionally, there is no mention of financial and human resources to ensure the full articulation and implementation of anti-discrimination education. The language used emphasizes diversity without there being any focus on systemic barriers, inequities and marginalization.

Other Manifestations of Anti-racism in Canada

The policy response of provincial governments in Canada in relation to equity is mixed, in that formal pronouncements are often followed by minimalist, nuanced programs and missed opportunities. When examining formal enunciations of diversity-related responses in ministries of education across the country, there is little that expressly addresses the intent of the Ontario policies of the early 1990s. In some cases, policies attempt to mollify equity-seeking groups by including vague and indirect provisions within citizenship education or similar educational themes. One example of the softer, more indirect trend in relation to equity in education is the 40-hour voluntary service requirement in Ontario, which is, ironically, a "mandatory" graduation requirement (Ontario Ministry of Education, 2000). This policy has no structured and progressive framework in that no funds are provided by the government to ensure that students have a meaningful community-service experience, and, further, schools are not required to interweave this potentially invaluable component with their formal educational program. One might ask if 40 hours over a four-year period is sufficient to actually do community work, especially since it may take that amount of time to be trained to undertake a particular task. Westheimer and Kahne (2004) have questioned the utility of community-service work without some direct political connection, and this is significantly lacking from the Ontario policy. Students should be made aware of the reasons for poverty, for example, and not just that a food bank serves food to people who are hungry, as this may reinforce the notion that somehow poor people are the authors of their own destiny; further, by donating a can of food, it is important to understand that the problem of poverty still exists. Similarly, do students engage in anti-racism activities grounded in the educational experience that are sustained, critical, action-based and relevant, or might they considered contrived, superficial and inauthentic?

A significant thread to the policy development conundrum pertains to the radically fluctuating international pressures from which educational policymaking must develop appropriate responses for local, territorial and national educational systems. Lund (2006a) has researched anti-racism social activism and policies in Canada, especially in Alberta, and concludes that, despite the booming economic prosperity in Canada's richest province, the neo-liberal stranglehold on education has had a significant impact on the educational experience of students: "So even though some government, community, and other organizations addressing diversity still exist in Alberta, many of them have faced restructuring and downsizing in recent years.... this lack of political will to address racism and other discrimination through policy and programming negatively influences the work they (teachers and students) do in this field (p. 36). In another study, Lund and Fidyk (2006) examined the availability and usage of anti-racism education resources in Canada, stressing that a "climate of constraint and additional demands for those (anti-racist) educators dedicated to these types of programs in schools" are barriers to implementing social justice measures (p. 60). A key consideration, however, relates to being able to support the usage of social justice materials through training, professional development, integration into and throughout the curriculum, and the establishment of an institutional culture conducive to addressing systemic issues related to (in)equity. Ultimately, the formal curriculum alone cannot transform the educational system, nor the experience of students; the informal, or hidden, curriculum must also be a major component in rectifying inequity and marginalization (Apple, 1996).

Considerations and Perspectives for Policy Development and Research

How do we know if we are making progress on the equity file (Leithwood & Riehl, 2003)? One visible way is to determine what data are collected on equity, how issues are defined, if there are standards and benchmarks indicating how we achieve equity, whether there is funding, staffing and resources especially dedicated to equity, and, finally, if there is a visible presence and dialog on the subject. In other words, outcomes, more so than counting heads, are important when thinking about social justice. What do ministry of education and national reports, such as the Pan-Canadian Indicators Program, say about equity? How does the formal structure for assessing achievement reconcile the indisputable need for equity (Kim & Sunderman, 2005)? Do educational systems have frameworks in place to effectively cultivate a social justice experience? Importantly, is there room for social justice in education within a time of a neo-liberal focus on competition, high standards, enhanced practical and business knowledge, and standardized testing (Lauder, Brown, Dillabough, & Halsey, 2006)? Also of critical importance is how the educational policy process and institutional culture take into consideration the decision-making process with marginalized groups, including those discussed in the earlier sections of the chapter.

Elsewhere (Carr, 2007a), in relation to how educational policy is developed, based, in part, on my experience working in the Ontario Ministry of Education (Carr, 2006b), I highlight five key considerations as to how the educational institutional culture responds to social justice concerns.

The question of accountability in education in relation to social justice is, therefore, pivotal to understanding the degree to which society, governments and decision-makers value progressive change. Accountability within the neo-liberal context has often focused on standards, which avoid addressing social justice or concrete spending and administrative milestones that are oblivious to the notion of inclusivity, power sharing, democratic learning and the contextual reality for marginalized groups (Kim & Sunderman, 2005; McLaren, 2007). The Ontario example highlighted in this paper underscores the superfluous commitment to accountability when it comes to antiracism education.

Figure 28. Key Considerations Related to Educational Institutional Culture and Social Justice

- *resisting change and rupturing progressive work* (how easily the equity agenda can be splintered, derailed and marginalized by competing interests and uncooperative institutional and leadership elements);
- *shaping the policy message* (the gulf between an idea and how that idea will be realized and implemented, characterized by a lack of knowledge, commitment, research base and diverse people involved in the formulation of the problem);
- *controlling the agenda* (the operational apparatus scaffolding the equity agenda can serve as an unnecessary deterrent to proceeding with tangible action, mired in institutional intransigence and layers of decision-making that are usually foreign to equity-seeking groups);
- *developing curriculum and educational policy* (the tussle over the formal policy terrain involves endless compromises and political trade-offs and can become disjointed, owing to non-integrated strategies);
- *White complicity and privilege* (involves a reluctance to acknowledge inequity and personal and collective implication based on racial group affiliation and also relates to preserving inequitable power imbalances).

In the US context, there is evidence that the "accountability requirements of the *No Child Left Behind Act* of 2001 place high-poverty schools and racially diverse schools at a disadvantage because they rely on mean proficiency scores and require all subgroups to meet the same goals for accountability" (Kim and Sunderman, 2005, p. 3). Further, Hoover and Shook (2003) question the relevance of teaching and learning within the era of strident accountability, highlighting that "the threat to teaching, experiencing, and realizing democratic ideals (which) has never been more real, especially as teaching convention is driven almost entirely by invalid proficiency tests and pseudo-accountability mechanisms" (p. 8). Therefore, accountability is a societal issue, involving all sectors, and requiring institutional engagement. Democratic leadership and a renewed commitment to social justice by educational administrators (Leithwood and Riehl, 2003) is a critical element in restoring credibility to, and for, the educational system. This leadership should be cognizant and conversant with the notion and impact of Whiteness.

The objective here, when thinking about *bona fide* accountability in relation to antiracist transformational change, is to specifically focus on social justice, of which anti-racism is a predominant feature, as opposed to the broader neo-liberal themes of financial accountability and academic outcomes that do not consider marginalization, identity and inequitable power relations. The people involved in this social justice accountability process, as well as the questions raised, distinguish it from traditional strategic planning exercises, which avoid stipulating how a meaningful social justice area will be achieved. Therefore, accountability for social justice in education within a time of pervasive neo-liberalism requires a comprehensive, systemic and institution-wide approach that fully interrogates identity and power relations at the base.

In the neo liberal era, the shift from, arguably, a more citizenship-based mission for public education to an extremely sophisticated and nuanced quest for employment-focused outcomes has filtered down throughout the education system. Without fully addressing the systemic barriers that prevent society from redistributing wealth and opportunity, public education has been widely considered as an important vehicle to facilitate some mobility between social classes (Dewey, 1916/1997; Freire, 1973/2005; Banks, 2008). A focus of this chapter has been on the frittering away of some of the equity and social justice gains that have been made, while also recognizing that there is significant need, and potential, to accomplish these worthy aims for public education. It is telling that such gains, as exemplified by the *equity waltz,* can be so quickly dismantled.

Ultimately, to suggest that equity, social justice and anti-racism are integral features to the educational experience, it would be necessary to establish formal standards, outcomes and policies, thus legitimating their place, and also ensuring that the myriad actors in the teaching and learning process are attuned to the diverse priorities in education, outside of the avalanche of prescriptive testing and curriculum milestones. The social context is, undoubtedly, a fundamental factor in understanding why some students do not achieve as well as others. More integrated and critical engagement around equity could help improve outcomes for all students, thereby providing a veritable learning experience that extends well beyond questionable standardized tests (Westheimer & Kahne, 2004). Recognizing and validating identity—as illustrated earlier in this paper (James, 2003)—and power structures are a key component to legitimizing the social justice agenda.

In sum, implementing anti-racism education is not a luxury or add-on activity to be drawn on in times of trouble; it should be an organizing principle, around which substantive and broad teaching and learning experiences are mobilized. In a multicultural society characterized by hope, vigor and dynamism, there are untold benefits to proceeding with sustained, integrated leadership, accountability measures and classroom learning, whereas the damage created by avoiding the inevitable is as equally far reaching[5]. Finally, critically interrogating the meaning and salience of Whiteness throughout the policy development, accountability and educational experience should be a necessary step to engaging debate and action around anti-racism and social justice. Otherwise, there is a serious potential to be locked in an *equity waltz*, in which tangible, meaningful social justice gains are always at risk of being overturned.

Chapter 9

Whiteness and Race Challenging Democracy[1]

Paul R. Carr in collaboration with Darren E. Lund

> People will be truly critical if they live the plenitude of the praxis, that is, if their action encompasses a critical reflection which increasingly organizes their thinking and thus leads them to move from a purely naïve knowledge of reality to a higher level, one which enables them to perceive the *causes* of reality. If revolutionary leaders deny this right to the people, they impair their own capacity to thinkor at least to think correctly. Revolutionary leaders cannot think *without* the people, nor *for* the people, but only *with* the people. (Freire, 1973/2005: p. 131)

Introduction

For the past few decades the issue of diversity has become increasingly relevant within the educational context (James, 2003). Whereas the formal recognition of pluralism was once contested as being inconsequential to educational success, educators, researchers, decision makers, activists and others have now made diversity a fundamental component to the educational experience (Banks, 2008). It would be unusual for schools, teachers' associations, ministries and departments of education, teacher-educator programs, and other entities involved in education *not* to endorse a commitment to diversity. In the same way that it would be difficult to oppose democracy, it is equally problematic to fail to embrace diversity. In this chapter, we challenge the traditional conception of diversity and the way that it is understood within the educational context, arguing that teaching and learning in relation to diversity must be tethered around a core belief to advance social justice (Carr, 2007b). Our central concern, building on the themes presented in the previous chapter, relates to the notion of Whiteness, and how White power and privilege can diminish the problematic of diversity to nothing more than a superficial manifestation of potentially stereotypical gestures and exchanges, thus raising important questions about democracy.

The foundation for this chapter is based on a book that we co-edited, *The Great White North? Exploring Whiteness, Privilege and Identity in Education*, published by Sense (Carr & Lund, 2007). The process of coordinating and writing the book, along with the numerous presentations, articles and interviews that have buttressed the dissemination of the concept of Whiteness, ultimately became more of a project than a discrete published contribution to the literature. As two White males from Canada, one from Toronto and the other from Calgary, who have been involved in anti-racism education for a number of years, the challenge of discussing, researching, learning about, and teaching on Whiteness has been enlightening and, in some ways, transformative. We have concluded that it is problematic and, perhaps, even counter-productive, at times, to entertain diversity without a solid comprehension of Whiteness. Our project concerns a critical engagement toward social justice, and we have found that Whiteness, despite being a concept and subject that many people wish to avoid, provides an effective platform to frame and analyze the lived experience of being part of a diverse, heterogeneous society (Sleeter, 2005).

This chapter contains three sections: the first will expose some of the ideas, debates and questions raised through *The Great White North* project; the second will propose some strategies, thoughts and cautionary notes in relation to teaching on Whiteness; and the last will involve a brief discussion of the problematic, concerns and consequences of Whiteness for society and the education-systems that must meaningfully deal with diversity.

Framing Whiteness

As *white as snow, pure white,* like *Snow White, The Great White North?*and dozens of related metaphors, analogies, images, and cultural landmarks speak to the sanctity, beauty, and the hypnotic predominance of the color *white* in the Western world. Not merely the opposite of black, white has been a signifier for global racial supremacy—good against evil, lightness versus darkness, and benevolence over malevolence,—and symbolizes cleanliness, kindness, serenity, and youth. White is associated with Europe the conqueror, while Black is inexorably fused to colonial notions of the "dark continent" of Africa.

White supremacist groups have coalesced in North America around virulent hatred based on the premise of biological superiority. Canada has long been a welcome home to the Ku Klux Klan and numerous other hate groups (Baergen, 2000; Kinsella, 2005). White supremacist propaganda has been used historically in a sophisticated manner to soften the message of xenophobia to reinforce White hegemony (Daniels, 1997). Slavery, colonialism of First Nations and other peoples, neo-colonialism, imperialism, and a host of other political, economic, and cultural strategic maneuvers and mind-sets have all been buttressed by the grandiose conceptualization of the White man as morally enlightened (Dei & Kempf, 2006). Supported for centuries by the Christian religion and the drive to expand the Empire, White people have colonized and ravaged much of the planet (Kincheloe & Steinberg, 2006). Willinsky (1998) reminds us that the racialized divisions of the past still shape our educational institutions, and that exposing privileges and inequities is part of what we owe our students. Further, he explains that students "need to see that such divisions have long been part of the fabric and structure of the state, including the schools, and they need to appreciate that challenging the structuring of those differences requires equally public acts of refusing their original and intended meanings." (p. 5)

Rather than regarding this as a sensationalistic depiction of the legacy of a diverse group of people, one need only look at the history of indigenous peoples in North America (Churchill, 1998) to understand the present day privilege and power held by White people (Dei, Karumanchery, & Karumanchery-Luik, 2004; Fine, Weis, Powell Pruitt, & Burns, 2004; Lund, 2006a).

The collection of writings assembled within *The Great White North?* speaks to the idea that Canada is an expansive country, richly diverse in its geography, shaped by the mesmerizing landscapes crafted by the Group of Seven artists in the early 1900s, with an undercurrent of the pioneer spirit defined in the literature of generations of great Canadian writers in the latter part of the twentieth century. One feature that defines the Canadian experience is the complex and often antagonistic relationship it has had with the United States since before Confederation. A common sentiment that binds Canadians together is the self-assured notion that Canada does not suffer from the same racial problems as in the US. We are less segregated, less discriminatory, less racist, and less divided, as we often remind ourselves. The Americans, on the other hand, have endless visible warts, including a long history of racial tensions and civil rights struggles, and we strive to convince ourselves that we Canadians have not followed their destiny (Lund, 2006c).

As educational researchers interested in the sociology of "race" and identity in education, the editors of this book sought to highlight the intricate, systemic, and pervasive nature of racism in Canada. Many anti-racism scholars have begun the work of acknowledging and documenting this racist past and present (e.g., Dei, Karumanchery, & Karumanchery-Luik, 2004; Fleras & Elliot, 2003; Henry & Tator, 2005; James, 2003; Trifonas, 2003). Starting with the first European contact with the Aboriginal peoples, through the existence of slavery in Canada—about which many Canadians have no knowledge—to the undulating waves of immigration, through the razing of Africville in Halifax, to the internment of Japanese Canadians during the Second World War, through the experience of Jamaican-Canadians in Toronto and Haitian-Canadians in Montreal, the history of racism in Canada is as rich as it is shrouded with resistance and denial (Fleras, 2002; Lund, 2006b). While there have been hundreds of studies on race relations and racism in Canada, there have been few, if any, scholarly works exclusively dedicated to exploring Whiteness in Canada.

We decided to compile such a book examining the multiple perspectives and vantage points on Whiteness in order to challenge the current complacency in the Canadian state and nation, and particularly among educators, to address deep-seated inequities and injustices. This volume builds on a growing desire to examine Whiteness without reifying its centrality in the anti-racism and other social justice movements. We have been, simultaneously, inspired by critical White scholars in the US who have undertaken critical self-examination of their own privileges as they take up the work of unlearning racism in their schools, communities, and faculties of education (e.g., Bush, 2005; Howard, 1999; Jensen, 2005; McIntosh, 1988; McIntyre, 1997; Rodriquez & Villaverde, 2000; Sleeter, 2005; Sullivan, 2006). Questions emerge that seem self-evident and yet confound our work: Do most White people even know that they are White? Do they use their privilege to deny or ignore their racial identity and, simultaneously, infer inherent racial attributes to the "Other"? If White people do not know that they are White, how can those who are in positions of power, many of whom are White, effectively understand and challenge racism and unearned privilege? The linkage to democracy and democratic education is clear and direct; if White power and privilege function, and even thrive, within what we consider to be a democracy, what are the implications for non-Whites?

We realize the oversimplification entailed in placing into one White category such heterogeneous ethnic, cultural, linguistic, religious, and other groups. Certainly, there are myriad international examples of nuanced experiences of oppression and struggle within and across nations of White people. For example, Francophones have historical differences with Anglophones in Canada, the Catholics and the Protestants have been at loggerheads for years in Northern Ireland, the Hungarian minority has not had a favorable experience with the majority Romanian population, and the Basque population has been involved in a separatist movement in Spain for generations, with all of these conflicts, struggles, and complexities involving White people. It would seem extremely unusual, and perhaps even unacceptable to most people, to hear news anchors speak of "the White community" during a daily newscast in North America, yet we commonly refer to the "Black community," the "Asian community," the "West Indian community" and so on, as if these racialized groups can so easily be confined within a tightly defined and coded category of identity and social experience.

The Great White North? asks: What does Whiteness look like, in general, and in Canada, in particular? The Canadian context is highly complex with the number and variety of exogamous relations and blending of peoples with complex and shifting ethnic, cultural, and racial identities. Almost infinite individual experiences make for a confusing notion of "race" in Canada; for example, the last two governor-generals are women from racialized minority groups, coincidentally with each being a former journalist married to a White man. Is it a coincidence that there has never been a non-White supreme court judge or a prime minister of color? Who maintains the predominance of power in cabinet, at the CBC/Radio-Canada, in boardrooms of the large corporations, the senates of Canadian universities, and so on? Power does have a color in Canada, despite official multiculturalism, making our nation appear superficially to be a harmonious society in which anyone can be successful with the right attitude and effort. The meritocratic myth has worked against people of color in Canada for hundreds of years. It is problematic that White people so effortlessly invoke deficits in individual efforts as an explanation of underachievement by some racial minorities.

Despite recent significant gains for (mainly White) women in the workforce and political life, there still remains an important and visible privilege gap between Whites and non-Whites in Canada. Clearly, women as a group still face numerous barriers and challenges in society, and for women of color the inequities are multiplied. The tumultuous rift and near dismantling of the *National Organization of Women* (NOW) in the 1980s is illustrative of the tension between White women and women of color. The latter did not see their needs being addressed, nor their voices being heard, through an organization dominated by middle-class White women, which eventually led to non-White women assuming leadership positions in the movement.

Are people generally overtly racist in Canada? While it is unlikely that blatant racist behaviour is currently condoned or tolerated by most Canadians, there is ample evidence that widespread systemic racism is a reality. Part of the problem in documenting trends is the absence of useful data collection (Carr & Thésée, 2008a). Many people resist indicating their racial origin on census forms, for a variety of reasons. People from racialized minority groups know that a chance at employment may later be tainted with the accusation that the employer simply wanted to "fill a quota." Playing the proverbial "race card" is perhaps most insidious when considering the trivialization and malignment of employment equity in Canada (Klassen & Cosgrove, 2002) and affirmative action in the US (Feagin & O'Brien, 2003). At some level, racial identity is obvious to everyone and, at the same time, is obscured by the false notion that human rights legislation, common decency, and religion all negate its existence. Where people live, the positions they ultimately attain, who they may befriend, employ, and marry, the types of associations, clubs, and organizations they belong to, and other markers of social integration all may have an explicit or implicit racialized component. Who most often attends private schools, private golf clubs, and private business circles has traditionally depended on, among other things, unspoken racial categories. How people choose to understand their own implication in racism relates to privilege and power, and ultimately, Whiteness is shrouded with justifications and denials that allow people to avoid discussion of how oppression continues to benefit White people in Canada (and elsewhere).

Therefore, we begin with the premise that "race" and racial identities are highly contested and problematic ideas for our consideration. Just as with politics and religion, these topics are not usually addressed openly in polite company. We emphasize that Canadian society cannot be understood without stripping away the layers of the "race" onion. Clearly, social relations are infinitely more complex than race relations. The social construction and intersectionality of identity provide a medium in which Whiteness can be deconstructed and problematized. Whether we are speaking about sexual orientation, ability, religion, gender identity, cultural group membership, or some other aspect of our identities, the racial template always affects the power relations inherent between groups and individuals (Kincheloe, 2007, 2008a, 2008b; McLaren, 2007). For instance, when a marginalized person is also a person of color, that individual's lived experience can become more complex.

Even before the launch of the edited collection (Carr & Lund, 2007), we were surprised at the strong reaction of some people to the notion of our studying Whiteness as a way of explaining and challenging racism in Canada. In fact, when a *Globe and Mail* newspaper reporter wrote an article (Church, 2007) covering a recent presentation about our research at a national conference, the reader responses were immediate and vociferous. In less than 24 hours, over 160 written items were posted to the newspaper's "Comments" on-line forum, most of them expressing what many would consider to be racist, xenophobic, or, otherwise, hateful viewpoints. In the following months, throughout a series of radio interviews, we were able to learn of a number of issues that people have in relation to race, and, importantly, how Whiteness is considered to be an offensive concept for many Whites in society. These experiences and observations reinforce our contention that education should be the forum for a more meaningful and critical engagement on diversity and the general theme of social justice (Howard, 1999; Banks, 2006; McLaren, 2007).

Teaching about Whiteness

Most teachers in North America are White, whereas an increasingly diverse demography is flourishing in schools and communities, most predominantly in urban centers but also edging into suburban and rural areas (Banks, 2006). We could interrogate why members of racialized minorities are not drawn to teaching in the same numbers as Whites, which could include an analysis of systemic barriers, the perception of teachers and teaching, the experience of minorities in education and the power structure overarching the decision-making processes in education, but our focus here is on the reality of how faculties of education and educational institutions, in general, can seek to address social justice throughout the educational programs.

How can we teach about Whiteness without alienating White students, and without placing racial minority students in an uncomfortable and marginalized position? Is it possible to teach about Whiteness without being disruptive or causing paralyzing White guilt? What type of preparation do Whites need in order to engage in Whiteness (Sleeter, 2005)? These questions frame the examples of activities below that we believe are an effective way to start the process of critical reflection and then move toward action in relation to Whiteness. It is necessary to highlight that there is no single list that can be magically produced to remedy the problems emerging around social justice, multiculturalism or diversity themes. Rather, we advocate an approach whereby students are engaged in critical reflection of their own identities and experiences, and then aim to draw them into a more dynamic, multi-faceted, dialectal dialog and process with other identities and experiences (James, 2003). Underpinning this philosophy and conceptual approach is a belief in Paulo Freire's (1973/2005) understanding of education being intertwined with the political, economic and socio-cultural milieu. In sum, education is politics (McLaren, 2007).

The first activity that we recommend as a way of commencing the dialog relates to a critical self-reflection on identity. It is important for education students to tease out their own educational experiences so as to be able to appreciate what led them to desire to become teachers. This activity with undergraduate education classes involves students writing a short paper on five personalities, experiences, factors, issues and/or events that have shaped their educational experience. When students present their papers in class, it proves to be extremely powerful to discover that the context is as important, if not more so, than the content in documenting their experiences. Students start to make linkages with each other, and also can see how peoples' identities are fundamental in determining educational success. Many students had unfavorable elementary and secondary school experiences, and it is important to deconstruct, contextualize and critique the meaning of the social context in shaping their educational experience.

Students can start to see trends in relation to how some were marginalized, ignored and diminished, whereas others seemed to have benefited from a relatively fluid, profitable and enjoyable experience. The process of documenting what shaped one's educational experience is powerful, especially as future teachers, in that students can start to connect the relevance of identity and cultural capital with the actual experience in the educational context. During this process, we also interrogate what diversity looked and felt like. We quickly learn that, if it was dealt with at all, diversity was often approached in a superficial manner, and the absence of an explicit and/or implicit approach to social justice can be extremely traumatic for some, and neutralizing for others. One of the focal points here is to determine how diversity shapes the educational experience and, moreover, how being White is not a neutral, raceless identity.

This activity allows us to engage in a discussion of the lived experiences of people from a range of identities and, significantly, to problematize Whiteness, even if we start to do this through an analysis of social class and poverty. Ultimately, this exercise, when framed with critical questions about the pertinence of the sociology of education (the context being as important as the content in the educational experience), can lead to a demystification of the notion that people succeed in education merely based on effort (meritocracy). The social construction of identity does, indeed, flavor the educational experience, and it also plays a role in affecting attitudes and behaviours, the organization of the school culture, the decision-making processes, and the fundamental relationships that students develop in their formative years. One cautionary note here is that it is necessary to avoid passing judgment on how students formulate the key events, personalities, issues, factors and/or experiences that they have highlighted; what is more important is to extract an analysis, and to seek a more critical vantage point, which will be indispensable in guiding these students as they become teachers.

The second strategy that could be used involves multicultural surveys, such as those developed by Paul Gorski (2008), a multicultural education activist and scholar. The activity highlights what we do and do not know and why. It is important for students to work first in small groups, debating issues and trying to work through what the answers to questions about diversity should be, and then come together in the larger group to discuss the answers one after another. One technique I have used is to get one group to read a question, and then have another group give their response with a justification, which may seem to be elementary, but the reiteration of the question in a large group serves another pedagogical purpose as opposed to the instructor simply conveying the answer. Other groups would then be invited to contribute, offering their analyses before the instructor reads the correct answer. From Gorski's basic multicultural quiz with twenty questions, the entire activity might take an hour to complete. The instructor should leave time after each answer is revealed to seek out a critical interpretation of how we came to believe, if that is the case, another conceptualization of reality (for example, in relation to US militarization, imprisonment rates based on race, and the distribution of wealth, all of which raise fundamental questions about the national narrative of *goodness* that is disseminated throughout society). This exercise allows us to critique what we learn in schools and elsewhere, including through the media, which can problematize stereotypes, fictitious images, and shortcomings in relation to diversity. In relation to Whiteness, it is important to consider how Whites are portrayed, in general, and how being White needs to be part of the equation of addressing racial discrimination. While this activity serves as a friendly and innocent icebreaker, it can also reinforce the salience of knowledge construction and the epistemology of identity. When does identity matter, and when does it not matter? How and why do we maintain that we are color-blind when there is so much evidence of racial discrimination and injustice? How is Whiteness connected to political literacy and democracy?

The third activity relates to the media (Chapters 10 and 11 deal with this in greater detail) and aims to heighten awareness of importance of media (and political) literacy. Do we teach about and for media literacy in our schools? What are the implications? How do the media pervade what we know and how we think? Do we critically analyze the media? The media can have the effect of creating a normative, universal presence for Whites and, as a corollary, may serve to further enhance stereotypes and discrimination. By not talking about White privilege, one might conclude that it does not exist. The activity is structured as followed: the class is broken down into five smaller groups, each with a different task (one watches the news, one times and documents everything, one focuses on the political messages, one monitors the news readers, journalists and others on the screen, and the last group focuses on race); the class then watches the 30-minute nightly news. It is important to point out that it does not make much of a difference what channel or jurisdiction is selected; after watching the news, each group, in the order outlined above, gives a report on what they saw. It is important to multi-layer the observations and analysis that each group comes up with and to not engage in a plenary discussion until each group has provided its input.

What I have found when using this activity with graduate students at the master's level is that students are generally surprised, and also disheartened, to see how little analysis is provided in the news and, moreover, how much it resembles entertainment more than a critical inquiry into what is important. Students start to question how the stories are selected and presented and why they are not critiqued, differentiated or contextualized in any meaningful way. Students can also observe a clear racialized organization to the news regarding who delivers the news and how, the angle selected, the lack of any critical discussion of race, and the reinforced image that Whiteness constitutes the norm. Students are then able to make the connection with their classrooms and how they address pivotal issues such as war, conflict, poverty and injustice, among others. Lund uses a similar media activity with the local daily newspaper, leading students through an analysis of the photos of people appearing throughout the entire edition. Whose faces do we see, and what roles do they play in our community? How fairly do these statistics reflect the community's demographics? Invariably, the predominant images are of White people, shown in a wide range of roles in the city and around the globe, while non-White images appear mainly in the sports and entertainment section, or in stories as the exotic "other" or positioned as criminals. These activities also raise questions as to why so much time is expended in the media on trivial matters, most typically about which Hollywood star has been seen with whomever. By leading our students through these exercises, we can start to assemble a picture of how racialized power works and, significantly, how White power and privilege are maintained in some very explicit and complex ways.

Conclusion: Whiteness and Diversity

Why focus on Whiteness? One of the reactions to the Great White North project has been: "This is very interesting but will White people ever agree to share power?" As Paulo Freire (1973, 1988, 2004, 1973/2005) has instructively pointed out, there must be hope in the proposition of educational transformation. Education is the core of societal hope, and not to desire social justice through education is to admit openly that empowerment, engagement and social change is undesirable. It is important to acknowledge the numerous barriers—historic, cultural, economic and political—that frame any discussion on education for social change. Within in the context of neo-liberalism, it is increasingly difficult to undertake meaningful social justice work that may challenge the balance of power. However, to fail to problematize Whiteness is to reinforce it, and this is the reason it is essential to attempt to address White power and privilege (Sleeter, 2005). The educative approach becomes extremely important, and poorly conceived or ineffective efforts at understanding, addressing and engaging in Whiteness may result in adverse effects (McCarthy, Crichlow, Dimitriadis, & Dolby, 2005). It is, therefore, essential to focus on Whiteness in order to seek the truth, to provide a legitimate moral foundation of knowledge, to provide hope to those marginalized by it, to empower Whites to be sensitized to their relationship to their racial origin, to give meaning to human rights, constitutions, and grand narratives espousing equality, to challenge the willing and unwilling complacency of those preaching a philosophy of color-blindness and, finally, to be able to strive for social justice (Sullivan 2006; Dei, 2008; Dei, Karumanchery & Larumanchery-Luik, 2004). If the qualitative experience of education does not include the tangible expression and representation of democracy, citizenship and social justice, then educators might question the relevance of merely stocking up on knowledge and skills, as exemplified by Freire's critique of students being perceived as empty vessels (1973/2005).

Whiteness is problematic for many reasons. That many White people do not see themselves as White, while simultaneously seeing non-Whites as people of "color" and, further, perceiving themselves as being "good" is problematic. There is a fear of being labelled racist, juxtaposed against an inability or unwillingness to become engaged, despite the preponderance of church and community groups that highlight the goodness and equality of all people. One student commented to me that "Sunday is the most racist day of the week because that is when we all go to our separate churches." Some White people are led to become fearful of the "other" based on the endless replaying of media and societal programming, not actual lived experiences, all of which often reinforces the entrenched sentiments that some hold. In the United States, for example, it is not uncommon to see large racial minority populations living in poorer conditions in the inner city with White populations living in relative harmony in "better" suburban neighbourhoods ringing the minority areas.

How should we consider "White flight," when White people leave a neighbourhood because Black people have moved in and, importantly, how should we learn to be together, to confront challenges collectively, to denounce inequitable situations and to create a more decent society, if we refuse to understand racism in a more collective sense? Individuals who choose to use the "N word" have faced public trauma and denunciation because of this; for example, in the past few years three prominent White Americans (Michael Richards from *Seinfeld*, Don Imus from radio fame, and Duane Chapman, who is *Dog, The Bounty Hunter* from the popular television show of the same name, have been the targets of the media for their overt expressions of racism. However, what is being done to understand that the individual acts are somehow connected to broader systemic, institutional and cultural practices, policies, programs and manifestations of racism? It would seem that education is the key piece to the puzzle in order to address, throughout myriad experiences, activities, courses, events and teaching and learning, what Whiteness is and how it can best be addressed.

Teaching for social justice requires a critical interrogation of the world around us (Solomon, Portelli, Daniel, & Campbell, 2005). Is it purely a coincidence that all of the Canadian prime ministers and US presidents have been White? What did each of them do to acknowledge and dismantle Whiteness? Why do we think of Canada and the US as being White, European, Christian countries? (The meaning of an African-American president of the US is explored further in Chapter 10). How do our schools reconcile the obvious reality that Aboriginal peoples were on these lands for thousands of years before the White man "discovered" them? We teach not only about what we know but also, importantly, what we do *not* know, and the students form their opinions, ideals and values, in part, based on knowledge from schools. While we should expect resistance, rejection and cynicism from White students when teaching about Whiteness, educators need to be vigilant, prepared, engaged and critical in demonstrating the transformative possibilities of being immersed in such an endeavor. Because this can be a disruptive and uncomfortable process, confrontation should be approached with caution as some students may not be sufficiently engaged to continue their reflection.

Dismantling Whiteness is not easy because it straddles the line of innocence and decency. It is much easier to argue that times have changed and that "we can't be blamed for what our ancestors did." We do know that having the "right" parents is a key ingredient to success in education, and that living in more well-off areas renders the schooling experience more enjoyable and less taxing than in poorer urban areas. White people, as Peggy McIntosh (1988) has effectively pointed out, need not reflect on their Whiteness in a range of daily activities, ultimately demonstrating the unearned privileges of being White. White people may reject their own implication in social justice, but this comes at a cost in terms of the impact on all learners and those involved in education.

Finally, White power and privilege is intertwined with neo-liberalism and the political systems that maintain hegemony. The notion of accountability, a major plank in educational reforms such as the *No Child Left Behind Act* in the US, does not willingly embrace the concept of social justice. Critically interrogating Whiteness, inequity, discrimination, marginalization and social justice is often considered an "extra" duty, something that falls outside of the purview of the teacher who must, in the words of some critics, "teach to the test." One comment we often received when teaching for social justice is, "How will we have time for that with so much else to cover?" This is where our understanding that teaching about and for social justice, with an aim to addressing Whiteness, is an ongoing process. It is not a list, and meaningful, sustained and critical engagement must be the cornerstone. The benefits to unmasking these concepts, regardless of the subject area or the cultural and institutional milieu, are numerous, and educators will find that the teaching and learning experience is enhanced, not diminished, by taking on such issues. Importantly, White people are uniquely positioned to play a crucial role in challenging White power and privilege.

Section 3:
Democracy and Power:
Can We Be Critical and Also Democratic?

Chapter 10

The Election of an African-American President: Does This Mean Democracy Is Working?[1]

Paul R. Carr in collaboration with Brad Porfilio

We can legitimately say that in the process of oppression someone oppresses someone else; we cannot say that in the process of revolution someone liberates someone else, nor yet that someone liberates himself, but rather that human beings in communion liberate each other. This affirmation is not meant to undervalue the importance of revolutionary leaders but, on the country, to emphasize the value. What could be more important than to live and work with the oppressed, with the "rejects of life, "with the "wretched of the earth"? In this communion, the revolutionary leaders should find not only their *raison d'etre* but a motive for rejoicing. By their very nature, revolutionary leaders can do what the dominate elites-by their very natureare unable to do in authentic terms. (Freire, 1973/2005: p. 133)

Introduction

At the normative level, one might easily be persuaded to believe that elections are the essence of democracy, that they reinforce democratic engagement, and that society is enhanced by the (supposedly) free and informed choice of citizens in selecting their government. The mainstream media, undoubtedly, plays a role in informing people about the state of affairs in relation to democracy, elections, and politics (Macedo & Steinberg, 2007). To varying degrees, most voters form their opinions about political candidates and what constitutes relevant issues based on the myriad reports and messages that flow from the print, electronic, radio, and computer (mass) media networks. The salience of media literacy in being able to critically understand bias, control, propaganda, misinformation, omission, ideology, and diverse vantage points must be considered, particularly when guiding pre-service and in-service teachers to gauge the vibrancy of representative/electoral democracy (Chomsky, 2008a; Gerstl-Pepin, 2007).

This chapter explores the 2008 US presidential campaign in relation to critical media literacy. Using the backdrop of research that I (Carr) have undertaken with teachers on critical media literacy (Carr & Porfilio, 2008; Porfilio & Carr, 2009), this chapter explores the (dis)connection between democracy and the media in the United States. Education should be a natural ally in forging a critical democratic society (Carr, 2007a, 2007b; Carr, 2008b; Lund & Carr, 2008). Unfortunately, educational institutions in North America function more often as appendages of the political and economic elite, blocking K-12 students and their teachers from questioning the constitutive forces and existing structures that perpetuate injustice and inequity, and from joining grassroots movements designed to remake the social world in line with the ideals of equity, justice, and democracy (McLaren, 2008). Therefore, we argue that critical media literacy must be taught, learned, practiced, and inculcated in schools if teachers and their students are to gain the critical insight necessary to understand what is responsible for power imbalances inside and outside of their classrooms, and to recognize why concerned citizens must struggle to create a truly democratic society, one that aims to meet the interests and needs of all citizens (Hoechsmann, 2006; Porfilio & Carr, 2009b).

This chapter presents various facets of the 2008 US presidential election within the framework of a critical media literacy vantage point, augmented by comments and analysis provided by in-service teachers, who are in a master's level class on the sociology of education. It also argues for a more robust and critical approach to media literacy in teacher education, concluding with a discussion on the connection between democracy, the media, and critical media literacy (Macedo & Steinberg, 2007). The central notion here is that critically analyzing the media during the recent electoral campaign throughout a period of time (in this case, a university course) can lead in-service teachers to hold socially just personas, allowing them to gain a stronger appreciation and sensitization of the salience of elections and democracy (Dautrich & Hartley, 1999).

Framing the 2008 US Presidential Campaign and the Media

This section includes a range of critical observations and analyses on the role of the media in shaping elections and ultimately democracy, paying particular attention to the 2008 US presidential election. The intention here is not to provide an exhaustive cataloguing of concerns with the media in relation to politics but rather to highlight some important concerns related to the influence of the media, as well as the implications for media literacy in schools of education, which would ultimately impact on political literacy and citizen engagement in democracy (Kellner & Share, 2007; Lund & Carr, 2008). By focusing on the 2008 US presidential electoral campaign, we are able to provide a conceptual framework to better understand the comments of the participants in this research. Each of the sub-sections contains an area of concern in relation to the media coverage of the election, followed by a reference to the participants in the study.

As reported elsewhere (Porfilio & Carr, 2009a), approximately sixty teachers participated in this study in three classes in 2008, which took place at a university in Ohio. The participants wrote blogs and papers on the role of the media, media literacy, and the connection to education, from which narrative comments are drawn for this paper. They were also introduced to readings on the media, such as those contained in Macedo and Steinberg (2007), providing them with a broad survey of media literacy concerns, techniques, critiques, and issues. Participants were asked to work in groups of two to four persons, and their comments are sited as such (i.e., Group 1, Group 2, etc.) below. The participants engaged in various activities to become sensitized to the notion of media literacy, and their final papers and blogs reflect their realization that the mainstream media does not necessarily serve a neutral, apolitical function, nor does it effectively cultivate broad and deep democratic engagement. The participants were predominantly White in-service teachers who educate youths in a range of elementary and secondary subject areas. It is also important to note that all teachers in Ohio are required to complete a master's degree in order to maintain their certification, which, for the purposes of this study, underscores that the participants, who are primarily from working-class backgrounds from the region in which the university is located, represent some of the beliefs, perceptions, and experiences of grassroots teachers, as opposed to those who have voluntarily opted for graduate studies.

It should briefly be emphasized here that, as has been well documented in the US and abroad, the 2008 US presidential election was a historic one, and the fact that an African-American candidate has now become president should not be diminished in any way. This is an important international event, one that merits support and critical examination at many levels. Will Obama be able to stem the tide of US hegemony, alter the deleterious US military presence abroad, and re-shape the visible power imbalance and poverty gap that is widening within the United States? These important questions will not be addressed in this paper, as this article's focus is on the media in relation to the campaign, but the reality that Obama is an African-American certainly plays into any discussion on media coverage.

1. Maintaining a Hegemonic View of the United States

There are many ways of understanding the 2008 US presidential electoral campaign. The official version is that this is an important event that bolsters democracy and American identity. Some argue that not to vote is to be anti-patriotic, and that one cannot complain if he/she has not participated in the election (Westheimer, 2007). Others go further in insisting that it is a privilege, a right, and a responsibility to vote, and that the United States is the bastion of democracy because of this supposedly unique characteristic enshrined through the electoral process (Macedo & Steinberg, 2007). The reality, as illustrated in Figure 29, is that the voter-participation rates for the United States are among the lowest in the Western, "democratic" world.

The mass media generally and uncritically support the official version of the electoral process: that it is about democracy, upholding the Constitution, framing, shaping and, some might say, controlling the agenda, and providing a vehicle for citizen engagement and participation (Chomsky, 2008). The official version is not open to incisive criticism about the role of the media in affecting the outcome of elections. In general, political and media literacy do not appear to be central to the debate on elections.

Students began to question the truthfulness of this national narrative as they started to critically examine how the media functions. This is not a natural process, but one that requires conscientious effort and vigilance. While sometimes surprised and disappointed, participants in the study became motivated to further their understanding of the media and its influence at the educational, political, and societal levels, as a result of the knowledge that to not do so would have a deleterious impact on their own lived experiences (Kincheloe, 2008).

> The mass media of the United States is a part of the national power structure and it therefore reflects its biases and mobilizes popular opinion to serve its interests. This is not accomplished by any conspiratorial plotting or explicit censorshipit is built into the structure of the system, and flows naturally and easily from the assorted ownership, sponsors, governmental and other interest group pressures that set limits within which media personnel can operate, and from the nature of the sources on which the media depend for their steady flow of news. Thus, what we observed was that there was a deliberate control as to who was allocating time, resources, and energy to the stories presented. (Group 3)

The challenge, as exemplified toward the end of the courses, relates to what participants can do to change their relationship with the media. One of the answers is that there is no one answer, that the work required involves a process, critical engagement, and an appreciation for inequitable power relations (Carr, 2008a).

Figure 29. Selected Comparative Voter Participation in "Democratic" Countries[2]

Country	Year	Population	Eligible voters	% who voted
Australia	2007	22M	14M	95%
Austria	2008	8M	6M	72%
Belgium	2007	11M	8M	91%
Canada	2008	34M	23M	59%
France	2007	65M	44M	84%
Germany	2009	82M	62M	71%
Great Britain	2005	62M	44M	61%
Netherlands	2006	16M	12M	80%
Portugal	2009	11M	9M	61%
Spain	2008	46M	35M	74%
Sweden	2006	9M	7M	82%
United States	2008	307M	230M	63%

[Note: a) figures have been rounded; b) some countries employ a two-phase voting system, and the figures provided in this table relate primarily to the first vote in those cases, although it was found that there was, generally, not much of a difference between the participation rates in the first and second rounds of voting; c) invalid (spoiled) votes are included in the percentage of those who actually voted (generally speaking, the data indicate that 1–3% of the votes in each election were spoiled); d) as electoral systems vary, there may be some differences in the meaning of legislative elections in each jurisdiction; e) voting is mandatory in Australia; f) for the elections contained in this chart, which are the most recent in each jurisdiction, they all relate to legislative seats, including, in some cases, the office of president and/or prime minister.]

2. Endorsing the Two-Party Model

As the media focuses on the two primary political parties (the Republicans and the Democrats) to the exclusion of other interests, the broader public is generally compelled to support and engage with these two voting blocks. Alternative voices are, ironically, shut out of the mainstream media debates, which further diminishes their chances of winning votes and support in elections. This is ironic because the notion of having the right to freedom of speech is an oft-cited refrain of those proclaiming the superiority of the democratic model (Carr, 2008b). Who ultimately has the right to speak? Who has the platform? Who is heard? What difference does it make? What are the implications of going against the grain when the mere mention of a criticism of patriotism, corporate control, or collusion of interests might permanently ostracize one from further debate?

It could be argued that the mass media in the US blocks the populace from forming popular movements that are able to organize, develop programs, groom candidates, and put them into office (Goodman, 2008a). As alluded to above, the mass media caters to the needs of the two major parties because these bodies represent the interests of the wealthy and powerful, the social actors who purchase airtime to sell their products and services across the globe. Chomsky highlights that elections in the United States are not watershed moments when the masses unite to bring about initiatives to "control resources, (support) cultural rights and social justice" (Goodman, 2008c). Echoing Tom Ferguson, Chomsky elaborates further that elections in the United States equate merely to "moments when groups of investors coalesce and invest to control the state and have quite the substantial predictive successes" (as cited in Goodman, 2008a). It is, in fact, improbable to be elected US president if a candidate fails to support "dominant authoritarian domestic and imperial structures and doctrine" (Street, 2008a). Thus, upholding certain mythologies—for example, that the United States is only a force of good in the world, that it is the exemplary model of democracy, that US democracy is based on ultimate fairness, that militarization is a necessity, and that the predominant economic model should not be critiqued—is generally accepted by the two main parties, in lockstep with the mass media, which undermines diverse and critical media coverage and options for the voting populace (Chomsky, 2008a; McChesney, 2008).

In undertaking their critical media literacy analysis, participants became highly attuned to the reality that the mainstream media generally cover the same stories from the same angles using the same experts to define the same events. At the same time, through careful observation, they came to realize that it is difficult to conceptualize diverse vantage points because of the *de facto* consensus that the two major political parties, necessarily, constitute the totality of the news.

> Throughout our analysis, the radio, the newspaper and the nightly news focused on the same story, the election. The two presidential candidates, Barack Obama (Democratic candidate) and John McCain (Republican candidate) were looked at closely especially during this week of news. The stories pertaining to the Democratic party ranged from a 109-year-old woman (daughter of a slave) casting her vote, and Barack Obama going out to vote with his family. On the other hand (Republican party), the media discussed the fact that Sarah Palin (McCain's running partner) was receiving prank phone calls. Another outlet reported on the fact that *Saturday Night Live* had exploited Sarah Palin's ideas and views as they continued to run specials as if to mock her and make fun of her. This outlet felt that the comedic skit weakened the Republican party's chance of being elected into office. (Group 6)

Participants could slowly start to witness how the news about the electoral campaign largely revolves around the two major candidates from the two mainstream parties, and, moreover, how trivial stories connected to this narrative flesh out newscasts, radio broadcasts and pages of newspapers.

3. Corporate Involvement in Ideas and Movements

The 2008 US presidential election resembled the past ten US presidential elections in many ways: the victors outspent their opponents. Although the campaign went on for an astounding almost two-year period, involving endless pronouncements, advertisements, tactics, media coverage, and manipulation, it is clear that Obama (the Democratic candidate) outspent McCain (the Republican candidate). Obama received "enormous, unprecedented contributions from corporate interests, Wall Street interests, and most interestingly, big corporate law firm attorneys" (Nader, 2008, para. 2), yet the media focused on how much the average person became involved in, and financed, the Obama campaign (Street, 2008a).

Traditionally, the candidate with the most funds is able to diminish his/her opponent, put him/her on the defensive, and use the media to his/her advantage, all of which pay dividends in the contemporary electoral process (Street, 2008b). While there is the sentiment that people and the media are not receptive to negative advertising, maligning one's opponent is generally accepted as a given in today's political world. This serves to obfuscate debate, narrowly constraining the issues and perspectives given to voters, which ultimately leads to citizen disenfranchisement rather than engagement. Furthermore, the media often spends innumerable hours covering negative attacks, rather than addressing more pertinent issues (Chomsky, 2008b).

Participants in the study critiqued the prevalence of the corporate sector in the media, something that many had not fully considered in the past. Some of the groups measured the amount of advertizing in newspapers or the number of commercials in the television and radio news. They found that superfluous corporate window dressing can have the effect of diminishing, downsizing, and mollifying what is packaged as newsworthy.

> We believe one of the overall implications from our findings was that the news concentrates all its forces on one or two issues.... In this way, they can keep us focused on one issue while preventing us from thinking about certain other issues. The owners are going to publicize what they want, either for personal gains and views, or for those of their sponsors. Another implication is that a lot of what they show is for entertainment value. Most of the articles and stories we read or saw did not require a lot of thought. It seems

the media does not want people knowledgeable on certain issues. In this way, they can't form their own opinions. They are trying to keep the masses complacent. (Group 1)

Newspapers rely on advertisements for financial support in producing a daily newspaper. The advertisements use catchphrases, not necessarily the truth, to draw in the consumer to market their products. For instance, one particular advertisement states: twelve months no payment, no interest, which lures people into buying products they really can't afford, thinking they have twelve months to pay, when actually they put off making payments and at the end of twelve months they have (to pay) the full year's interest.... These are several examples of how the media uses bold print catchphrases to appeal to the public's eye. (Group 7)

Participants learned through the media literacy section of the courses that the corporate architecture framing the news can have an influence on what type of news is reported, ultimately affecting the state of democracy (Porfilio & Carr, 2008). Is it possible for the mainstream media to critique those who purchase the very advertising space that secures their profits? Since the media is dependent on the two mainstream parties for purchasing airtime, what type of room remains for the media to introduce topics, issues, and concerns of those not involved in maintaining the two-party structure?

4. Marketing the Candidate

In keeping the vast majority of US citizens passive through an uncritical media, business interests create marketing campaigns and advertisements, which lead US voters to "make irrational choices based on the success of illusion, slander, and effective body language or whatever else is supposed to be significant" (Goodman, 2008a). In fact, Obama was recently selected by the Association of National Advertisers (ANA) as the "Marketer of the Year" (Street, 2008b), beating out Apple (the computer company) for this award. He "built his brand with grand gestures, and his campaign demonstrated an understanding of ground-level marketing strategies and tactics, everything from audience segmentation and database management to the creation and maintenance of online communities" (Creamer, 2008, para. 6). The importance of the way Obama understood, handled, and negotiated with the media was highlighted by the candidate, the media, and observers at all levels (Street, 2008b). Sussman (2005) highlights how there is now an accepted trend that "sees political consultants as deliberately pushing expensive media-based campaigning as a way of obstructing the grassroots in public decision-making" (p. 175).

Mazzoleni and Schultz (1999) frame how formal politics, especially in relation to elections, is being debased as the focus is increasingly focused on candidates' trivial personality traits:

> Critics argue that the media's presentation of politics in the United States as well as in many other countries—as 'show-biz' based on battles of images, conflicts between characters, polls, and marketing, all typical frenzies of a journalism that is increasingly commercial in its outlook—has diminished if not supplanted altogether debate about issues, ideals, and people's vital interests, has debased voters by treating them not as citizens but as passive "consumers" of mediated politics. (p. 248)

Rhetoric generated by both political candidates in the mass media ensured that specific large private and economic interests pervaded the electoral process. For instance, Obama and McCain used the public rhetoric that their presidencies would offer significant "change" to the US public. Obama's corporate handlers crafted a media-political image of a rockstar-like persona, positioning Obama as representing "amorphous symbols of 'Hope,' 'Change,' and 'Unity' to absorb the diverse and often confused aspirations and dreams of a mass constituency containing numerous and often contradictory values and positions" (Street, 2008a, para. 18). As Sussman (2005) relates, elections allow the elites to construct moralistic, freedom-loving, natural interest, and "other diversionary public rhetoric" to "disguise the actual workings of the political economy" (p. 173).

The narrative provided below highlights how several teachers hold the critical capacity to recognize that the mass media focus on "entertainment" more so than on informing and enlightening citizens on "life's problems." The prevailing question posed in this course was, "Is the media presenting news or entertainment?"

From this analysis it is clear that very little of what we call news is actually relevant information needed to make positive change in society. The half-hour time slots must be filled with something, and while the time is being filled, it might as well be profitable. The bottom line here is that news is an industry. People will not buy the product if it is not entertaining. The problem lays in the fact that entertainment and news may always be at odds with each other. Entertainment is meant to distract us and reroute our attention away from life's problems. W. H. Auden said, "What the mass media offers is not popular art, but entertainment which is intended to be consumed like food, forgotten and replaced by a new dish." If we want to be entertained, the media simply cannot burden us with stories of social injustice or need for change. We need weather and cooking segments and information on how to best clean out our gutters.

News should inform and enlighten us. It should present facts that spark critical questions that then move us toward action that produces positive changes in society. We should see a news broadcast about Darfur and scream for justice. This, of course, would not be entertaining. It would require action. After a hard day's work, middle class America just wants to sit down, relax and read the paper. We are tired. We need a little distraction from life's problems. So, until society requires the media to provide thought provoking news that requires action, we will continue to be entertained. News reports will not have any effect on society until we decide to analyze the facts involved in the reporting. Then, we will move to action and social change. (Group 6)

The participants in the study also reveal that, without media literacy, there is a harsh reality in K-12 classrooms: often, there is a simple consumption of the mainstream media in a neutral fashion, which may actually be harmful to promoting democracy, and moving "to action and social change." Participants could infer that the electoral campaign was more about getting candidates elected and supporting business interests than it was about focusing on how to build a better society.

5. *Avoiding the Issues*

It is questionable whether the two predominant parties focused on issues of importance during the campaign, and also, significantly, whether the media probed candidates and parties to force a meaningful debate. Chomsky (2008b) is extremely critical and insightful about how the 2008 campaign was configured to trivialize important issues.

> The McCain campaign was honest enough to announce clearly that the election wouldn't be about issues. Sarah Palin's hairdresser received twice the salary of McCain's foreign policy adviser, *The Financial Times* reported, probably an accurate reflection of significance for the campaign. Obama's message of "hope" and "change" offered a blank slate on which supporters could write their wishes. One could search websites for position papers, but correlation of these to policies is hardly spectacular, and in any event, what influences voters' choices is what the campaign places front and center, as party managers know well.

The media's complicity in continually looking for a hook or an angle to obscure relevant debate on issues impacting US society and other social contexts is, perhaps, best exemplified by the massive coverage allocated to an Ohio man called "Joe the plumber." This man (who, as it turns out is not named Joe, nor is he a plumber) was able to occupy endless hours of debate in the mainstream media. He became a celebrity, hit the campaign trail with McCain, was interviewed on numerous news programs, had his name invoked in presidential debates, and, generally, served to obfuscate a real and necessary discussion on a range of important issues (Palermo, 2008).

Participants in the study, through careful and critical documentation, could see that many of the issues occupying the greatest amount of space and time in the media were not relevant.

> As we critically analyzed our notes we found many disheartening things. We found that both [media] outlets [that the group studied] presented biased information, made use of word trickery, and contained an obvious lack of many important issues. Nor did they represent the minority population to any great extent. Had it not been for the presidential campaign, coverage of African Americans would have been seen primarily in the sports section. (Group 1)
>
> Researching and investigating the *Vindicator* newspaper for a week brought to my attention that the media has their own hidden agenda when reporting and writing about newsworthy events. In the *Vindicator*, many of the new articles come from the Associated Press. As a result, not as many stories were actually even written by *Vindicator* staff writers. Also, it appears as though much of the news was simply stated and lacked any real depth or meaning. Therefore, not all vantage points were covered in most of the articles. (Group 5)

Participants noted that the vast majority of stories lacked context and meaningful analysis. They found that, by stating issues as facts devoid of *bona fide* journalistic due diligence, the broader public is (mis)led to believe that these are the only issues that count, reinforced by endless references in the mainstream media.

6. Curtailing Non-Mainstream Voices

The dominant US media also purposely keep out the perspective of third-party candidates who seek a shift in the power agenda, push to eliminate the corporate agenda of the "duopology" party system, and desire that Americans take the reigns over their government and control over their lives (Nader, 2008). Not coincidently, both parties "have moved very heavily in the direction of corporate contracts, subsidies, handouts, giveaways, and the swelling of this enormous, corrupt, wasteful military budget that is draining money" (Goodman, 2008d, para. 44).

While the mainstream media incessantly focused on the positions of the two primary candidates, whose policies on a range of issues did not differ greatly, scant attention was paid to other political parties or interests. The Green Party, for example, which has members of parliament in a number of European countries, and is a force in a number of political contexts, also has a political party in the United States, which supported former Congress member Cynthia McKinney in the election. She was "the first African American women to win a congressional seat in Georgia" (Goodman, 2008b, para. 9). *Democracy Now*, an alternative media program without corporate ties, provides a forum for interests and groups such as the Green Party and other independent candidates and political activists, who may not share the common hegemonic narrative generally portrayed in the mainstream media. *Democracy Now*'s Amy Goodman provides a window into a more critical, independent, and alternative media. The transcript highlights below from two interviews underscore the differences that exist between the Green Party position, third-party candidates, and those of the two traditional parties:

Amy Goodman: Where do you differ with Barack Obama most, (Green Party candidate) Cynthia McKinney? I mean, you, too, to say the least, broke barriers as the first African American woman to win a congressional seat in Georgia.

Cynthia McKinney: I reject the continuation of the occupation of Iraq and, of course, reject any surge into Afghanistan. There was silence over the most recent US raid over Syria, the incursions into Pakistan, the virtual blaming of Russia for a provocation that actually was initiated by Georgia, the push to include NATO membership for countries that are right up to the border of Russia and China. Then, of course, I would never have been for the bailout, put out my own fourteen points with respect to the bailout, would never have supported FISA, the illegal spying, the unwarranted spying on US citizens, and at the same time granting of immunity to telecoms that were complicit in that. There are many areas of disagreement with the Obama administration. (Goodman, 2008b, para. 9–10)

Amy Goodman: Ralph Nader, your response to Joe the plumber...

Ralph Nader: [There] would be an obligation of the government to provide full health insurance. It's much more efficient. Free choice of doctor and hospital, quality and cost control on the private delivery of healthcare. It's supported by a majority of the people and a majority of the physicians in a recent poll, 59 percent of them. We also say to Joe plumber that we're going to revise the tax system so we tax things wesociety likes the least or dislikes the most before we tax human labor. That is, a securities derivative tax. We tax gambling industry more, addictive industry more, corporate crime and pollution, like a carbon tax. Notice, throughout the debate, so-called, between Obama and McCain, they avoided anything that would challenge corporate power. They didn't talk about a crackdown on corporate crime. They didn't talk about ending corporate welfare. They didn't talk about cutting the huge bloated military budget of the military-industrial complex that Eisenhower warned us about. They didn't talk about shifting this into a major public works program to repair America at the community level. What we're seeing today on your program is how a larger frame of reference should have been given to tens of millions of people, what Cynthia McKinney and I have been denied reaching. (Goodman, 2008a, para. 116).

Participants in the study were sometimes surprised to learn that there are alternative voices, interests, and parties outside of the two mainstream parties. They would often ask: Why is this information not known in the broader public? Their understanding of how corporate interests infuse the media process enhanced their textual analysis in critiquing the mainstream media.

> While the intent of news is to provide information that is unbiased, and without consideration of political vantage points, our observations indicate that this is not the case. Ultimately, one must remember that the media is a business, and so it functions like a business, designed to serve those who support it monetarily. Sponsorship and advertisements are the two main entities that provide the necessary resources to maintain the existence of the television news channel and the newspaper. Therefore, if the majority of sponsors and advertisers are of a certain race, it is probable that news stories aired and published will cater to that same race. Often times, the media is used as a tool to influence uninformed viewers. Stories are selectively edited to be skewed in such a way that people will interpret information in a certain way, which is designed to benefit the media's stakeholders. For example, rather than providing the actual details of an issue or incident, the media will instead choose to provide only those details which will sway viewers in a direction that will serve their purpose. (Group 10)

Participants in the study came to realize that the average citizens, especially social actors from traditionally marginalized groups, are negatively affected by a lack of media literacy (Carr, 2008a). Passively consuming what the mainstream media delivers as pertinent news can cloud the reality of how power works, and can also keep in place policies, practices, and structures that favor the few at the expense of masses.

7. The (Non-)Debate Over Education and the Media

The educational policies of the candidates were not very different, and the debate on and around education seemed to play a negligible role in the campaign. Although Obama was consistently labelled as liberal or even a radical, his educational platform was clearly moderate to conservative, and the media avoided any critical examination of education in general. Barack Obama promised Tuesday to double funding for charter schools, pay teachers based on performance and replace those who aren't up to the job, embracing education proposals normally more popular with Republican candidates (*USA Today*, 2008).

The participants in the study highlighted how they were generally surprised to learn how little the media focus on education, especially in any meaningful way. The result is that education and educators are not seen to be directly linked to the formal political process. This can diminish the connection between education and elections, and also reinforce the notion that democracy in education should be focused on a thin interpretation (teaching and learning about candidates, parties, and electoral processes) as opposed to a more robust, thicker vision of democracy (challenging students to become more engaged, critical, and conscious about their own identities, social justice, inequitable power relations, and how they are involved in politically shaping society) (Carr, 2007a, 2007b, 2008b; Lund & Carr, 2008a; Porfilio & Carr, 2009a, 2009b).

> Refraining from being media illiterate is the challenge of our times. As citizens, our political and social lives have become disrupted and distorted by powerful, impersonal, and corrosive forcescommercialism and American capitalism. The "real" world is being defined by what is seen on TV, browsed on the Internet, and viewed in passing on the cover of sensational magazines on the newsstand at the grocery check-out. As responsible citizens, it has become imperative that we come to realize that we have the ability to choose, to understand, to evaluate, to create, and to respond thoughtfully to the media we consume in mass quantities on a daily basis. As educators, we should impart upon our students the skills and strategies needed to become effective at analyzing the barrage of information that they must sift through on a daily basis. The classroom is a perfect forum to encourage discussion and conversation about meaningful issues affecting our society today—human rights, politics, and even education. We must work to create a generation of critical thinkers who question inequalities—a generation that uses their voice for purpose and change. (Group 2)
>
> The lack of coverage is evidence that education, which is supposed to support and maintain our democratic communities and ideals, has taken a back seat to other corporate agendas. When media sources publish information on schools, it focuses on low-test scores, high salaries of teachers, and student misconduct. Media seems to be an avenue to confirm America's view that money should not be invested in education. Media seems to publish stories that audiences want to read rather than what they need to read. Instead of focusing on what is happening and why, media is caught up in personalities and processes. They focus on what they can find as problems, instead of highlighting what good is happening in education or among marginalized people. (Group 3)

Participants in the study underscored the importance of media literacy in education, in light of the preponderance and effect of the mainstream media on the thoughts, images, and issues that young people are exposed to (Hoechsmann, 2006). The importance in relation to education is obvious when thinking about how and where people learn to address political issues (Kincheloe, 2008). If schools are disengaged or "neutral," they may be feeding into the fallacy that the news is unbiased and truthful, which would be detrimental at many levels (Macedo & Steinberg, 2007).

8. The Media's Obsession with Polling, and the Reality Not Revealed in the Polls

The media is enmeshed in the business of polling, forecasting results, and positioning almost the way one might do for a horserace. The attention the media pays to polls, many of which are generated by corporate interests and the media outlets themselves, can be a distraction to advancing democratic interests and engagement, and it is unclear how much such polls influence the voting behavior of citizens. Voting strategically, or not voting at all, is one direct result from the avalanche of polling. Landes (2005) further clarifies how corporate officials have the power to cloak the intricacies surrounding how polls operate, and to keep the legitimacy of the data generated from polls on election night from public scrutiny:

> Exit-polling, in particular, needs to be scrutinized by outside sources without a corporate interest. In America, the networks completely control the exit poll operation on election night through their National Election Pool (NEP). It's a top secret operation. They allow no observers and provide no proof that their data is real. They completely stonewall reporters' inquiries. This is what the Collier brothers, late-authors of the book, *Votescam: The Stealing of America* discovered, and so did I. Worse yet, back in the 1970's in Miami, the Colliers caught the networks simply making up the exit poll numbers. My theory is that the networks do extensive pre-election polling to get a good lay-of-the-land, and then on Election Night perform a squeeze play on candidates. And although the networks' polling organization has changed its name over the decades from News Election Service to Voter News Service to National Election Pool, it's pretty much the same cast of characters. (Landes, 2005)

An interesting phenomenon during the 2008 US presidential campaign relates to the incessant reporting by mainstream media outlets about how Americans were much more involved in this election than in previous elections. The reality, as shown in the table below, provides some details on voting behaviour during the last several elections.

Figure 30. Voter Participation in US Presidential Elections[3]

Year	1980	1984	1988	1992	1996	2000	2004	2008
% participation	59%	60%	57%	61%	54%	60%	64%	65%

Although the mainstream media played up the "unprecedented" interest in this election, it was not matched by actual voter participation. As the media followed the trajectory, planning, fundraising, detailed profiles of the candidates, and the daily agendas of each of the two predominant political parties, there was little analysis on a fundamental reality of the electoral process, including (US Census Bureau, 2008):

- Education (75% of college graduates voted in 2000 as opposed to 38% of high school drop-outs);
- Employment (60% in 2004 versus 46% of those who are unemployed);
- Race (61% of Whites voted in 2000 as opposed to Blacks (57%) and Hispanics (45%); and
- Age (only 32% of the 18–24 age-group voted in 2004 as opposed to 68% for the 65+ group).

Another critical fact that was not generally elucidated by the mainstream media is that more and more citizens are becoming independent voters, rather than aligning themselves with the two traditional parties. In essence, the roughly 35% of Americans who do not vote constitute the majority, followed by the two predominant political parties, who generally share the remaining two-thirds of the vote. Yet none of the mainstream media outlets' reporting, analysis, polling, experts, or other information reflected the reality that the citizens of the country are leaning in a different direction than the fabricated or manufactured scenario that was presented as fact (Goodman, 2008c). In addition, and what is pivotal to understanding the nuance between *thin* and *thick* democracy, is that the presidential electoral campaign in and of itself constitutes only a limited portion of democratic engagement and participation, which was rarely if ever alluded to by the mainstream media. (Carr, 2007a, 2008b; Porfilio & Carr, 2008a). Participants in the study questioned the salience of the proliferation of media outlets, which, logically, should provide more choice, vantage points, and platforms from which a thicker, more critical form of democracy could be explored.

> The Internet and new technologies have become a popular source for media. News information is now available at anytime. However, because popular news sites are simply spinoffs of television and radio news, these sources are not providing citizens with anymore of an in-depth look at news stories or issues. For example, there is truly no difference in a story that is produced by any Fox News media. The story is the exact same whether it is viewed on Fox television, read on Fox News on the Internet, or heard on Fox News radio. Internet sources carry their own biases as well. Links that contain news stories advertise for higher education opportunities, lending agencies, and retirement investment options, but entertainment links within the same site have advertisements for beauty aids, sweepstakes, movie rentals, and medicines. These prejudices imply that only upper class, educated citizens view actual news sites, and lower class, uneducated citizens view entertainment sites and have no need for higher education or retirement opportunities. (Group 6)

As exemplified by the comment above, participants did not feel that the inundation of media stories in and around the presidential campaign served to generally mobilize and/or inform people to challenge the predominant national narrative.

Participants noted that, in general, polling served to (ironically) disenfranchise voters. An example of this is the blame heaped on Ralph Nader during the 2000 presidential election, as a pretext to indict his campaign. Major media outlets incorrectly claimed that the percentage of the votes he received was the deciding factor leading to the defeat of Al Gore, the Democratic candidate.

The Misrepresentation and Omission of Issues

Chomsky (2008a) has written extensively about how consent is manufactured, which involves the shaping and dissemination of propaganda. Thought control and compliance of the masses are at work through the incessant reporting of a limited range of issues, generally from the same vantage point. This may not be obvious at first glance, but through careful examination, as the participants in this study have reported, the overall effect can be far reaching. In the aftermath of September 11th, he illustrates how the slogan "*we* are good, and *they* are evil" (p. 344) was used to suppress debate, omit important and divergent vantage points, and entice citizens into a nefarious form of patriotism (Westheimer, 2006). At the political level, omission takes place in the daily barrage of news wherein political and public affairs are framed by "experts" who come from a very limited range of perspectives, identities, and backgrounds. Within the US context, the standard format is to have one or two representatives from each of the mainstream parties, the Republicans and the Democrats, to the exclusion of other interests, parties and voices.

> It was evident that media does not present multiple perspectives and shows definite biases and stereotyping. Our research… illustrates how people of color are represented negatively by the news stories in print and visual form. Further evidence collection from the media demonstrated that corporate interests with their emphasis on maximum profits drive the media and dictate largely what stories are given what degree of attention. Also, it was our observation of what was excluded during the broadcasts and print articles (or given minimal detail and explanation) that sometimes spoke the loudest…. there are essentially two ways that information about social groups can be presented: By inclusion and by exclusion…. The summation of our research efforts clearly indicated that it is our responsibility as educators is to inform students of how such power, bias, and control occur in media and to teach our students to be analytical and critical in their reception of information. (Group 3)

> One significant weakness of the Mahoning Valley newscast is that stories are reported on in isolation, and reporters fail to provide a context surrounding the report. For example, a lead story on soaring gas prices included an interview with a mechanic and a lengthy segment on an innovative electrical car. Although the report detailed ways for consumers to save gasoline, it failed to provide a context that addressed the reason for high oil prices and steps the government should be taking to alleviate the burden. An overall lack of perspective is obviously absent in the news media, and this accounts for its lack of critical analysis. (Group 6)

Participants learned, as underscored in the above comments, that what is not said is as important as what is said in the mainstream media. The context for the news is critical, and overlooking peoples' identities on a broad and systemic scale can be deleterious to society. Participants were particularly intrigued and enlightened by the numerous ways that the mainstream media collectively serve to create, reinforce, and sustain nefarious stereotypes aimed at minorities and marginalized groups. The 2008 US presidential campaign is an interesting case study because of the way that there seemed to be a quasi-consensus in the media that racial origin was not a significant variable, yet it was continually alluded to in polls, advertisements, and the presentation of issues, even if it was done so in a subtle way. Critical media literacy, therefore, becomes an indispensable resource not only to understand issues and realities, but also to be able to take action and construct alternative visions to the media's hegemonic, propagandized caricatures (Hoechsmann, 2006; Porfilio & Carr, 2009a).

Discussion: Implications for Media Literacy

This research has raised concerns about the relevance of representative democracy, which is predicated on electoral politics, as opposed to participatory democracy, which seeks to be more responsive to the needs, concerns and interests of all citizens. While the former could be considered *thin* democracy, and the latter *thick* democracy, one of the primary distinctions is the attention paid to social justice, effectively expanding the debate and action on concerns affecting all groups, including historically marginalized ones (Lund & Carr, 2008). Critical media literacy would fit nicely within a framework focused on thick democracy, and this study validates that teachers can benefit from exposure to theoretical, conceptual, and applied media analysis (Hoechsmann, 2006; Macedo & Steinberg, 2007). Translating the *concientization* (Freire, 1973/2005) that students have been exposed to would involve a process of reflection and praxis, culminating in challenging themselves and the students they teach to further think through issues of propaganda, corporate control, bias, manipulation, omission, misrepresentation, and the quest for the truth. Critical media literacy, therefore, is connected to a never-ending process of critical engagement, far surpassing the rudimentary concept of generating checklists to flag if there is, for example, bias or openness in the media (Kellner & Share, 2007; Macedo & Steinberg, 2007; Porfilio & Carr, 2009a).

Participants in this study acknowledge that they had not considered the media in a very critical way at the beginning of the course. Their views changed as they started to systematically examine the media. Many of the participants began to question their own strongly held beliefs about democracy and the role of the US government at home and abroad. The goal here was not to tell participants how to think, but to facilitate a process, as supported by critical pedagogical theorists (Kincheloe, 2008a; McLaren & Kincheloe, 2007), that would allow them to determine their socially mediated realities. In other words, critical media literacy requires a dialectical process of engagement, combined with exposure to concepts, themes, and issues that may not be readily accessible or apparent, especially given the closed nature of the mainstream media (Macedo & Steinberg, 2007).

The form of pedagogy offered to most American K-12 students surrounding the presidential campaign tends not to position students to get beyond the way in which the two major parties address salient issues affecting US society and the wider world. Typically, students are invited to take part in debates representing the Young Democrats or Young Republicans, advancing arguments that the two parties have staked out, such as the economy, pork barrel spending, health care, and the War in Iraq (Normand, 2008). Rather than doing investigative and critical work to find multiple insights from scholars, alternative websites, and people in their communities on the topics they debate, students are deemed debate winners and "critical thinkers" based upon how well they analyze topics through the platforms generated by the two major parties. Consequently, these academic exercises do little to nudge students toward recognizing the need to assess the value of supporting grassroots movements and third-party candidates, who challenge current institutional policies, arrangements, and practices, such as the commercialization of political elections (Porfilio & Carr, 2008). They also do not require them to discuss other salient issues that are absent from the major parties' platforms or investigate how the US political system could be altered to more effectively involve citizens in making political and economic decisions. The result could be a re-entrenchment toward a compliant patriotism (Westheimer, 2006a).

In juxtaposition, alternative formats have been proffered by progressive organizations, such as C-Span and the Public Broadcasting Service (PBS), to assist US schoolteachers to teach their students to understand how the current configuration of presidential politics in the United States keep in place the interests of the corporate and political elite over the interests of the vast majority of citizens. For instance, rather than keeping students from thinking critically about how the media influences US presidential elections and their own social world, students from several high schools in the United States have engaged in critical discussion with members from C-Span about "how media plays a role in presidential campaigns" and "the role of the media in informing the people about government and politics" ("Riverview Gardens High School students aired on C-SPAN," 2008, para. 12, 13). Moreover, PBS has generated instructional resources to help classroom teachers guide youths to understand the role media technology has played in influencing campaigns (Public Broadcasting Service, 2008). These resources encourage students to develop possible solutions to diminish corporate control over the election process, over US social and economic institutions, and over how knowledge is constructed and consumed in the United States and across the globe.

Could studies like the one highlighted in this article make for better elections? Would enhanced media literacy lead to a *thicker* democracy? Would the issues and candidates be more responsive if there were a greater level of media literacy in society? What are the challenges to teaching for media literacy? Is there a place within the prescriptive curriculum, mandated standards, and narrow focus of reforms such as the *No Child Left Behind* Act to do critical media literacy? The study presented in this paper advances the argument that significant progress, both at the educational and democratic engagement levels, can be made if teacher educators guide in-service teachers to develop critical frames of reference to the mass media. Studying elections from diverse and critical vantage points, problematizing and critiquing them, and exposing inequities, bias, omission and propaganda, among other things, can lead to a more responsive and democratic experience for schoolteachers and their students. Arguably, this would then enhance youths' participation in society after their formative school years, where they would struggle to build a society that accounts for the needs and concerns of all citizens.

In sum, a critical media approach to the study and experience of elections can be beneficial to all those concerned, especially in the educational system. Demystifying and questioning how power is connected to elections, as was exemplified in this study, can be empowering for teachers. This pedagogical approach also has the potency to lead to more authentic and meaningful engagement in the electoral process, amongst other forms of democratic participation. Students, educators, social activists, corporate interests, observers, and citizens alike need to keep in mind that no government has a (clear) mandate, and, moreover, democracy must be constantly cultivated and lived, which puts into context the punctual and somewhat static nature of elections in the United States. Thus, a *thicker* interpretation of democracy necessarily involves critical media literacy.

Chapter 11

The Media, Media Literacy and Democratic Education[1]

This is another fundamental dimension of the theory of oppressive action which is as old as oppression itself. As the oppressor minority subordinates and dominates the majority, it must divide it and keep it divided in order to remain in power. The minority cannot permit itself the luxury of tolerating the unification of the people, which would undoubtedly signify a serious threat to their own hegemony. Accordingly, the oppressors halt by any method (including violence) any action which in even incipient fashion could awaken the oppressed to the need for unity. Concepts such as unity, organization, and struggle are immediately labeled as dangerous—to the oppressors—for their realization is necessary to actions of liberation. (Freire, 1973/2005: p. 141)

Introduction

People with high levels of media literacy will have a better understanding of the world, adopt a position, make their own conclusions, discern truth from fiction, not follow trends, and can have a better opinion and judgment on critical issues. On the other hand people with low levels of media literacy will be vulnerable, affected, impressed, and will have conflicts when digesting the information they receive. (Jack, a teacher-participant in the research)

During a time of globalized turbulence, or "permanent war" as Peter McLaren (2007) has described the quest for neo-liberal hegemony, is it fair to ask if there is any pertinence to the media in relation to education? Is the patriotic fervour of the intense drumbeat of conformity (McChesney, 199a, 2008) too overwhelming for there to be any meaningful learning experiences from and about the media? Are educators themselves critically engaged in using, dissecting and translating the media in the classroom (Giroux, 1988; Kellner & Share, 2007)? Do the media connect with education in any substantive way that offers hope for critical engagement (Macedo, 2006)? In sum, what can be learned from the interplay between the mainstream media and education (Macedo & Steinberg, 2007)?

These questions, which are the focus of this chapter, are important because a fundamental part of critical and engaged learning is the quest for political literacy, which, necessarily, involves media literacy (Carr, 2008a; Hoechsmann, 2006). If educators are ill informed, discouraged and weakly supported in promoting critical discussions, analysis and action in relation to the media, then there will be clear implications for democracy (Chomsky, 2003). Therefore, the process leading to political engagement and political literacy (a form of *conscientization*) is, or should be, an important component to achieving a more robust and meaningful democratic experience in education (Lund and Carr, 2008).

From a pedagogical vantage point, little can be gained from avoiding a vigorous and broadly infused critical approach to the media (McLaren & Kincheloe, 2007). Critical pedagogy, as outlined by Kincheloe (2008a, 2008b), McLaren, Steinberg and Freire, among others, along with the seminal work on the political economy of the media undertaken by McChesney (2008) and Herman and Chomsky (2002), provide an indispensable framework through which the connection between the media and education can be interrogated and critiqued. Macedo (2006), Giroux (1988, 1997, 2005a, 2007) and Kellner (1995, 2005) have also contributed significantly to the field of critical pedagogy, undertaking detailed studies of the media, as well as the linkage to (critical and political) literacy, within a neo-liberal context, and, thus, their work provides a substantive underpinning to how media, media literacy and political literacy are developed and analyzed in this chapter. Studying media literacy is another entry point into how democracy works, if there is transformational potential within it, and also how hegemonic forces can be disrupted in order to achieve *thicker,* more meaningful approaches to democracy outside of the traditional representative election model.

At today's historical juncture, media culture has arguably become the most dominant force defining the sense of self, driving our understanding of the 'Other,' and providing "symbols, myths and resources" for generating a common culture (Kellner, 1995). Western corporate leaders have not only consolidated their power over the content, production, and distribution of cultural texts in the world of entertainment, but also they have utilized their influence to create a "media oligarchy," which allows them to propagate corporate and commercial interests as well as denigrating or ignoring what cannot fulfill their agendas (McChesney, 1999, 2008). Specifically, corporate leaders rely heavily "on mass media and global technologies to disseminate" (Richardson, 2007, p. 790) ideologies that often trivialize, demonize, or miniaturize the Other, while concomitantly reifying the socially constructed supremacy of Whiteness, heterosexism, patriarchy and capitalism (Fleras & Kutz, 2001).

One of the major areas in which corporate leaders spawn their agendas and perpetuate hegemonic commercial and social ideologies is via youth culture. Today's youth, whether through MTV, the Internet, the gaming world, the

Western music industry, or Hollywood, consume myriad digitized texts and goods to embody the 'cool' lifestyles of Western pop icons, which marketers, advertisers and corporations configure to net the excess of dollars that children and their caregivers have increasingly spent to amuse themselves through marketed forms of leisure for the past 20 years (Muehlenberg, 2002; Schor, 2004). This spate of goods, texts, products, and trends collectively reinscribe to youth, throughout their childhood and into adulthood, dominant ideologies that do not represent a challenge to neo-liberalism, which ultimately shelters the existence of racism, sexism, classicism, and homophobia (Kahn & Kellner, 2004).

Hoechsmann (2006) provides a useful interpretation of media education, which he contrasts with media literacy.

> Media education provides teachers and learners the opportunity to engage in the study of contemporary social and cultural values and to situate the curriculum in a meaningful manner in the lived realities of the students. It is a realm of inquiry that treats contemporary forms and practices as historically situated and thus enables the study of resonant social and cultural matters faced by young people. It is at once consumption and production oriented. Central to the project of media education is the teaching of critical interpretation techniques for decoding media texts and phenomena and technical skills for producing, or encoding, media products. (p. 27)

He teases out the notion of media literacy, arguing that it is "not something only learned from teachers," maintaining that "On the one hand, there is the hand of the powerful in the mixmedia corporations and those corporations whose products are pitched in the media. On the other hand, there is an insider knowledge already possessed by the learner, one which in many instances outstrips that of the teacher" (p. 28).

Complementing the above formulation, Kellner and Share (2007) focus on *critical* media literacy, which:

> expands the notion of literacy to include different forms of mass communication and popular culture as well as deepens the potential of education to critically analyze relations between media and audiences, information and power. It involves cultivating skills in analyzing media codes and conventions, abilities to criticize stereotypes, dominant values, and ideologies, and competencies to interpret the multiple meanings and messages generated by media texts. Media literacy helps people to discriminate and evaluate content, to critically dissect media forms, to investigate media effects and uses, to use media intelligently, and to construct alternative media. (p. 4)

Significantly, Kellner and Share (2007) emphasize the importance of having an understanding of "ideology, power, and domination that challenges relativist and apolitical notions of much media education in order to guide teachers and students in their explorations of how power, media, and information are linked" (p. 8).

Thus, together, Kellner and Share (2007) and Hoechsmann (2006) provide a critical framework that is underpinned by Kincheloe's (2008a) work in critical pedagogy to understand the media literacy dynamic, emphasizing that the "vast majority of our students are consumers and fans of at least some media texts, and these texts are sites not only of pleasure and entertainment, but also of learning" (p. 28). In sum, the explicit as well as the implicit connection between the media, education and power is a primary concern of this chapter.

This chapter examines data drawn from two master's level sociology of education classes at a university in Ohio with students who are already teachers. The course raises important questions about the potential for doing critical media literacy in schools as well as the general positioning of the subject by teachers. The focus on the media in a class for educators may not have seemed to be overly relevant to them in the beginning, but, based on comments and completed surveys provided by the students at the end of the course, the connection to education and democracy is considered to be direct, deep and fundamental. The concern over how educators view or do not view education as a political enterprise underscores the analysis.

The Process of Engaging Teachers in Media Literacy

As part of the class I teach to roughly twenty teachers each time, I have designed several activities to sensitize them to the widespread, yet somewhat nefarious, influence of the mainstream media. The objective here is to determine how the media affects teaching and learning, and, more importantly, to be able to formulate strategies to more effectively inculcate media literacy in education. Although this course, in isolation to other parts of the formal educational program, may only have a limited impact, the response, thus far, has been overwhelmingly positive. Students have often expressed stupefaction that people are generally such casual consumers of the media in spite of the far-reaching effect of the media at the macro-level, cultural level. I have no reason to believe that the teachers in my class are not effective, engaged and determined educators, which makes the findings of the study all the more interesting. Being in north-east Ohio, where there has been a staggering dislocation of the economy over the past three decades, in an area with a large working-class population divided by a visible African-American inner-city and a donut-ring of White suburbs, there are many features to this landscape that undoubtedly resonate throughout the US.

The course involves several weeks of discussions around the role of the media, especially in relation to education. The major culminating project has students, either individually or in small groups, monitoring, documenting and analyzing at least two media outlets (within the television, newspaper, internet and radio sectors) for a one-week period. They are to track what is said, how, by whom, when, and to what degree, and, then, importantly, formulate a daily analysis, which is then rolled into a more comprehensive global analysis at the end of the process. Some of the questions that are specifically asked are:

- What is the context for the news?
- What perspectives are elucidated?
- Does the news vary from medium to medium or from newscast to newscast?
- How is race (and social justice) portrayed?
- What are the particular political vantage points?
- How do the media connect with and to education?

In sum, we are concerned with the shaping or "manufacturing" of consent, as Herman and Chomsky (2002) have labelled it, and what this might mean for social justice, democracy and the potential for transformational change in education. Being able to independently decode, filter, contextualize, analyse and critique media messages is, or I would argue, should be, a fundamental part of the educational process and experience.

In order to prepare students, there are two fundamental activities. The first involves a critical analysis of the local newspaper, in which students comb through every page and section to dissect how the news is organized, where it is placed, what is prioritized, how advertising is infused throughout, how equity, and, particularly, race are treated, and, lastly, attempting to determine the editorial content and orientation.

The second preparatory activity employs a similar critical analysis of a thirty-minute local nightly newscast. It is important to highlight that it is not considered consequential which station or evening is selected, as will be seen, since the mainstream news is presented, packaged, and developed in a similar way through-out the nation. In order to augment reflection and discussion afterwards, students are divided into five groups, each of which is asked to watch the news from one of the vantage points outlined below:

Figure 31. Critical Media Analysis Activity

<table>
<tr><td>

Group 1 – watch the news as you would normally;

Group 2 – watch the news to determine the political perspectives and nuances that are evident and/or implicit;

Group 3 – time the news, monitoring the flow, cadence and prioritization given to each segment;

Group 4 – observe how race (and identity) is a part of the newscast, including who is reporting on the news as well as what is reported on;

Group 5 – monitor how the newscasters and reporters present the news, from what angles and how.

</td></tr>
</table>

In both of these activities, students engaged in small group and, thereafter, plenary discussions. My role was to get students talking about the media together, after which a more layered, contextualized analysis was developed. An important part of the process is to debate diverse vantage points, aiming for a more nuanced critique of the media. It is helpful to undertake these preparatory activities without much background into the global economy of the media (McChesney, 2008), which then enhances the learning experience afterward.

This is the first time that many of the students will be looking at the media critically so the exercise of discovering for themselves, in a structured way, the impact, nature and formula of the media constitutes an important learning experience. It is necessary to stress that the objective is not to preach a certain, prescribed response or conclusion about the media but, rather, to expose students to a critical pedagogical approach to understanding the media, especially in relation to education, and, significantly, extending this to the implications for democracy (Dewey, 1916/1997; Herman & Chomsky, 2002; Freire, 1973/2005; McLaren, 2007; McChesney, 2008).

Toward the end of the course, students started to blog on the need for and existence of media literacy in education. Students were encouraged to structure a critical analysis, including the implications for education, and engage in dialog with their colleagues. This component of the course was extremely insightful and useful because it encouraged students to reflect on and interrogate the material and concepts covered together outside of the structures of the classroom environment. Several techniques aimed at critically analyzing the media or other phenomena were introduced in order to assist students as they undertake their media projects (Figure 31).

Figure 32. Types of Analysis to Critique the Media

- a *factor analysis*, stressing legal, economic, political, social, educational and other factors;
- a *stakeholder analysis*, seeking to understand issues from the diverse vantage points of different groups (for example, minorities, teachers, students, administrators);
- an *ideological analysis*, examining ideological considerations and principles underpinning issues and approaches;
- a *bias analysis*, illustrating how everyone has biases, and that social phenomena should not be approached neutrally; and
- a *power relation analysis*, elucidating how (inequitable) power relations are infused into the media and throughout decision-making processes.

The routine, seemingly natural experience of watching, reading and listening to the news is, therefore, the focal point of this academic exercise. One of the underlying motivations for this activity is to underscore how the media are not neutral, and, further, how the extremely selective and homogenized view of the world portrayed though the plethora of media outlets, despite the illusion of competition and diversity of opinion, can serve to constrain debate and political literacy (Winter, 2007). Similar, another key reason for undertaking this project is to emphasize the direct linkage to education, especially in relation to the entrenchment and reproduction of social and class relations as well as a viscerally ingrained patriotism as a result of a less-than-vibrant and culturally relevant mass media. The resultant connections to democracy, with the well-known narratives of "freedom of press" and "freedom of speech," therefore, hinge, to varying degrees, on the viability of the media to "hold the government to account" and to assist in providing a vehicle through which citizens can be empowered to achieve "liberty." The media literacy of teachers, and their students, then, becomes critical as it significantly influences the orientation and salience of reality, affecting the degree to which people are engaged and are able to contest hegemonic representations of what is considered to be in the collective interest of society, including wars, policies to deal with the environment, racism, and poverty, and the framing of the role of education in society (McChesney, 2008).

Methodology

The electronic discussions (or blog) through WebCT that students undertook in the last part of the course, which focus on the media and media literacy, are analyzed, generating several themes, trends, reflections and strategies. Students provided their consent to use their work on an anonymous basis, and their comments are provided as they were originally presented. All names attached to the narrative comments are pseudonyms.

In the state of Ohio, all teachers must complete a master's degree to maintain their certification. The students in these classes, who are teachers, are therefore largely representative of the general teaching population, as they are not a self-selected group that is pursuing graduate studies for purely academic reasons. Almost all of the teachers participating in this study are White, the majority of whom are female, with most of the sample coming from the regional area within close proximity to the university. Although there is a diverse ethnic demography in the sample, most are from working-class backgrounds.

It should be emphasized that, although I (the instructor) do have some definitive ideas about politics and education, my role was to facilitate, cultivate and provoke critical thinking around media literacy, and not to elicit a particular response. Rather, I view the notion of media (and political) literacy as a process, one that is strongly supported by the critical pedagogical approach, to become engaged and to seek to critically interrogate the meaning of identity, societal justice, politics, and (inequitable) power relations (Kincheloe, 2008b).

The actual sifting through the blogs, categorizing, organizing and developing themes is undertaken within the lens of a critical pedagogical framework (Kincheloe, 2008a; McLaren & Kincheloe, 2007), using the tools enunciated for a research *bricolage* (Tobin & Kincheloe, 2006), which calls for the blending of methodological approaches and vantage points. Similarly, within the qualitative methodological approach (Berg, 2007; Merriam, 1988; Schram, 2006), I analyzed the data from a range of perspectives, seeking to crystallize themes that resonate and speak clearly to subject matter explored. The research, inevitably, is aimed at bolstering media literacy, and is not meant to be judgmental of the particular identities, realities and experiences of the participants. Teasing out the meaning of the narratives provided by participants required a certain depth and range of knowledge and exposure to critical media literacy, which enables a more robust and critical assessment of the themes generated.

Findings

During our on-line discussions, students were asked to respond to the following question: Do we teach about and for media literacy in education? By this time, we have covered a certain number of issues, concepts and concerns in relation to the media, media literacy and media education, and students also became engaged in group projects that served to immerse themselves in critically assessing the media.

As eluded to earlier in this chapter, students become significantly more critical about their own implication in education as the course progressed to the role, effect and presence of the media in education. What follows are seven themes that emerged from the research:

Theme 1: Superficial Treatment of Media Literacy in Schools

Most of the students concurred that they felt that their particular school environments were not predisposed to a concerted effort to inculcate media literacy in the classroom. Several participants enunciated a common refrain, that efforts aimed at addressing the media were generally superficial.

> Although I might think that I am trying to teach students to understand media and question things that are going on around them, I'm not sure that they necessarily get that from my lessons. In most cases they are just trying to get done with whatever they are doing so that can move on to the next thing. We do look at different websites and talk about their validity or at different articles that are written in magazines and newspapers... but I'm not sure that they really understand why. So in my thoughts, some schools and teachers may be trying to implement the use of media literacy in their classrooms, (but) they just don't explain what it is to their students. (David)

> In my opinion, there is very little instruction about and for media literacy in schools. While some classes do receive newspapers to examine, how much classroom time is really available to analyze the newspaper's content critically? I do think students need to receive instruction about how the media operates, along with using critical thinking skills to decipher what motives are behind news presentations. (Joanne)

> I have found no evidence that my school supports teaching media literacy in school. Yes, it should and can be taught in school, but is it? ... Technology continues to influence how we teach and we have all too often heard the stories of media used by students in inappropriate ways.... Students need to understand beyond the fun and games how very serious the media is whether it is good or bad. (Suzanne)

Participants raise concerns here about how teachers may be out of step with the plurality of technologies and media that young people are exposed to and use. In highlighting how critical media literacy is not a common feature of the formal education experience, they are also raising issues about how school boards, departments of education and governments, in general, do not place a premium on media literacy at the same level as the standards, evaluation regimes and neo-liberal conceptual frameworks that are well known to educators.

Participants may have differed on the reasons for which media literacy was not taught in schools, but there was almost universal agreement that media literacy was not a focus of either the general or specific curriculum.

> Teachers are supposed to teach about media literacy in our schools but unfortunately this does not happen for various reasons. There is a great demand on the teacher's time, especially in preparing students for the standardized test to an extent that there is no time left for media literacy lessons. On the other hand, School district curriculum does not accommodate media literacy, as a subject matter to be taught is schools. (Nathan)

> I do not feel that we educate our youth very much about media literacy. Due to the fact that we are responsible for so many other concepts such as standardized tests, we have been ignorant toward teaching them about this topic. That certainly does not mean that it is not a significant topic, however. In my opinion, I think that we need to make a more collective effort to expose them to the current events that are taking shape in their local communities, their state, their country, and even the world. (Eugene)

The reality of a significant time constraint combined with a prescriptive, limited curriculum make it extremely difficult to engage students in meaningful media literacy activities and processes. Macdeo (2007) argues strongly that the "media represent a mechanism of ideological control," and the "disarticulation between what goes on in the classroom and socio-cultural, economic, and political realities that shape, guide, and determine the educational enterprise have led to a de facto construction of not seeing, proving once again the old proverb, 'The eyes do not see; they only record while the mind sees'" (p. xix).

Theme 2: The Media includes more than Traditional Outlets (Newspaper, Television, Radio)

Students became sensitized to the all-encompassing nature of the media, and started to view it as a force that is infused into and through education, either overtly or covertly, something that is not always acknowledged. For example, in addition to the traditional media outlets, such as the newspapers and the written press, television and the radio, today's educators must also now contend with myriad other forces, including the Internet, advertising, political messaging, and diverse forms of social organization. Therefore, it can be quite difficult to teach about media literacy simply because of the type of information it exposes our children to.

> The information presented in the news can be complicated all on its own; let alone the advertisements we have to deal with in order to get through media. No matter how the

> news is presented to our students, they will be subject to some form of advertisement....
> We as teachers need to be critical of the media findings we present. (Beverly)

> I do not believe that we teach students enough information on how to fully analyze and
> critique the media. Not every source is credible and students may have a hard time
> understanding that at a young age. Also, think of all the media advertisements that
> students are surrounded by on a daily basis. Almost everything we read, hear or listen to
> has some sort of hidden message on trying to shape who we are by telling us what to buy
> or how to dress. How are students supposed to be creative and unique individuals, when
> much of our media portrays how a person should look, feel and act? (John)

As Hoechsman (2006) underscores, young people are now engaged in social networking networks (sometimes referred to as Web 2.0), such as Facebook and MySpace, that are largely foreign to most teachers. Information travels quickly, and there is great potential for both engagement and alienation. At the same time, cyber-bullying is now a concern that did not exist a decade ago. Youth now make and disseminate their own media through YouTube video clips, blogs and Internet discussion groups. As noted in the participants' comments above, there is also significant concern about the effect of explicit and implicit advertising and marketing, which makes it imperative for teachers to be able to assist students in understanding the ramifications and potential harm they may cause if not examined critically. The predominance of pop-cultural manifestations—reality shows such as *American Idol*, *Survivor*, and *Do You Want to Be a Millionaire?*, and movie stars and musicians—flood the formal airwaves and educational space, creating the illusion that diverse representations of reality are insignificant. Educators need to be not only aware of this but also prepared and encouraged to engage students in deconstructing how the media plays a role in propagating certain (sur)realities, which may be detrimental to minority and marginalized voices, and also reinforce stereotypes and inequitable power relations without critical interrogation (Macedo & Steinberg, 2007).

Theme 3: The Corporate Infiltration in the Mass Media

The concern over the corporate domination of the media was a common theme highlighted by students, and many commented that they were previously unaware of how much of media is infused with corporate messages and control. This led to some interesting discussions about how the media may be dissuaded from, or timid about, examining certain issues, policies, products and/or personalities owing to corporate oversight. Participants critiqued the corporate sector in how it buttresses, shapes and "manufactures" the reality generated and espoused by the mass media. This corporatization has myriad implications for how schools address the media, and also for how teachers and students understand and are able to dig under, around and between the messages generated for mass consumption.

> Corporations gain the opportunity to promote their product by using the media communications in schools. Schools use the items with the companies' logos as incentives for activities and special events and teachers use them as part of their curriculum to motivate students. In other words, schools and teachers get free give always and the company gets and easy and cheaper way of marketing their company and the products. (Jack)

> Personally, I watched Channel One every morning from 1993–1997 and yet I feel I was totally illiterate to what was taking place around the world.   As an educator I feel to improve our media illiteracy is not only to watch Channel One but also to read newspapers, watch other news channels and take time to discuss and have assignments on what we view in the media. (Sandra)

These comments highlight the direct, yet what some might consider necessary, infusion of the corporate sector into the classroom. Within the neo-liberal sphere of contemporary education (Hill, 2008), schools need to look elsewhere for basic funding, beyond the scope of the State, thus exposing the obvious inequalities between schools and districts. What schools receive the contracts, and what are the stipulations? Can educators critique these contracts that provide schools with football stadiums, uniforms and equipment but not necessarily any enhancements to teacher salaries, service learning, and educational materials, etc.? The news that is funnelled into the classroom, replete with commercials, can have a deleterious effect on the educational experience of young people as well as an obvious societal impact of not cultivating a politically literate populace.

Theme 4: The Omni-presence of (Neo-liberal) Standards Overrides Media Literacy

Another hindrance to media literacy pertains to having the relevant and appropriate media resources available to educators. Given the over-arching framework of neo-liberal reforms, which privilege standardized testing, currricula and outcomes, critical media literacy, or even just a moderate approach to critiquing the media, may be considered too lightweight and superfluous to find a place within the formal educational program.

> In my district, I am not allowed to read the newspaper or even have it out in my room during the day. The principal does not want students or teachers looking at it during the school day because it will take away from the learning time that students need to spend on OGT standards. (David)

> Why isn't media literacy a mainstay of US education? The answer is complicated, but a major obstacle to media literacy is simply that Americans generally don't see the media as an important influence on our lives. With budget crises, testing, and the need to teach basic skills, many educators see media literacy as a waste of resources. But there are many compelling reasons to include media literacy programs in the schools. However, convincing those that control the educational process of its importance is another story. (Gene)

Another specific concern, and perhaps a reticence, about teaching for and about media literacy is the overarching mission of education, which can coalesce into a quasi-obsession at some levels, to generate certain learning outcomes aimed at meeting the "standards."

> And there it is again, standardized curriculums are not critical thinking skill oriented. In order to function in our democratic society, citizens need to be able to analyze media reports as to the motive that fuels them. With so much emphasis on test scores and teaching content for the test, little time is left to teach about media literacy. In order to make good decisions based on what the media presents, media literacy needs to be a part of a student's education. (Joanne)

> Teachers are supposed to teach about media literacy in our schools but unfortunately this does not happen for various reasons. There is a great demand on the teacher's time, especially in preparing students for the standardized test to an extent that there is no time left for media literacy lessons. On the other hand, School district curriculum does not accommodate media literacy as a subject matter to be taught is schools. (Nathan)

> As with teaching everything else, media literacy is another bystander that gets pushed to the side by the demands to teach ONLY the curriculum.... as educators we need to take time to ensure that our students understand the difference between the "good life" and real life and how to pick out and critique the news they are presented with. (Cynthia)

These comments underscore the stark difference between the formal and informal (hidden) curriculum; and addressing the former only will certainly have a negligible effect on the latter (Kincheloe, 2008a). Students are exposed to a broad and never-ending range of mass media images, messages and content that can be influential in how they construct their identities, experiences and perspectives, which, if left unchecked, can diminish the attachment that they may have to democracy and their own involvement in society.

Theme 5. Media Literacy Needs to be Approached from Multiple Vantage Points

The debate over media literacy, ultimately, needs to involve a range of sectors, stakeholders and interests, and should not be isolated to a single course or teacher.

While there seems to be strong agreement around the need to teach for and about media literacy, participants in this research argued for a broader level of political literacy in order to engage students as a means of enhancing a critical awareness of the media. As is the case when thinking about social justice and democracy, media literacy can, and should, be incorporated into, and interwoven throughout, the educational experience. It is interesting to note that participants suggested many innovative ways to approach media literacy.

> I don't believe that we as educators really do teach about media literacy in our class rooms today. I guess in this fast-paced, digital world in which we teach and live, how much of this "stuff" do we as teachers really understand? Let's face it, our students (or at least a great majority of them) are more technologically savvy than we are. What a great learning opportunity, whereby the tables are turned and the students can now teach the teachers. But media literacy is more than being able to use the latest technology to access information, it is how you critique and analyze the information for making sound, wise judgments? Media literacy would serve as a great opportunity for Language Arts and Social Studies teachers to get together and team teach concepts which would help our students to become better informed citizens and provide them with opportunities to become better critical thinkers. (Jordan)

> Media by definition is the form of communication used to influence a wide amount of people. Literacy is being able to read or write. Media literacy is the ability to read and discern the communication that you are presented. I now see the importance of empowering my students to be their own person and think for themselves. I use music as a vehicle to teach media literacy because often times young people are influenced by the music they allow themselves to be engrossed in because of the superstar that they see daily on television. I ask them what type of music they listen to and why. The majority of them listen to RAP, rhythm and poetry, and R & B, Rhythm and Blues. I do not condemn them for what they listen to but I do have them listen to the words of the songs and tell me what the writer was trying to get across. After studying the lyrics they are shocked to see what they allowed themselves to digest in their minds. After doing this activity, I find that students are more critical in their thinking pattern when observing the news, videos, music, books, etc. (Anthony)

> English class always seems like the gateway to address the media, but other core content subjects can easily contribute to teaching media literacy. Social studies can tie in current events as well as comparing and contrasting news around the world. Science can use the news to discuss environmental changes taking place, the weather patterns and reading weather maps. Math on the other hand can be a little more challenging, but even in math class the students need to learn about the misleading graphs and data analysis represented by corporations in order to get you to buy their products. Even though teaching media literacy may not be a large topic of interest in schools, it can and should be incorporated into the curriculum when possible. (Angie)

In other words, any subject can (and should) be addressed from a critical vantage point, thus augmenting the teaching and learning from a range of perspectives and lived experiences (Banks, 2008; Gorski, 2008). Macedo (2007) warns that not confronting that problematic nature of bias and propaganda can lead to the perpetuation of grave injustices and catastrophe, thus strongly making the case for confronting patriotism. While acknowledging that media literacy should not be marginalized to a single area, discipline or educator, it is equally important to ensure that educators know how to teach, and are engaged in the process, about and for media literacy, which requires training, materials, support and a critical thinking framework to provide teachers with concepts, principles and strategies to teach about the media in a critical way.

Theme 6: The Marginalization of Diverse Groups in the Mass Media

The final media projects that students completed, in particular, emphasized how racial minorities were visibly marginalized in the content and presentation of the mass media news. They discovered, through their projects, that newscasters, journalists, analysts, and others of importance in delivering the news were largely White, although, at certain times, there might be a small number of minority people, especially on weekends and later at night. The concern is not only about who is packaging the news but, more importantly, who decides on what stories and angles will be covered.

> Media can actually shape a culture or possibly your view concerning a culture or a people. For some time now, the media has presented African Americans as people who are criminals, people who are slaves, and people who are dropouts or possibly video girls. The media has presented young African American children the false reality of becoming millionaires overnight by challenging them to become rap stars or famous athletes. It is sad that the media does not advertise youth excellence as much in the black community. In the school where I teach, I now see the importance of making my students aware of the options that they have in choosing their destiny. (Anthony)

As exemplified above, and this came through in class discussions, the media can be extremely disempowering for some individuals and groups, who are either routinely omitted or portrayed as not being a full part of society (for example, the overrepresentation of African-Americans in crime and sports stories). An important realization for participants is the demystification of what Winter (2007) terms as the "myth of competition" and the "cult of objectivity." In essence, minorities are often stigmatized and marginalized under the guise of an open flow of ideas and "fair and balanced" (the moniker of FOX News) reporting in spite of the mass media being tightly controlled by special interests that are generally disinterested in social justice. Therefore, educators need to be vigilant about not engaging in critical media literacy, as avoidance to do so may reinforce disengagement and vilification of the "other."

Theme 7: The Effect of the Course on Media Literacy

One of the areas of interest in this research, apart from attempting to understand how educators perceive and work with media literacy in education, is to determine if a university course focused on media literacy can have an impact on educators' conceptualization of, and engagement with, media literacy. Although it is not possible at this time to gage how participants are actually using what they have learned, it is fair to note that, in general, all participants experienced change in their attitudes and commitment to media literacy as a result of the process of critical reflection and interrogation. It is equally unclear if this change, if that is what has occurred, will it be sustainable, meaningful, and of a critical nature. Many found the experience to be enlightening, as they had not considered the media in a critical manner before. For some, the deconstruction of the media, which involved trying to understand propaganda, bias, corporate control and the editorial hegemony exercised by a small group of interests, led to discomfort as it altered the conceptualization of society. The process could, therefore, be empowering in some cases.

> Personally, I have never put much thought into what I watched on television or heard on the radio before this course. The media was just entertainment or a way to pacify time. Now, I am looking more critically about how ads are portrayed and trying to figure out the messages that are being sent. I do not think that in education there is a strong urge to deal with media literacy. It is something that should be more important, but at the same time we need to teach educators about media literacy before they can pass on this knowledge to the students that they teach. Also, from this course I am definitely more in tune to what the media is showing and I see the effects that it could potentially have on children, but I also strongly feel that no matter what is shown on television it ultimately comes down to parenting and how you raise your children. (Melissa)

> After taking this class, I have realized that our educational system is lacking in teaching for media literacy. Most of us are focused on standards and how to fit everything else in that is expected of us. ... we do not take the time that is needed to really have students critically think or analyze the media. Partially, I feel that we were never taught this way and this class has been an eye opening experience to the different vantage points that certain media sources can take. On the other hand, as teachers, when teaching for media literacy, we must be careful to not persuade our students according to our viewpoints but to teach

them how to make an educated decision after researching many sources. ... As a high school student, the teachers really never made an effort to help us connect to the news or to inspire us to question what was being said. Maybe they felt that if we began to question the news we would begin to question their ways as well. (Julia)

As educators we must do our best to promote media literacy in our students by making them aware of how to analyze and critically think for themselves. Honestly, before taking this class I wasn't even aware of how much of the media is very straightforward and simplistic. Students need to be taught that not all vantage points are normally discussed in the media and therefore students have to be like detectives, in a sense that they must do their own researching and investigating to really understand what is going on in our world. (Maria)

While participants appear to feel that focused exposure to critical media literacy, as was the case in the course framing this research, is beneficial at many levels, they also exhibit apprehension owing to the structure and neo-liberal framework in education. A common question, therefore, is: how do you teach about and for media literacy when there doesn't seem to be the required (institutional) support to do so (Carr, 2008a)? A connected area of concern pertains to the notion of being perceived as impartial or doctrinaire, which seems to be overwhelming for many educators. Educators must feel a certain comfort in how they address controversial issues, and also how they understand the notions of bias, propaganda and power (Brinkley, 1999; Claire & Holden, 2007). There is, or I contend should, not be any shame in acknowledging that not only may we not have all the answers but, importantly, that knowledge is constructed (Kincheloe, 2008b). This notion underpins my formulation, as enunciated in the first section, of a *democratic* critical pedagogy.

Connecting Media Literacy to Critical Pedagogy

There has been an explosion of corporatist imperatives and practices launched in K-12 schools and education faculties in the US and other countries. The focus on the US is important because how Americans understand, construct, critique and engage in and with the media will have an effect on the international community, given the political, economic, cultural and hegemony that has been manifest since the Second World War. Developing a coherent media literacy curriculum in educational institutions at all levels has, therefore, been difficult to achieve. Notwithstanding, educators have been able to access several key sources to find fissures in the corporatist status quo, which has allowed them to understand how the mass media influences events in their lived worlds. The events unfolding in diverse social and economic contexts require a more critical interrogation in order to understand the impact of various "teaching machines," such as advertisements, film, television programs, video games, the Internet, music and toys in relation to youths' understanding of self and relationship with the "Other." This is fundamental to understanding the meaning, depth and power relations inherent in a multicultural society. Therefore, initiating critical media projects and experiences aimed at eliminating entrenched social inequalities, such as racism, sexism, classism, and homophobia, overshadowing the celebratory aspect of intercultural or multicultural relations and awareness, should be an important concern for schoolteachers, concerned citizens and social activists.

Several critical scholar-practitioners have influenced numerous pre-service and in-service teachers as well as teacher educators with their theoretical insights and empirical projects aimed at bringing awareness to how social, political and economic forces shape the mass media. Conversely, these critical pedagogues also demonstrate how media culture is often complicit in perpetuating injustice and oppression in schools and in society (Macedo & Steinberg, 2007). Other scholars and educators have been instrumental in documenting how teachers can harness the cultural texts that their students consume, such as music, video games, advertisements, and television programs, in order to nudge them to recognize, often for the first time, injustice and marginalization (Wishart Leard & Lashua, 2006).

There is still much to be done to make media literacy a critical centerpiece in promoting a culturally relevant education. A critical pedagogy that helps students make sense of their lived realities in a society that often privileges individualism and materialism over the imperatives of social justice, critical thinking, equity, and democracy needs to be considered (Carr & Lund, 2008; Porfilio & Carr 2008a). Torres and Mercado's (2006) call for teacher-educators to team up with schoolteachers and other concerned citizens to develop a common critical literacy curriculum for schools of education would seem to be a logical and necessary step in the quest for a more critical (media) pedagogy. Accreditation bodies that focus only on functional literary skills for youths, which may prepare them to become compliant workers rather than enlightened individuals who are capable, as suggested by Freire, of reading the "word and the world," must be critiqued. To this end, the common denominator of the unprecedented level of corporate control over knowledge production in schools, in the mass media, and other social institutions must be considered (Carr & Lund, 2008; Chomsky, 2008b; Porfilio & Malott, 2008; Torres and Mercado, 2006). In sum, a common critical literacy curriculum could ensure that media literacy does not become an appendage to the aforementioned functional, corporatist literacy movement.

According to Livingstone (2004), the form of media proposed by functional literacy proponents is designed to equip youths with skills to use particular pieces of technology, as teachers train them to "access, analyze and evaluate" new media. However, providing individuals these skills will not necessarily link media literacy to critical multicultural education. This curriculum is also designed to guide social actors to detect how the mass media are complicit in perpetuating asymmetrical institutional arrangements, which seeks to explicitly and implicitly address social justice concerns (Flores-Koulish 2006; Kincheloe 2008). There is also a dire need to show current teachers, administrators and caregivers the relevancy of incorporating critical media literacy into K-12 schools.

There are a number progressive organizations and alternative media sources dedicated to promoting critical media literacy. For instance, *Rethinking Schools Online* provides teachers, caregivers, and teacher-educators with information on several non-profit organizations designed to pinpoint how corporate agendas are infiltrating Western political, economic and educational policies, which, collectively, have an effect on developing countries. There are numerous media literacy projects and networks, which have formed over the past twenty years, to promote educational conferences, highlight professional development opportunities, and to share media literacy initiatives with concerned citizens and educators, such as: *The Association for Media Literacy, Media Awareness Network*, the *New Mexico Literacy Project, Center for Media Literacy*, and *About-Face*. The content and approach may vary from jurisdiction to jurisdiction, and a deep examination of how the media obfuscates social justice and inequitable power relations may not immediately occur in K–12 classrooms or in schools of education on a broad scale, but it is important to underscore that there is an increasing concern about how to understand the media. The connection to the social justice component within a multicultural society is clear and inextricable.

Discussion

This research raises a number of questions about the contemporary state of education, which, undoubtedly, connect with the potential for transformation within a context of neo-liberal reforms (Hill, 2008). If there is a tendency for teachers to not be overly engaged in, or exposed to, media literacy, it is important to understand the degree to which this is facilitated and codified by the overarching framework of neo-liberalism, which has de-emphasized social justice to the behest of employability, the marketplace and a pedagogical regime aimed at meeting established standards. The importance of infusing more relevant and critical media literacy into the education experience was flagged by virtually all of the participants in this study.

The debilitating discourses and narratives that numb, mollify and obfuscate youth culture are designed to help the elite forces gain the public's consent to implement policies and practices that concentrate wealth and power. For instance, many large corporations have continually characterized urban youths as aberrant, violent, dim-witted, and lazy so as to convince the public that youths are not deserving of social entitlements, such as health care, public education, and housing (Giroux, 2005a). Rather than having the state provide social support for our children, most voters in the United States (of the roughly 50–60% who actually participate in elections) have willingly or unwillingly endorsed neo-liberal ideologies, which allow these transnational corporations to implement policies that hold youths accountable for their "transgressions." For instance, most of the public has opted to have corporations implement "kill and drill" teaching strategies and standardized forms of assessment, advertise and sell their products to children in exchange for providing schools with a small pool of resources, and fold in zero-tolerance policies, security equipment, and private security guards to quell the growing spate of youth violence committed in schools (Casella, 2008; Kozol, 2005; Giroux, 2004). This happens rather than supporting policies aimed at improving youths' educational performance and fostering their social development, such as providing resources to repair crumbling school facilities and purchasing textbooks and technology, hiring qualified teachers, reducing classroom size, providing quality preschool education for all learners, and designing curricula that focus on promoting critical thinking skills, building community, eliminating hate, and focusing on peace and social justice. Media literacy is sadly lacking in the classroom, in general, which raises concerns about how students will become actively and critically engaged in democracy (Carr, 2008a).

Hoechsmann (2006) reminds us that "the best education is dialogic and foregrounds the background and experience of the learner" (p. 34), thus making the case for a more critical engagement on the part of educators, who may not be in touch with the diverse media exposure that youths are exposed to. He also stresses the importance of educators being immersed in the actual development of media: "Media educators do need to have the conceptual tools to undertake analysis and interpretation of media texts and the sources of media production. As well, media educators increasingly need to have the capacity to produce media of all types though the interesting wrinkle that has emerged as new technologies became cheaper and more accessible is that learners across multiple spectrums began to come into media education settings with adequate or better knowledge bases in production" (p. 34).

This enhanced engagement with media literacy links to political literacy, which underscores the political nature of education (Freire, 2005). Critical pedagogy offers a conceptual framework to think through the process of critical engagement in relation to the media in education (Kincheloe, 2008). There are several concerns here that, collectively, participants have enunciated as requiring attention (see Figure 32).

This study also speaks of the importance of culture and identity in relation to the media. Since the media is everywhere, and is infused into people's daily lives, it is imperative that educators are aware of who is included and excluded. In other words, if a critical media literacy approach is not advocated, it is likely that rampant stereotypes in the media about, for example, African-Americans, Hispanics and Aboriginal peoples (American Indians) will be perpetuated largely unchecked. The marginalization of diverse groups and peoples would be further entrenched given the absence of a politically literate and engaged populace. White power and privilege, which has been gratuitously presented as the norm in society through the media, and by extension in education, should be understood through the lens of a critical pedagogical approach to media literacy (Carr & Lund, 2007).

Lastly, it is important to emphasize that media literacy is not about a lesson plan, a list or menu of options, a resource or an individual event or personality. Rather, media literacy is about a process of engagement, one that offers the opportunity for reflection, interrogation and debate (Macedo and Steinberg, 2007). While there is a definite formal component required for media literacy in education (i.e., standards, curriculum, resources, the requirement to teach the subject, etc.), as per the main principles of critical pedagogy (Kincheloe, 2008), the more fundamental aspect of media literacy pertains to the commitment to, and process of, personal and collective critical engagement. To teach about and for democracy (or "radical democracy," as Kellner and Share label it), anti-racism, social justice and citizenship, the formal structure and requirements will only go so far. To have a meaningful impact, there needs to be a more comprehensive and broad-based approach to critiquing the shape, form and meaning of education, and media literacy, bolstered by educators who are willing to be innovative, critical and cognizant of inequities and power relations, can be a significant enhancement to the education of all parties involved.

Figure 33. Concerns Emanating from Research on Media Literacy

- how teachers are trained, certified, and supported in their quest to be media literate;
- the absence of a clear and relevant conceptual framework in education that creates the conditions and impetus to undertake media literacy in schools;
- if standards, high-stakes tests and other barometers of the neo-liberal reform period continue to rule the day, it would be important to, at the very least, develop and require the usage of specific standards and outcomes related to media literacy, the absence of which will further perpetuate the myth that this is an add-on or supplementary concern only;
- a support network and curriculum base from which teachers could draw on appropriate resources, activities, strategies and evaluation measures to formalize the media literacy experience in schools is needed;
- students, as exemplified in the educational experiences of the participants, are not generally afforded an educational experience that fully and freely acknowledges political and media literacy, which can be a significant impediment to creating a more robust and critical educational experience;
- the media plays a significant role in defining the youth educational and cultural experience, and to omit or diminish a concerted effort at media literacy in schools would have the effect of, ultimately, working against the interests of an engaged and productive citizenry which will be called on to make decisions about social justice, war, poverty, and the fabric of democracy (Lund & Carr, 2008a; Westheimer, 2006).

Many things can be done to counter the trend of not critically assessing the influence of the media. Various standards and reforms should include guidelines for media literacy, and the curriculum should be more focused on the qualitative experience of understanding and critiquing the media, in addition to producing and constructing media and technological-based projects that strive to be more connected to the diversity of youth experiences. Literacy should not be evaluated and understood in narrow terms but should embrace a more holistic, critical vantage point (Kincheloe, 2008a, 2008b; Provenzo, 2005). Educators, including in teacher-education programs, should be resourced, trained and encouraged to become critically engaged, meaning that alternative vantage points, methods, strategies, assessments, and experiences should become part of the educational journey. Ultimately, a critical examination of democracy, one that extends well beyond elections (Lund & Carr, 2008), should become a part of the renewed vision for media literacy, with a sharpened view on the youth experience, one that challenges subservience, consumerism, and patriotism (Westheminer, 2006a).

Chapter 12

"Shocked and Awed" Into and Out of Democracy: Can There Be War and Democracy Simultaneously?[1]

Dialog, as essential communication, must underlie any cooperation. In the theory of dialogical action, there is no place for conquering the people on behalf of the revolutionary cause, but only for gaining their adherence. Dialog does not impose, does not manipulate, does not domesticate, does not "sloganize." This does not mean, however, that the theory of dialogical action leads nowhere; nor does it mean that the dialogical human does not have a clear idea of what she wants, or of the objectives to which she is committed. (Freire, 1973/2005: p. 168)

Introduction

"Shock and Awe" is the celebrated expression used to characterize the initiation of the American invasion in Iraq, a spectacular show of force and strength that lit up the sky like a fireworks extravaganza (Altheide, 2009). As the incessant bombing rained down on Baghdad, media commentators repeated the mantra of "shock and awe" as if this were a natural and appropriate depiction of the destruction caused on the ground from the thousands of sorties being skilfully orchestrated with laser precision from above. Kellner (2004) highlights that embedded journalists and the proclivity to avoid showing the real horror of the assault, combined with censorship, propaganda and editorialization tethered to a patriotic narrative, served to further silence the American public. Hammering the Iraqi capital with hi-tech guided missiles and sophisticated weaponry was portrayed in the media as a necessary action. The military enterprise, exemplified by "shock and awe," is devastating at several levels.

One extremely relevant factor in this scenario is the absence of concern and attention paid to the environment in times of war. Is the environment a consideration during military conflicts? How do the media cover the environmental impact of war? Who is most affected by the militarization of the environment? What are the consequences of environmental war? It is somewhat ironic that the issue of global warming has become a priority internationally at the United Nations and in most countries around the world, yet there is little scrutiny of the environmental destruction caused by war. The ways that the mainstream media have covered the military invasion into Iraq exemplifies word tricks, propagandistic techniques, "a rhetoric of deceit and deception," the obfuscation of the truth, a manipulative blurring of a panoply of those outside hegemonic circles to equate terrorism, and a limited portrayal of reality, all of which serves to boost further patriotic hegemony (Engels, 2007; Goodall, 2008; Gordon, Smyth & Diehl, 2008; Ivie, 2005)

One theme suggested in this chapter is that marginalized peoples, whether they are in developing countries, such as Iraq, Lebanon, Angola, Rwanda, Vietnam, or Nicaragua, or in developed countries, are disproportionately affected by environmental destruction. Differential power relations determine how the environment is to be treated within war situations, and this is also true when considering resource allocation within countries that are not directly affected by local military conflict. Within the United States, for example, the vast majority of toxic waste sites are located in lower-income, minority neighbourhoods, leading to untold health, social, and economic problems. Another example is the Hurricane Katrina tragedy in New Orleans, which was largely foreseeable, given the debate in Congress concerning levies two years earlier; the tragedy only became formalized as a priority once international and national attention uncovered the racialization of poverty in the light of the political commitment by the US government, whose military investment in Iraq did not allow for a proactive, effective deployment of resources.

This chapter will, therefore, discuss the far-reaching impact on marginalized groups in times of environmental destruction, who are more vulnerable, owing to the neo-liberal drive to maintain power and profits. War is never rational, nor proportionate. It is difficult to fully comprehend the simplistic leitmotif of war having a moral fibre or that it will determine the "winners and losers." With such death, injury, scarring, torture, hatred and ideological dementia, some might conclude that there can only be losers. Some estimates, for example, place the death toll in Iraq (since the US invasion) at 1,000,000; the religious conflict and civil war caused by the military intervention does not appear close to being extinguished. The official claims that the United States could not simply "cut and run" are, therefore, somewhat incomprehensible, especially to those who have directly been affected by the loss of life, property, security, livelihood, and their environment. War, it has been argued, especially in light of the Vietnam War, cannot be won on military might alone; as Victor Hugo said, "An idea is more powerful than all of the armies of the world." The internationalization of the impact of war on the social and physical environments is ultimately considered, if at all, long after the military decisions have been implemented. The patriotic fervor buttressing the US military campaign in Iraq could be attributed to the reaction to the returning troops during the Vietnam War in the 1960s and 1970s. People are extremely careful to emphasize that it is necessary to "support the troops," which seems to be a prominent feature on automobiles throughout the United States in the form of magnetic ribbon-shaped decals.

The general reticence to debate the Iraq conflict and war in public education denotes an obvious malaise in society and also a long-term threat to democracy and social justice (Altheide, 2009). If young people are not engaged in their formative years, society will be at a deficit to understand and challenge decision making and power later on (Westheimer & Kahne, 2004). The connection to education is key in that war, conflict, strife, famine, poverty, and problems at an international level always have a local connection, illustrating the interdependence between developed and developing countries (Lund & Carr, 2008a). The average person may not consider that there is a strong link between actions of her or his government abroad and at home, but the visible, tangible manifestations of these actions—immigration, migration, employment dislocation, economic fluctuation, access to resources, armed conflict, terrorism, and ecological shifts—demonstrate both the need to become engaged and the pertinence of political literacy (Chomsky, 2008a).

Environmental and human destruction caused by military action

The Vietnam War, which ended some thirty years ago, provides evidence of sustained damage to the environment at several levels. A significant part of the environmental destruction caused by war in Vietnam concerns the US program of blanketing the local topography with millions of tons of chemical spray, known as Agent Orange, which ravaged forests and contaminated the landscape for generations to come. The loss of trees, arable land, foodstuffs, livestock, and medicinal products cannot be quantified in simple economic terms. The Peace Pledge Union provides a detailed description of the damage caused by chemical weapons: people exposed to the spray suffered headaches, vomiting, diarrhoea, weakness and chest complaints. Meanwhile, Agent Orange's carcinogenic dioxin was sinking into the soil, washing into the sea, and entering the food chain, where it is still at work today. Children born since the war have consumed high levels of dioxin, and many fathered by men exposed to the spray (many of whom are now dead or suffering from cancers) have spina bifida and other congenital abnormalities. The latent social, health and psychological effects of Agent Orange linger on in the Vietnamese population as well as those American soldiers exposed to the chemical.

It is somewhat paradoxical that one of the key motivations to invading Iraq was that the Iraqi leader had used chemical weapons within his own territory. Where did he get these weapons, and why was he not stopped by the United States at that time from using them? To what degree did the fact that Iraq was considered an ally against Iran during its bloody eight-year war in the 1980s influence the level of criticism of its militarization? With over one million deaths, tens of thousands murdered by chemical weapons, a plethora of countries involved in supplying the warring countries (Iraq and Iran) with armaments, and an undeniable destruction of the environment, why was there no public, formal denunciation by the United States at that time of Saddam Hussein's despotic dictatorship? This trend of supporting despots when they are "our despots" haunts human history, and raises questions about the fundamental reasons for armed conflict.

Information for Action (undated) estimates that there are between 60 and 110 million landmines presently in areas where conflict has taken place, and, significantly, that approximately 30,000 people die or are maimed annually from exposure to these weapons, with a far greater number of animals being affected. Wildlife and livestock are common causalities of landmine explosions. There have been reports of antelopes and elephants killed by landmines during the civil war in Angola. Elephants have also been killed by landmines planted along the border between Burma and Bangladesh. Brown bears were killed by landmines in Bosnia and Croatia. Native tigers are threatened by landmines in Cambodia. In Tibet, rare species of clouded leopard, barking deer, snow leopard, and Royal Bengal tiger have been reported as casualties of landmines—either maimed or killed. In the Congo Democratic Republic, rebel forces tested some fields for the presence of landmines by herding cattle across them. The hundreds of thousands of landmines planted in Vietnam, Laos, and Kampuchea have terrorized local populations, rendering untold numbers of civilians maimed and permanently disabled, as well as decimating the arable and cultivable land, infusing it with toxicity. Clearing the landmines has proven to be an extremely costly, problematic, and challenging task, one that involves inherent risks. Campaigns to remove landmines in Angola, after years of civil war and agitation from South Africa, and in Lebanon, after the recent Israeli invasion in that country, demonstrate how this work is not fully supported by the international community, receiving sporadic injections of resources and media attention but never becoming the priority required to ensure that local populations can freely access their environment without fear. One estimate is that the removal of a landmine costs more than thirty times the cost of the weaponry. Once the conflict is over, the war continues because the environment is seething with the potential to harm local populations.

The negligible value of natural resources

During the Iraq war in 1991, as reported by the World Resources Institute, Iraqi forces ignited some 600 oil wells, causing a long-term environmental catastrophe: Oil spilled into the Persian Gulf, tarred beaches and killed more than 25,000 birds. Scientists predict the toxic residue will continue to affect fisheries in the Gulf for over 100 years. Oil spilled on land formed huge pools in lowlands, covering fertile croplands. The deposition of oil, soot, sulphur, and acid rain on croplands up to 1,200 miles in all directions from the oil fires turned fields untillable and led to food shortages. The fires released nearly half a billion tons of carbon dioxide, the leading cause of global warming, emissions greater than all but the eight largest polluting countries for 1991 that will remain in the atmosphere for more than a century. The oil that did not burn in the fires traveled on the wind in the form of nearly invisible droplets resulting in an oil mist or fog that poisoned trees and grazing sheep, contaminated fresh water supplies, and found refuge in the lungs of people and animals throughout the Gulf. Perhaps the most dangerous example of the armaments industry in relation to destroying the environment concerns nuclear bombs. According to the Peace Pledge Union:

> Nuclear waste is a global problem that won't go away, threatening environmental disaster on a vast scale: its poison, and toxic chemicals which accompany all weapon production, have travelled round the globe in the atmosphere and ocean currents as well as water and air, they harm earth, plants that grow in it, and subsistent livestock and wildlife. Human exposure to nuclear and chemical tests and factories, or via the food chain, results in miscarriages, malformed foetuses, high infant mortality and congenital disorders, leukaemia and other cancers, tumours, thyroid disorders, and complex debilitating and life-shortening syndromes.

During the nuclear arms race, in which the United States and the former Soviet Union were locked into what seems like an incredulous demonstration of fatalism, each country built a nuclear arsenal that could destroy the world hundreds of times over. The manufacturing of these weapons involves a range of risks, and the handling, maintenance, and disposal of materials related to nuclear arms has considerably damaged the environment. Radioactive waste has become a substantial concern for the international community in light of the very public testimony concerning a Russian submarine that sunk in 2000 containing extremely hazardous weaponry. Less known is that there has been a series of mishaps involving nuclear submarines since their proliferation in the 1960s, although much of the information documenting the gravity of the destruction has never been released by official bodies.

The military labelling of killing and destruction that is unintentional is often referred to as "collateral damage." This does not necessarily include environmental concerns, and collateral damage is usually only considered when there is intense media scrutiny. The coverage of "accidental" deaths and destruction detracts from the mission of winning the war, can be considered anti-patriotic, thus raising questions about the effectiveness of war to proverbially "win the hearts and minds" of the opposition. Conquering others because they are not democratic, a common refrain in the Iraq War as well as many others since the ending of World War II, is rife with contradictions and potential for long-term stability.

The disproportionate impact against marginalized groups

The militarization of the environment also means that people in conflict zones are vulnerable to the long-term effects of being isolated. It is not uncommon, for example, for people to deplete the indispensable foliage of forests to be used for cooking oil, heat, and building materials. With the elimination of the forest comes a host of problems affecting the bio-diversity of local and global contexts, serious erosion of the earth (as exemplified by Haiti), which further compounds problems related to housing and potable water as well as the quality of air in the local environment. Similarly, the displacement and mass migration of people fleeing conflicts hampers the local environment by endangering wildlife and changing living patterns in often previously under-populated areas. According to Ecology News (2007), environmental war can be defined as: [1] the intentional modification of a system of the natural ecology, such climate and weather, earth systems such as the ionosphere, magnetosphere, tectonic plate system, and/or the triggering of seismic events (earthquakes), [2] to cause intentional physical, economic, and psycho-social, and physical destruction to an intended target geophysical or population location, (and) [3] part of strategic or tactical war.

The Rio Declaration on Environment and Development in 1992 formally condemned the environmental destruction caused by military conflict: "warfare is inherently destructive of sustainable development. States shall therefore respect international law providing protection for the environment in times of armed conflict and cooperate in its further development, as necessary." Some fifteen years earlier, the United Nations Treaty against Modification of the Environment prohibited environmental war, yet weapons have continually been developed that threaten the world's ecology. Interestingly, despite the organized efforts of nongovernmental organizations, weapons developed to destroy the environment, either directly or indirectly, are often conceived and used in covert ways. Although international law prohibits harm to the environment, legal protocols, instruments, conventions, and processes have been extremely difficult to enforce.

Tara Weinstein (2005) points out that no state has ever been prosecuted for environmental war crimes, "The reasons range from the political problem of holding victors and their vanquished opponents responsible for the same actions to the prosecutorial barriers embedded in environmental war crime statutes, and from the values of the international community to the potential for environmental crimes to be overshadowed by other atrocities." Weinstein further elaborates an intricate argument on how international law works, and how it might be used to prosecute those guilty of "eco-terrorism" and environmental crimes against humanity.

The question of accountability and responsibility is paramount when considering the pursuit of environmental war crimes offenders. Would only the losing countries be prosecuted? How is destruction measured, and by whom? Could global warming, at the very least partially, be considered an environmental war crime? Can developing countries, without the same level of resources as developed countries, be held to the same standard, especially when considering the types of weapons and strategies available to the latter? With the advent of increasingly sophisticated war technology, it is quite conceivable the future military conflicts will involve more insidious mechanisms for destroying the environment, including contaminating water sources, infecting agricultural stocks, and poisoning the environment. It is telling that many countries, including the United States, maintain substantial reserves of chemical weapons, which are problematic to control and dispose of, as is the case for nuclear weapons and the uranium they contain.

An important consideration, therefore, in the discussion on environmental war is the disproportionate impact toward marginalized groups, principally minorities, and the poor. The elite class in most conflicts is able to flee before significant damage is inflicted, or is able to buy their way out of intolerable conditions. Moreover, they often have contacts, linkages, and networks established in developed countries that are able to facilitate their non-implication in hostilities. In many cases, the economic and political elites may already have vast sums of money placed outside of their countries once conflicts commence. It is important to caution, however, that there is no reason to believe that these elites desire or promote the destruction of their countries and environments. In effect, being able to identify the perpetrators of environmental war is a complex undertaking.

Conclusion

To conclude with the "shock and awe" metaphor, what do we know of the environment in Iraq following the military invasion some four years later? What do we know of the wildlife, the arable land, the potable water, the bacteria, infections, diseases and health problems, the re-shaped and permanently scarred landscapes, the radiation sifting through the air, and all other factors that might define the environment? Similarly, outside of the meticulously presented data and quantification of scoring the war, what do we know of the people who are affected by the "shock and awe" of war in Iraq, not the American soldiers or those they are fighting but the multitudes of innocent civilians caught in the crossfire? Do official presidential press conferences and military briefings accurately capture the essence of what is happening to the environment? What voices are heard in the cacophony of clatter about fighting "against terror"? Are minority and marginalized groups fully considered in how the war is affecting their rights, culture(s), and livelihoods?

The current debate internationally over global warming and fluctuation in the world's environment seems to have omitted the direct and insidious impact of war and military conflict. It is difficult to link the two phenomena given the pressure to pursue neo-liberal political and economic objectives, which Peter McLaren (2007) argues is closely linked to the "permanent war on terror." The human, cultural, and economic cost of war to the environment is substantial. What is most destabilizing is that the environment is generally not included in calculations of costs and benefits. The unmitigated, uncalculated long-term costs to local peoples are generally inconsequential to war planners. According to Altheide (2009), "The mass media are inextricably linked to the propaganda project through their reliance on institutionalized news sources within an entertainment format promoting fear" (p. 14). Moreover, he argues that human rights atrocities are generally omitted, whenever possible, because they are considered "disturbing, and not entertaining for journalism" (p. 18).

The media, in lock-step with hegemonic forces, refuse to focus or are prevented from focusing on the environment. The massive resources spent on recycling, energy conservation, finding alternative environmental options, and researching climate change pales in comparison to the destruction caused by war. The disconnect between the public willingness to acknowledge the importance of the environment and the patriotic backlash against critiquing the war in Iraq illustrates the problem of having a tightly controlled political agenda that avoids considering local as well as global environmental concerns.

The connection between the environment and democracy and democratic education is transparently clear (Hill & Boxley, 2007). In order to understand and engage in the issue of militaristic destruction of the planet, the teaching and learning process has a legitimate role in facilitating critical inquiry. Critical pedagogy can be an indispensable voice in the sea of patriotic clamouring about the rightness of military invasion, or it can also silence any public thinking on the subject. This chapter illustrates the tight linkage between political and media literacy in the hopes of building a more authentic and tangible democratic experience and democratic platform for all peoples.

Section 4:
"The End Is the Beginning"

Chapter 13

"But What Can I Do?"[1]

To divide the oppressed, an ideology of oppression is indispensable. In contrast, achieving their unity requires a form of cultural action through which they come to know the *why* and *how* of their adhesion to reality—it requires de-ideologizing. Hence, the effort to unify the oppressed does not call for mere ideological "sloganizing." The latter, by distorting the authentic relation between the Subject and objective reality, also separates the *cognitive,* the *affective,* and the *active* aspects of the total, indivisible personality. (Freire, 1973/2005: p. 173)

Introduction

In a "land of milk and honey," the "American dream," a place where freedom is supposedly enshrined in the cornerstones of its history, is it surprising, dumbfounding or simply incomprehensible that so many education students, those who will become, or who are currently, teachers, often throw their hands up and say "But what can *I* do?" To be clear, this is not merely an indictment of young people seeking a university education. The issue is broader than that as it leads to questions about the structure and organization of society (McLaren, 2007). The problem is multi-layered, and relates to patriotism (Westheimer, 2006), critical analysis (Noll, 2007), cultural trends (Banks, 2008), political literacy (Provenzo, 2005), societal representations of education (Sadovnik, Cookson & Semel, 2006), and the struggle to articulate a vision of social justice (Vincent, 2003). Ultimately, it concerns power and political literacy (Freire, 1973/2005), two issues that must be considered in education if there is the realistic hope that society will be (critically) engaged in democracy during and after the formative schooling years.

The context for this paper is a series of experiences and observations stemming from two classes—a third year education and society course for students who aspire to be teachers, and a master's level sociological basis of education course for teachers who are pursuing graduate education—I have taught several times in the past few years. These two classes focus on diversity, equity, multiculturalism and social justice. They are required courses in their respective programs, and each is often the most extensive and meaningful exposure that students have to a sociological vantage point. This is not to suggest that the other required courses and practicum are not instructive and necessary components to their formal educational training but, rather, to underscore that the methods, strategies, approaches and processes of teaching and learning in these two particular courses are, arguably, different, and more attuned to the social construction of identity and the place of education within the broader political context than the regular methods courses (Nieto, 1999). The focus in these courses is more on the context than the content, more on the informal (hidden) than the formal curriculum, and more on critical analysis than the development of lesson plans and classroom management strategies. Significantly, the sociological courses do, I believe, help future and current teachers prepare for integral aspects of teaching by providing a deeper, more nuanced, reflective and critical understanding of who the students are, and how their educational experience is mediated by socio-political factors (Nieto, 1999; Sadovnik, Cookson & Semel, 2006). However, for change to take place, there must be transformation and infusion of concepts, approaches and processes throughout the educational experience, not only in designated classes (Banks, 2008).

It is important to highlight that the analysis provided in this article is not intended to be a myopic, introspective profile of a couple of groups of students. Rather, picking up on trends, concerns, innovative practices and sociological research, this paper proposes fifteen considerations for instilling critical engagement among individual educators. For whatever reason, many education students often feel that their small contribution to the education world cannot make a difference. When this attitude is multiplied across the board, the overall effect is enormous. Ultimately, those with the cultural capital (Delpit, 1988) often succeed academically regardless of the nefarious democratic educational experience they encounter, whereas a large number of students will not benefit from a critical learning experience (Duarte & Smith, 2000). At this point, some teachers may even say that they do not wish to be "political," yet the sociological literature on education clearly indicates that teaching is a political process (McLaren, 2007).

Some students want to be more engaged when they learn of racism, classism, sexism and other forms of discrimination, when they make the connection between neo-liberalism and sustained under-development at home and abroad, or when they understand that the *status quo* may be simply re-producing inequitable power relations. Their interest in moving forward is often challenged and derailed by what they perceive as an inhospitable social environment, one that does not encourage critical debate on fundamental issues. Thus, the reason for this paper is to provide education students with strategies, concepts and considerations for becoming engaged, and, significantly, for taking action aimed at ethical, relevant, social justice-based change.

A cautionary note about the list of fifteen suggestions that educators can consider to make for a better educational experience for themselves and the plurality of students is necessary. One of the recurring problems one encounters when teaching one of the few mandatory sociological courses in a jam-packed undergraduate or graduate curriculum is that many of the students have the rather unfortunate conception that these courses are less central, less relevant, less substantive and, without reserve, less related to the science of teaching and pedagogy. Not uncoincidentally, many students openly request lists that will enable them to teach, for example, multicultural education. The notion that a quick 8-step approach could be used to have people become engaged in culture, learning, institutional change, diversity, racism and many other highly complex areas of inquiry conflicts with the notion that critical learning and engagement involves an ongoing process, not just a lesson plan that will allow one to solidify relations with students. While content certainly has a place in education, the context is pivotal to education and schooling (Nieto & Bode, 2008). Therefore, my list is intended to be an anti-list of sorts, one that encourages thought, introspection, reflection and critical dialog and action but does not limit the progressive and transformative work required to become a better teacher, one who is more attuned and responsive to the needs of all students.

The "But what can I do?" list: Fifteen suggestions

1. Accept that no one knows everything, and that we can always learn

> *If fifty million people say a foolish thing, it is still a foolish thing.*
> —Anatole France (1844–1924)

Even after studying an area of interest for years, it is difficult to fully understand all of the aspects, issues, concerns, perspectives, data, analysis, and related components of a particular field of study. For example, the area of racism includes dozens of peer-reviewed academic journals, local, national and international conferences, workshops, study groups, associations, educational programs, and a plethora of studies, reports and books. There are also daily findings and incidents documented in the media (mainstream, alternative, and local as well as international, etc.) that require an understanding of how race is socially constructed and shaped. There are theoretical, historical, conceptual, applied and various other ways of examining racism in society. Different approaches, including structuralist, functionalist, feminist, post-modern, Marxist, and others, will also influence our understanding of race, racialization and racism in society. The field of methodology, inquiry and data collection can also be a significant area of concern when considering race in society. An example of the evolution of the field of anti-racism, race and ethnic studies and multiculturalism is the relatively recent introduction of the concept of Whiteness (Fine, Weis, Powell-Pruitt & Burns, 2004), which has transformed how we understand the power and privilege of Whites in maintaining systemic barriers and racism. In other words, we have to be open to new ways of thinking about old issues because we should be wary of believing that we have all the knowledge and, importantly, experience we require to understand how students experience their educational journey. We need to challenge ourselves to always learn more, to become engaged, to comprehend the interplay between theory and practice (praxis), and to accept that people experience phenomena differently. Being able to critique divergent viewpoints is an integral part of teaching and learning, and, therefore, conscientious listening and dialog are important skills to acquire (Provenzo, 2005). Teachers should be cognizant of how their teaching can shape the context for students as well as how their ability to accept that their own learning is never complete and, equally, is a factor in establishing the parameters for critical engagement (Noel, 2000; Nieto & Bode, 2008).

2. Content is never devoid of context

> *How can one not speak about war, poverty, and inequality when people who suffer from these afflictions don't have a voice to speak?*
>
> —Isabel Allende (b. 1942)

It is odd that when theory emphasizes that we take into account the context of instruction that there is more and more content to teach and to learn. The current educational context (How, what and why we learn? Who decides? How is the human condition factored into the equation? What are the implications?) is submerged in a deluge of content (expectations, standards, objectives, lesson plans, prescriptive curriculum documents, etc.). The context also includes where students are from, where they are at, how they experience phenomena, and the myriad issues that frame how culture is shaped (Nieto, 1999). While students need to learn some common and specialized curricular content, they also need to learn how to learn, how to be, how to think, how to relate, how to critically examine, and how to understand and be a part of society. Freire (2005) cautions that a focus on the content without the context can lead to the "banking" model, in which students are considered empty vessels that must be filled with knowledge in a staid, unilateral learning process. From a sociological perspective—contrary to the neo-liberal approach of emphasizing the marketplace, competition, employment, standards, uniformity and a "back-to-basics" focus to learning (Hill, 2003)—we are more than individuals and consumers, and public education is a formative period in binding together a society. Moreover, one might insist that students need to learn how to transform society, how to move it in the direction of a more humane, decent, caring, and noble place (McLaren, 2007). Giroux (1988) speaks of *emancipatory* learning as a means of positioning students to be able to critique, understand and politically negotiate their educational environment. What should be the equilibrium between the content and the context? Can we teach the content without a critical appreciation of the context? How do we understand the vast educational attainment gaps between groups without examining the context? If we focus on the content, how do we explain the rejection of the curriculum and schooling process by large numbers of students (Ogbu, 1990), particularly with regard to the under-achievement of African-American and Aboriginal students? Teachers must understand that they are not neutral, that insisting on such a stance only reinforces normative values that privilege White, male, middle-class, European origin, heterosexual, Christian hegemony. In sum, the content is always more appropriate, relevant and engaging when it is contextualized, and when it takes into consideration the needs and realities of the students.

3. Work locally but make the linkage with the international milieu

> *A man of humanity is one who, in seeking to establish himself, finds a foothold for others and who, desiring attainment for himself, helps others to attain.*
>
> —Confucius (551–479 BC)

Understanding that what happens locally, and getting involved locally, is an important step to making connections with the international sphere. The questioning, for example, of how the "out-sourcing of jobs in America," as CNN's Lou Dobbs has characterized it in his almost nightly attack on what he perceives as unfair foreign intervention into the US market, must be critically interwoven into the decades of American exploitation of labor, resources and politics in other countries. Who is responsible for sending American jobs overseas, especially when considering that US investors and executives are making decisions based on increasing profits for themselves and their shareholders? It is also important to question who is profiting from illegal immigration to the US, and whether as many people would still come to this country if no one would employ, or rather exploit, them. There is an undeniable interdependence in world affairs—illustrated by constantly shifting waves of people through migration, the exchange of goods, the global environment, travel, the drug trade, and wars and military conflict—and it is, therefore, imperative to critically understand how issues are inter-connected. Thinking and acting locally infers a comprehension of why local factories are being shut down, who prospers from the dislocation of labor, and, importantly, the implications for diverse peoples around the world locked out of the decision-making process from such measures. Macedo and Gounari (2006) have written about the "globalization of racism," and Klein (2005) exposes the insidious labor practices worldwide that serve to render subservient large segments of diverse national populations. In effect, national boundaries do not stop racism, sexism, poverty, AIDS, exploitation and other concerns. Interrogating how education prepares students and society to better and more critically engage in/with international phenomena is fundamental to achieving a more just society, both locally and internationally (Guttman, 1999; Holm & Farber, 2002). Therefore, local issues are also international issues, and achieving change at a smaller, local level should not be unnecessarily dissected from the broader political space. Teachers should strive to make connections within the formal and informal curriculum (Apple, 1996) and with the international context, elucidating the linkages, inter-dependencies and implications of the impact and reality of local concerns. Thinking critically about globalization is also an important area for consideration for teachers (Gandin & Apple, 2005).

4. Media literacy is not a soundbite

> *Washing one's hands of the conflict between the powerful and the powerless means to side with the powerful, not to be neutral.*
>
> —Paulo Freire (1921–1997)

The mainstream media has become so encompassing, widespread, and infused into the broader culture that a large number of people no longer read to acquire knowledge and develop their own original analysis (Curran & Gurevitch, 2000). One can easily notice how the corporate radio, print and television media work in unison to produce virtually the same reports, images and messages from the same vantage points (Herman & Chomsky, 2002). In relation to the nightly news, it is astounding to realize how much time is spent on discussing the weather, which is interspersed with generous portions of banter between the smiling co-hosts as well as the constant advertising segments. Similarly, although newspapers can devote more space and time to presenting editorial positions, it is obvious that the vast majority of content in the media is purchased from the large press agencies, which generally construct homogenous stories that have a clear uncritical thread running through them. The corporate media has a highly nefarious effect on developing a national culture and mind-set, and teachers should be aware of how the "medium is the message," as Marshal McLuhan (with Fiore, 2001) put it, or how the media's main function is "manufacturing consent" (Herman & Chomsky, 2002). Given the corporate media's impact on society, in terms of basic information, swelling the notion of collective identity, and tempering social justice movements, being able to critically deconstruct the validity of the organization, the utilization and presentation of information is something that teachers should address. Basic literacy reposes, in part, on the capacity to comprehend, dissect and critique the media. One example could be the US invasion in Iraq, which has shown the media to have been equally manipulated, complicit and ineffectual in offering a supposedly neutral, objective, truthful and critical voice to allow citizens to understand the rationale, implications, and options for embarking on a path of a "permanent war against terror," as Peter McLaren (2007) puts it. Teachers should be aware of diverse media outlets and perspectives in the alternative sector, either on the radio, television, in print or through the internet, and also be prepared to understand how a diverse student body is affected by a mainstream media that traditionally avoids acknowledging and validating the experience of myriad sectors of society. Moreover, the media's role in undermining education and supporting hegemonic forces that support neo-liberalism should become a mandatory part of teaching and learning in schools.

5. History is not uni-dimensional

He who passively accepts evil is as much involved in it as he who helps perpetuate it.
—Martin Luther King, Jr. (1929–1968)

Students and teachers should be concerned about the multidimensional way that history is shaped, defined, presented and connected to contemporary times. Who writes history? Who is not involved in mainstream history? We learn about the virtues of the US Constitution and liberty for all, but how do we reconcile that philosophy with the fact that all of the Founding Fathers were slave owners, that the land was virtually stolen from Indigenous peoples, and that numerous laws, practices and incidents of a racialist and racist flavor swept through the diverse non-White and non-Christian communities of the US for generations? Who has been persecuted, and why? What role have women played in the construction of society? How are labor, social action and peace groups represented? Is there a connection between slavery, segregation, Jim Crow laws and continuous discrimination against African-Americans and the fact that, presently, the latter experience, in comparison to the White population, a lower rate of home ownership, less wealth accumulation, more poverty, higher rates of incarceration, lower postsecondary participation rates and, using a range of indicators, less access to decision-making and political power? How do we critically understand the linkage to historical phenomena, especially when considering the traditional method of teaching about wars and conquests without articulating the human dimension? Do we learn as much about peace as we do about war, about social justice as much as injustice, and about minorities as much as the majority? Therefore, the context for discussing, teaching and learning about history should be critical, and should concern itself with diverse perspectives and issues that are not traditionally understood in the formal curriculum (Kincheloe & Weil, 2004). The US, like other countries, is not *only* a benevolent regime that has brought liberty, fraternity and goodness to its own people and others but, as well, it is a regime that has used its power disproportionately and in an abusive manner (McLaren, 2007; Shapiro & Purpel, 2005). In sum, teachers should be concerned with the construction and various interpretations of history.

6. Culture is more than sombreros, tacos and mariachis

One does not sell the earth upon which the people walk.

—Crazy Horse (1838–1877)

While culture can be used negatively to produce stereotypes, understanding culture is fundamental to breaking down stereotypes, and also to building a textured analysis of individual and collective identity (Banks, 2008). In the undergraduate course I teach, a common refrain by the end of the course is that "I had no idea that culture was so complex." Although it is dangerous to narrowly and uncritically define culture as food and festivals, the practice of identifying people based on perceived cultural traits such as ethnic origin and everything that that implies is commonplace in education (Nieto, 1999). The implications for not understanding that not all Hispanics speak Spanish, not all people of Chinese origin are Buddhist, not all Italians are predisposed to large family dinners on Sunday, and so on are numerous. Culture involves race, class, gender, religion, ethnicity, sexual orientation, family, and, importantly, lived experience, and, therefore, identity is considered to be socially constructed (Nieto & Bode, 2008). People have their own individual identity, and this intersects with collective identity. Someone's racial identity will mean different things in different contexts, as will their religion, language and citizenship status. Culture is dynamic, shifting and transforming according to local, national and international phenomena and is, significantly, affected by power (Duarte & Smith, 2000). To be a Japanese-American during the Second World War was to face internment, which, ultimately, had an impact on the succeeding years. Who can be American (Westheimer, 2006)? Is it necessary to be White (Fine, Weis, Powell-Pruitt & Burns, 2004)? Would it be unfair to generalize about Whites, who clearly are in a position of power and privilege? Would it be equally unfair to generalize about other racial groups? What are the implications of a limited understanding of culture (Delpit, 1988)? Do teachers have a natural lower expectation for African-American students and higher expectations for Asian-American students? Teachers should strive to understand that there may be many reasons for a student's success or underachievement, and that it is critical to examine one's own identity as well as the multi-faceted ways that people form their unique cultural identities. Understanding how groups perform should be contextualized in relation to how education systems institutionally and systemically function to work for the success of certain sectors of society over other sectors of society. Teachers should be open to discussing and examining what they do not know about others, and also to accepting that understanding culture is a key component to providing a level playing field for all students. As a last point, it is important to highlight that understanding culture critically does not infer that one must learn dozens of languages, and the traits, traditions, histories and contexts for myriad cultures around the world; rather, the emphasis here should be placed on being appreciative of difference and divergent perspectives, and on being engaged with others without succumbing to the hegemonic notion of Western cultural superiority (Banks et al., 2005) Ultimately, engaging in a critical way with diverse cultures can lead not only to greater understanding and harmony, but also, significantly to peace. Instead of a reflex of annihilation, there should be an instinctive call for comprehension in times of conflict.

7. Problematize war, and fight for peace

A country cannot simultaneously prepare and prevent war.
—Albert Einstein (1879–1955)

Is education intended, at some level, to allow us to avoid using violence as a means of resolving our disputes? This may sound, at the same time, too esoteric and simplistic, but the point is directly related to international events. Do our schools prepare students to challenge solutions based on military might and the concomitant suffering and annihilation associated with it? Is it political and "indoctrinating" to discuss the war in Iraq, not to mention the dozens of other ongoing military conflicts around the world, or not to discuss the war? What are the implications of not working toward peace? How do we understand the ethical and moral implications of foreign military intervention, the arms industry, the militarization of education, with the Pentagon being publicly mandated through legislation to be able to recruit at the high school level, and the human and financial costs of maintaining large military infrastructures? How do we critically analyze the racialization of a government-sponsored military, with a disproportionate number of minorities at the bottom being locked into battle operations? What can schools do to encourage a critical understanding of war and military conflict, and also to work for peace? Similarly, what is the relationship between military action and the environment? These questions should be considered by teachers in a critical way. It is not unpatriotic to question war as a reasonable, acceptable or lasting solution to conflict. If students are not exposed to a range of perspectives, experiences and contexts during their formative education years, how will they be prepared to fight for peace in the future? Teachers can offer the space and context to students for discussing, understanding and examining issues that will have a tangible impact on their immediate and future prospects. Therefore, teachers need to understand the limitations and nefarious nature of the tightly prescriptive formal curriculum, and also seek out opportunities to make it more relevant, meaningful and critical. Lastly, the notion of strict discipline, anti-bullying programs and concern about weapons in schools should be contextualized within the framework of the need to reduce and eliminate violence at all levels, including within the national sphere.

8. Humility is an unbelievable virtue

> *The life that is unexamined is not worth living.*
>
> —Plato (427–347 BC)

We live in a time that when wars are started, rather than reflecting on the reason, morality and legality of such actions, the debate is often turned on its head: we are involved in a war, we must win it, and we cannot divide ourselves with senseless debate. On the basketball court, multi-millionaires are often involved in what is politely called "trash-talk." In some circles of society, it is not uncommon to be physically maligned and even killed for "dissing" (disrespecting) another. When Enron continued to fabricate surrealistic balance sheets, arrogantly—i.e., we can do anything and get away with it—doctored by one of the world's largest accounting firms, the profits rolled on until the house of cards crumbled, leaving thousands of people without any savings. Donald Trump has made a career out of the extravagant, unapologetic drive to make money, and to boast about it, very loudly. To be elected as president of the United States, it would appear that it is important, first, to have military experience, and, second, to demonstrate a strong resolve to use military force, two qualities that bend the mind when one considers the values that are supposedly enshrined in communities that see themselves as charitable, kind, open, embracing and "a good place to raise children." In sum, as the above examples attempt to illustrate, the notion of humility seems to have a diminishing status in our society, some might argue as a function of neo-liberalism, which places a premium on individualism and materialism (Hill, 2003). Yet, in general, religions do not ordinarily encourage such audacious, un-humble behavior, nor do parents when a newborn arrives. Traditionally, educators are thought of as people who have garnered some respect in the community, individuals who exemplify decency and fairness and, further, who attempt to inculcate values of fairness and respect. Are most people disrespectful, audacious, and purposefully self-centered? Or is it the culture that promotes and condones such behavior? Does it make a difference to comport oneself with dignity, decorum and decency avoiding some of the pomposity alluded to above? Teachers should be aware of the various aspects of the cultural life of individuals, groups and society, and should also reflect on their own approach to human interaction. This is not to suggest that educators are naturally predisposed to unacceptable behavior, only to highlight that the broader cultural and political framework forces us to consider the implications of the lack of humility in society. Humility can lead to a panoply of authentic dialog, rapprochement, and action as people recognize that the truth often lies well outside the parameters of the marketplace. Top-down, hierarchical, exclusionary leadership can only further distance and dislocate people (Ryan, 2006). Humility is a means of starting the process of understanding. Lastly, I acknowledge that some forms of humility can lead to a passive condoning of the reprehensible, or of being a follower (see next section), that being humble may be construed as being disengaged and obedient, but the argument presented above centers the debate more around the humaneness and humanity of humility, as espoused by Freire, than the acceptance of oppression.

9. Be wary of being a follower

> *Don't walk in front of me, I may not follow; don't walk behind me, I may not lead; walk beside me, and just be my friend.*
>
> —Albert Camus (1913–1960)

It is often common in education circles to be predisposed to group-think, the process of achieving a common, unitary notion of reality, one that limits divergent, original, critical thought (Leithwood, Jantzi, & Steinbach, 1999). The implications for this are numerous, including, in particular, the strong potential to disregard and undermine minority opinion and viewpoints. Are educators trained and encouraged to critically assess the tools—learning materials, standards, rubrics, teaching methods, lesson plans, professional development, business plans—at their disposition? Teachers can influence the texture, shape and even the content of the educational environment in which they find themselves if they become engaged in the context (Nieto, 1999). More than a trite slogan, teachers can question the potential impact of reforms and decisions, especially when they are not directly involved in the implementation. If they do not believe in the education that they are implementing, then this will inextricably flow through to the students (Leithwood, Steinbach & Jantzi, 2002). Being kind is not enough to transform the educational experience for students, and, therefore, striving to improve and connect the teaching and learning to the needs and lived experiences of the students requires careful consideration and initiative (Noel, 2007). Institutionally, it is often difficult to be the person who stands out, the "lone wolf" so to speak, but there are also numerous examples of those who choose to stand on principle, and who make proposals based on solid foundation and reasoning, which can then have a lasting impact on the direction of reforms. As Ryan, (2006) points out, leadership is a multi-faceted art, and being in sync and being willing to address social justice needs is pivotal to transforming educational systems; as a corollary, being silent on such issues sends the message that they are not to be considered in spite of policies that might indicate positive movement. This is clearly problematic territory because being part of a team is highly valued in educational institutions. However, in a wide range of employment advertisements for progressive and leadership positions, this is often counter-balanced with the popular mantra of being a "free thinker," "having a critical vantage point" and being a "risk taker," which are considered positive virtues. Being a follower means being "color-blind" to racial inequities, not speaking up to counter injustice, and potentially, albeit indirectly and implicitly, partaking in further marginalization in education.

10. Accept that you are a political being

> *How, critical researchers ask, can we remain disinterested and anonymous when our concerns, values, experiences, ideology, language, race, class, gender, and sexuality help shape everything we do in a study.*
>
> —Joe Kincheloe (1950–2008)

In mainstream society there seems to be the general sentiment that education is an apolitical enterprise whereas the literature on the role played by teachers develops that notion that understanding the political nature of teaching and learning is pivotal to serving the interests of the students (Marshall & Gerstl-Pepin, 2005). Being political does not mean being a member of the Republicans or Democrats, or even participating in the electoral process, but rather it is associated with grasping the nature of power in our actions, our thinking and our societal conventions. Developing a critical analysis of decision-making related to the curriculum, policy development, parental involvement, school culture, and student achievement surpasses the simple pedagogical process of examining issues from a neutral vantage point. Not acting to implement social justice is a political decision, as is the priority placed on purchasing computers or developing an anti-bullying policy (Ryan, 2006). Teachers' unions clearly lobby for the interests of their constituents, and school board members have clear ideological antecedents, even if they argue in the firmest tone that they are simply there "for the students." Ultimately, education is a political enterprise, and teachers, therefore, need to understand how their own politics and political experience plays into their approach to teaching and learning (McLaren, 2007). This leads to the question of political literacy, and whether we should teach to promote it (Giroux, 1988). Fearing the label of being *political*, which, unfortunately, has been used to discredit and marginalize some views, is a cultural reality facing educators who desire change and a movement toward social justice within their schools. Teachers should consider closely their own views as well as others on a range of matters outside of the narrow electoral process that has been conflated to represent the totality of democracy and democratic action. Making the connection to the qualitative educational experience, which includes citizenship, democracy and social justice, through service learning, school activities and especially the curriculum, should be taken up as a necessary part of the political education of teachers (Freire, 1970). Teachers should not be inhibited to consider the how (the context) of education in addition to the what (the content) (Nieto, 1999).

11. Read and write, and seek out authors far from mainstream culture

> *Hatred does not cease by hatred, but only by love; this is the eternal rule.*
>
> —Buddha

It is disheartening to see how the written word is occupying a more limited place in the lives of many people. While the Internet has opened up a plethora of avenues for reading, researching and consuming knowledge and culture, it is also clear that many people are not reading thoughtful pieces in a critical way, forcing them to reflect and develop their own arguments (Shor, 1997). This is clear in colleges of education in relation to using peer-reviewed resources and writing papers, which seems to be less of concern for a standards-based teacher education program that emphasizes content, lesson plans, the practice of teaching and classroom management. Through reading thoughtful, well-developed arguments in books or peer-reviewed articles, one can escape the temptation to repeat populist slogans that have served to limit constructive debate in education and society. In the era of soundbites, blogs and Wikipedia where anyone can post an opinion, text-messaging, and an over-zealous corporate media, it is sometimes difficult to develop original, critical arguments. Reading authors with whom one may not initially agree can stimulate the neurons to reformulate why one thinks a certain way. Writing is equally important to develop important communication skills, and also to critically engage in substantiating a position. As Shor (1997), McLaren (2007), Giroux (1988) and (1970) argue, it is important to contextualize learning for students, and to use sources, resources and situations that relate to their realities, straying from the traditional conundrum of teaching all students the same way with the same techniques based on the same worldview. Teachers can easily cover the content requirements of the curriculum by engaging students in experiences and scenarios that resonate with youth culture. The benefits for such an approach would include, principally, that students are more likely to stay in school, to learn, and to share this learning with others in their schools and communities, thus making the teaching process a more meaningful one (Kincheloe & Weil, 2004; McLaren, 2007).

12. Problematize the discrepancy in wealth, but also the importance of money as an indicator of worth or value

> *Where justice is denied, where poverty is enforced, where ignorance prevails, and where any one class is made to feel that society is in an organized conspiracy to oppress, rob, and degrade them, neither persons nor property will be safe.*
>
> —Frederick Douglas (1818–1895)

What is the value of money in our society (McLaren, 2007)? Do we need money to live? What is the value of one's life? Is it logical to pay a basketball player $10M and a teacher $35,000? Should companies be given financial incentives, including an exemption from paying tax, while average citizens must pay a percentage of their wages to subsidize the profits of these companies? Is there a connection between funds spent on education and those spent on war? Is education a right or a privilege? Should money be spent on early childhood education, literacy, wealth distribution, meaningful employment, healthcare and housing support for lower socio-economic status groups, or on prisons, policing and welfare later on? Are these questions too categorical and not nuanced enough to take into account the complexity of our society? Teachers need to be concerned with how money influences the quality of, and access to, education. Some children already have significant cultural capital before entering school, are not required to take part-time jobs, and can have the luxury of educational visits, reading and exposure to activities and personalities that further reinforce their learning in school, whereas others are tracked because of what is considered to be poor language skills and limited cultural knowledge (Delpit, 1988). Teachers should be critical of the over-emphasis in the curriculum on employment in relation to earning power (Hill, 2003). Why are some students streamed into programs that will assure that they will be ineligible for university admission, and, therefore, be subject to low-skilled jobs that have limited remuneration and opportunities (Nieto, 1999)? Teaching and learning, as Kozol (1992) has effectively illustrated, should not be conducted in an abstract manner isolated from the myriad financial factors influencing how education is organized: the structure and maintenance of the physical plant of the building, the availability of textbooks, computers, laboratory and related equipment, the status of extracurricular activities, including field trips, gymnasium and sports centers, and the human resources supporting the school, the attractiveness of the cafeteria, and other related features that encourage students to appropriate their schools. Funding also plays a role in the retention of teachers. Therefore, teachers should be concerned with the economic equation in education, and understand that this may have an impact on how students perform in school. It is, therefore, not a coincidence that school boards from more affluent areas generally having higher academic outcomes than those in which poverty is more evident.

13. Consider the proposition that there is hope

> *There is one thing stronger than all the armies in the world, and that is an idea whose time has come.*
>
> —Victor Hugo (1802–1885)

Two of the key factors in ensuring effective educational achievement are high teacher expectations and parental involvement. Teachers need to believe that all students can learn, which sounds rather simplistic and even pedantic but is worth repeating because decades of research on streaming indicate that some students have been routinely placed in lower learning tracks, effectively ensuring that they will not continue their studies at the postsecondary level (Banks, 2008; Kincheloe & Weil, 2004). Students need to believe that there is hope; otherwise, as Ogbu (1990) has illustrated, scores of young African-American students may believe that schooling is only for Whites, exemplifying a culture of resistance, culminating in their under-achievement. If there is no hope for education to lead to transformational change in individuals, in communities, in societies, and at the international level, then the neo-liberal focus on employability and competition will translate into the simple reproduction of social relations (Bourdieu & Passeron, 1977; Hill, 2003). Much of the sociological literature aims to empower students and teachers (Banks, 2008; Delpit, 1988; Nieto, 1999), and this can be realized through forward-thinking approaches and acknowledgement on the part of teachers who refuse to close their eyes to institutional intransigence. In addition to individual appropriation of one's reality, hope requires engagement and action. The field of critical pedagogy has spawned largely because of the notion that goodwill alone will not break down systemic barriers (McLaren, 2007), that it also necessitates the political imperative of not giving up on those who are marginalized. Having hope can also mean understanding what American society looks like for different individuals and groups, who is silenced and who has voice, how power works to advantage some and not others, and why some appear to be more comfortably positioned to demonstrate the virtues of a democratic society whereas others are locked into permanent struggle. Without hope for all students, education will become nothing more than a holding cell in which large numbers of students will not be able to realize their potential.

14. Examine important events, personalities and experiences in your own education

Everything has been figured out, except how to live.

—Jean-Paul Sartre (1905–1980)

By critically examining our own educational experience we can become more attuned to how students might be experiencing teaching and learning. This activity, which Foundations professors integrate into the undergraduate course at our University, ultimately allows students to retrospectively understand the salience of the content they learned in their formative years in juxtaposition to the context. Almost universally, students refer to incidents of inclusion or exclusion, peer pressure, the school culture, the involvement or lack thereof on the part of their parents, their own social situation at home, their feelings of marginalization based on social class, culture, ethnicity, race and other markers of identity, and, importantly, how one or more teachers was disrespectful, discouraging and even detrimental to the educational journey and aspirations they had. Few students point out how easy school was, how there were no issues that affected them, and how the school experience effectively reflected their particular needs. The goal of the exercise is not to denigrate education but, rather, to reflect on how and why some people do not succeed while others do. It is enlightening for many to discover that their underachievement, even their abandonment of education, had little to do with their intellectual capacity, which is borne out by the fact that they are in the midst of completing a degree in education. Sometimes we believe that major happenings are merely coincidences, devaluing the broad impact of institutional practices that undermine some people more than others (Provenzo, 2005). As we look back in a critical way, we may start to see how the curriculum was exclusionary, how racial minorities were routinely ostracized, and how the learning we undertook did not effectively allow us to appreciate our own complicity in sustaining or undermining social justice (Apple, 1996). This activity also leads us to understand how the context for learning is pivotal to learning the standardized content that is generally insisted upon through the standards movement symbolized by No Child Left Behind. To be a good teacher, one must be aware of the impact of one's gestures, comportment, language, thinking, values, and approach to teaching and learning. Critical reflection on one's own challenges in education, as exemplified by Nieto (1999), can lead to important discoveries of how schooling, despite goodwill on the part of teachers, generates inequitable experiences for many students (McLaren, 2007).

15. Affirm That "I Can Do What I Can Do"

You must be the change you wish to see in the world.

—Mahatma Gandhi (1869–1948)

The starting point of this chapter—But what can *I* do?—raises the issue of the perceived impotence, disenfranchisement, solitary individualism and hopelessness of a certain current running through the educational field. This does not take away from those educators who see hope, and who act in ways that demonstrate that something can be done. However, it is clear that individuals—for example, Rosa Parks, Martin Luther King Jr., Nelson Mandela, Mahatma Gandhi, and others—can make a difference. Recognizing that individual action takes place within a broader context, and also involves the infinite stories and manifestations of others, it remains that individuals can influence their immediate, and sometimes the broader, environment on a number of issues on a daily basis. Our personal actions can be infused with ethical reflection, introspection, comprehension of others, an examination of the implications as well as the unique consequences of demonstrating decency, or they can be equally devoid of such processes. How we talk to people, how we share and discuss matters, how we move, how we consider, embrace, respect and debate, how we include, validate and name, how we openly consider our own infallibility, how we strive to understand issues, how we accept the political nature of political phenomena, such as education, and how we accept to learn through teaching and learning will all have an effect on the educational environment. Is it too Pollyannaish and simplistic to consider that we can be a proverbial "agent of change"? Is it too cynical and fatalistic that none of our actions matter? Teachers need to grapple with how they can participate in the change process and the social justice dialectic. Affirming that something can be done, but that there is no prescriptive list that will quickly answer how to deal with such far-reaching issues as those discussed in this chapter is a necessary precursor to transforming education, but this can only be obtained if teachers engage in critically examining themselves, the teaching and learning context, the local as well as the macro-level context, and the fundamental factors underpinning the learning experience for *all* students.

Conclusion

This chapter has argued for a more lucid, constructive, meaningful, and critical engagement in the process of teaching and learning. Considering the context in addition to the content of what is being taught is crucial. What is fundamental in this process, and for it to have some salience and meaning, is the involvement of teachers themselves. Educators need to interrogate their own implication in shaping the educational experience of others, those who may or may not share similar identities, experiences, ideologies, opportunities and perspectives. Education for educators need not stop after the end of a teacher-education program. On the contrary, it only starts once one finds him/herself in the classroom. Transformational change, which has become somewhat of a campaign slogan of late, can take place if educators challenge the practices that have served to reproduce inequitable power relations. This critical dialog involving educators needs to take place at several levels, involving a range of contentious and controversial subjects but also allowing for genuine critical reflection. Educators are well placed to initiate debate on the state of schools. Merely adopting an apolitical, neutral stance toward students, parents and communities would only serve to further entrench socio-economic marginalization and disenfranchisement. It is hopeful that the list of fifteen suggestions that educators can consider might serve as a startingpoint for such a process to question and disrupt educational practices that do not seek to enhance political literacy and social justice.

Chapter 14

Conclusion: Some Thoughts on, and Options for, a Critical Pedagogy of Democracy

In order for the oppressed to unite, they must first cut the umbilical cord of magic and myth which binds them to the world of oppression; the unity which links them to each other must be of a different nature. To achieve this indispensable unity the revolutionary process must be, from the beginning, *cultural action*. The methods used to achieve the unity of the oppressed will depend on the latter's historical and existential experience within the social structure. (Freire, 1973/2005: p. 175)

Introduction

What can be done, or, as suggested in the previous chapter, "what can I do?," to contribute to democracy? Clearly, there is no one answer, especially not an easy or simplistic one. This book has argued that education must be part of the equation. But, one must ask, what kind of education? Part of the formulation of a response comes in the form of how we choose to elucidate what we mean by democracy. As argued throughout this book, my interpretation surpasses the electoral politics (representative) model, embracing a *thicker* version of inclusion, participation, dialog, interrogation and critical engagement, which is underpinned by a vigorously and humbly formulated critical pedagogy. This form of democratic education seeks to embrace the experiences and perspectives of diverse peoples, including those traditionally marginalized from the national narratives that have enshrined a partisan allegiance to patriotism, which often included and accepted military conquest as a normative value, and, conversely, often excluded and rejected those groups and actions that run counter to hegemonic reasoning. It is problematic, therefore, to consider democracy in exclusion of a meaningful analysis of inequitable power relations.

Consistent with the theme of this book, I caution that there is no one thing, menu or recipe that can be produced to inculcate a democratic state, government, citizen and/or education system. Indeed, even addressing an amalgam of concerns is no guarantee of reinforcing democracy. However, the desire for a more meaningful, just, decent form of democracy is something that requires, borrowing from the contemporary vernacular within mainstream politics, a certain measure of *hope*. One must remain confident and strident to improve the current situation because to simply endorse it uncritically is to further entrench vast swaths of the landscape, figuratively and literally, to a permanently deceptive existence in which the quest for human rights becomes a mere fictional, legal maneuver, reserved largely for those with their hands firmly on the economic levers of power.

Ultimately, seeking a more democratic society in and through education is tantamount to seeking the truth. Never comfortable, nor easily achieved, such a proposition requires a multitude of measures as well as the belief that people can, ultimately, function together without self-destruction. War is not *the* answer, nor is violence. Corruption and greed are also areas that can be addressed, provided that the will of the people is respected. Racism, sexism and poverty are not virtues; they are man/woman-made, and can be addressed. Cycles of disenfranchisement do not mesh well with the oft-repeated mantra of American "greatness" and the superiority of a highly developed, advanced nation, one often invoked as being blessed by God. Rather than reducing inequities, society is actually (according to all of the standard measures used to demonstrate development and superiority) becoming less united, less equal, less resolutely inclusive, and, ultimately, I would argue, less democratic. The space provided for elections has usurped the place of education in many regards.

One hundred proposals that could contribute to democracy through education

Building on the content and arguments made throughout this book, at the risk of being criticized for including some ideas that may not mesh with a democratic education focus or others that seem to be superfluous to the debate or may not seem too original or innovative, below is a list of one hundred proposals that could contribute to a *thicker* democratic education. As articulated throughout the book, these proposals should be considered as an ensemble, not disparate, individual efforts at reform.

1. Make education a *societal* responsibility, removing the false narrative of it somehow being only a *local* responsibility. The (nation-)state should undertake a public education campaign to acknowledge and promote public education as the engine behind societal growth, development, harmony and ingenuity.

2. Democratic *conscientization* should be integrated into educational planning, and political, media and critical forms of literacy should become mandatory aspects of teaching and learning.

3. Eradicate the mainstream representation of education as being neutral, devoid of politics. Emphasize that education can lead to change, and that regressive forms of education can lead to docile, compliant citizens, the antithesis of *thick* democracy.

4. Re-define the notion of accountability in education to more centrally focus on ethics, *bona fide* diversity, social justice and *thick* democracy. Just because NCLB declares that there is greater accountability does not necessarily mean that this is true.

5. The state should only fund public education, and charters, vouchers, private schools and other offshoots should be discouraged and not receive public support. Public education is a public good, benefitting all of society, and it should be viewed as a collective, global responsibility.

6. End the ranking of schools and school boards. They are divisive, punish the marginalized, are not appropriately contextualized, and serve to disintegrate rather integrate, diminishing the possibility of enhancing the public good and the notion of education being a fundamental pillar to solidifying the *thicker* and more humane elements of a democracy.

7. Do not let high *cultural capital* areas—those with high property values and other advantages—graduate their high schools without having them work closely with schools in their areas that are facing serious challenges. The notion here is that all schools will see that they are part of a common struggle, existence and society, not simply, within the neo-liberal mindset, individuals demonstrating how hard they work as opposed to others who are supposedly not committed.

8. All subject areas of the curriculum should explicitly diagnose how power works as well as the meaning of social justice. This should include a critical pedagogical analysis of Whiteness, racial, gender and class inequities, and other forms of marginalization, discrimination and disenfranchisement. It may be considered impolite to discuss such matters, but to avoid them is to only further entrench and ingratiate harm, damage and the antithesis of democracy.

9. The educational program and curriculum should specifically address indigenous knowledge and peoples. To celebrate the arrival of White Europeans to the United States some five hundred years ago without critically interrogating the relationship with Aboriginal peoples, who had occupied this land for 10,000–20,000 years, is extremely problematic.

10. Focus education on the critical journey of constructing knowledge, in addition to learning knowledge.

11. Education systems and educators should embrace the following saying: *"The more I know, the less I know."* If education is to sincerely be about life-long learning, then it should involve an endless process of critical interrogation, lived experiences, and dialectical questioning and dialog, which far overshadows the notion of standards, high-stakes testing, and a prescriptive curriculum.

12. Men and women of all origins, races, ethnicities, and backgrounds should be involved in teaching and education. Some elementary schools lack male teachers, and some schools have no racial minorities or females in leadership positions, which can further lead to false stereotypes about leadership, role models and learning.

13. Educational policymaking and curriculum development should involve more consultation and collaboration with diverse groups and interests, and the decision-making process should necessarily become more transparent. Educators, parents, students and the broader community should be able to understand how decisions are made and why, and they should be involved in these processes that will, ultimately, have an effect on all of society.

14. As with the previous point, people of all origins need to be involved in developing education policy and curriculum. The reaction to formal education by some ethno-cultural and racial groups that formal education is largely meant to benefits Whites must be addressed.

15. All schools should be twinned within local areas (for example, an urban school could be twinned with a suburban school, and a suburban school twinned with a rural school, or schools from different demographic areas could be twinned in the same area). This twinning would involve *bona fide* academic and curriculum work in addition to cultural exchange. No student should be allowed to say that they do not know, understand or experience diversity because "everyone in their school is White," which does not sufficiently encapsulate a *thicker* version of critical thinking and engagement with pluralism.

16. School boards should use technology to twin classrooms in the US with those around the world to exchange language and culture with colleagues in other countries. The Government should provide seed funding to schools that require it in order to undertake this program.

17. *No Child Left Behind* should be replaced by a more meaningful and qualitatively responsive framework as suggested by some of the models presented in this book. Decreeing that 2014 will be the end of illiteracy and underachievement needs to be replaced with questioning related to why there are such vast inequities in the most "developed" country in the world.

18. If there must be standards in education, there should be standards for democratic education, citizenship education, peace education, media literacy and social justice. Standards should be focused on building a more decent society, not on testing basic skills that are pre-defined largely because of cultural capital. Consideration should be given to the *Social justice accountability framework* presented in this book.

19. Teachers should not be remunerated on how well their students do. Teachers' salaries should be increased, and other measures of acknowledgement for their contribution should be pursued. The objective should not be to diminish those working in more challenging situations or those whose students have lower levels of cultural capital. The role of the teacher has to be understood in a broader societal context, not simply related to mercantilist outcomes.

20. The curriculum should be significantly revamped. Freire's generative themes and Dewey's constructivism should be incorporated within classrooms at all levels, instilling values of respect, critical interrogation, engagement, and appreciation of how power works.

21. All subject areas should systematically encourage critical enquiry, dialog and debate. Mathematicians, musicians and biologists all need to be able to communicate, to understand others, and to advance social justice as much as social scientists, and everyone involved in education should appropriate the re-defining of a progressive, socially just, democratic educational experience.

22. All schools should emphasize deliberative democracy, and young people should learn how to listen, articulate, debate, and diagnose difference. Significantly, students should learn how to respectively seek to construct further knowledge in a peaceful way. Condemning those with critical opinions needs to be stopped as *group-think* can lead to societal paralysis and a nefarious form of patriotism.

23. Rather than protecting students from controversial subject matter, they should be encouraged to critically understand not only the *what* but also the *how* and *why* behind significant events,

issues and concerns. The mythology that politics is about Democrats and Republicans needs to be rectified, and students need to learn that critical reflection can lead to more appropriate and effective resolutions of systemic problems and conflicts than the use of force, whether it be wars, racial profiling or the neglect of impoverished groups.

24. Howard Zinn's *A People's History of the United States* should be studied in every school in the nation. Taking up some of the cultural forms of seeking historical knowledge through the stories of average or non-elite and military figures should be encouraged.

25. When teaching about historical as well as contemporary issues and problems, students should be presented with a broad, *thicker* representation of events, far outstripping the military and patriotic version of reality. The connection between national and international events should be explored, as well as military interventions, genocides and present-day racial, environmental and social problems in connection to our individual and collective responsibilities.

26. Peace and peace education should become centerpieces to the educational project. If peace is not a fundamental part of education, what then is its purpose?

27. A *thicker* interpretation of the environment and environmental education should be taught throughout the educational program. The effects of war and military conflict on the environment, for example, should be interrogated.

28. Parks with green spaces, accessible, safe equipment, and a welcoming environment should be constructed at every school, and be open to school communities year-round. Sporting venues, including basketball courts, baseball diamonds, football/soccer fields, and general playing spaces, should be included in these parks. Serious efforts should be made to ensure that the parks are used for the purpose of leisure, sportsmanlike conduct, and positive intercultural and intergenerational contact. Poorer areas should not be punished because of wealth concentration, and everyone should be able to enjoy the outdoors without cost.

29. Sports, in general, should be de-emphasized within the educational system. Large, elaborate football programs, alongside mediocre academic programs, must be problematized. The reality of numerous coaches, vast sports complexes, and Friday-night televised high school football games must be reevaluated in relation to the values that are advanced. Accessible, fair-play, sportsmanlike values should be re-asserted in place of a win-at-all-costs mission and the drive for notoriety and the supremacy of money.

30. Sports scholarships and the sports industry at the college level must be re-thought. Why is tuition so high when college-level sports programs supposedly generate so much revenue? The reality that few working-class students benefit from sports scholarships must be reexamined. Why do college football coaches make substantially more than college presidents and faculty?

31. Building football stadiums at high schools should not be the responsibility of local communities. The state should be charged with the responsibility of developing a comprehensive plan for athletics, documenting how much money is allocated for which services, and substantiating how athletics can be made accessible to all students as well as how they benefit the academic environment and the health of local communities.

32. All students should be introduced to critical service learning. The experiences should be accompanied by courses and debriefings on why societal problems exist. To do a service-

learning placement without some socio-political contextualization may only reinforce the opposite of what is sought through the actual experience.

33. Governments and school boards should clearly articulate the framework for critical service learning, including budgets, measures and the connection to a *thicker* democratic experience in education.

34. Contracts for superintendents of education and principals should contain a clause that they will be evaluated on how well they inculcate democratic education, political literacy and social justice. Their renewal should hinge, in part, on how well they address these matters within their educational institutions.

35. There should be no place in schools for military recruitment, especially not in schools in poorer areas. All students should be afforded the possibility of higher education, not just those with higher levels of cultural capital, and the message should not be transmitted, either explicitly or implicitly, that poor people have no other option than to join the army.

36. All American students should learn at least one foreign language starting in First Grade, and then be introduced to a second language in high school. The notion that English will get Americans everywhere they wish to go at all times and will lead to intercultural development, not to mention the visible concern of achieving peace and good relations with the world, must be recast in a more holistic and democratic form of education.

37. All states and school boards should publicize the socio-linguistic research on learning languages so as to demystify and rehabilitate the mythology within mainstream society about the danger of learning more than one language. Quite simply, speaking more languages than English will not harm one's capacity to speak English.

38. The enticement to enter into contracts with for-profit enterprises as a way of funding schools should be eliminated. Communities should be made aware of economic situations that pressure and coerce some localities more than others and should also be invited to critique the role of marketing, advertising, and the drive to capture market-share. Educational policymaking should also address this area.

39. Programs such as Channel One, as per the preceding point, should be prohibited in schools. They are not benevolent services; moreover, they come with strings attached, and are not problematized.

40. The differentiated experiences of schools that have a larger wealth base, as compared to poorer districts, should be addressed. The research on this reality, including the social context, should be concisely and critically presented to parents, students, educators and the broader community. The approach should not be to illustrate blame, pity, guilt or incompetence but, rather, to seek to underscore systemic problems, resource allocation, and ineffectual curriculum and policy development.

41. Citizens should be presented with a clear analysis on the costs of not investing in education early on, especially in relation to incarceration, retraining, illiteracy, welfare, etc., and also be presented with research on the benefits of investing in early childhood education. This should not simply be the posting of charts and graphs on a website but, rather, a vigorous, sustained, open dialog between all sectors of society.

42. The limited accessibility to trips to museums, cultural events, and even foreign countries only serves to further increase the educational, cultural and political gap between Americans. Governments should provide an appropriate level of funding so that all schools can benefit from such indispensable activities.

43. Parents should be required, except in extraordinary circumstances, to provide one-half day of service per month to their childrens' schools. The objective is to make all parents knowledgeable of what happens at school, to create support for progressive activities, and to provide a vehicle to discuss education and democracy. Legislation should be passed to ensure that no parent would be penalized for participating in such a program. School principals should be supported in finding the appropriate ways to liaise with parents.

44. Teacher-education programs should focus on qualitative teaching and learning experiences, and develop assessment schemes that monitor and support innovation, engagement, collaboration, and critical pedagogical work that emphasizes learning and the construction of knowledge over the acquisition of knowledge.

45. Teacher-education programs should forge meaningful relationships with local school boards. All education faculty should have some form of a formal relationship with schools.

46. Accreditation for teacher-education programs should not be predicated on quantitative measures and rubrics but on critical engagement among the faculty and students. Before embarking on accreditation, all interested parties should collectively determine if the educational system will benefit from the accreditation process (in other words, if we were to construct an effective education system, would we consecrate the time, energy and focus on the present (neo-liberal) accreditation process, or some other process?).

47. All schools should implement a guest program whereby a range of professionals, academics, and people with diverse experiences could liaise with students. The access to a diversity of guests should be distributed equally throughout all schools, and no school should be without some form of a regular, regimented and engaging program in place. Special attention should be paid to diversity and the public good (i.e., high cultural capital schools should not be the only ones exposed to leading business and political figures; conversely, critical alternative movements and grassroots figures should not be invited only to working-class schools).

48. Public officials, including politicians, diplomats and mainstream media, should be invited into schools to dialog with students, all the while being open to critical questions about social justice, bias, patriotism, propaganda and why systemic issues exist in addition to the traditional reasons that such figures visit schools (e.g., to extol the virtues of democracy, to sell support for a particular platform, career choices, being a good citizen, etc.).

49. All schools should embark on a range of community projects, which could count for credit toward graduation. These projects could involve service-learning, undertaking research, writing narratives and ethnographies, and making presentations on how social problems might be addressed.

50. When students are required to work part-time jobs in order to sustain themselves, special provisions should be made in order for them to critically analyze their experiences and also to receive credit for the related academic projects that they construct.

51. State departments of education, overseen by a board of professionals and activists, should gather data on inputs and outputs of the education system, and report on how diversity, social justice, media literacy, democracy and other program areas are relevant. These reports should be available online, free of cost, through the department of education's website.

52. When elections are discussed in schools, every effort possible should be made to clarify how many people do not vote and why, as well as explicating the problematic nature of there being only two mainstream parties. Students should critically interrogate the role of money, polling, media manipulation and political parties in enhancing or constraining democracy. Students should also be made aware of and study comparative (international) models and systems of democracy.

53. The study of democracy and/or elections should not be concentrated within a single course (often labelled as a Civics or Government course). Democracy must be demonstrated, acted upon, and lived, not ghettoized within a course that focuses on encouraging voting.

54. Require school boards and schools to implement participatory budgeting in an inclusive and meaningful fashion, involving diverse interests in determining the allocation of funds for education.

55. The state, overseen by an advisory board of non-political appointees, should review and make recommendations on the textbooks and other education matters to be used in schools. Monopoly practices for textbooks that exclude inclusive, critical thinking should be addressed.

56. Prohibit fundraising within schools, and have educators focus exclusively on critical teaching, learning and engagement. If schools are not concerned with raising funds, they will then be able to freely target the best interests of the students, and also not be beholden to any outside interests.

57. Schools should focus on the prevention of bullying and violence, and work with communities, families and students at various levels to establish a conducive environment for learning, and, at the same time, seek to avoid the nefarious *zero tolerance*, criminalization route.

58. Schools should undertake community violence and criminality projects, examining the form, substance and degree of violence and criminality in their localities. The data collection and analysis should include White-collar crime, corruption, racial profiling and un- and under-documented crimes, including abuse against women, gang activities and police misconduct. The results, which form part of a process of critical interrogation, could be publicly presented on an ongoing basis in order to lead to a more rigorous understanding of how and why criminal activities and violence take place and, moreover, what is done about it.

59. Similar to the point above, schools should undertake community health projects to determine the types of diseases, infections and illnesses that exist in local communities with a view to undertaking critical comparative analysis. Are poorer people more a risk, do they live shorter lives, do they have access to adequate health care, do they contribute equally to the formulation of health policy, etc? The ongoing results of the research should be exposed, and acted upon.

60. In order to undertake critical democratic projects, such as those highlighted above, teachers will need professional development that responds to their needs, cultivates critical epistemological reflection, and allows for a dialectical teaching and learning experience. This will not decrease

educational achievement and outcomes; arguably, it will make the educational experience more meaningful, authentic, engaging, critical and relevant.

61. Incorporating social workers and community activists in a meaningful way can be effective in detecting problems and concerns, and should be interwoven into educational programming.

62. Have teachers construct two one-week school experiences that can complement the formal curriculum. Formal education need not be top-down, and teachers can offer insight, expertise, strategies and enthusiasm to de-center neo-liberal education. Teachers could have students work together in multi-grade or multi-group assignments with a view to inculcating cooperative learning, mediation, anti-racism education, etc.. Students could present their work at the end of the week, seeking input into how to respond to societal needs.

63. Students should be invited, as per Lawrence Kohlberg's moral development model, to determine some of the rules, guidelines and conditions of their school experience. Students should not be uniquely the recipients of the formal education experience but should also be full participants in shaping their knowledge and reality.

64. Media literacy should be a mandatory part of the educational experience, and critical media activities should be part of the curriculum at every grade level.

65. Professional development for educators should focus on how knowledge is constructed as well as critical thinking and engagement. Educators should be able to understand the direction of educational reforms, and also be able to have a say in how they should be shaped, especially since they will be called upon to implement them. As research indicates that these reforms can only be considered effective if educators understand, appropriate and are permitted to question the shape, form and dimension of implementation, politically expedient neo-liberal reforms should be open to dialog and suggested change on the part of educators.

66. Schools, educators and students should problematize and critique what is meant by "the United States is the greatest nation." Repeating this mantra uncritically can lead to a delusionary sentiment of superiority, which could culminate in indifference, ignorance and antagonism toward the world. No country, people, race, culture, ethnic group, religion or nationality is superior, nor should there be the generalized belief that that is the case.

67. When studying economics, an explicit area of discussion should be inequities that exist and have existed emanating from the prevailing political and economic system. The supposed benefits of the free-market system should be contextualized and challenged in a critical fashion.

68. Alternative visions of democracy and comparative analysis of international systems, problems and issues should be part of the formal curriculum. We should not be able to discard that which we do not know.

69. Diverse methods, examples, processes and approaches to mediation, peace and reconciliation should be taught within the formal educational experience. Acceptance of war, torture, state-sanctioned executions, and other forms of violence should be critically diagnosed.

70. Teachers should be consulted on the planning of the courses, scheduling and the configuration of classes. Staid, neo liberal school planning should be open to innovative proposals on the part of teachers.

71. Teachers in the primary grades should stay with cohorts for a three-year period.

72. As per the previous point, groups of 2–3 teachers should work together with each cohort in order to provide stability and coherence in relation to the teaching and learning experience.

73. The school year need not be artificially structured around the agricultural calendar of the early twentieth century and should be expanded so as to offer fluid, constructive learning opportunities.

74. Class sizes, especially in the primary grades, should be limited to 15–20 students.

75. Gifted classes should be eliminated, and all students should be considered to have exceptional interests, talents, skills and abilities. For students with advanced academic standing, teachers should be attuned to differentiated learning needs and styles but should not separate those who excel more easily. All students can and should learn individually as well as collectively.

76. No child should be placed in special education without a full determination of the socio-economic context, thus diminishing the possibility of marginalized and racialized communities being disproportionately streamed into these programs. Despite formal procedures outlined in present processes, there is still widespread concern about the types of children directed to special education.

77. All universities and colleges should be involved in research, professional development and policy support with schools and school boards. A committee should be formed in each higher education institution to act as a clearinghouse to assist school boards.

78. Make humility a virtue for teaching and learning and downgrade the emphasis placed on economic gain accrued by business leaders, actors and professional athletes.

79. Provide teachers every seven years, when they have exhibited engaged and exemplary educational practices, and when they have a plan for learning, followed by a contribution to the school upon their return, a one-semester sabbatical to further enhance their abilities, approaches, pedagogies and critical engagement.

80. All schools should have a garden that produces fruits and vegetables. While working 1–2 hours a week on the garden, students will also learn and have opportunities to make concrete curricular connections to the environment, agriculture, nutrition, the economics of food, and globalization. The fruits and vegetables produced could also be consumed by the students.

81. A national education strategy should be formulated, taking into account the social justice framework, the *thin versus thick* typology, and other components of a critical pedagogy of democracy.

82. Civic society and alternative groups and movements, such as women's, environmental, peace, anti-racism, anti-poverty, and immigrant groups, should be accorded a formal place at the decision-making table alongside the traditional power brokers (bankers, the military, the wealthy, business CEOs, etc.).

83. All schools should have music, arts and physical education programs. Funding and wealth should not be an impediment to children having access to a broad liberal arts education.

84. Schools should be open in the evening for communities to be able to access them, without paying, in order to play sports, practice music and dance, and undertake scholarly and/or other activities.

85. The education sector should make a clear distinction between technology as a tool to assist in learning versus technology as the goal of education. Technology does not replace the brain, nor

does it create social justice. Similarly, technology does not create political literacy, nor does it make for a more media-literate populace, as exemplified in earlier chapters. Educators should clearly contextualize how technology might be beneficial while focusing on the fundamental aspects of critical democratic *conscientization*.

86. Students should construct critical ethnographies of their lives, building on a corpus of reflective and analytical work each year, which could serve to challenge epistemological intransigence. By seeing the evolution and transformation of their thinking over time and in relation to various events, personalities and experiences, students can start to make critical observations about their identities, societies and the way that knowledge is constructed. Toward the end of each year, students could review their analysis from the previous years, and then add to it by commenting on their previous thoughts as well as elaborating on changes in their thinking.

87. Make schools and society safer by eliminating firearms and weapons from the public domain. Gun control should be enforced, and carrying guns should be made a punishable offence.

88. Tuition to postsecondary education should be eliminated.

89. A war tax of 20% should be applied to all spending on the military and militarization, and the resultant funding should be applied to education. In present times, with approximately $1 trillion being spent annually on the military in the US, the government would be obliged to allocate an additional $200 billion to the education section. Education should not be used to subsidize war, nor should poorer people be forced into fighting *other people's battles*.

90. The federal government should organize an annual Education Summit, in which diverse civil society, educational and *alter-mondialiste* organizations could contribute to a debate around formal measures, data, policies, resources and goals of public education. This Education Summit could be considered as an *accountability* forum for governments and education authorities. The Summit would generate a detailed annual report and plan, which would be reviewed the following year.

91. At the broader political level, politicians and political parties should be prohibited from fundraising, especially while in office, and from buying advertising and the dissemination of promotional materials, including environmental-unfriendly campaign signs.

92. Election campaigns should be restricted to an enforced four-week period. There is no legitimate reason for having two-year campaigns, and they have not proven to increase voter turnout, nor democratic engagement. Moreover, they seem to monopolize the mainstream media cycle, which further marginalizes critical debate and analysis on a plethora of other relevant news items.

93. All political announcements, debates and arguments should be presented, without cost, through the mainstream, community, and alternative media. Candidates and parties should use websites to publicize their platforms. The focus should be on engagement, ideas, interaction with the plurality of society, and on eliminating money from the political system, which is surely at odds with what democracy was intended to be.

94. The political and economic configuration of the society should be openly critiqued and debated, and the fundamental question of inequitable power relations should be problematized. If change is (supposedly) inevitable, why then is there still unacceptably high levels of poverty

and marginalization, and, moreover, why is the gap between rich and poor increasing, not decreasing?

95.   For a country as diverse as the United States, any elections with only two parties should be cancelled. The Republicans and Democrats should not be permitted to monopolize elected, representative decision-making. Elections should be about people, and the collusion of the media, the military and the two corporate-focused/dependent parties will only further disenfranchise the population. Elections should be open to all peoples, not only those capable of raising untold millions, and even billions, of dollars.

96.   Privilege of all kinds should be examined critically before, during and after elections. Systemic inequities need to be contextualized, and made evident, rather than propagating the myth that simple hard work will lead to success.

97.   Any elections should necessarily be required to involve schools and the education sector in meaningful meetings at educational sites, with explications on how the macro-level economy, foreign policy, military ventures and social policy are related to education, including the potential effects, outcomes and costs and benefits.

98.   Freedom of speech should include uncomfortable (and, using Al Gore's language, inconvenient) truths, without retribution. If so many people in education are uncomfortable, for example, with NCLB, they should be able to enunciate their concerns without fear of being marginalized.

99.   Humility should be emphasized over nationalism and patriotism.

100.   *Radical love* should be the starting point for the conceptualization of education.

Whether or not the above proposals appear to be realistic is not the critical question to be asked. The reality that there are diverse proposals, movements, interests and people seeking a different kind of democracy should be kept in mind.

A democratic education planning model

This democratic education planning model (Figure 33) can assist in mapping what individuals, schools and communities are thinking and experiencing in relation to democracy and democratic engagement. Schools could document the context, the content, the experiences and the outcomes of what takes place within the realm of education. There are many ways of promoting constructive collaboration, and I would encourage critical, dialectical and harmonious efforts aimed at understanding and constructing more meaningful experiences, not imposing haphazard, incongruent and inauthentic ones. For this model, schools could work with diverse interests, or stakeholders in public policy jargon, who are not, using the neo-liberal terminology, "clients." Involving teachers, parents, students, members of the community and others, and being cognizant of differential power relations, may facilitate some important synergetic planning as well as the formulation of proposals. This approach is inspired by the participatory budget planning process (Gandin & Apple, 2005), established in Porto Alegre, Brazil, in which the community comes together to consider how portions of the budget will be spent. Using a critical pedagogical analysis, participants in the democratic education planning model should be highly sensitized to systemic and institutional barriers to change, and should also consider the *lived* experiences of individuals and groups, being vigilant to grasp the nuanced existence of marginalized interests.

Figure 33. Democratic education planning model

	Context	Content	Experiences	Outcomes
Individual				
School				
Community				

The model does not seek the typical (supposed) accountability report that is skewed toward illustrating the virtue of the funder or the institutional interest. Rather, the focus should be on *bona fide*, tangible critical engagement, questioning why policies and programs have been developed, in whose interest, and to what end. For example, how do individuals, the school and the community contribute to the democratic foundation, growth and tension of what takes place locally within an educational site?

One way to use this model would be to chart out the context for democratic education, to define it, to highlight the historic and contemporary achievement, issues and challenges, and to address such fundamental concerns as those related to patriotism, socio-economic development, and political participation in an inclusive and *thick* way. The notion is not to draft volumes here but, rather, to attempt to link the epistemological and philosophical underpinning to what we know and how we know and believe it to our actions (Kincheloe, 2008b). Often education policies seem to drop from the sky, disconnected from the lived realities of students, and inconsistent with scientific research (although NCLB specifically prescribes that reforms be based on scientific research, can educational leaders enumerate the literature that has informed their philosophies?)(Gordon, Smyth & Diehl, 2008).

Returning to democratic literacy and critical pedagogy

Can we have democracy without democratic literacy? Without democratic engagement? Is critical pedagogy an appropriate means for achieving democratic literacy and democratic engagement? Relying, in large part, on the critical pedagogical foundation of Paulo Freire, it is helpful here to highlight the epistemological salience of Freire's work, which Au (2007) argues is steeped in the Marxist tradition. Epistemological interrogation is a necessary function to the quest for transformational change in education. Although the terminology may change from context to context, Freire's *conscientization* has meaning across diverse milieus and environments. Achieving meaningful experiences in and through education, cognizant of differential power relations, is the core of a critical pedagogical democratic education. Whether or not a critical Marxist perspective is germane in nurturing democratic education should not obfuscate the reality that critical pedagogy can lead to the process of personal and collective transformation.

Brosio (2003), in citing Michael Parenti, a leading radical political philosopher, highlights that normative neo-liberal, capitalistic structures have, and continue to have, a significant effect on people and societal development.

> What we need is a 180 degree shift away from unilateral global domination and toward equitable and sustainable development among the peoples of the world. This means US leaders would have to stop acting like self-willed unaccountable rulers of the planet. They must stop supporting despots, and stop opposing those democratic movements and governments that challenge the status quo. The struggle is between those who believe that the land, labor, capital, technology, markets, and natural resources of society should be used as expendable resources for transnational profit accumulation, and those who believe that such things should b used for the mutual benefit of the populace. What we need is to move away from liberal complaints about how bad things are and toward a radical analysis that explains *why* [the current writer's emphasis] they are so, away from treating every situation as a perfectly new and befuddling happening unrelated to broader politico-economic interests and class power structures. What we need is a global anti-imperialist movement that can challenge the dominant paradigm with an alternative one that circumvents the monopoly ideological control of officialdom and corporate America.

Bellamy Foster, Holleman and McChesney (2008) support this perspective, arguing for a more comprehensive, critical and global analysis of American empire, suggesting that the degree to which US society is controlled by militarization is only poorly understood by the population, which then leads to far-reaching potential to dominate, marginalize and diminish the vibrancy of vast swaths of society. Willinsky (1998) further addresses the need to critique empire as a necessary step to bringing forth the prospect for change, which relates to Freire's (1973/2005) oppressor-oppressed dichotomy. Anti-colonial education should, therefore, not be uniquely a discussion reserved for the archives as the historical is intertwined with the present, and appreciating how current problems and issues have a relationship with previous actions is pivotal to avoiding simplistic, essentialized education responses.

Taking account of the dialectical relationship between hegemony and ideology (Fishman & McLaren, 2005) is a pivotal part of the critical pedagogical equation. As highlighted in the first section of the book, critical epistemological interrogation is fundamental to the dissection and unravelling of how power is infused in and through (supposed) democratic processes. The relevance for education, therefore, is clear.

> Critical pedagogy problematizes the relationship between education and politics, between socio-political relations and pedagogical practices, between the reproduction of dependent hierarchies of power and privilege in the domain of everyday social life and that of the classroom and institutions. In doing so, it advances an agenda for educational transformation by encouraging educators to understand the socio-political contexts of educative acts and the importance of radically democratizing both educational and larger social formations. In such processes, educators take on intellectual roles by adapting to, resisting, and challenging curriculum, school policy, educational philosophies, and pedagogical traditions. (Fishman & McLaren, 2005, p. 425)

A critical pedagogy of democracy can cultivate a vigorous and meaningful interrogation of the various strands underpinning power structures, including the functioning of the military, limited but populism-laden visions of politics, and the infusion of right-wing Christian fundamentalist religious infiltration into decision-making (Giroux, 2005; Steinberg & Kincheloe, 2009). Giroux and Giroux (2006) provide a thoughtful synthesis of critical democratic pedagogy:

> The democratic character of critical pedagogy is defined largely through a set of basic assumptions, which holds that power, values, and institutions must be made available to critical scrutiny, be understood as a product of human labor (as opposed to God-given), and evaluated in terms of how they might open up or close down democratic practices and experiences. Yet, critical pedagogy is about more than simply holding authority accountable through the close reading of texts, the creation of radical classroom practices, or the promotion of critical literacy. It is also about linking learning to social change, education to democracy, and knowledge to acts of intervention in public life. Critical pedagogy encourages students to learn to register dissent, as well as to take risks in creating the conditions for forms of individual and social agency that are conducive to a substantive democracy. (p. 28)

Challenging neo-liberalism is a central feature to this project, shining a light on nefarious practices, marginalization, and conservative interpretations of success that serve to blame the victim rather than critique the trappings and inner-working of power (Giroux & Giroux, 2006). De-coding signals, omissions, directives, and the meaning of rhetoric is a key component to the critical pedagogy of democracy (Engels, 2007; Kellner & Share, 2007; Macedo & Steinberg, 2007). State authority is not obliged to be oppressive, and ingratiating students with a critical pedagogy of democracy can lead to *thicker* experiences and interpretations of democracy.

A radical democratic pedagogy, as outlined by Denzin (2009), speaks to hope: "Hope is ethical. Hope is moral. Hope is peaceful and nonviolent. Hope seeks truth of life's sufferings. Hope gives meaning to the struggles to change the world. Hope is grounded in concrete performative practices, in struggles and interventions that espouse sacred values of love, care, community, trust, and well-being" (p. 385).

Compelling arguments can be made for a more deliberately conscious, engaged and loving connection to others (Darder & Miron, 2006). Freire spoke of radical love, and the inescapable prospect of indignation, which need not be considered weakness, cynicism or hopelessness (Freire, 2004). The capacity and necessity to love is enraptured in the very essence of the human condition. Accepting human and humane interactions and relations, without exploitation and discrimination, is a fundamental consideration for a critical pedagogy of democracy. Darder and Miron (2006) emphasize that our experiences are not disconnected from the broader poltico-economic context but, as Brosio (2003, 2004) maintains, are inter-woven in a socially constructed narrative.

> [c]apitalism disembodies and alienates our daily existence. As our consciousness becomes more and more abstracted, we become more and more detached from our bodies. For this reason, it is absolutely imperative that critical educators and scholars acknowledge that the origin of emancipator possibility and human solidarity resides in our body. (p. 16)

As Darder and Miron (2006) argue, and as was advanced in the previous chapter, everyone is capable of contesting, resisting and challenging nefarious neo-liberal policies and manifestations: "If we, as citizens of the Empire, do not use every opportunity to voice our dissent, we shamefully leave the great task of dissent to our brothers and sisters around the world who daily suffer greater conditions of social, political, and economic impoverishment and uncertainty than we will ever know. For how long will our teaching and politics fail to address the relevant and concrete issues that affect people's daily lives?" (p. 18). Not every action or gesture need be representative of a grandiose, sweepingly transformative manifestation. As alluded to earlier in this book, individuals can make their voices heard, they can resist imperialism, hegemony and patriotic oppression, and, importantly, they can choose love over hate, peace over war, and humanity over inhumanity.

Concluding Thoughts

While focusing on democracy throughout this book, is it clear that a *thicker*, more critical version of democracy, outside of representative, electoral politics, necessarily involves an inter-disciplinary approach (sociology, history, philosophy, political science, economics, education, cultural studies and the social sciences, in general) with close consideration to a number of directly related subjects/issues (peace studies, media literacy, environmental education, intercultural relations, etc.). There is no set answer, list or menu to the question of how to *do* democracy, or how to create a *thicker* democracy. Rather, as suggested in the cluster of what might be done above, an amalgam of thinking, interrogation, critical analysis, experience and humility may lead to a more meaningful and sustainable democracy, one that seeks to engage and cultivate critical engagement of all people and interests. A more radical determination toward a more radical democracy requires thinking well outside of constricted, hegemonic boundaries, and must address how power works (Hill & Boxley, 2007).

Neither Paulo Freire, nor Joe Kincheloe, nor other well-known critical pedagogues, I believe, would want students, educators and others to simply replicate what they've done, or to believe simply that what they've experienced and developed in theory and in praxis is the penultimate answer. The quest for critical humility and radical love encourages all of us to seek new, innovative and reflective thoughts and actions in the quest for a more decent society. What Freire, Kincheloe and others offer us, however, is an enormous wealth and insightful archive of *constructed* knowledge, something that is, I would argue, of tremendous value to those wishing to have a more *conscious* connection to what society was, is and is evolving into. The critical pedagogy of democracy is not about counting votes but relates more fundamentally to an unending critical interrogation of the human experience, focused on humane encounters, social justice, peace, a more equitable and respectful distribution of resources, a more dignified and just recognition of indigenous cultures, and an acknowledgement that hegemonic forces marginalize peoples at home and abroad.

Does your vote count? It could... but there are a multitude of other factors that are most likely more germane, not to mention that voting, in and of itself, does not make a democracy. As argued throughout this book, any definition of democracy that omits a central place for a meaningful, engaged, critical education is problematic. People construct a democracy, not political parties and institutions, albeit they are relevant, and, therefore, people must construct their political, economic, social, cultural and philosophic destinies. The people are the ones who define their circumstances, values, affiliations, interpersonal relations and essence to live. Yet, as per the central hypothesis of this book, the people must also be vigilant and suspicious of how power affects their daily lives, their abilities, their relations, and their connection to the world. Education is the key intersecting vehicle that can reinforce or, conversely, interrupt patriotic bondage, racialized marginalization, essentialized visions of poverty and impoverishment, and an uncritical assessment of how power works. Freire and Kincheloe offer much inspiration for this journey, and their willingness to question and accept questions provides for a vibrant, dynamic and engaged democracy within the spirit of critical pedagogy. Alongside the mantra of the *alter-mondialiste* movement that *another world is possible*, I would like to conclude by suggesting that... *another democracy is possible.*

Chapter 15

Postscript:
Quoting Democracy and Other Subversive Acts

Throughout the ages, many people have commented on the meaning of democracy. Below are a few quotes, which are not representative of the world but do give a flavor of some of the hopes, desires, concerns and images of the concept. Although these quotes could be organized in a number of ways, given the broad historical, multicultural, and inter-disciplinary nature of those cited, I have chosen to simply list them in alphabetical order. It should be noted that it is not always easy, nor appropriate, to place a label on those cited below, but I have chosen to do so in order to contextualize the quotes, understanding that these historic figures represent more than the moniker I have placed beside their names.

> *The one pervading evil of democracy is the tyranny of the party that succeeds, by force or fraud, in carrying elections.*
>
> —Acton, Lord [English historian (1834–1902)]

> *Democracy... while it lasts is more bloody than either [aristocracy or monarchy]. Remember, democracy never lasts long. It soon wastes, exhausts, and murders itself. There is never a democracy that did not commit suicide.*
>
> —Adams, John [President of the US (1735–1826)]

> *We have learned to say that the good must be extended to all of society before it can be held secure by any one person or any one class. But we have not yet learned to add to that statement, that unless all [people] and all classes contribute to a good, we cannot even be sure that it is worth having.*
>
> —Addams, Jane [American sociologist (1860–1935)]

> *Change means movement. Movement means friction. Only in the frictionless vacuum of a nonexistent abstract world can movement or change occur without that abrasive friction of conflict.*
>
> —Alinsky, Saul [American scholar and community organizer (1909–1972)]

> *If liberty and equality, as is thought by some, are chiefly to be found in democracy, they will be best attained when all persons alike share in the government to the utmost.*
>
> —Aristotle [Greek philosopher (284BC–322BC)]

Voting is one of the few things where boycotting in protest clearly makes the problem worse rather than better.

> —Auer, Jane [American novelist and playwright (1917–1973)]

Fear is not the natural state of civilized people.

> —Aung San Suu Kyi [Myanmar politician (b. 1945)]

There is an idea of democracy produced by one-sided thinking.

> —Bongo, Omar [President of Gabon (1935–2009)]

There are only two families in the world, my old grandmother used to say, the Haves and the Have-nots.

> —(de) Cervantes, Miguel [Spanish novelist (1547–1616)]

Democracy, as has been said of Christianity, has never really been tried.

> —Chase, Stuart [American economist (1888–1985)]

The unconscious democracy of America is a very fine thing. It is a true and deep and instinctive assumption of the equality of citizens, which even voting and elections have not destroyed.

> —Chesterton, G. K. [English author (1874–1936)]

Propaganda is to a democracy what the bludgeon is to a totalitarian state.

Capitalism is a system in which the central institutions of society are, in principle, under autocratic control. Thus, a corporation or an industry is, if we were to think of it in political terms, fascist, that is, it has tight control at the top and strict obedience has to be established at every level... Just as I'm opposed to political fascism, I am opposed to economic fascism. I think that until the major institutions of society are under the popular control of participants and communities, it's pointless to talk about democracy.

The most effective way to restrict democracy is to transfer decision-making from the public arena to unaccountable institutions: kings and princes, priestly castes, military juntas, party dictatorships, or modern corporations.

> —Chomsky, Noam [American scholar and activist (b. 1928)]

The best argument against democracy is a five-minute conversation with the average voter.

> —Churchill, Winston [(British Prime Minister (1874–1965)]

I'm not willing to be tolerated. That wounds my love of love and liberty.

> —Cocteau, Jean [French poet (1889–1963)]

Abraham Lincoln did not go to Gettysburg having commissioned a poll to find out what would sell in Gettysburg. There were no people with percentages for him, cautioning him about this group or that group or what they found in exit polls a year earlier. When will we have the courage of Lincoln?

> —Coles, Robert [Child psychiatrist (b. 1929)]

He who merely knows right principles is not equal to him who loves them.
—Confucius [Philosopher (551–479 BC)]

One does not sell the earth upon which the people walk.
—Crazy Horse [Native American (1838–1877)]

When great changes occur in history, when great principles are involved, as a rule the majority are wrong. The minority are right.
—Debs, Eugene V. [Union leader and politician (1855–1926)]

The surface of American society is covered with a layer of democratic paint, but from time to time one can see the old aristocratic colors breaking through.
—(de) Tocqueville, Alexis [French author (1805–1859)]

The aim of education is to enable individuals to continue their education ... (and) the object and reward of learning is continued capacity for growth. Now this idea cannot be applied to all the members of a society except where intercourse of man with man is mutual, and except where there is adequate provision for the reconstruction of social habits and institutions by means of wide stimulation arising from equitably distributed interests. And this means a democratic society.
—Dewey, John [American philosopher (1859–1952)]

Originality and the feeling of one's own dignity are achieved only through work and struggle.
—Dostoevsky, Fyodor [Russian novelist (1821–1881)]

Where justice is denied, where poverty is enforced, where ignorance prevails, and where any one class is made to feel that society is in an organized conspiracy to oppress, rob, and degrade them, neither persons nor property will be safe.
  No man can put a chain about the ankle of his fellow man without at last finding the other end fastened about his own neck.
—Douglas, Frederick [American abolitionist (1818–1895)]

The cost of liberty is less than the price of repression.
—Du Bois, W. E. B. [American civil rights activist (1868–1963)]

The two greatest obstacles to democracy in the United States are, first, the widespread delusion among the poor that we have a democracy, and second, the chronic terror among the rich, lest we get it.
—Dowling, Edward [Anglican priest and historian (1838–1920)]

Democracy don't rule the world, You'd better get that in your head; This world is ruled by violence, But I guess that's better left unsaid.
—Dylan, Bob [(American folksinger (b.1941)]

That's free enterprise, friends: freedom to gamble, freedom to lose. And the great thing—the truly democratic thing about it—is that you don't even have to be a player to lose.
> —Ehrenreich, Barbara [American author and feminist (b. 1941)]

A country cannot simultaneously prepare and prevent war.

I know not with what weapons World War III will be fought, but World War IV will be fought with sticks and stones.

The distinctions separating the social classes are false; in the last analysis they rest on force.
> —Einstein, Albert [Physicist (1879–1955)]

Every revolution was first a thought in one man's mind; and when the same thought occurs to another man, it is the key to that era.
> —Emerson, Ralph Waldo [American essayist (1803–1882)]

If fifty million people say a foolish thing, it is still a foolish thing.
> —France, Anatole [French poet and journalist (1844–1924)]

Education either functions as an instrument which is used to facilitate integration of the younger generation into the logic of the present system and bring about conformity or it becomes the practice of freedom, the means by which men and women deal critically and creatively with reality and discover how to participate in the transformation of their world.

Washing one's hands of the conflict between the powerful and the powerless means to side with the powerful, not to be neutral.

> —Freire, Paulo [Brazilian educator (1921–1997)]

In a democracy, dissent is an act of faith.
> —Fulbright, J. William [US Senator from Arkansas (1905–1995)]

If I seem to take part in politics, it is only because politics encircles us today like the coil of a snake from which one cannot get out, no matter how much one tries. I wish therefore to wrestle with the snake.

You must be the change you wish to see in the world.

An eye for eye only ends up making the whole world blind.

The spirit of democracy cannot be imposed from without. It has to come from within.

The spirit of democracy cannot be established in the midst of terrorism, whether governmental or popular.

What difference does it make to the dead, the orphans, and the homeless, whether the mad destruction is wrought under the name of totalitarianism or the holy name of liberty and democracy?

—Gandhi, Mohandas [Leader of India (1869–1948)]

The essence of democracy is its assurance that every human being should so respect himself and should be so respected in his own personality that he should have opportunity equal to that of every other human being to show what he was meant to become.

—Garlin Spencer, Anna [American minister (1851–1931)]

Naturally the common people don't want war; neither in Russia, nor in England, nor in America, nor in Germany. That is understood. But after all, it is the leaders of the country who determine policy, and it is always a simple matter to drag the people along, whether it is a democracy, or a fascist dictatorship, or a parliament, or a communist dictatorship. Voice or no voice, the people can always be brought to the bidding of the leaders. That is easy. All you have to do is to tell them they are being attacked, and denounce the pacifists for lack of patriotism and exposing the country to danger. It works the same in any country.

—Goering, Hermann [German politician and Nazi official (1893–1946)]

Everybody's for democracy in principle. It's only in practice that the thing gives rise to stiff objections.

—Greenfield, Meg [American columnist (1930–1999)]

Democracy! Bah! When I hear that I reach for my feather boa!

—Ginsberg, Allen [American poet (b. 1941)]

They wrote in the old days that it is sweet and fitting to die for one's country. But in modern war, there is nothing sweet nor fitting in your dying. You will die like a dog for no good reason.

—Hemingway, Ernest [American writer (1899–1961)]

There is one thing stronger than all the armies in the world, and that is an idea whose time has come.

Hugo, Victor [French writer (1802–1885)]

The right to be heard does not automatically include the right to be taken seriously.

—Humphrey, Hubert H. [Vice President of the US (1830–1902)]

The death of democracy is not likely to be an assassination from ambush. It will be a slow extinction from apathy, indifference, and undernourishment.

—Hutchins, Robert M. [American educator (1899–1977)]

A democracy which makes or even effectively prepares for modern, scientific war must necessarily cease to be democratic. No country can be really well prepared for modern war unless it is governed by a tyrant, at the head of a highly trained and perfectly obedient bureaucracy.

—Huxley, Aldous [English writer (1894–1963)]

The thing about democracy, beloveds, is that it is not neat, orderly, or quiet. It requires a certain relish for confusion.

—Ivins, Molly [American columnist (1944–2007)]

A democracy is nothing more than mob rule, where fifty-one percent of the people may take away the rights of the other forty-nine.

The care of human life and happiness, and not their destruction, is the first and only object of good government.

—Jefferson, Thomas [President of the United States (1743–1825)]

We are not afraid to entrust the American people with unpleasant facts, foreign ideas, alien philosophies, and competitive values. For a nation that is afraid to let its people judge the truth and falsehood in an open market is a nation that is afraid of its people.

—Kennedy, John F. [President of the United States (1917–1963)]

He who passively accepts evil is as much involved in it as he who helps perpetrate it.

Injustice anywhere is a threat to justice everywhere.

Philanthropy is commendable, but it must not cause the philanthropist to overlook the circumstances of economic injustice that make philanthropy necessary.

—King Jr., Martin Luther [American minister and activist (1929–1968)]

Democracy does not guarantee equality of conditions—it only guarantees equality of opportunity.

—Kristol, Irving [American columnist (1920–2009)]

Democracy is indispensable to socialism.

—Lenin, Vladimir [Russian leader and revolutionary (1970–1924)]

Without general elections, without unrestricted freedom of press and assembly, without a free struggle of opinion, life dies out in every public institution, becomes a mere semblance of life, in which only the bureaucracy remains as the active element.

—Luxemburg, Rosa [Polish (Jewish) revolutionary (1871–1919)]

A modern democracy is a tyranny whose borders are undefined; one discovers how far one can go only by traveling in a straight line until one is stopped.

—Mailer, Norman [American writer (1923–2008)]

Habit creates the appearance of justice; progress has no greater enemy than habit.
—Marti, Jose [Cuban writer (1853–1895)]

Democracy is the road to socialism.

Catch a man a fish, and you can sell it to him. Teach a man to fish, and you ruin a wonderful business opportunity.
—Marx, Karl [German philosopher and revolutionary (1818–1883)]

Democracy is a pathetic belief in the collective wisdom of individual ignorance.

Democracy is only a dream: it should be put in the same category as Arcadia, Santa Claus, and Heaven.

A good politician under democracy is quite as unthinkable as an honest burglar.
—Mencken, H. L. [American journalist (1880–1956)]

Liberation means you don't have to be silenced.

If you're going to hold someone down you're going to have to hold on by the other end of the chain. You are confined by your own repression.

The function of freedom is to free somebody else.
—Morrison, Toni [American author [(b. 1931)]

The survival of democracy depends on the renunciation of violence and the development of nonviolent means to combat evil and advance the good.
—Muste, A. J. [American pacifist (1885–1967)]

In a time of universal deceit, telling the truth becomes a revolutionary act.
—Orwell, George [English novelist (1903–1950)]

Democracy is a process by which the people are free to choose the man who will get the blame.
—Peter, Laurence J. [American writer (1919–1990)]

Governments exist to protect the rights of minorities. The loved and the rich need no protection: they have many friends and few enemies.
—Phillips, Wendell [American abolitionist (1811–1884)]

Computers are useless. They can only give you answers.
—Picasso, Pablo [Spanish artist (1881–1973)]

Tyranny naturally arises out of democracy.

An imbalance between rich and poor is the oldest and most fatal ailment of all republics.

The life that is unexamined is not worth living.
> —Plato [Greek philosopher (427BC–367BC)]

The answer to injustice is not to silence the critic but to end the injustice.
> —Robeson, Paul [American actor and activist (1898–1976)]

Terror is only justice: prompt, severe and inflexible; it is then an emanation of virtue; it is less a distinct principle than a natural consequence of the general principle of democracy, applied to the most pressing wants of the country.
> —Robespierre, Maximilien [French revolutionary (1758–1794)]

Elections are a good deal like marriages. There's no accounting for anyone's taste. Every time we see a bridegroom we wonder why she ever picked him, and it's the same with public officials.
> —Rogers, Will [American actor (1879–1935)]

Pure logic is the ruin of the spirit.
> —(de) Saint-Exupery, Antoine [French writer (1900–1944)]

Everything has been figured out, except how to live.
> —Sartre, Jean-Paul [French philosopher (1905–1980)]

Democracy is a device that ensures we shall be governed no better than we deserve.
> —Shaw, George Bernard [American playwright (1856–1950)]

Democracy encourages the majority to decide things about which the majority is ignorant.
> —Simon, John [American theater critic (b. 1925)]

Of all tyrannies, a tyranny exercised for the good of its victims may be the most oppressive. It may be better to live under robber barons than under omnipotent moral busybodies. The robber baron's cruelty may sometimes sleep, his cupidity may at some point be satiated; but those who torment us for our own good will torment us without end, for they do so with the approval of their own conscience.
> —Staples Lewis, Clive [English author (1898–1963)]

It is not the fact of liberty but the way in which liberty is exercised that ultimately determines whether liberty itself survives.
> —Thompson, Dorothy [American journalist (1894–1961)]

If you are neutral in situations of injustice, you have chosen the side of the oppressor. If an elephant has its foot on the tail of a mouse and you say that you are neutral, the mouse will not appreciate your neutrality.

—Tutu, Desmond [South African minister and activist (b. 1931)]

Citizenship is what makes a republic—monarchies can get along without it.

We adore titles and heredities in our hearts and ridicule them with our mouths. This is our democratic privilege.

—Twain, Mark [American writer (1835–1910)]

Politics is the art of preventing people from taking part in affairs which properly concern them.

—Valéry, Paul [French philosopher (1871–1945)]

Democracy is supposed to give you the feeling of choice, like Painkiller X and Painkiller Y. But they're both just aspirin.

Apparently, a democracy is a place where numerous elections are held at great cost without issues and with interchangeable candidates.

—Vidal, Gore [American novelist (b. 1925)]

So long as the people do not care to exercise their freedom, those who wish to tyrannize will do so; for tyrants are active and ardent, and will devote themselves in the name of any number of gods, religious and otherwise, to put shackles upon sleeping men.

—Voltaire (François-Marie Arouet) [French writer (1694–1778)]

No person is your friend who demands your silence, or denies your right to grow.

—Walker, Alice [American writer and activist (b. 1944)]

As Mankind becomes more liberal, they will be more apt to allow that all those who conduct themselves as worthy members of the community are equally entitled to the protections of civil government. I hope ever to see America among the foremost nations of justice and liberality.

—Washington, George [President of the United States (1732–1799)]

In Switzerland they had brotherly love, five hundred years of democracy and peace, and what did they produce? The cuckoo clock!

—Weil, Simone [French philosopher and activist (1909–1943)]

I have learned the guilt of indifference. The opposite of love is not hate but indifference.

—Wiesel, Elie [(b. 1928)]

Democracy is the recurrent suspicion that more than half of the people are right more than half of the time.

—White, E. B. [American Writer (1899–1985)]

Did you, too, O friend, suppose democracy was only for elections, for politics, and for a party name? I say democracy is only of use there that it may pass on and come to its flower and fruit in manners, in the highest forms of interaction between [people], and their beliefs—in religion, literature, colleges and schools—democracy in all public and private life....

The purpose of democracy—supplanting old belief in the necessary absoluteness of establish'd dynastic rulership, temporal, ecclesiastical, and scholastic, as furnishing the only security against chaos, crime, and ignorance—is, through many transmigrations, and amid endless ridicules, arguments, and ostensible failures.

—Whitman, Walt [American poet (1819–1892)]

Democracy means simply the bludgeoning of the people by the people for the people.

—Wilde, Oscar [Irish writer (1854–1900)]

When people refuse to obey, then democracy comes alive.

—Zinn, Howard [American historian and activist (b. 1922)]

Afterword

Joel Westheimer
University Research Chair and Professor, University of Ottawa

More than 60 years ago, former Supreme Court Justice Louis Brandeis is purported to have warned that: "We can have democracy in this country or we can have great wealth concentrated in the hands of a few, but we can't have both." If he was right, then democracy today is in grave danger. As this book painstakingly details, *econ-ocracy*–which might be described as government of the wealthy, by the wealthy, and for the wealthy–is a concept that is, today, frighteningly apt. The most salient decisions about how we choose to spend our resources, who will benefit, and who will suffer are now concentrated in the hands of a very few people. Carr rightly sees education as a critical vehicle out of this mess. If we are to make each of our votes count, then there are a great number of changes that have to be made not only in the way government works, but also in the way we educate our children to take part in shaping their future.

Yet, as many readers of this volume already know, education reform in the United States, Canada, and elsewhere, has generally run in the opposite direction. *No Child Left Behind* (which in previous writing I have called 'No Child Left Thinking') has done more than any previous education reform to ensure that curriculum is aimed squarely away from deep and critical thinking about social and political matters. Furthermore, NCLB's successor–Obama's Race-to-the-Top legislation–promises no better. With this context in mind, I want to revisit three brief themes that emerge from the previous pages of this book: the conflation of economic and political power; a complicit media; and critical education reform that could help to reinvigorate democratic well-being.

Money Madness: Stranger than Fiction

As a graduate student of sociology, Ari Rosner wrote a fictional account of life in the year 2983 in which transnational corporations (TNCs) wield enormous economic, civic, and social power. Poorer, developing countries rapidly trade their independence for a guarantee of jobs for their citizens, and eventually even powerful governments have struck deals with the TNCs for the provision of essential human services.

Somewhere in the middle of Rosner's story, the TNCs that end up employing a vast majority of the world's population give their employees a choice between citizenship and their jobs. This leads to a new population of "citizen-employees," each of whom has renounced their national citizenship in exchange for their job. Each corporation then develops its own company constitution, its own utilities for clean water and air, its own company laws, company prisons, and so on.

Although the fanciful case study of what *could* happen seems ominous, the reality of economic and political control today is already worrisome. As in Rosner's story, citizenship has come to mean less about civic participation, and more about economic control. The ever-growing gap between the wealthy and the poor in many industrialized countries around the world signals a return to an aristocratic political-economic system. The news is not new but recent research and writing indicates that the situation may be quite a lot worse than many believe. We may be aware that poor and middle-class Americans have been left behind economically in the wake of the Bush years, but many of us have always assumed that at least wealthy Americans benefitted.

Well, that depends on how you define wealthy. According to an exhaustive analysis by David Cay Johnston, the only American citizens who leapt ahead during the Bush years were those in the top one-tenth or even *one-hundredth of one percent* of the nation. Maybe you have even heard those figures, but it is difficult to imagine exactly what that means. How many people is one-hundredth of one percent of the population of the United States? About 30, 700–the population of Beverly Hills or less than one *one-thousandth* of the population of California. In fact, as Johnston argues in his 2008 book, *Free Lunch: How the Wealthiest Americans Enrich Themselves at Government Expense,* the level of inequality in contemporary America puts it in the company not of Canada, Europe, Australia, or Japan, but rather Mexico, Brazil, or Russia–countries, as Johnston argues, "in which adults have the right to vote, but real political power is wielded by a relatively narrow, and rich, segment of the population."

Perhaps the most amazing thing about the decline of democratic control is that those most brutally affected by it do not seek its reinstitution, but rather hope to rise to the level of the elites. Currently, the total income of the top one-hundredth of one percent that I referred to above equals the total income of the poorest 20 million households. In the last 30 years, the income of CEOs of major corporations has risen 2,500 percent in adjusted dollars. But as Daniel Brook writes in *The Nation*, members of those poorest 20 million households "aspire not to roll back inequality but to benefit from it." Recall the episode of the television show *West Wing* when fictional President Jeb Bartlett explains why Americans seem to vote against their own interests by protecting a tax system that benefits only the super rich. "It doesn't matter if most voters don't benefit," he explains, "They all believe that someday they will. That's the problem with the American dream. It makes everyone concerned for the day they're going to be rich." The question, then, becomes one of education or as Brook puts it, how to turn a nation of gamblers into a nation of citizens. As this book and others emphasize, two central sources for such an effort are the media and the schools. Yet, although both these institutions are potentially powerful catalysts for democratic participation and action, each instead avoids or actively works against those goals, at least within the formal sphere.

The Power of the Media

In *Manufacturing Consent: The Political Economy of the Mass Media* (1988), Noam Chomsky and Edward S. Herman argue that ordinary people in a democracy can and should participate in making informed political decisions, but that the information required to make these decisions is constrained by a system of half truths or misinformation promulgated primarily by the media.[1] In a dictatorship, they argue, what people think is of little importance because the state enforces its will (which represents the interests of a small elite) through force: do what we say or else. But in a democracy, means of control need to be more subtle; since citizens are allowed to voice their opinions, it becomes necessary to control their opinions ("propaganda is to democracy what violence is to totalitarianism"). To exercise control over what might be unpopular political decisions, then, the state must direct the range of perspectives that are voiced.

One of the ways to do this, Chomsky contends, is to ensure that political debate appears to embrace many opinions (what he calls *necessary illusions*), but actually stays within very narrow margins. This strategy should be familiar to any viewers of late-night news shows such as ABC News' *Nightline* or CNN's *Larry King Live*. The manufacture of consent–a phrase Chomsky and Herman borrow from the influential journalist Walter Lippman (1922)–provides government with coercive power and control while maintaining the illusion of democracy.

Not only are the consequences of such restricted debate devastating to fundamental principles of real democracy, but they are also self reinforcing. *the more narrow the range of ideas to which people are exposed, the less they inquire about or imagine alternatives.* In time, it becomes unnecessary for the state to restrict legitimate debate because citizens and non-governmental institutions do it on their own. In sharp contrast, then, to the dystopic vision of an authoritarian, repressive government represented by works of fiction such as Orwell's *Nineteen-Eighty-Four*, media-driven propaganda relies on the atrophied politics of the people themselves. The repression is not top-down but rather bottom-up. In other words, as the popular 1950s comic strip character Pogo famously said, "We have met the enemy, and he is us."

The consequences of the anemic media discourse and restricted debate around issues of vast social, political, and economic importance are, indeed, serious. The lead up to the American-led war in Iraq is one example. In 2003, before the war had started, Fox News commentator Bill O'Reilly proclaimed that when the war against Saddam Hussein begins, "We expect every American to support our military, and if they can't do that, to shut up...Americans and, indeed, our allies who actively work against our military once the war is under way will be considered enemies of the state by me" (cited in Tomasky, 2003: 22). Curiously, wartime almost always invites a majority of media outlets to call for "closing ranks." much in the same way Bill O'Reilly described above. Wartime is no time to critically evaluate government decisions on US engagement, the thinking goes. The idea that citizens should not publicly criticize the government is, of course, central to every aspiring fascist nation in the history of the world. If you criticize us, you are supporting the enemy. It should be evident that any democratic society must respect dissent, especially when it is unpopular and when the issue being debated is of such monumental consequence. When thousands, tens of thousands, or even hundreds of thousands of lives are at stake, suppressing or ignoring dissenting views that might inform policy decisions seems especially worrisome. One can only wonder whether those who advocate a wartime doctrine of follow-the-leader-no-matter-what realize what is at stake. Some factual reminders about the Iraq war include the following:

- The ongoing Iraq war has lasted more than 7 years (as of the publication of this book) and counting;
- The combined duration of US participation in World War I, World War II, and the 1991 Gulf War is 5.5 years. The Korean War lasted 3 years, and the War in Vietnam lasted more than 10 years.
- 2,974 US civilians were killed in the attacks on the World Trade Center, the Pentagon, and United Airlines flight 93.
- As of this writing, close to twice that number of American soldiers have been killed in the US invasions of Iraq and Afghanistan (this does not include fatalities among coalition member-nations).

- According to a Johns Hopkins study, the same number (2,974) of Iraqi civilians have been killed *every week for the past six years* (even far more conservative estimates of Iraqi civilian fatalities would mean that more civilians are killed each *month* than died in the September 11 attack).
- More than 2,000 US children have lost a mother or a father in Iraq.
- There are no accurate estimates of Iraqi children who have lost a parent, but the number surely exceeds two million.
- The number of Iraqis who have left their homes and are now refugees or internally displaced persons (at least 4.4 million according to CIA and Congressional Research Service reports[2]) now surpasses the populations of the states of Alaska, North and South Dakota, Wyoming, Montana, and Delaware, combined.

As the actual human cost of the war far exceeds Americans' estimations of these costs, so too do the economic opportunity costs. The following figures pertain to US operations in Iraq only:

- Operation "Iraqi Freedom" is costing US taxpayers, according to conservative estimates, $343 million per day.
- This means that for one day's expenditure on the war, we could hire 6,000 new teachers and pay their salaries for a year, or enroll 45,000 children in Head Start.
- We could have bought 130,000 uninsured Americans health insurance or eliminate 27 million tons of carbon dioxide from the atmosphere.[3]

Former chairman of the Council of Economic Advisers Joseph E. Stiglitz estimates the final cost of the war will be three trillion dollars (Washington Post, 2008). If we decide that the actual cost will be only *half* of that final estimate (an unrealistically conservative prediction), then the Bush administration chose to spend 1.5 trillion dollars that might have been spent elsewhere. This number—only half of Stiglitz' estimate—requires effort of the imagination to fully comprehend:

- 1.5 trillion dollars could have paid for 73 million full four-year scholarships to public universities—nothing to scoff at since fewer than three million students graduated from all US high schools this year.[4]
- This money could have provided 14 years of health insurance to all 42.6 million uninsured Americans.

- If, instead, we focused on health insurance for uninsured children only, then we could have provided the nation's uninsured children with health insurance for about one and a half centuries.

The federal budget allocation is always a matter of choices–given a limited budget pie, choices must be made on how to spend slices of varying size. It is perhaps a political inevitability that administration officials, members of congress, and candidates in local, state, and federal elections will rarely choose to frame budget allocation questions in terms of choices: if we fund x, then we will not fund y. But these are exactly the kinds of terms in which a robust media in a democratic society should function.

Most importantly, the active cultivation of multiple perspectives is a prerequisite to democratic discourse. Much as Darwin's theory of natural selection depends on genetic variation, any theory of democracy depends on a multiplicity of ideas. It is the responsibility of the citizenry, the media, and the schools to safeguard the expression of those ideas.

School Reform and Democracy: Critical Pedagogy vs. the Tyranny of Facts

Given the state of affairs I outlined above, schools remain an essential point of leverage for building democratic habits of mind and action. Carr and many others have written extensively about the negative effect of school reform on these goals. Yet in virtually every US state, every Canadian province, and every school district in most countries around the globe, lessons on democratic thought and action do take place. They tend to be opportunistic rather than bureaucratic, based on an individual teacher's courage rather than on legislative muscle, and episodic rather than consistent and enduring. All of these kinds of lessons, however, reflect a steadfast resistance to the idea that school is an arm of the economy. Practicing what Carr labels as "critical engagement," they also reject the notion that the acquisition of disconnected facts should be the sole measure of school success.

Somehow, critics of the kind of school reform that is essential for democracy to flourish have become convinced that those who say they want students to think for themselves do not care whether students can read, write, or perform addition or subtraction. This is nonsense, but it is the kind of nonsense that fills the rhetoric of *No Child Left Behind*, *Race To The Top*, and talk about standards and accountability generally. As Carr argues in this book, educators who aim for critical pedagogy do not ignore facts. But many want students to know more than facts and formulas. They want the knowledge that students acquire to be embedded in the service of something bigger. It is not enough for students to learn how to read; they also need to learn to decide what is worth reading and why. In other words, they need to learn how to think, and how to use knowledge in the service of community life.

Critical education for democracy will require reclaiming common assumptions about what democratic thinking requires. There are few educators who believe that facts are unimportant components of a proper (and appropriate) education. But at a time when vast databases of information are at our fingertips in seconds, facts alone represent a profoundly impoverished goal for educational achievement. Furthermore, although students tend to learn more "facts" through thoughtful participation in meaningful projects of concern, engagement in such projects of democratic importance is, sadly, rarely driven by the acquisition of facts only. In short, the kind of knowledge that comes from a limited focus on standardized measures of school success does not necessarily lead to thoughtful participation. In many programs colleagues and I have studied that emphasized teaching about the workings of democratic government, legislative procedures, elections, and so on, students gained solid factual knowledge without necessarily gaining the inclination or the conviction required to participate in democratic community life (Kahne & Middaugh, 2008; Hess, 2009; Llewellyn et al., 2007). In fact, we found that often it worked the other way around: participation led to the quest for knowledge. Once students gained experiences in the community, they tended to ask deep and substantive questions that led them to research information they knew little about and, until then, had little inclination to learn.

Critical pedagogy is firmly rooted in the Deweyan notion that experience should drive the curriculum and not the other way around. In a popular but generally unattributed quotation, John Dewey is purported to have said that "any genuine teaching will result, if successful, in someone's knowing how to bring about a better condition of things than existed earlier." This is the heart of education that has gone lost in the last decade of school reform, and which this book reclaims so thoughtfully.

Notes

Foreword by Daniel Schugurensky

1   The "new cooperativism" emerged as a response by workers and other grassroots groups to the crisis of the neoliberal model, does not have strong links to the traditional cooperative movement, has more horizontal labour processes, democratic decision-making structures, and egalitarian pay schemes than older cooperative experiences in the region, and has strong connections with surrounding communities and with local initiatives of community economic development.

2   FLISOL (Festival Latinoamericano de Instalación de Software Libre, or Latin American Festival of Installation of Free Software) is the largest event of the diffusion of free software that takes place in different countries simultaneously. It started in 2005, and in 2008 involved more than 200 cities in 18 countries of Latin America.

3   I am not implying here that most politicians are self-serving and corrupt (the opposite is probably true) but am highlighting the fact that many people believe so, generating an anti political sentiment that provides a dangerous fertile soil for authoritarian regimes.

4   Even if we leave arms trading aside, we spend more money on ice cream and pet food than on water, sanitation, and primary education for all. Our priorities seem to be out of whack.

Chapter 1

1   All of the quotes at the beginning of the chapters in the book are from Paulo Freire's *Pedagogy of the Oppressed* (1973/2005).

2   The notion of *thick* and *thin* democracy is borrowed from Gandin and Apple (2005), who build on the seminal work of Benjamin Barber (1984). Barber raises pivotal questions on the saliency of liberal democracy, including the tension between individualism and the rights of all citizens.

3   See, for example, McLaren & Kincheloe, 2007, and Kincheloe, 2008a, for an account of numerous scholars who have contributed to this area, including, in addition to McLaren, Kincheloe and Paulo Freire, W. E. B. Du Bois, Anotonio Gramsci, Lev Vygotsky, Stanley Aronowitz, Henry Giroux, Michael Apple, bell hooks, Donaldo Macedo, Ira Shor, Jesus "Pato" Gomez, Deborah Britzman, Philip Wexler, Patti Lather, Antonia Darder, John Wilinsky, Shirley Steinberg, Ana Cruz, and others.

4   The United Nations has held an annual vote condemning the US blockade against Cuba since 1992. Every year, the vast majority of countries have denounced the US blockade. In 2008, virtually every country in the world voted with Cuba (185 countries against the blockade, and 3 in favor [US, Israel and Palau]). See http://links.org.au/node/716 and http://www.usatoday.com/news/world/2007-10-30-cuba_N.htm for details of the UN vote. Interestingly, coverage of this matter has been extremely slim in the US, and the predominant narrative of Cuba being a "communist dictatorship" prevails without any analysis, contextualization, alternative vantage points and critical interrogation of the US relationship

with Cuba. The general assumption that Cuba is not *democratic* is widely accepted in the mainstream media.

5   Paulo Freire's book *Pedagogy of the Oppressed* was first published in 1970 in the original Portuguese, and has been the object of great interest by activists, scholars and educators. This book became the gateway to numerous relationships and collaborations with those who have advanced critical pedagogy in the past three decades.

6   See Kincheloe (2008b, p. 10).

7   See Kincheloe (2008b, p. 23).

8   I have cited Kincheloe liberally here because of his over-arching importance in the field of critical pedagogy as well as the direct and indirect influence on my own elaboration of some of the fundamental issues dealt with in this manuscript.

9   See the February 23, 2005 Media Matters for America article entitled "FOX News doctors AP reports to mimic White House terminology" at http://mediamatters.org/research/200502230006.

10   There is some questioning around how many people vote in *American Idol* but the point here is that there is a significant level of engagement of monitoring, analyzing and participating in the lives of the performers on this show.

11   The notion of *goodness* has been explored in the vast literature on Whiteness, related to White power and privilege despite a hegemonic mindset favoring color-blindness and meritocracy. Epistemologically, the national narrative of being a force of decency and benevolence enveloped within various forms of patriotism (Westheimer, 2006) has made it difficult to openly and critically critique misdeeds and injustice. See Carr and Lund (2007a), Ellesworth (1997), Feagin and O`Brien (2003), Feagin, Vera and Batur (2001), and Fine, Weis, Powell Pruitt and Burns (2004) for a discussion of Whiteness.

12   See the article by Kalle Lasn (undated) entitled "The unofficial history of America™" at http://silent-nation.com/the-unofficial-history-of-america. Her hypothesis is as follows: "The unofficial history of America," which continues to be written, is not a story of rugged individualism and heroic personal sacrifice in the pursuit of a dream. It is a story of democracy derailed, of a revolutionary spirit suppressed, and of a once-proud people reduced to servitude."

13.   See http://www.informationclearinghouse.info/article18562.htm.

14   At the risk of overlooking some of those, whether directly or through their writing, who have influenced my thinking on critical pedagogy, I would refer readers to the Paulo and Nita Freire International Project for Critical Pedagogy website, located at McGill University, where a listing of biographies of scholars can be found: http://www.freireproject.org/.

Chapter 2

1   See http://www.merriam-webster.com/dictionary/democracy

2   See http://www.ask.com/web?q=dictionary%3A+democracy&content=ahdict|61593&o= 2832 &l=dir.

3   See the *Stanford Encyclopedia of Philosophy* at http://plato.stanford.edu/entries/democracy/.

4   Ibid.

5   See Paul Treanor's (2006) analysis at http://web.inter.nl.net/users/Paul.Treanor/democracy. html.

6   See Democracy Watch's website: http://www.dwatch.ca/democracy.html

7   Ibid.

8   Noam Chomsky's book, *Hegemony or survival—America's quest for global dominance*, published in 2003 by Metropolitan Books, became the object of international attention when Venezuelan President Hugo Chavez presented it to the United Nations General Assembly as he attacked US foreign policy. See, for example, http://www.thepeoplesvoice.org/cgi-bin/blogs/books.php/2006/09/23/p11005.

9   See http://www.answers.com/topic/polyarchy and also Dahl (1972), *Polyarchy: Participation and Opposition*. New Haven: Yale University Press.

10   See http://www.answers.com/topic/polyarchy and also Dahl (1972), *Polyarchy: Participation and Opposition*. New Haven: Yale University Press.

11   See http://www.chomsky.info/books/survival01.htm.

12   See http://www.secularhumanism.org/index.php?section=library&page=britt_23_2

13   This figure is based on information provided by War Resisters League (www.warresisters.org), which draws on analysis produced by the for Arms Control and Non-Proliferation: www.armscontrolcenter.org.

14   Cited from http://jcoward1.home.mindspring.com/EOH.htm.

15   See, for example, http://www.bowlingalone.com/.

Chapter 3

1   I make this comment based on my 17-year experience as a Senior Policy Advisor in the Ontario Ministry of Education, and not based on any scientific study. From what I personally experienced, in addition to my reading of formal educational policy development in diverse jurisdictions throughout North America, there appears to be little evidence that critical theory and thought has penetrated mainstream educational reforms. Elsewhere, I (2006b) have written about Whiteness in educational policy-making, emphasizing how the range of policy discussion often explicitly or implicitly marginalizes critical theory, which can manifest itself through ignorance, omission and a purposeful control of the agenda in opposition to social justice-based thinking.

2   See, for example, the critical work of: Bob McChesney at http://will.illinois.edu/mediamatters/; Amy Goodman at democracynow.org; the Monthly Review at *http://mrzine.monthlyreview.org;* The Center for Research on Globalization at *http://www.globalresearch.ca/index.php.*

3   See http://www.swamppolitics.com/news/politics/blog/2007/04/john_edwardss_400_hair cuts_fee.html.

4   See http://www.pbs.org/moyers/journal/04252008/profile.html.

5   See http://www.greenleft.org.au/2009/806/41460.

6   The media spent an inordinate amount of time and energy on the extramarital activities of Governor Elliot Spitzer in 2008 (see, for example, the *New York Times* report at http://www.nytimes.com/2008/03/10/nyregion/10cnd-spitzer.html).

7   Incoming Governor David Patterson strategically sought to remove this potential irritant before commencing his mandate. See the *New York Times* report at http://cityroom.blogs.nytimes.com/2008/03/18/paterson-to-hold-news-conference/?scp=5&sq=Gov.%20Patterson%202008%20installation%20sex%20scandle&st=cse.

8   There are a plethora of reports on this topic, with detailed analysis about Clinton's relationships from his time as governor through his presidency. See, for example, CNN for a chronology of the Lewinsky affair: http://www.cnn.com/ALLPOLITICS/1998/resources/lewinsky/timeline/.

9   Interestingly, Churchill's quote has been taken up by a number of people who adapt it accordingly to their diverse perspectives. For example, I attended a lecture given by Aleida Guevara, Che's daughter, in 1998 in Toronto where she stated: "Socialism is the worst form of government except for all those others that have been tried."

10 See http://www.associatedcontent.com/article/725199/american_idol_versus_the_presidential.html.

11 See http://www.americanidol.com/idolgivesback/foundation/.

12 In late 2009, the National Priorities Project pegged the amount spend on wars in Iraq and Afghanistan at roughly $1 trillion (http://costofwar.com/); in March 2008, the *Washington Post* estimated that the Iraq conflict could cost $3 trillion, once associated costs such healthcare for veterans, is imputed (http://www.washingtonpost.com/wp-dyn/content/article/2008/03/07/ AR2008030702846.html); in March 2006, MSNBC was already predicting that the war would cost more than $1 trillion (http://www.msnbc.msn.com/id/11880954/); a study compiled by scholars from Columbia University and Harvard University in 2006 foresaw that the war would cost over $2 trillion (http://www.npr.org/templates/story/story.php?storyId =5156416). In all cases, the amounts estimated by outside observers, scholars, activists and journalists are considerably higher than the official figures presented by government sources (see http://www.warresisters.org/).

13 See, for example, Toward Freedom's discussion of how international interests have dumped nuclear waste in Somalia's waters in addition to pillaging the fish stocks: http://toward freedom.com/home/content/view/1567/1/.

14 Of the many reports, the majority in the mainstream media focused on rioting and instability (see, for example, CNN's http://www.cnn.com/2008/WORLD/americas/04/14/world. food.crisis/) whereas a minority examined the needs of the population, such as this one by the NGO Doctors Without Borders, http://doctorswithoutborders.org/press/release.cfm?id= 3140&cat=press-release&ref=tag-index.

15 Evidence of this can be seen in the vibrant Haitian community activities and organizations that are clearly visible in Montreal, New York and Miami, which include professional, media, political and other networks.

16 See, for example, the exposé by Haiti 2004 on Haitian tourism at http://homepage.mac.com/intersocietal/interso/h2004/h2004english/h2004_23.html.

17 There was some debate on whether the president should attend the Olympic Games in Beijing, given the situation in Tibet and human rights concerns. Then-Senator Hillary Clinton demanded that President Bush not attend whereas former President Clinton advised Hollywood producer Steven Spielberg to stay involved in the Games despite the massive pressure on him to withdraw his participation. See, for example, this report by ABC News at http://blogs.abcnews.com/politicalpunch/2008/04/hillary-clinton.html.

18 See the Center's report at http://www.newsdesk.umd.edu/culture/release.cfm?ArticleID =1736.

19   See, for example, the work of Amnesty International (http://www.amnesty.org/en), Human
     Rights Watch (http://www.hrw.org/), the United Nations Human Rights network
     (http://www.un.org/en/rights/), and Madre (http://www.madre.org/index.php?video=1).

20   See http://www.nationmaster.com/graph/spo_sum_oly_med_all_tim_percap-medals-all-time-
     per-capita.

21   See "Global Issues: Social, Political, Economic and Environmental Issues That Affect Us All" at
     http://www.globalissues.org/article/35/us-and-foreign-aid-assistance#GovernmentsCutting
     BackonPromisedResponsibilities.

22   This is commonly referred to as tied aid, meaning assistance that requires recipient countries to
     adhere to certain conditions, such as purchasing services and products from the donor country.
     Even donor countries acknowledge the practice, underpinning their actions with arguments
     about the need to extend domestic markets and interests. See, for example, the Organization for
     Economic Co-operation and Development document on the subject (2005):
     http://www.oecd.org/document/24/0,3343,en_2649_34171_2668440_1_1_1_1,00.html.

23   From the US Department of State at http://www.state.gov/f/releases/iab/fy2009cbj/. This
     table is reproduced from a synthesis produced by Parade at http://www.parade.com/
     news/intelligence-report/archive/who-gets-us-foreign-aid.html. Without providing the
     context on comparative amounts with other countries, the amount of aid flowing from the
     South to the North, and the relevance of the US aid to developing countries, this table would
     seem to argue for a reduction in aid but not for the same reasons enunciated earlier above.

24   See http://www.stwr.org/aid-debt-development/the-south-has-repaid-it-external-debts-to-the-
     north-but-the-north-denies-its-debt-to-the-south.html.

25   See Sharp, Jeremy M. (2008). *US Foreign Aid to Israel (CRS Report for Congress)*. Washington:
     Congressional Research Serve (p. 18). http://www.au.af.mil/au/awc/awcgate/crs/rl33222.pdf.

26   According to its website, "Freedom House, an independent nongovernmental organization
     that supports the expansion of freedom in the world, has been monitoring political rights and
     civil liberties worldwide since 1972." Freedom House compiles an annual survey of
     democracies, focusing on "free" societies, distinguishing between *electoral* and *liberal*
     democracies, the latter of which involves greater civil liberties.
         "To qualify as an electoral democracy, a state must have satisfied the following criteria:
     1.A competitive, multiparty political system; 2. Universal adult suffrage for all citizens (with
     exceptions for restrictions that states may legitimately place on citizens as sanctions for criminal
     offenses); 3. Regularly contested elections conducted in conditions of ballot secrecy, reasonable
     ballot security, and in the absence of massive voter fraud, and that yield results that are
     representative of the public will; 4. Significant public access of major political parties to the
     electorate through the media and through generally open political campaigning." (http://www.
     freedomhouse.org/template.cfm?page=2)

27   See http://silent-nation.com/us-foreign-policy-1940-present for a summary of significant acts
     perpetrated by the US against other nations.

28   This table was constructed from a range an amalgam of sources, including:
     www.infoplease.com/ce6/people/A0835878.html,icarusfilms.com/new2000/mob.html,yalibn
     an.com/site/archives/2006/12/saddam_husseins.php,www.iranchamber.com/history/moham
     madrezashah/mohammad_rezashah.php,www.moreorless.au.com/killers/montt.html,en.wikip
     edia.org/wiki/Anwar_El_Sadat#Unpopularity_and_conspiracy_theories,en.wikipedia.org/wiki/Ho

sni_Mubarak#Mubarak_and_corruption,www.nytimes.com/2006/08/16/ world/americas/16cnd-stroessner.html?pagewanted=all,www.economicexpert.com/a/Hugo:Banzer:Suarez.htm, www. moreorless.au.com/killers/duvalier.html,newworldencyclopedia.org/entry/Batista#Aftermath _and_legacyuselectionatlas.org/FORUM/index.php?topic=22806.0, news.bbc.co.uk/2/hi/amer icas/1203355.stm,uk.reuters.com/article/idUKJAK2399420080127?pageNumber=2&virtual BrandChannel=0, www.stanford.edu/group/ arts/nicaragua/discovery_eng/timeline/

29 Center for Bhutan Studies. (2009a). *Gross National Happiness: Explanation of GNH index.* http://www.grossnationalhappiness.com/gnhIndex/intruductionGNH.aspx

30 The United Nations Development Program outlines the program as follows: "Each year since 1990 the Human Development Report has published the human development index (HDI) which looks beyond GDP to a broader definition of well-being. The HDI provides a composite measure of three dimensions of human development: living a long and healthy life (measured by life expectancy), being educated (measured by adult literacy and gross enrolment in education) and having a decent standard of living (measured by purchasing power parity, PPP, income). The index is not in any sense a comprehensive measure of human development. It does not, for example, include important indicators such as gender or income inequality nor more difficult to measure concepts like respect for human rights and political freedoms. What it does provide is a broadened prism for viewing human progress and the complex relationship between income and well-being." See http://hdr.undp.org/en/.

Chapter 4

1 This chapter is a version of the introduction of the book*Doing Democracy: Striving for Political Literacy and Social Justice* (Lund & Carr, 2008) that I co-edited with Darren E. Lund.

Chapter 5

1 This text is a version of a published article: Carr, Paul R. (2007d). "Standards, accountability and democracy: Addressing inequities through a social justice accountability framework," *Democracy and Education*, 17(1), 1–16.

2 Two common features of this trend are: 1) the propensity to advertise widely about how a given school board has met the required standards, thus affecting and shaping public perceptions; and 2) the institutional policy response to the conceptualization and promotion of standards, which involves ranking—often without providing a significant sociological context—and rewarding schools based on their success in standardized tests. An unfortunate outcome of this process is the punishment of schools not achieving high standards, often dismantling the schools or pushing the students into charter schools. Henry Giroux (2005a, 2007, 2009) has written widely on this phenomenon.

3 Many of the concepts that I have formulated in this article were cultivated during my tenure as a Senior Policy Advisor in the Ontario Ministry of Education, where I worked on and co-coordinated a number of equity issues in education.

Chapter 6

1   This chapter is based on: Carr, Paul R. & Thésée, Gina. (2008b). "The quest for political (il)literacy: Responding to, and attempting to counter, the neo-liberal agenda." In Malott, C. & Porfilio, B. (eds.), *The Destructive path of neo-liberalism: An international examination of education* (pp. 173–194). Rotterdam: Sense Publishers.

Chapter 7

1   This chapter is based on two published articles and a book chapter: Carr, Paul R. (2007b). "Experiencing Democracy through Neo-liberalism: The Role of Social Justice in Democratic Education," *Journal for Critical Education Policy Studies*, 5 (2). http://www.jceps. com/?pageID=article&articleID=104; Carr, Paul R. (2008b). "Educators and education for democracy: Moving beyond "thin" democracy," *Inter-American Journal of Education and Democracy*, 1(2), 147-165. http://www.ried-ijed.org/english/articulo.php?idRevista=4&id Articulo=16; Carr, Paul R. & Thésée, Gina. (2009). "The critical pedagogy of understanding how educators relate to democracy." In Schugerensky, D., Daly, K. and Lopes, K. (eds.), *Learning Democracy by Doing: Alternative Practices in Citizenship Learning and Participatory Democracy* (pp. 274–283). Toronto: University of Toronto, Transformational Learning Center.

2   This research continues to expand as part of the Global Doing Democracy Research Project, for which I am a co-director along with David Zyngier of Monash University in Australia. In 2009/2010, there were some 15 projects in eight countries seeking to use the methodology and approach I developed (Carr, 2007a, 2008b) to determine how democracy varies in diverse contexts, how education cultivates democracy, and, significantly, how political literacy and social justice can be achieved through "doing" democracy.

3   For the purposes of this book, social justice is intended to mean the political, social, cultural, economic and legal components of society, especially in relation to education, which address the explicit as well as implicit manifestations of identity, difference, marginalization, discrimination and inequitable power relations. Similarly, it seeks to address the intersectionality of identity, far out-stretching normative notions of racial diversity as enveloping the totality of diversity. Lastly, the focus herein is on critical and political literacy, which are key elements to social justice (Freire, 1973; McLaren, 2007; Portelli & Solomon, 2001).

4   The notions and underlying principles of citizenship education and democratic education are often conflated to mean the same thing, although there can be specifically narrow interpretations of each (Sears & Hughes, 2006). In this chapter, the focus is on the critical aspects of democracy that lead to political literacy, which encompasses the more progressive and democratic education (Kincheloe, 2008a; Parker, 2003; Patrick, 2003).

5   The name of the university is less important than the fact that the study actually took place. Although the university is described and some demographic data are provided based on publicly available information, it was determined that naming the university would not add to the overall presentation and analysis, and might even diminish the strength of the research. While the study was conducted within one university, given the contextualization provided, readers are invited to determine the generalizability of the findings. Whereas the institution is

named within the French-language sample, given that readers would most likely not have any difficulty identifying it as there are only two such universities in Montreal, the university in question within the US context is not as easily identifiable, and it was, therefore, not considered necessary to name it.

6   This research was not conceptualized as being quantitative in nature, although some questions sought a quantitative ranking (see the next note). Rather, the focus was on eliciting reaction, commentary, narratives and understanding of the participants' engagement with democracy. The answers to the questions with a Likert scale were further fleshed out and elaborated on through the subsequent narrative comments. In sum, no quantitative methodological tests were undertaken to determine if the sample was deemed large enough to allow for the formulation of generalizations and analysis.

7   To clarify, survey questionnaires contained explanatory information with each question containing a Likert scale. For example, for the question "Do you think that the US is democratic?," instructions were provided indicating that a 1 would represent not very democratic at all and a 5 would indicate extremely democratic. The narrative comments provided after the quantitative score further helped to flesh out the strength of the data.

8   See UQAM's website: http://www.registrariat.uqam.ca/Pdf/Pop_etudiante/0506/population.pdf.

9   Carr and Thésée (2006) have found that the data-collection based on racial origin in Quebec has traditionally been problematic and limited. This is not to suggest that race data are necessarily easily collected elsewhere in Canada but that there have been some programs in that direction, especially in Ontario (Potvin and Carr, 2008).

10   See the official website of the Consultation Commission on Accommodation Practices Related to Cultural Differences at http://www.accommodements.qc.ca/index-en.html. There was extensive media coverage of the Commission's work during 2007 and 2008, and the debates that ensued created controversy and tension, juxtaposing diverse visions of Québécois society. The reality between the immigrant-rich region of Montreal and the regions was brought to light throughout the process.

11   Note that the quotations from this study for the Quebec sample have been translated from the original French into English.

Chapter 8

1   This chapter is a version of a published article: Carr, Paul R. (2008). "The 'Equity Waltz' in Canada: Whiteness and the informal realities of racism in education," *Journal of Contemporary Issues in Education, 3(2)*, 4–23.

2   The Human Development Index and other international comparisons using social, educational, economic and political indicators consistently rank Canada within the best countries in which to live. Canada has even been awarded the top honours a few times in the past fifteen years.

3   A comprehensive resource documenting Black-Canadian history, produced by *Historica Black History of Canada,* can be found at http://blackhistorycanada.ca/.

4   The City of Toronto's Black history website at ww.toronto.ca/blackhistory/victorian-exhibit.htm notes that approximately 1,200 of Toronto's 45,000 residents in 1860 were Black, and also that there was a vibrant Black business community there at that time.

5   An illustration of the problem of not having a concrete, visible equity strategy could be the
     post-1995 period in Ontario, where there has been a flurry of accusations that school violence
     and gang activity have increased, in part because of a lack of focus on building school
     communities through social justice programs. There are many complexities to the problematic,
     but it is clear that eliminating anti-racism from the formal educational map has made the task
     of ensuring that prevention and social cohesion, rather than "zero tolerance" and "strict
     discipline," all the more difficult.

Chapter 9

1   This chapter is a version of a published article: Carr, Paul R. & Darren E. Lund. (2009). "The
     unspoken color of diversity: White privilege and critical engagement in education." In
     Steinberg, S. (ed.), *Diversity: A Reader* (pp. 45–55). New York: Peter Lang Publishing.

Chapter 10

1   This chapter is a version of a published article: Carr, Paul R. & Porfilio, Brad, J. (2009b). "The
     2008 US presidential campaign, democracy and media literacy," *International Journal of
     Critical Pedagogy*, 2(1), 119–138.
2   The data for this chart were gathered from Adam Carr's election archive website http://pseph
     os. adam -carr.net/.
3   See the US Census Bureau Statistical Abstract (2008). There are varying interpretations of the
     actual percentage of eligible voters voting in the 2008 election but the difference seems to be
     minimal with most agreeing that it was 64% or 65%.

Chapter 11

1   This chapter is a version of a published article: Carr, Paul R. (2009). "Political conscientization
     and media (il)literacy: Critiquing the mainstream media as a form of democratic engagement,"
     Multicultural Education, 17(1), 2–10. It also contains small portions of a published article:
     Porfilio, Brad J. & Paul R. Carr. (2008). "Youth culture, the mass media and democratic
     education," *Academic Exchange Quarterly*, 12(4). http://www.rapidintellect.com/AEQweb/
     cho4255w9.htm.

Chapter 12

1   This chapter is a version of a published article: Carr, Paul R. (2007c). "*Shock and awe* and the
     environment," *Peace Review*, 19(3), 335–343.

Chapter 13

1   This text is a version of a published article: Carr, Paul R. (2008a). "But What Can I Do?"
     Fifteen Things Education Students Can Do to Transform Themselves in/through/with
     Education," *International Journal of Critical Pedagogy*, 1(2), 81–97.

Afterword by Joel Westheimer

1 It is important to note that Chomsky does not imply a conspiracy, but rather an alignment of interests among a small portion of society including what Chomsky calls the "ruling elites" and the corporate owners of mainstream media.

2 See https://www.cia.gov/library/publications/the-world-factbook/fields/2194.html and https://www.policyarchive.org/bitstream /handle/10207/3195/RL33936_20070323.pdf.

3 See www.ahipresearch.org, *Individual health insurance 2006–2007: A Comprehensive survey of premiums, availability, and benefits.* AHIP Center for Policy and Research, December 2007, www.vattenfall.com/climatemap

4 From National Center for Education Statistics, 2008353rev.http://nces.ed.gov/pubsearch/pubsinfo.asp?pubid=2008353rev.

References

Adams, M., Bell, L. & Griffen, P. (eds.). (1997). *Teaching for diversity and social justice: A sourcebook*. New York: Routledge.

Adley, J., & Grant, A. (2003). *The environmental consequences of war (A report prepared for the Sierra Club of Canada)*. http://www.sierraclub.ca/national/postings/warandenvironment.

Agger, B. (2009). The pulpless generation: Why young people don't protest the Iraq war (or anything else), and why it's not entirely their fault. *Cultural Studies-Critical Methodologies, 9*, 41–51.

Agostinone-Wilson, F. (2005). Fair and balanced to death: Confronting the cult of neutrality in the teacher education classroom, *Journal For Critical Education Policy Studies*, 3(1). http://www.jceps.com/?pageID=article&articleID=37.

Aldous Bergeron, A. (2003). Critical race theory and white racism: Is there room for white scholars in fighting racism in education? *Qualitative Studies in Education, 16(1)*, 51–63.

Alexander, G. (1999). Schools as communities: Purveyors of democratic values and the cornerstones of a public philosophy. *Systemic Practice and Action Research, 12(2)*, 183–193.

Altheide, D. L. (2009). War and mass mediated evidence. *Cultural Studies-Critical Methodologies, 9*, 14–22.

Apple, M. (1996). The hidden curriculum and the nature of conflict. In W.C. Parker (ed.), *Educating the democratic mind* (pp. 173–200). Albany: State University of New York Press.

Applebaum, B. (2005). In the name of morality: Moral responsibility, whiteness, and social justice education. *Journal of Moral Education, 34(3)*, 277–290.

Aronowitz, S. (2006). Left turn: Forging a new political future. Boulder, CO: Paradigm Publishers.

Au, W. (2007). Epistemology of the oppressed: The dialectics of Paulo Freire's Theory of Knowledge. *Journal for Critical Education Policy Studies*, 5(2), http://www.jceps.com/index.php?pageID= article&articleID=100.

Avery, P. G. (2003). Using research about civic education to improve courses in the methods of teaching social studies. In Patrick, J.J., Hamot, G.E., & Leming, R.S. (eds.). *Civic learning in teacher education: International perspectives on education for democracy in the preparation of teachers* (pp. 45–65). Bloomington, IN: ERIC Clearinghouse for Social Studies/Social Science.

———. (2002). Political tolerance, democracy, and adolescents. In Parker, W. C. (Ed). *Education for democracy: Contexts, curricula, assessments* (pp. 113–130). Greenwich, CT: Information Age Publishing.

Avila, E. (2004). *Popular culture in the age of white flight fear and fantasy in suburban Los Angeles*. Los Angeles: University of California Press.

Ayers, W., Hunt, J. A., & Quinn, T. (1998). *Teaching for social justice*. New York: The New Press.

Baergen, W. P. (2000). *The Ku Klux Klan in central Alberta*. Red Deer: Central Alberta Historical Society.

Bagdikian, B. H. (2004). *The new media monopoly*. Boston: Beacon Press.

Bales, B. (2006). Teacher education policies in the United States: The accountability shift since 1980. *Teaching and Teacher Education, 22*, 395–407.

Baltodano, M. P. (2006). The accreditation of schools and education and the appropriation of diversity. *Cultural Studies-Critical Methodologies, 6*, 123–142.

Banks, J., McGee Banks, C. A., Cortés, C. E., Hahn, C. L., Merryfield, M. M., Moodley, K. A., et al. (2005). *Democracy and diversity: Principles and concepts for educating citizens in a global age.* Seattle: Center for Multicultural Education.

Banks, J. A. (2008). *An introduction to multicultural education.* Boston: Allyn & Bacon.

———. (2006). *Race, culture, and education: The selected works of James A. Banks.* New York: Routledge.

Barber, B. (2004). *Strong democracy: Participatory politics for a new age.* Berkeley: University of California Press.

Bellamy Foster, J. (2009). *The ecological revolution: Making peace with the planet.* New York: Monthly Review Press.

Bellamy Foster, J., Holleman, H., & McChesney, R. (2008). The US imperial triangle and military spending, *Monthly Review,* 60(5), 1–19.

Berg, B. (2007). *Qualitative research methods for the social sciences.* Boston: Allyn and Bacon.

Berry, D. & Theobald, J. (eds). (2006). *Radical mass media criticism: A cultural genealogy.* New York: Black Rose Books.

Bjork, L. & Alsbury, T. (2005). Politics and normative expectations for democratic leadership in the superintendency. Paper presented, University Council for Educational Administration conference, Nashville, TN.

Black, K. (2003). Erasing anti-racism: A decade later, anti-racism education is still nonexistent in the classroom, *NOW Magazine, 23(7).* http://www.nowtoronto.com/issues/2003-10-16/news _story4.php.

Boertlein, J. (2010). *Presidential confidential: Sex, scandal, murder and mayhem in the oval office.* Cincinnati: Clerisy Press.

Borg, C. & Mayo, P. (2007). Public intellectuals, radical democracy, and social movements: A book of interviews. New York: Peter Lang.

Bourdieu, P. (1970). *La reproduction: Éléments pour un système d'enseignement.* Paris: Édition de Minuit.

Bourdieu, P. & Passeron, J-C. (1990). *Reproduction in education, society and culture.* New York: Sage Publications.

Bowles, S. & Gintis, H. (2001). Schooling in capitalist America revisited. *Sociology of Education, 75(1),* 1–18.

———. (1977). *Schooling in capitalist America: Educational reform and the contradictions of economic life.* New York: Harper & Row Publishers.

Bradley, R. (2005). Paranoia, conspiracy theories, and the presidential election of 2004. *Cultural Studies-Critical Methodologies,* 5(3), 338–345.

Brauer, J. (2000). "The Effect of War on the Natural Environment." http://www.aug.edu/_sbajmb/ paper-london3.PDF.

Brinkley, E. (1999). *Caught off guard: Teachers rethinking censorship and controversy.* Needham Heights, MA: Allyn & Bacon.

Brosio, R. (2004). Civil society: Concepts and critique, from a radical democratic perspective. *Journal for Critical Education Policy Studies, 2(2),* http://www.jceps.com /index.php?pageID= home&issueID=27.

———. (2003). High-stakes tests: Reasons to strive for better Marx. *Journal For Critical Education Policy Studies, 1(2),* http://www.jceps.com/index.php?pageID= home&issueID=17.

Brown, R. (1999). *A study of the grade 9 cohort of 1993 (1993–1998): The last grade 9 cohort of the Toronto Board of Education.* Toronto: Toronto District School Board.

Burke, B. (2005) Antonio Gramsci, schooling and education. *The Encyclopedia of Informal Education,* http://www.infed.org/thinkers/et-gram.htm.

Bush, M. E. L. (2005). *Breaking the code of good intentions: Everyday forms of whiteness.* Lanham, MD: Rowman & Littlefield.

Campbell, D. (2000). *Choosing democracy: A practical guide to multicultural education.* Upper Saddle River, NJ: Pearson Education.

Canadian Council on Social Development. (2003). *Aboriginal children in poverty in urban communities: Social exclusion and the growing racialization of poverty in Canada.* Ottawa: Canadian Council on Social Development.

Carlson, D., & Gause, C., eds. (2007). *Keeping the promise: Essays on leadership, democracy, and education.* New York: Peter Lang.

Carr, P. R. (2008a). "But what can I do?": Fifteen things education students can do to transform themselves in/through/with education, *International Journal of Critical Pedagogy, 1(2),* 81–97. http://freire.mcgill.ca/ojs/index.php/home/article/view/56/31.

———. (2008b). Educating for democracy: With or without social justice?, *Teacher Education Quarterly, Fall,* 117–136.

———. (2008c). Educators and education for democracy: Moving beyond "thin" democracy, *Inter-American Journal of Education and Democracy, 1(2),* 147–165. http://www.ried-ijed.org/english/ articulo.php?idRevista=4&idArticulo=16.

———. (2008d). The "Equity Waltz" in Canada: Whiteness and the informal realities of racism in education, *Journal of Contemporary Issues in Education, 3(2),* 4–23. http://ejournals.library.ualberta.ca/index.php/JCIE/article/view/4575/3735.

———. (2007a). Educational policy and the social justice dilemma. In H. Claire & C. Holden (eds.), *Controversial issues in education.* London: Trentham.

———. (2007b). Experiencing democracy through neo-liberalism: The role of social justice in education, *Journal of Critical Education Policy Studies, 5(2).* http://www.jceps.com/index.php?pageID= article&articleID=104.

———. (2007c). Shock and awe and the environment, *Peace Review, 19(3),* 335–343.

———. (2007d). Standards, accountability and democracy: Addressing inequities through a social justice accountability framework, *Democracy and Education, 17(1),* 1–16.

———. (2006a). Democracy in the classroom?, *Academic Exchange Quarterly, 10(2),* 7–12. http://www.rapidintellect.com/AEQweb/cho34206.htm.

———. (2006b). Social justice and whiteness in education. Color-blind policymaking and racism, *Journal For Critical Education Policy Studies, 4,* 2. http://www.jceps.com/index.php?pageID=article &articleID=77.

———. (1999). Transforming the institution, or institutionalizing the transformation? Racial diversity and anti-racism in education in Toronto, *McGill Journal of Education, 34 (1),* 49–77.

———. (1997). Reflections on identity formation. Is it easier to embrace or reject Canadian citizenship?, *Multiculturalism, 2,* 1–7.

Carr, P. R. & Klassen, T. (1997). Different perceptions of race in education: Racial minority and white teachers, *Canadian Journal of Education, 1(Winter),* 68–81. http://www.csse.ca/CJE/Articles/FullText/CJE22-1/CJE22-1-Carr.pdf.

———. (1996). The role of racial minority teachers in anti-racist education, *Canadian Ethnic Studies, 28(2),* 126–138.

Carr, P. R. & Lund, D. E. (2009). The unspoken color of diversity: White privilege and critical engagement in education. In Steinberg, S. (ed.), *Diversity: A reader* (pp. 45–55). New York: Peter Lang Publishing.

———. (2008). Antiracist education. In Provenzo, E. (ed.), *SAGE Encyclopedia of Cultural and Social Foundations of Education* (pp.48–52). Thousand Oaks: SAGE Publications.

———. (eds). (2007). *The great white north? Exploring whiteness, privilege and identity in education.* Rotterdam: Sense Publishers.

Carr, P. R. & Porfilio, B. J. (2009a). Computers, the media and multicultural education: Seeking engagement and political literacy, *Journal of Intercultural Studies, 20(2),* 91–107.

———. (2009b). The 2008 US presidential campaign, democracy and media literacy, *International Journal of Critical Pedagogy, 2(1),* 119–138. http://freire.mcgill.ca/ojs/index.php/ home/article/view/110 /51.

Carr, P. R. & Thésée, G. (2009). The critical pedagogy of understanding how educators relate to democracy. In Schugerensky, D., Daly, K. and Lopes, K. (eds.), *Learning democracy by doing: Alternative practices in citizenship learning and participatory democracy* (pp. 274–283). Toronto: University of Toronto, Transformational Learning Center.

———. (2008a). Educational institutions negotiating democracy and social justice: The (im)balance of power and accountability, *Journal of Canadian and International Education, 36(3),* 32–46.

———. (2008b). The quest for political (il)literacy: Responding to, and attempting to counter, the neo-liberal agenda. In Porfilio, B. and Malott, C. (eds.), *An international examination of urban education: The destructive path of neo-liberalism* (pp. 173–194). Rotterdam: Sense Publishers.

———. (2006). Race and identity in education in Quebec, *DIRECTIONS: Research and policy on eliminating racism, 3(1),* 18–23.

Casella, R. (2008). Security, pedagogy, and the free-market approach to "troubled youth." In Porfilio, B. and Malott, C. (eds.), *An international examination of urban education: The destructive path of neo-liberalism* (pp. 63–79). Rotterdam: Sense Publishers.

Center for Bhutan Studies. (2009a). *Gross National Happiness: Explanation of GNH index.* http://www. grossnationalhappiness.com/gnhIndex/intruductionGNH.aspx.

———. (2009b). *Proceedings of the Fourth International Conference Held in Bhutan, November 24– 26, 2008.* http:// www.bhutanstudies.org.bt/main/gnh4.php.

Center for Information and Research on Civic Learning and Engagement (CIRCLE). (2003). *The civic mission of schools.* New York: Carnegie Corporation.

Center for Research and Information on Canada. (2001). *Voter participation in Canada: Is Canadian democracy in crisis?* Montreal: Center for Research and Information on Canada.

Chomsky, N. (2008a). The election, economy, war and peace. *Znet.* http://www.zmag. org/znet/view Article/19749.

———. (2008b). *The essential Chomsky* (edited by Anthony Arnove). New York: The New Press.

———. (2007). *Failed states: The abuse of power and the assault on democracy (American Empire Project).* New York: Holt.

———. (2003). *Chomsky on democracy and education.* New York: Routledge Falmer.

———. (2000). *Chomsky on miseducation.* Oxford: Roman & Littlefield.

————.Chomsky, N. & Herman, E. S. (1998). *Manufacturing consent: The political economy of the mass media.* New York: Pantheon.

Chossudovsky, M. (2005). *America's "war on terrorism" in the name of 9/11.* Montreal: Center for Research on Globalization.

————. (2003). *Globalization of poverty and the new world order.* Montreal: Center for Research on Globalization.

Church, E. (2007, May 31). White people need to face role in racism, academics say. *Globe and Mail, A5.*

Churchill, W. (1998). *A little matter of genocide: Holocaust and denial in the Americas, 1492 to the present.* San Francisco: City Lights.

Clarke, H. et al. (1984). *Absent mandate : The politics of discontent in Canada.* Toronto: Gage.Coelho, E., Costiniuk, B. & Newton, C. (1995). *Antiracism education: Getting started: A practical guide for educators.* Toronto: Ontario Secondary Schools Teachers' Federation.

Collaborative for Academic, Social and Emotional Learning. (2003). *Safe and sound: An educational leader's guide to evidence-based social and emotional learning (SEL) programs.* Chicago, US Department of Education, Mid-Atlantic Regional Education Laboratory.

Comber, M. (2006). Group discussion skills and civic education content. Paper delivered at the annual International Civic Education Conference, Orlando, FL.

Cook, S. (2004). Learning to be a full Canadian citizen: Youth, elections and ignorance. *Canadian Issues Magazine,* 17–20.

Cook, S. & Westheimer, J. (2006). Introduction: Democracy and education, *Canadian Journal of Education,* 29(2), 347–358.

Cooper, J. & Weaver, K. (2003). *Gender and computers: Understanding the digital divide.* New York. Lawrence Erlbaum.

Corporation for National and Community Service. (2001) *A guide to effective citizenship through AmeriCorps.* New York: Corporation for National Service.

Corson, D. (2001). Ontario students as a means to the government's end, *Our Schools Our Selves,* 10(4), 57–80.

Crow, G. (2006). Democracy and educational work in an age of complexity. *UCEA Review,* Winter, 1–5.

Curran, J., & Gurevitch, M. (2000). *Mass media and society.* London: Arnold.

Dahl, R. A. (1972). *Polyarchy: Participation and Opposition.* New Haven, CT: Yale University Press.

————. (1956) *A Preface to Democratic Theory.* Chicago: The University of Chicago Press.

Daniels, J. (1997). *White lies: Race, class, gender, and sexuality in white supremacist discourse.* New York: Routledge.

Dantley, M. & Tillman, L. (2006) Social justice and moral transformative leadership. In Marshall, C. & Oliva, M. (eds.), *Leadership for social justice: Making revolutions in education* (pp. 16–30). Boston: Allyn and Bacon.

Darder, A. (2002). *Reinventing Paulo Freire. A pedagogy of love.* Boulder, CO: Westview.

Darder, A. & Miron, L. F. (2006). Critical pedagogy in a time of uncertainty: A call to action. *Cultural Studies—Critical Methodologies,* 6(1), 5–20.

Darling-Hammond, L., French, J., & Garcia-Lopez, S. P. (2002). *Learning to teach for social justice.* New York: Teachers College, Columbia University.

Davies, I., & Hogarth, S. (2004). Political literacy: Issues for teachers and learners. In J. Demaine (ed.), *Citizenship and political education today* (pp. 181–199). Hampshire, UK: Palgrave Macmillan.

De Tocqueville, Alexis. (2007). *Democracy in America*. Bel Air, California: Echo Library.

Dei, G. J. S. (2008). *Racists beware: Uncovering racial politics in the post modern society*. Rotterdam, Netherlands: Sense.

———. (2007). Foreword. In Carr, P. & Lund, D. (eds)., *The great white north: Exploring Whiteness, privilege and identity in education* (pp. vii–xii). Rotterdam: Sense Publishers.

———. (1996). *Antiracism education: Theory and practice*. Halifax: Fernwood Publishing.

Dei, G. & Karumanchery, L. (2001). School reforms in Ontario: The 'Marketization of education' and the resulting silence on equity. In Portelli, J. and Solomon, P. (Eds.), *The Erosion of Democracy in Education* (pp. 189–215). Calgary: Detselig Enterprises Ltd.

Dei, G. J. S., Karumanchery, L. L., & Karumanchery-Luik, N. (2004). *Playing the race card: Exposing white power and privilege*. New York: Peter Lang.

Dei, G. J. S., & Kempf, A. (2006). *Anti-colonialism and education: The politics of resistance*. Rotterdam: Sense.

Dei, G., Mazzuca, J., McIsaac, E. & Zine, J. (1997). *Reconstructing 'drop-out': A critical ethnography of the dynamics of Black students' disengagement from school*. Chapel Hill, NC: University of Toronto Press.

De Lissovoy, N. (2008). Conceptualizing oppression in educational theory: Toward a compound standpoint. *Cultural Studies—Critical Methodologies*, 8(1), 82–105.

Delpit, L. (1996). *Other people's children: Cultural conflict in the classroom*. New York: The New Press.

———. (1988). The silenced dialog: power and pedagogy in educating other people's children. *Harvard Educational Review*, 58(3), 280–298.

Demaine, J. (2004). *Citizenship and political education today*. Hampshire, England: Palgrave MacMillan.

Denzin, N. K. (2009). Critical pedagogy and democratic life or a radical democratic pedagogy. *Cultural Studies—Critical Methodologies*, 9(3), 379–397.

———. (2007). Flags in the window: Dispatches from the American war zone. New York: Peter Lang.

———. (2005). Homegrown democracy, homegrown democrats. *Cultural Studies—Critical Methodologies*, 5(1), 126–131.

Dewey, J. (1916/1997). *Democracy and education: An introduction to the philosophy of education*. New York: Free Press.

Diamond, L., & Morlino, L. (2005). *Assessing the quality of democracy*. Baltimore, MD: Johns Hopkins University Press.

Dreher, A., Kotsogiannis, C. & McCorriston, S. (2004). Corruption around the world: Evidence from a structural model. http://129.3.20.41/eps/pe/papers/0406/0406004.pdf.

Duarte, E. M., & Smith, S. (2000). *Foundational perspectives in multicultural education*. New York: Longman.

Dudley, R. L., & Gitelson, A. R. (2002). Political literacy, civic education, and civic engagement: A return to political socialization? *Applied Developmental Science*, 6(4), 175–182.

Ecology News. (2007). Environmental War: A Primer & FAQ. http://www.ecologynews. com/cuenews16.html.

Economist, The. (2008). The Economist intelligence Unit's Index of Democracy 2008. http:// graphics.eiu.com/PDF/Democracy%20Index%202008.pdf.

Ellsworth, E. (1997). Double blinds in whiteness. In M. Fine, L. Weis, L. Powell, & M. Wong (eds.), *Off White: Readings on Power, Privilege, and Resistance.* New York: Routledge.

Engels, J. (2007). Floating bombs encircling our shores: Post-9/11 rhetorics of piracy and terrorism. *Cultural Studies—Critical Methodologies,* 7(3), 326–349.

Essex, N. (2006) *What every teacher should know about no child left behind.* Boston: Pearson.

Feagin, J., & O'Brien, E. (2003). *White men on race: Power, privilege, and the shaping of cultural consciousness.* Boston: Beacon Press.

Feagin, J., Vera, H. & Batur, P. (2001). *White racism.* New York: Routledge.

Fenimore-Smith, J. K. (2004). Democratic practices and dialogic frameworks: Efforts toward transcending the cultural myths of teaching. *Journal of Teacher Education,* 55(3), 227–239.

Fielding, K. (2002). Tales from the crypt or writing the Ontario Canadian and World Studies curriculum. Our Schools Our Selves, (March). http://www.policyalternatives.ca/ index.cfm?act=news&call=789&do=article&pA

Fine, M., Weis, L, Powell Pruitt, L. & Burns, A. (2004). *Off White: Readings on power, privilege, and resistance.* New York: Routledge.

Fischman, G. E. & McLaren, P. (2005). Rethinking critical pedagogy and the Gramscian and Freirean legacies: from organic to committed intellectuals or critical pedagogy, commitment, and Praxis. *Cultural Studies—Critical Methodologies,* 5(4), 425–447.

Fleras, A. (2002). *Engaging diversity: Multiculturalism in Canada.* Toronto: Nelson Thomson Learning.

Fleras, A., & Elliot, J. L. (2003). *Unequal relations: An introduction to race and ethnic dynamics in Canada.* Toronto: Prentice Hall.

Fleras, A. & Kunz, J. (2001). *Media and minorities: Representing diversity in a multicultural Canada.* Toronto: Thompson

Frank, A. G. (1979). *Dependent accumulation and underdevelopment.* New York: Monthly Review Press.

Freire, P. (1973/2005). *Pedagogy of the oppressed.* New York: Continuum.

———. (2004). *Pedagogy of Indignation.* Boulder, CO: Paradigm Publishers.

———. (1998). *Pedagogy of freedom: Ethics, democracy, and civic courage.* Lanham, MD: Rowman & Littlefield.

———. (1985). *The Politics of Education.* South Hadley, MA: Bergin & Garvey Publishers.

———. (1973). *Education for Critical Consciousness.* New York: The Continuum Publishing Company.

Friedland, L. & Morimoto, S. (2005). *Why young people are volunteering in record numbers* (CIRCLE Working Paper 40). The Center for Information and Research on Civic Learning and Engagement. 3, 2. http://civicyouth.org/PopUps/WorkingPapers/WP40 Friedland. pdf.

Fukuyama, F. (1992). *The end of history and the last man.* New York: Free Press.

Fullan, M. (2005). *Leadership and sustainability: System thinkers in action.* Thousand Oaks, CA: Corwin Press.

Galeano, E. (1973). *Open veins of Latin America: Five centuries of the pillage of a continent.* New York: Monthly Review Press.

Galston, W. (2003). Civic education and political participation. *Phi Delta Kappan,* 85(1), 29–33.

Gandin, L. A., & Apple, M. (2005). Thin versus thick democracy in education: Porto Alegre and the creation of alternatives to neo-liberalism. *International Studies in Sociology of Education,* 12(2), 99–116.

———. (2002). Challenging neo-liberalism, building democracy: Creating the citizen school in Porto Alegre, Brazil. *Journal of Education Policy,* 17(2), 259–279.

Gerstl-Pepin, C. (2007). Introduction to the special issue on the media, democracy, and the politics of education, *Peabody Journal of Education,* 82(1), 1–9.

Ghosh, R. (2001). *Redefining multicultural education.* Toronto: Nelson Thomas Learning.

Gilborn, D. (2006). Citizenship education as placebo: 'Standards,' institutional racism and education policy, *Education, Citizenship and Social Policy,* 1(1), 83–104.

Giroux, H. (2009a). The attack on higher education and the necessity of critical pedagogy. In Macrine, S. (ed.). (2009). *Critical pedagogy in uncertain times: Hopes and possibilities* (pp. 11–26). New York: Palgrave MacMillan.

———. (2009b). The spectacle of illiteracy and the crisis of democracy, *truthout* (September 15). http://www.truthout.org/091509A.

———. (2007). Democracy, education, and the politics of critical pedagogy. In McLaren, P. & Kincheloe, J. (eds). *Critical pedagogy: Where are we now?* (pp. 1–5). New York: Peter Lang.

———. (2005a). Kids for sale: Corporate culture and the challenge of public schooling. In S. Shapiro & D. Purpel (eds.), *Critical social issues in American education: Democracy and meaning in a globalizing world* (pp. 143–162). Mahwah, NJ: Lawrence Erlbaum Associates, Publishers.

———. (2005b). The passion of the right: Religious fundamentalism and the crisis of democracy. *Cultural Studies—Critical Methodologies,* 5(3), 309–317.

———. (2004). Class casualties: Disappearing youth in the age of George W. Bush. *Workplace: A Journal of Academic Labor* 6(1).

———. (1998). *Channel surfing: Race talk and the destruction of today's youth.* New York: St. Martin's Press.

———. (1997). *Pedagogy and the politics of hope: Theory, culture and schooling.* Boulder, CO: Westview Press.

———. (1993). Paulo Freire and the politics of postcolonialism. In McLaren, P. & Leonard, P. (eds.), *Paulo Freire: A critical encounter* (pp. 177–188). New York: Routledge.

———. (1988a). Literacy and the pedagogy of voice and political empowerment. *Educational Theory* 38(1), 61–75.

———. (1988b). *Teachers as intellectuals: Toward a critical pedagogy of learning.* South Hadley, MA: Bergin & Garvey.

Giroux, H. & Giroux, S. S. (2006). Challenging neo-liberalism's new world order: The promise of critical pedagogy. *Cultural Studies—Critical Methodologies,* 6(1), 21–32.

Goodall, H. L. (2008). Twice betrayed by the truth: A narrative about the cultural similarities between the Cold War and the global war on terror. *Cultural Studies—Critical Methodologies,* 8(3), 353–368.

Goodall, H. L. & Wiener, S. (2008). Creating the right reality: Communication message strategies and the Republican party. *Cultural Studies—Critical Methodologies,* 8(2), 135–158.

Goodman, A. (2008a). Breaking the sound barrier: Third-party candidates Ralph Nader & Cynthia McKinney respond to final McCain-Obama debate. (October 16) [Radio News Program]. Democracy Now! The War and Peace Report. http://www.democracynow.org/2008/10/16/breaking_the_sound_barrier_third_party.

———. (2008b). Green Party presidential candidate Cynthia McKinney responds to Obama win. (November 5). [Radio News Program]. Democracy Now! The War and Peace Report. http://www.democracynow.org/2008/11/5/green_party_presidential_candidate_cynthia_mckinney.

———. (2008c). Noam Chomsky: "What next? The elections, the economy, and the world (November 24). Truth, war, and consequences. [Radio News Program]. Democracy Now! The War and Peace Report. http://www.democracynow.org/2008/11/24/ noam_chomsky_what_next_the_elections.

———. (2008d). Ralph Nader on Barack Obama: "It is quite clear he is corporate candidate from A to Z." (June 18). [Radio New Program]. Democracy Now! The War and Peace Report. http://www.democracynow.org/2008/6/18/ralph_nader_on_barack_ obama _it.

Gordon, S. P., Smyth, J. & Diehl, J. (2008). The Iraq War, "Sound Science," and "Evidence-Based" educational reform: How the Bush administration uses deception, manipulation, and subterfuge to advance its chosen ideology. *Journal for Critical Education Policy Studies*, 6(2), 173–204. http://www.jceps.com/PDFs/6-2-10.pdf.

Gore, J., Griffiths, T., & Ladwig, J. (2004). *Towards better teaching: Productive pedagogy as a frame of work for teacher.* Newcastle: Faculty of Education, University of Newcastle.

Gorski, P. (2008). EdChange: Professional development, scholarship and activism for diversity, social justice, and community growth [on-line resource]. St. Paul, MN: Author.

Gramsci, A. & Forgacs, D. (2000). *The Antonio Gramsci reader: Selected writings.* New York: NYU Press.

Greene, M. (2009). Teaching as possibility: A light in dark times. In Macrine, S. (ed.). *Critical pedagogy in uncertain times: Hopes and possibilities* (pp. 137–150). New York: Palgrave MacMillan.

Greene, S. (2008) *Literacy as a civil right: Reclaiming social justice in literacy teaching and learning.* New York: Peter Lang.

Gregg, S. (2000). The tragedy of democracy: 'Rights,' tolerance and moral 'neutrality.' *Policy*, Winter, 39–43.

Gross, S., & Shapiro, L. (2005). Our new era requires a new DEEL: Towards a democratic ethical educational leadership. *UCEA Review,* Fall, 1–4.

Guttman, A. (1999) *Democratic education.* Princeton, N.J.: Princeton University Press.

Hartman, A. (2008). *Education and the Cold War. The battle for the American school.* New York: Palgrave Macmillan.

Held, D. (2006). *Models of democracy.* Palo Alto, CA: Stanford University Press.

Henry, F. & Tator, C. (2005). *The color of democracy: racism in Canadian society.* Toronto: Nelson Thompson.

Herman, E. & Chomsky, N. (2002). *Manufacturing consent: The political economy of the mass media.* New York: Pantheon.

Hess, D. (2009). *Controversy in the classroom: The Democratic Power of Discussion.* New York: Routledge

———. (2004). Discussion in social studies: Is it worth the trouble? *Social Education*, 68(2), 151–155.

Hill, D. (2008). Resisting neo-liberal global capitalism and its depredations: Education for a new democracy. In Lund, D. and Carr, P. (eds.), *Doing democracy: Striving for political literacy and social justice* (XIV). New York: Peter Lang.

———. (2003). Global neo-liberalism, the deformation of education and resistance, *Journal for Critical Education Policy Studies*,1, 1. www.jceps.com/?pageID=article&articleID=7.

Hill, D. & Boxley, S. (2007). Critical teacher education for economic, Environmental and social justice: an ecosocialist Manifesto. *Journal for Critical Education Policy Studies*, 5(2). http://www.jceps.com/index.php?pageID=article&articleID=96.

Hoechsmann, M. (2006). Bono for pope? A case for cultural studies in media education, *Taboo*, 10(2), 25–35.

Hoffman, S. (2006). The foreign policy the US needs. *The New York Review of Books*, LIII, 3(August 10), 60–64.

Holden, C., & Hicks, D. (2007) *Making global connections: The knowledge, understanding and motivation of trainee teachers.* 23 (1): 13–23.

Holm, G. & Farber, P. (2002). Teaching in the dark: The geopolitical knowledge and global awareness of the next generation of American teachers, *International Studies in Sociology of Education*, 12(2), 129–144.

Hooley, N. (2009) *Narrative life: Democratic curriculum and indigenous learning.* New York: Springer.

Hoover, R. & Shook, K. (2003) School reform and accountability: Some implications and issues for democracy and fair play, *Democracy and Education*, 14(4). Pages 81–86.

Howard, G. R. (1999). *We can't teach what we don't know: White teachers, multiracial schools.* New York: Teachers College Press.

Hursh, D., & Martina, C. (2003). Neo-liberalism and schooling in the US: How state and federal government education policies perpetuate inequality. *Journal of Critical Education Policy Studies,* 1(2). wwwjceps.com/?pageID=article&articleID=12.

Hyslop-Margison, E. J. & Thayer, J. (2009) Teaching democracy: Citizenship education as critical pedagogy. Rotterdam: Sense Publishers.

Information for Action. (undated) "The impact of war and weapons on humans and the environment." http://www.informaction.org/cgi-bin/gPage.pl?menu¼menua.txt&main¼ weapons _effects.

Ivie, R. L. (2005). Democratic Dissent and the Trick of Rhetorical Critique. *Cultural Studies – Critical Methodologies*, 5(3), 276–293.

Jacobs, J. (2006). Supervision for social justice: Supporting critical reflection. *Teacher Education Quarterly,* Fall, 23–39.

James, C. E. (2003). *Seeing ourselves: Exploring race, ethnicity and culture* (3rd ed.). Toronto: Thompson.

James, C. L. R. (1989). *The Black Jacobins: Toussaint L'Ouverture and the San Domingo revolution.* London: Vintage Books.

Jello Biafra. (2007). www.jellobiafra.org/.

Jensen, R. (2005). *The heart of whiteness: Confronting race, racism, and white privilege.* San Francisco: City Lights.

Joshee, R. & Johnson, L. (2007). *Multicultural education policies in Canada and the United States.* Vancouver: UBC Press.

Kahn, R. & Kellner, D. (2004). Global youth culture. http://www.gseis.ucla.edu/faculty/kellner/essays.html.

Kahne, J. & Westheimer, J. (2003). Teaching democracy: What schools need to do, *Phi Delta Kappan*, 85(1), 34–40 & 58–66.

Kahne, J., Westheimer, J. & Rogers, J. (2000). Service learning and citizenship: Directions in research, *Michigan Journal of Community Service Learning*, Fall, 42–51.

Kahne, J., & Middaugh, E. (2008). Democracy for some: The civic opportunity gap in high school. Working Paper #59. Washington, DC: Center for Information and Research on Civic Learning [CIRCLE].

Kaplan, R. (1997). Was democracy just a moment? *The Atlantic*. http://www.theatlantic.com/doc/199712/democracy-kaplan.

Karatnycky, A. (2002) *Freedom in the world 2000–2001: The annual survey of political rights and civil liberties, 2000–2001*. (New York: Freedom House, 1991–2001)

Karumanchery, L. L. & Portelli, J. (2005). Democratic values in bureaucratic structures: Interrogating the essential tensions. In Bascia, N. et al. (eds), *International Handbook of Educational Policy* (pp. 329–349). New York: Springer.

Kellner, D. (2007). Lying in politics: The case of George W. Bush and Iraq. *Cultural Studies – Critical Methodologies*, 7(2), 132–144.

———. (2005). The media and election 2004. *Cultural Studies—Critical Methodologies*, 5(3), 298–308.

———. (2002). "The axis of evil," Operation infinite war, and Bush's attacks on democracy. *Cultural Studies—Critical Methodologies*, 2(3), 343–347.

———. (1997). Critical theory and British cultural studies: The missed articulation. In J. McGuigan (ed.), *Cultural* Methodologies. London: Sage, 12–41.

———. (1995) *Media culture: Cultural studies, identity, and politics between the modern and the postmodern*. London and New York: Routledge.

Kellner, D. & Share, J. (2007). Critical media literacy, democracy, and the reconstruction of education. In Macedo, D. and Steinberg, S. (eds.), *Media literacy: A reader*. (pp. 3–23). New York: Peter Lang.

Khan, Ali L. (2001). *A theory of universal democracy: Beyond the end of history*. The Hague, Netherlands: Kluwer Law International.

Kim, J. & Sunderman, G. (2005). Measuring academic proficiency under the No Child Left Behind Act: Implications for Educational Equity. *Educational Researcher*, vol. 34, no. 8, pp. 3–12.

Kincheloe, J. L. (2008a). *Critical pedagogy: Primer*. New York: Peter Lang.

———. (2008b). *Knowledge and Critical Pedagogy: An Introduction*. London: Springer.

———. (2007). Critical pedagogy in the twenty-first century. In McLaren, P. & Kincheloe J. (eds), *Critical pedagogy: Where are we now?* (pp. 9–42). New York: Peter Lang.

———. (1993). *Toward a critical politics of teacher thinking: Mapping the postmodern*. Westport, CT: Greewood Publishing Group.

Kincheloe, J. L. & Steinberg, S. R. (2006). An ideology of miseducation: Countering the pedagogy of empire. *Cultural Studies—Critical Methodologies*, 6(1), 33–51.

Kincheloe, J. L. & Weil, D. (2004).*Critical thinking and learning: An encyclopedia for parents and teachers*. Westport, CT: Greenwood Publishing Group.

King, C. R. (2009). Some academics try to push back: Ward Churchill, the war on truth, and the improbabilities of interruption. *Cultural Studies—Critical Methodologies*, 9(1), 31–40.

Kinsella, W. (2001). *Web of hate: Inside Canada's far right network* (2nd ed.). Toronto: HarperCollins.

Klassen, T., & Cosgrove, J. (2002). *Ideology and inequality: Newspaper coverage of the employment equity legislation in Canada* (Working Paper Series No. 28). Toronto: Center for Research on Work and Society at York University.

Klein, N. (2008). *The shock doctrine: The rise of disaster capitalism.* New York: Picador.

———. (2005). Threats and temps. In Shapiro, S., & Purpel, D.E. (Eds.), *Critical issues in American education: Democracy and meaning in a globalizing world* (pp. 373–397). Mahwah, New Jersey: Lawrence Erlbaum Associates.

Knight, T. & Pearl, A. (2000). Democratic education and critical pedagogy, *The Urban Review*, 32(3), 197–226.

Kozol, J. (2005). *The shame of the nation: Restoration of apartheid schooling in America.* New York: Random House.

———. (1992). *Savage inequalities: Children in America's schools.* New York: HarperCollins.

Kurth-Schai, R., & Green, C. (2006). *Re-envisioning education and democracy.* Greenwich, CT: Information Age.

Kymlicka, W. (1995). *Multicultural citizenship.* Oxford: Oxford University Press.

Lambsdorff, J. G. (2007). *The Institutional economics of corruption and reform: Theory, evidence and policy.* New York: Cambridge University Press.

Landes, L. (2005). Did networks fake exit polls, while AP accessed 2,995 mainframe computers? www.dissidentvoice.org

Larson, C., & Ovando, C. (2001). *The color of bureaucracy.* Belmont, CA: Wadsworth.

Lauder, H., Brown, P., Dillabough, J. & Halsey, A.H. (2006). *Education, globalization and social change.* London: Oxford

Lebrun, N. (2006). Représentations de la notion de démocratie chez des groups de futures enseignants du primaire, *Canadian Journal of Education* 29(3), 635–649.

Lee, E. (1985). *Letters to Marcia: A teacher's guide to anti-racist education.* Toronto: Cross Cultural Communication Center.

Leithwood, K. (2001). 5 Reasons why most accountability policies don't work (and what you can do about it). *Orbit*, 32, (1), 1–5.

Leithwood, K., Jantzi, D., & Steinbach, R. (1999). Do school councils matter? *Educational Policy* 13(4), 467–493.

Leithwood, K. & Riehl, C. (2003). *What we know about successful school leadership.* Philadelphia: Laboratory for Student Success, Temple University.

Leithwood, K., Steinbach, R. and Jantzi, D. (2002). School leadership and teachers' motivation to implement accountability policies. *Educational Administration Quarterly*, February (38), pp. 94–119.

Levin, B. (2005). *Governing education.* Toronto: University of Toronto Press.

———. (1994). Democracy and education, students and schools. Paper presented at the conference Under Scrutiny Again: What Kind of Secondary Schools Do We Need?, Simon Fraser University, Vancouver, B.C., February 24.

Linn, S. (2008). Commercializing childhood: The corporate takeover of kids' lives. *Multinational Monitor,* 30(1), pp. 32–38.

Lintner, T. (2007). Critical race theory and the teaching of American history: Power, perspective, and practice, *Social Studies Research and Practice*, 2(1), 103–116.

Lipman, P. (2004). Education accountability and repression of democracy Post-9/11. *Journal for Critical Education Policy Studies*, 2(1). http://www.jceps.com/index.php?pageID=article&articleID=23.

Lippman, W. (1922). *Public opinion*. New York: Free Press.

Llewellyn, K., Cook, S., Westheimer, J., Molina-Giron, L., & Suurtamm, K. (2007). *The state and potential of civic learning in Canada*. Ottawa: Canadian Policy Research Network.

Lopez, C. (2000). Neo-liberalism and teachers. http://www.vcn.bc.ca/ idea/neolib.html.

Lund, D. E. (2006a). Everyday racism in Canada: Learning and teaching respect for aboriginal people. *Multicultural Education*, 14(1), 49–51.

———. (2006b). Rocking the racism boat: School-based activists speak out on denial and avoidance. *Race, Ethnicity and Education*, 9(2), 203–221.

———. (2006c). Waking up the neighbors: Surveying multicultural and antiracist education in Canada, the United Kingdom, and the United States. *Multicultural Perspectives*, 8(1), 35–43.

———. (1998). Nurturing democracy in the schools: Engaging youth in social justice activism. *Multiculturalism/Interculturalisme*, 17(2), 26–31.

———. (2005). Addressing multicultural and antiracist practice and theory with Canadian teacher activists. In B. J. McMahon & D. E. Armstrong (Eds.), *Inclusion in urban educational environments: Addressing issues of diversity, equity, and social justice* (pp. 255–274). Greenwich, CT: Information Age.

Lund, D. E. & Carr, P. R. (eds). (2008). *"Doing" democracy: Striving for political literacy and social justice*. New York: Peter Lang Publishing.

Lund, D. E., & Fidyk, A. (2006). Desperately seeking anti-racism education resources. *Directions: Research and* Policy on Eliminating Racism, 3(1), 53–64.

Macedo, D. (2009). Unmasking prepackaged democracy. In Macrine, S. (ed.). (2009). *Critical pedagogy in uncertain times: Hopes and possibilities* (pp. 79–96). New York: Palgrave MacMillan.

———. (2006). *Literacies of power: What Americans are not allowed to know*. Boulder, Colorado: Westview Press.

Macedo, D. & Gounari, P. (2006). *The globalization of racism*. Boulder, CO: Paradigm.

Macedo, D. & Steinberg, S. (2007). *Media literacy: A reader*. New York: Peter Lang.

Macrine, S. (ed.). (2009). *Critical pedagogy in uncertain times: Hopes and possibilities*. New York: Palgrave MacMillan.

Magdoff, H. (2003). Imperialism without colonies. New York: Monthly Review Press.

Mairles, H & Gilchrist, I (2005) 'We're citizens now'· The development of positive values through a democratic approach to learning, *Journal for Critical Education Policy Studies*, 3(1). www.jceps.com/?pageID=article&articleID=45.

Malott, C. & Miranda-Carol, J. (2003). Punkore scenes as revolutionary street pedagogy. *Journal for Critical Education Policy Studies* 1(2). http://www.jceps.com/?pageID=article &article ID=7.

Marshall, C. & Gerstl-Pepin, C. (2005) *Re-framing educational politics for social justice* Boston· Pearson A&B.

Marshall, C. & Oliva, M. (2006). *Leadership for social justice: Making revolutions in education*. Boston: Pearson Education.

Martin, G. (2005). You can't be neutral on a moving bus: Critical pedagogy as community praxis. *Journal for Critical Education Policy Studies*, 3(2).

Martinez, E., & Garcia, A. (1996). What is neo-liberalism? A brief definition for activists. http://www.corpwatch.org/article.php?id=376.

Marx, S. and Pennington, J. (2003). Pedagogies of critical race theory: Experimentations with white preservice teachers, *Qualitative Studies in Education,* 16(1), 91–110.

Mazzoleni, G. & Schultz, W. (1999). "Mediatization" politics: A challenge for democracy? *Political Communication*, 16, 247–261.

Mbakpuo, V. (2005). *The conscience of a nation: Clinton, sex and politics around the world.* Charleston, SC: BookSurge Publishing.

McCarthy, C., Crichlow, W., Dimitriadis, G., & Dolby, N. (2005). *Race, identity and representation in education* (2nd ed.). New York: Taylor & Francis.

McCaskell, T. (2005). *Race to equity: Disrupting education inequality.* Toronto: Between the Lines.

McChesney, R. (2008). *The political economy of media: Enduring issues, emerging dilemmas.* New York: Monthly Review.

———. (1999a). *Rich media, poor democracy: Communication politics in dubious time.* New York: Free Press.

———. (1999b). The new global media: It's a small world of big conglomerates. *The Nation*, 29, 11–15.

McGinn, N. (1994). Politics of educational planning. In T. Husen and N. Postlehwaite (eds.), *International encyclopedia of education* (pp. 4595–4602). Oxford: Pergamon Press.

McHugh, D. (2006). A cost-benefit analysis of an Olympic games (Queen's Economics Department Working Paper No. 1097). Kingston, Ontario: Queen's University.

McIntosh, P. (1988). White privilege and male privilege: A personal account of coming to see correspondences through work in women's studies. Wellesley, MA: Wellesley College Center for Research on Women (Working Paper No. 189). http://www.feinberg.northwestern.edu/diversity/uploaded_docs/UnpackingTheKnapsack.pdf.

McIntyre, A. (1997). *Making meaning of whiteness: Exploring racial identity with white teachers.* Albany, NY: SUNY Press.

McLaren, P. (2008). Capitalism's bestiary: Rebuilding urban education. In B. Porfilio and C. Malott's (eds.) *The destructive path of neo-liberalism: An international examination of urban education* (pp. vii–xv). The Netherlands: Sense Publishers.

———. (2007) *Life in schools: An introduction to critical pedagogy in the foundations of education.* Boston: Pearson Education, Inc.

———. (2005a). *Capitalists and conquerors: A critical pedagogy against empire.* New York: Rowman and Littlefield.

———. (2005b). Critical Pedagogy reloaded: Dispatches from Las Entranas de La Bestia. *Cultural Studies—Critical Methodologies*, 5(3), 318–337.

McLaren, P. & Jaramillo, N. (2007). *Pedagogy and praxis in the age of empire.* Netherlands: Sense Publishers.

McLaren, P. & Kincheloe J. L. (eds). (2007). *Critical pedagogy: Where are we now?* New York: Peter Lang.

McLuhan, M. (1967). *The medium is the message.* Toronto: Bantam Books/Random House.

McLuhan, M., & Fiore, Q. (2001). *The medium is the message: An inventory of effects.* Corte Madera, California: Gingko Press.

Mendelson, M. (2006). *Aboriginal peoples and postsecondary education in Canada.* Ottawa: The Caledon Institute of Social Policy.

Merriam, S. (1998). *Qualitative research and case study applications in education.* San Francisco: Jossey-Bass.

Millar, S. M. (1998). *Cracking the gender code: Who rules the wired world?* Toronto: Secondary Story Press.

Morse, J. (2006). Social justice and federal intervention in education. Paper presented at an international conference on America's least wanted: Urban children and urban youth, Buffalo, NY.

Moyo, D. (2009). *Dead aid: Why aid is not working and how there is a better way for Africa.* New York: Farrar, Straus and Giroux.

Nader, R. (2008). Open letter to Senator Barack Obama. http://www.votenader.org/media /2008/11/03/lettertoobama/

National Institute for Literacy (US). (2006). Facts and statistics. www.nifl.govinifl/ facts/facts.html

Nicholson-Goodman, Jovictoria (2009). *Autobiography of a democratic nation at risk: The currere of culture and citizenship.* New York: Peter Lang.

Nieto, S. (1999). *The light in their eyes: Creating multicultural learning communities.* New York: Teachers College Press.

Nieto, S., & Bode, P. (2008). *Affirming diversity: The sociopolitical context of multicultural education,* 5th ed. Boston/NY: Allyn & Bacon/Longman.

Noel, J. (2000). *Developing multicultural educators.* New York: Longman.

Noll, J.W. (2007). *Taking sides: Clashing views on educational issues.* Dubuque: McGraw-Hill.

Normand, S. (2008). Antioch students examine presidential election issues. The Tennessean. http://www.tennessean.com/article/20081107/ COUNTY0104/811070333/1196

Ogbu, J. (1991). Immigrant and involuntary minorities in comparative perspective. In M. Gibson & J. Ogbu (Eds.), *Minority status and schooling: A comparative study of immigrant and involuntary minorities* (pp. 3–33). New York: Garland.

———. (1990). Minority education in comparative perspective. *Journal of Negro Education,* 59(1), 45–57.

Ontario Ministry of Education. (2002). *Ontario secondary school diploma requirement: Community involvement activities in English-language schools* (Policy/Program Memorandum No. 124a). Toronto: Ontario Ministry of Education. http://www.edu.gov.on.ca/ extra/eng/ppm/124a.html.

———. (2000). *Ontario secondary school diploma requirement: Community involvement activities in English-Language Schools.* Toronto: Ontario Ministry of Education.

———. (1999). *Ontario secondary schools, grades 9 to 12: Program and diploma requirements.* Toronto: Ontario Ministry of Education. http://www.edu.gov.on.ca/eng/document/ curricul/secondary/oss/oss.pdf.

———. (1993) *Antiracism and ethnocultural equity in school boards.* Toronto: Ontario Ministry of Education.

———. (1992). *Changing perspectives.* Toronto: Ontario Ministry of Education and Training.

Ontario Royal Commission on Learning. (2005). *For the love of learning.* Toronto: Queen's Printer for Ontario.

Ornstein, M. (2000). *Ethno-racial inequality in Toronto: Analysis of the 1996 census.* Toronto: City of Toronto.

Osborn, K. (2001). Democracy, democratic citizenship and education. In Portelli, J. & Solomon, P. (eds.), *The erosion of democracy in education: From critique to possibilities.* Calgary: Detselig Enterprises Ltd.

O'Toole, T., Marsh, D., & Jones, S. (2003). Political literacy cuts both ways: The politics of non-participation among young people. *Political Quarterly,* 74(3), 349–360.

Palast, G. (2004). *The best democracy money can buy.* New York: Plume.

Palermo, J. (2008). The "Joe the plumber" debate. The Huffington Post. http://www.huffingtonpost.com/joseph-a-palermo/the-joe-theplumber-debate.

Parker, W. (2006). Public discourses in schools: Purposes, problems, possibilities, *Educational Researcher,* 35(8), 11–18.

———. (2003). *Teaching democracy: Unity and diversity in public life.* New York: Teachers College Press.

———. (2002). *Education for democracy: Contexts, curricula, assessments.* Greenwich, CT: Information Age.

Patrick, J. (2003). *Teaching democracy (ERIC Digest).* Bloomington, IN: ERIC Clearinghouse for Social Studies/Social Science Education.

———. (2002). *Improving civic education in schools.* Bloomington, IN: ERIC clearinghouse for social studies/social science education. www.ericdigests.org/2003-3/civic.htm.

Patterson, D. (2001). *Liberalism and conservatism, 1846–1905.* Oxford: Heinemann Educational Publishers.

Patterson, T. (2003) *The vanishing voter: Public involvement in an age of uncertainty.* New York: Vintage Books.

Payne, C. (2003) More than a symbol of freedom: Education for liberation and democracy, *Phi Delta Kappan,* 85(1), 22–28.

Pearl, A., & Pryor, A. (2005). *Democratic practices in education: Implications for teacher education.* Lanham, MD: Rowman & Littlefield.

Perkins, John. (2007). *The secret history of the American empire: Economic hit men, jackals, and the truth about global corruption.* New York: Dutton.

Pon, G. (2000). The art of war or the wedding banquet? Asian-Canadians, masculinity, and antiracism education, *Canadian Journal of Education.* 25(2): 139–151.

Porfilio, B. & Malott, C. (eds.). (2008). *The destructive path of neo-liberalism: An international examination of education.* Rotterdam: Sense Publishers.

Porfilio, B. J. & Carr, P. R. (in press). *Youth Culture, Education and Resistance: Subverting the Commercial Ordering of Life.* Rotterdam: Sense Publishers.

———.(2008). Youth culture, the mass media and democratic education, *Academic Exchange Quarterly,* 12(4). http://www.rapidintellect.com/AEQweb/cho4255w9.htm.

Portelli, J. (2001). Democracy in education: Beyond the conservative or progressive stances. In W. Hare and J. Portelli (eds.), *Philosophy of education* (pp. 279–293). Calgary: Detselig Enterprises Ltd.

Portelli, J. & Solomon, P. (eds.) (2001). *The erosion of democracy in education: from critique to possibilities.* Calgary: Detselig Enterprises Ltd..

Porter, J. (1965). *The vertical mosaic: An analysis of social class and power in Canada.* Toronto: University of Toronto Press.

Potvin, M. & Carr, P. R. (2008). La conceptualisation et la mise en œuvre de l'éducation antiraciste : Les cas de l'Ontario et du Québec. *Éducation et francophonie*, XXXVI(1), 197–216. www.acelf.ca/c/revue/pdf/XXXVI_1_197.pdf.

Potvin, M., McAndrew, M. & Kanouté, F. (2006) L'éducation antiraciste en milieu scolaire francophone à Montréal : diagnostic et prospectives. Rapport de recherche, CRSH-ministère du Patrimoine Canadien, Chaire en relations ethniques, Université de Montréal, mai 2006.

Prins, N. (2009). *It takes a pillage: Behind the bailouts, bonuses, and backroom deals from Washington to Wall Street*. Indianapolis, IN: Wiley.

Provenzo, E. (2005). *Critical literacy: What every American ought to know*. Boulder, CO: Paradigm Publishers.

Public Broadcasting Service (2008). Lesson plan: Changing media, changing campaigns. www.pbs.org/teachers/vote2008/blueprint/pdfs/pbs-teachers-vote2008-lp-2.1.pdf.

Putnam, R. (2001). *Bowling alone: The collapse and revival of American community*. New York: Simon & Schuster.

Ravitch, D., & Viteritti, J. P. (2001). *Making good citizens: Education and civil society*. New Haven, CT: Yale University Press.

Reiss, M. (2003). Science education for social justice. In Vincent, C. (ed.), *Social justice, education and identity* (pp. 153–165). London: Routledge/Falmer.

Reitz, J. & Banerjee, R. (2006). Racial inequality, social cohesion, and policy issues in Canada. In Courchene, T., Banting, K. (eds.), Belonging? Diversity, recognition and shared citizenship in Canada (pp. 1–57). Montreal: Institute for Research on Public Policy. http://www.irpp.org/books/archive/AOTS3/reitz.pdf.

Rezai-Rashti, G. (2003). Educational policy reform and its impact on equity work in Ontario Global challenges and local possibilities, *Education Policy Analysis Archives*, 11(51), 1–15.

Riverview Gardens High School Students Aired on C-SPAN (2008, May 21). http://rgsd.k12.mo.us/153310310141628230/blank/browse.asp?A=383&BMDRN=2000&BCOB=0&C=77459.

RMC Research Corporation. (2005) Citizenship and service-learning in K–12 Schools. www.service learning.org.

Robbins, C. (2003). Racism and the authority of neo-liberalism: A review of three new books on the persistence of racial inequality in a color-blind era. *Journal for Critical Education Policy Studies*, 2(2). wwwjceps.com/?pagelD=article&aticielD=35.

Rodriquez, N. M., & Villaverde, L. E. (eds.) (2000) *Dismantling white privilege: Pedagogy, politics, and whiteness*. New York: Peter Lang.

Royal Commission on Aboriginal Peoples (1996). *Report of the royal commission on Aboriginal peoples*. Ottawa. Department of Indian and Northern Affairs.

Rury, J. (2005). Democracy's high school? Social change and American education in the post-modern era. In S. Shapiro and D. Purpel (eds.), *Critical social issues in American education: Democracy and meaning in a globalizing world* (pp. 45–88). Mahwah, NJ: Lawrence Erlbaum Associates, Publishers.

Ryan, J. (2006). *Inclusive leadership*. Toronto: Jossey-Bass.

Sadovnik, A.R., Cookson Jr., P.W., & Semel, S.F. (2006). *Exploring education: An introduction to the foundations of education*. Boston: Pearson A&B.

Saltman, K. (2009). Schooling in disaster capitalism: How the political right is using disaster to privatize public schooling. In Macrine, S. (ed.). (2009). *Critical pedagogy in uncertain times: Hopes and possibilities* (pp. 27–54). New York: Palgrave MacMillan.

Santora, E. (2006). "Disturbing spaces": Struggling for identity and democracy in culturally diverse collaborative groups. Paper presented at the second annual symposium: Urban education and intercultural learning, Buffalo, NY.

Scatamburlo-D'Annibale, J. S., Jaramillo, N. & McLaren, P. (2006). Farewell to the "bewildered herd": Paulo Freire's revolutionary dialogical communication in the age of corporate globalization. *Journal for Critical Education Policy Studies*, 4(2). http://www.jceps. com/index.php?pageID=article&articleID=65.

Schmitz, D. (2006). *The United States and right-wing dictatorships, 1965–1989.* New York: Cambridge University Press.

Schor, J. (2004). *Born to buy: The commercialized child and the new consumer culture.* New York: Scribner.

Schram, Thomas H. (2006). *Conceptualizing and Proposing Qualitative Research.* Upper Saddle River, NJ: Pearson.

Schugurensky, D. (2003). Civic participation—on active citizenship, social capital and public policy, *Canadian Diversity*, 2(1), 10–12.

———. (2000). Citizenship learning and democratic engagement: Political capital revisited. Proceedings of the 2000 Adult Education Research Conference, Vancouver, BC. http://www. edst.educ.ubc.ca/aerc/2000/schugurenskyd1-web.htm.

Sharp, Jeremy M. (2008). *US Foreign Aid to Israel (CRS Report for Congress).* Washington: Congressional Research Service.

Sears, A., & Hughes, A. (2006). Citizenship: Education or indoctrination? Citizenship and Teacher Education, 2(1), 3–17.

———. (1996) Citizenship education and current educational reform. *Canadian Journal of Education,* 21(2), 123–142.

Shapiro, S., & Purpel, D.E. (2005). *Critical issues in American education: Democracy and meaning in a globalizing world.* Mahwah, NJ: Lawrence Erlbaum Associates.

Shenton, S. G-M. (2009). A New Sun: Democracy, the public, and journalism education. *Cultural Studies—Critical Methodologies,* 9(3), 425–437.

Shor, I. (1997). What is critical literacy? *Journal of Pedagogy, Pluralism & Practice.* http://www.lesley. edu/ journals/jppp/4/shor.html.

Simpson, D., Jackson, M., & Aycock, J. (2005). *John Dewey and the art of teaching: Toward reflective and imaginative practice.* Thousand Oaks, CA: Sage.

Sleeter, C. (ed.). (2007). *Facing accountability in education: Democracy and equity at risk.* New York: Teachers College Press.

———. (2005). How white teachers construct race. In C. McCarthy, W. Crichlow, G. Dimitriadis, & N. Dolby (Eds.), *Race, identity and representation in education* (2nd ed.). New York: Routledge.

———. (2000). Multicultural education, social positionality, and whiteness, in: E. Manuel Duarte & S. Smith (eds.). *Foundational perspectives in multicultural education* (pp.118–134). New York: Longman.

Smiley, T. (2006). *The covenant with black America.* Chicago: Third World Press.

Soder, R. (1996). *Democracy, education, and the schools.* San Francisco: Jossey Bass.

Solomon, R.P. & Daniel, B.J. (2007). Discourses on race and 'White privilege' in the next generation of teachers. In Carr, P. & Lund, D. *The great White north?: Exploring Whiteness, privilege and identity in education* (pp. 161–172). Rotterdam: Sense Publishers.

Spring, J. (2004). Deculturalization and the struggle for equality: A brief history of the education of dominated cultures in the United States. New York: McGraw Hill.

Steinberg, S. & Kincheloe, J. (eds). (2009). *Christotainment: Selling Jesus through popular culture.* Boulder, CO: Westview Press

———. (2004). *Kinderculture: The corporate construction of childhood.* New York: Westview Press.

Stevick, E. D. & Levinson, B. A. U. (2007). Introduction: Cultural context and diversity in the study of democratic citizenship education. In Stevick, E. D. and Levinson, B. A. (eds.), *Reimagining civic education: How diverse societies form democratic citizens* (pp. 1–14). Lanham, MD: Rowman & Littlefield.

Stockton, J. (undated). CIA secret wars. http://silent-nation.com/quotes /cia-secret-wars.

Strama, M. (1998). Overcoming cynicism: Youth participation and electoral politics. *National Civic Review,* 87(I),71–77.

Street, P. (2008a). "Brand Obama," "brand USA," and "the audacity of marketing": Some candid reflections at advertising age. *Znet.* www.zmag.org/znet/viewArticle/19692.

———. (2008b). Our challenge, not Obama's: Hope and change beyond the great man theory of history. *Znet.* www.zmag.org/znet/viewArticle/19795.

Sullivan, S. (2006). *Revealing whiteness: The unconscious habits of racial privilege.* Indianapolis: Indiana University Press.

Swift, R. (2002). *The Nonsense guide to democracy.* Toronto: New International Publications.

Tabb, W. (2001). Globalization and education as a commodity. *Clarion.* www.psc-cuny.org/ jcglobalization.html.

Taft-Morales, M. & Drummer, D. A. (2007). *Haiti's development needs and a statistical overview of conditions of poverty.* Washington: Congressional Research Service.

Tator, C. & Henry, F. (2002). *Discourses of domination: Racial bias in the Canadian English Canadian Press.* Toronto: University of Toronto Press.

Tatum, B. (1992). Talking about race, learning about racism: An application of racial identity development theory in the classroom. *Harvard Educational Review,* 62(1), 1–24.

Thésée, G. (2006). A tool of massive erosion: Scientific knowledge in the neo-colonial enterprise. In G. L. Sefa Dei & A. Kempf (Eds.), *Anti-colonialism and education: The politics of resistance* (pp. 25–42). Rotterdam: Sense Publishers.

———. (2003). Le rapport au savoir scientifique en contexte d'acculturation. Application a l'étude de l'expérience scolaire en sciences d'élèves d'origine haïtienne. Doctoral dissertation at the Université du Québec a Montréal.

Thésée, G. & Carr, P. R. (2008). L'interculturel en environnement: Où justice sociale devrait rimer avec justice environnementale, *Journal of Canadian and International Education,* 7(1), 45–70.

Thompson, A. (2003). Tiffany, friend of people of color: White investments in antiracism, *Qualitative Studies in Education,* 16(1), 7–29.

Tinder, G. (2004). *Political thinking: The perennial questions.* New York: Pearson Longman.

Tobin, K. & Kincheloe, J. (2006). *Doing educational research: A handbook.* Rotterdam: Sense Publishers.

Tomasky, M. (2003). *Dissent in America. The American Prospect.* 14(4): 22.

Toohey, K. & Veal, A. J. (2007). *The Olympic games: A social science perspective.* Oxfordshire: CAB International.

Torney-Purta, J., & Richardson, W. K. (2002). Sources of civic behavior and knowledge: School related experiences and organizational membership among adolescents in a 28-country comparative study. Presented at *Citizenship on trial: Interdisciplinary perspectives on political socialization of adolescents,* McGill University (June).

Torney-Purta, J., Kland Richardson, W., & Henry Barber, C. (2005). Teachers' educational experience and confidence in relation to students' civic knowledge across countries. *Citized,* 1(1), 32–57. www.citized.info/index.asp?strand=6&r_menu=prev-v1-n1.

Torney-Purta, J., Schwille, J., & Amadeo, J. (1999). *Civic education across countries: Twenty-four national studies from the IEA civic education project.* Christchurch, New Zealand: Eburon.

Torney-Purta, J. & Vermeer S. (2004). *Developing citizenship competencies from kindergarten through grade 12.* Denver, CO: Education Commission of the States.

Torres, C. (2005). No child left behind: A brainchild of neo-liberalism and American politics. New Politics,(2). www.wputtjedu/newpol/issue38/ torres38.1itin.

Treanor, P. (2006). Why democracy is wrong? http://web.inter.nl.net/users/Paul.Treanor/ democracy.html.

———. (2005). Neo-liberalism: origins, theory, definition. http://web.intermlmet/users/Paul. Treanor /neo-liberalism.html.

Trifonas, P. P. (ed.). (2003). *Pedagogies of difference: Rethinking education for social change.* New York: RoutledgeFalmer.

United Nations Environment Program. (2003). A Strategy for protecting the people and the environment in post-war Iraq. http://postconflict.unep.ch/publications/iraq_ds.pdf.

US Census Bureau (2008). US census bureau statistical abstract 2008. http://www.census.gov/ compendia/statab/.

USA Today. (2008). Obama unveils plans for education reform. http://www.usatoday.com/ news/politics/election2008/2008-09-09-obamaeducation _N.html.

Vincent, C. (2003) *Social justice, education and identity.* London: RoutledgeFalmer.

Waggener, T. (2006) Citizenship and Service Learning, *Academic Exchange Quarterly,* 10(1), 1–5.

Walsh, J. (2009). The critical role of discourse in education for democracy. *Journal for Critical Education Policy Studies,* 6(2), 54–76. http://www.jceps.com/index.php? pageID=article& articleID=131.

Washington Post. (2008). Expenditures on the war as of the writing of this chapter was more than $600 billion. March 9, B01.

Webster Brandon, W. (2003). Toward a white teachers' guide to playing fair: Exploring the cultural politics of multicultural teaching, *Qualitative Studies in Education,* 16(1), 31–50.

Weinstein, T. (2005). Prosecuting attacks that destroy the environment: Environmental crimes or humanitarian atrocities?, *Georgetown International Environmental Law Review* (Summer). http://www.airapparent.ca/library/full_text/prosecuting_environmental_attacks5.htm.

West, C. (1999). *The Cornel West reader.* New York: Civitas.

Westheimer, J. (2008). *No child left thinking: Democracy at-risk in American schools.* Democratic Dialog Series, No. 17. Ottawa: Democratic Dialog, University of Ottawa.

———. (2006a). Patriotism and education: An introduction. *Phi Delta Kappan,* 87(8), 569–572.

————. (2006b). *Pledging allegiance: The politics of patriotism in America's schools*. New York: Teachers College Press.

Westheimer, J., & Kahne, J. (2004) What kind of citizen?: The politics of educating for democracy, *American Educational Research Journal*, 41(2), 237–269.

————. (2003). Reconnecting education to democracy: Democratic dialogs. *Phi Delta Kappan*, 85(1), 9–14.

Willinsky, J. (1998). *Learning to divide the world: Education at empire's end*. Minneapolis: University of Minnesota Press.

Wilson Cooper, C. (2006). Refining social justice commitments through collaborative inquiry: Key reward and challenges for teacher educators, *Teacher Education Quarterly*, Summer, 115–132.

Wink, J. (2005). *Critical pedagogy: Notes from the real world*. Boston: Pearson Education, Inc.

Wrage, A. (2007). *Bribery and extortion: Undermining business, governments, and security*. New York: Praeger Security International.

Yates, M. & Youniss, J. (1998) Community service and political identity development in adolescence, *Journal of Social Issues*, 54(3), 495–512.

Zinn, H. (2003). *A people's history of the United States: 1492–Present*. New York: Harper Perennial.

Zinn, H., & Macedo, D. (2005). *Howard Zinn on democratic education*. Boulder, CO: Paradigm Publishers.

Zunes, S. (2007). Pakistan's dictatorships and the United States foreign policy in focus. http://www.fpif.org/fpiftxt/4718

Index

Studies in the Postmodern Theory of Education

General Editor
Shirley R. Steinberg

Counterpoints publishes the most compelling and imaginative books being written in education today. Grounded on the theoretical advances in criticalism, feminism, and postmodernism in the last two decades of the twentieth century, Counterpoints engages the meaning of these innovations in various forms of educational expression. Committed to the proposition that theoretical literature should be accessible to a variety of audiences, the series insists that its authors avoid esoteric and jargonistic languages that transform educational scholarship into an elite discourse for the initiated. Scholarly work matters only to the degree it affects consciousness and practice at multiple sites. Counterpoints' editorial policy is based on these principles and the ability of scholars to break new ground, to open new conversations, to go where educators have never gone before.

For additional information about this series or for the submission of manuscripts, please contact:

> Shirley R. Steinberg
> c/o Peter Lang Publishing, Inc.
> 29 Broadway, 18th floor
> New York, New York 10006

To order other books in this series, please contact our Customer Service Department:

> (800) 770-LANG (within the U.S.)
> (212) 647-7706 (outside the U.S.)
> (212) 647-7707 FAX

Or browse online by series:
> www.peterlang.com